24.26

D1010442

THE HAPPIEST CORPSE I'VE EVER SEEN

THE LAST TWENTY-FIVE YEARS OF THE BROADWAY MUSICAL

The Last
Twenty-five Years
of the Broadway
Musical

ETHAN MORDDEN

THE HAPPIEST CORPSE I'VE EVER SEEN

palgrave
macmillan

First published 2004 by
PALGRAVE MACMILLAN™
175 Fifth Avenue, New York, N.Y. 10010 and
Houndmills, Basingstoke, Hampshire, England RG21 6XS
Companies and representatives throughout the world.

PALGRAVE MACMILLAN is the global academic imprint of the Palgrave Macmillan division of St. Martin's Press, LLC and of Palgrave Macmillan Ltd. Macmillan® is a registered trademark in the United States, United Kingdom and other countries. Palgrave is a registered trademark in the European Union and other countries.

ISBN 0–312–23954–8

Library of Congress Cataloging-in-Publication Data
Mordden, Ethan
    The happiest corpse I've ever seen : twenty-five years of the Broadway musical / by Ethan Mordden.
        p. cm.
    Includes index.
    ISBN 0–312–23954–8
    1. Musicals—United States—History and criticism. I. Title.
    ML2054.M66 2004
    782.1′4′0973—dc22   2004044304

A catalogue record for this book is available from the British Library.

First edition: October 2004
10 9 8 7 6 5 4 3 2 1

Printed in the United States of America.

To My Marvelous Editor
Michael Flamini

CONTENTS

INTRODUCTION   I

1. THE GREAT TRADITION   3

2. CLOSE A LITTLE FASTER   45

3. THE MUSIC OF THE NIGHT   71

4. BIG DEALS   93

5. LIE TO ME   111

6. NEW TALENT   133

7. WHAT EXACTLY IS AN OFF-BROADWAY MUSICAL?   155

8. VICTORS/VICTORIAS   169

9. FIVE SPECIAL SHOWS   195

10. JUNK IS A GENRE   221

11. WHY CAN'T SUSAN SMITH AND TIMOTHY
MCVEIGH HAVE A MUSICAL? HITLER HAS ONE   241

12. I Dreamed I Saw Fosse in My Maidenform
   Bra; or, the Last Five Years   269

Index   300

INTRODUCTION

Under separate cover, in six volumes, I have been tracing the development of the American musical from the 1920s through the 1970s. That was the Golden Age, because the culture was smart and the musical its smartest popular form. It was universal in appeal yet sophisticated, coaching the imagination, independent, even subversive. It preached on such texts as racial tolerance and pacifism even while entertaining. It was *Anything Goes* and *Hello, Dolly!* but also *Lady in the Dark* and *West Side Story*. Above all, it was *Show Boat* and *Oklahoma!*, authentic national art built on the very meaning of America. The musical attracted the most gifted artists, earning them the covers of *Time* and *Life*, the certain sign that the genre's maximum leaders were cultural avatars.

Today the musical is suffering dislocation and alienation. It no longer leads the culture. It follows, adopting the degenerative policies of schlock. Smart creators share the stage with inarticulate idiots specializing in worthless forms based on exhausted old song catalogues and the staging of movies. Present-day America has summoned up a new kind of musical, coarse and uneducated, Broadway's equivalent of the lower life-forms that have become our national idols—Adam Sandler, Anna Nicole Smith, Eminem, the Osbournes. In the decade books, I have discussed every important or interesting title, or even virtually any show that ran at least a few months. In this book's period, 1978 to 2003, shows that ran years might not deserve discussion, even mention.

Many have commented on the traditional musical's humanitarian liberalism, but few note how enlightening it was not only socially but pedagogically. Golden Age lyricists routinely widened one's knowledge with impish allusions to lit and history and ontological wisdoms veiled in bons mots. They were wits; they were poets. Challenging *Carousel*'s Julie Jordan to explain herself through the observations of her pal Carrie Pipperidge, Oscar Hammerstein II lets Julie put Carrie off with evasions. But when Carrie wonders why Julie is up early every morning, gazing out the window—at what?—hear how laden is Julie's "empty" response: "I like to watch the river meet the sea."

It's the dreamer and her symbols—an existentialist rebus, a character study, a denial. Julie Jordan isn't a queer one; she's an easy solution in a place of self-replicating problems. In a dysfunctional world, the sensible seem queer. This dreamgirl is the musical's Ockham's Razor, cutting through the excepts and hesitations to the simple truth. All of this Hammerstein catches in a single line, set to ten notes of Richard Rodgers at his most logical, with a capricious little flip to finalize the exchange.

It was thought at the time of *Carousel* that (to quote a more recent work) dreamgirls will never leave you: because writers in the Golden Age knew what people were. They knew life. Today, many writers can't even rhyme properly, and what they know is pop. Pop music, pop politics, pop language, pop ideas. After two generations in which musicals were hits or flops, or entertaining or dull, or operetta or musical comedy, these new writers have invented something once inconceivable: the inaccurate musical. It brays with self-confidence because it has no idea how ignorant it is. And that is what ignorance means.

Meanwhile, the last decade of the Golden Age fell under the control of the super-director, as if making up for the concomitant passing of the personality star. The wild magic was now to be made behind the scenes— but such magicians as Jerome Robbins, Bob Fosse, and Michael Bennett died without proper successors. As the current narrative starts, in 1978, Robbins has finished with Broadway and Fosse and Bennett have but two shows each to deliver.

So the six volumes that precede this one are chronicles; this volume is a rant, in defense of an enlightened genre hijacked by pop. Dreamgirls *will* leave you: with a cast of vapid kids phoning in sick as often as they can get away with. The stories run on an automatic pilot of poses, and the music makes one long for the whoopee-cushion melodies of Marc Blitzstein. The artistry is that of a graffito artist, and the attitude that of a Kinko's clerk. And that's the new pop fun on Broadway.

I

THE GREAT TRADITION

They knew how to write a musical comedy in the 1920s. There was the Cinderella show, usually set in New York and often Irish in flavor. There was the legacy-with-a-catch plot left over from the 1910s: heroine must keep her temper for a year, hero must marry mysterious stranger, and so on. There was the rustic-conquers-the-city premise; also its converse, the slicker-among-the-peasantry tale.

Most dependable of all was the engagement-threatened-by-a-snag setup, with farcical plot development involving mistaken identity, jokes about marriage and politics, out-of-story gags such as byplay with the orchestra (who by logic's rights are not part of the narrative reality), the sudden appearance of dancers who don't even bother to check into the plot before launching their act, and other extraneous fun.

This describes many a twenties title, but especially one of the most successful of the kind. Of course, it had a touch of novelty. Shows had to, with so much monotony of genre. *Kid Boots* (1923) had golf. *The Cocoanuts* (1925) had Florida real-estate scamming. *A Connecticut Yankee* (1927) had time travel. And *this* show had a homosexual romance bonding its two leading men. I'm thinking of the last of the twenties musicals, *La Cage aux Folles* (1983).

This was not the first musical to include a gay couple. The little-known *Sextet* (1974) presented a party hosted by two male lovers, and some three months before *La Cage aux Folles* opened, *Dance a Little Closer* offered a pair of airline stewards who actually asked a clergyman to marry them, leading to a full-scale musical scene on this matter a generation before gay marriage became even a controversy.

But *La Cage aux Folles* unprecedentedly *starred* its gay lovers, George Hearn and Gene Barry. Moreover, they played not merely sweethearts but a couple of twenty years' standing who have raised a son (John Weiner). It is the son's engagement that rests in jeopardy in Harvey Fierstein's script, drawn from Jean Poiret's play of the same name. The title translates as *The House of Crazies* and refers to the Saint-Tropez cabaret that Barry runs and over which drag artiste Hearn presides.

One can only guess how the show might have gone over if key producer Allan Carr had hired not these two straights for the leads but, say, Noël Coward and Liberace. The production, directed by Arthur Laurents and choreographed by Scott Salmon, was conservative generally—traditional, let us say—with a heavy scene plot necessitating old-fashioned blackouts and motorized set changes over orchestral distraction. And Jerry Herman, who defines mainstream simply by showing up, wrote the score.

Still. Two gay guys dominating the evening in domesticated security and no one calls the cops? Herman even provisioned the cabaret's drag-queen chorus with the merrily unapologetic "We Are What We Are." The engagement's snag is that son Weiner loves the daughter (Leslie Stevens) of a homophobic politician, and thus Hearn finds himself excrescent in his own family. This inspires the defiantly unapologetic "I Am What I Am," capped by Hearn's throwing his wig at Barry and storming up the theatre aisle to end Act One. And *this* of course becomes a revolutionary gay anthem in real life, as Herman, Carr, Fierstein, and Laurents must have known it would.

A bold twenties musical comedy! There weren't many others, though the American theatre's inclination toward tolerance of minorities and unique opinions roots *La Cage* in history. Indeed, of all the cast, only the homophobic politician (Jay Garner) and, to an extent, his wife (Merle Louise) see anything unusual in gay. The people of Saint-Tropez can't even be called "accepting": they don't notice it. Garner's daughter, too, can't be roused to hatred. When Garner demands that she accompany her parents as they stomp out of Sodom, she refuses.

In fact, the one genuine snag in the love plot is not the bigoted politician but rather the son, because he wants to accommodate bigotry. Like Patrick, the adopted son in another Jerry Herman show, *Mame* (1966), who repudiates governess Agnes Gooch because her single-mother pregnancy will offend his in-laws-to-be, Hearn's son wants Hearn out of sight when the bigots show up. This prompts "Look Over There," Barry's gentle rebuke of the young man's monumental disloyalty. It is one of Herman's more emotional numbers, but understated, even repressed: so embarrassed to have to be sung at all that its waltz melody rides on a wave of angry broken chords. We see what patient, loving parents Barry and Hearn have been, and Weiner sees it, too. Humiliated, he runs offstage during the song, leaving Barry to finish it as a valentine to Hearn.

Nothing so subtly intense could have graced a twenties musical comedy in the 1920s. Not, at least, before *Show Boat*, near decade's end. But then *La Cage* returns to its generical roots, for Hearn both leaves *and* stays, turning himself into a drag Mother, complete with prim maroon suit, white print blouse, and sensible slingbacks. The masquerade was a staple of twenties shows, in *Two Little Girls in Blue* (1921), *Just Because* (1922), *Lady, Be Good!* (1924), *China Rose* (1925), *Tell Me More* (1925), *The Five O'Clock Girl* (1927), *Fifty Million Frenchmen* (1929), and literally scores of others. It was how musical comedy saw the world: a place of games.

However, *La Cage* treats serious issues, if in its own unserious way, and Hearn's disguise is a kind of pun on the strict construction of gender meaning. Hearn's a better parent—a better person—than the more conventional parents Garner and Louise. And this disguise also brings about a conclusion to Weiner's conflict, when he addresses Garner:

> WEINER: I apologize for what happened tonight. I made a terrible mistake, but . . . I hope, one day, I'll receive forgiveness for being stupid and thoughtless.
>
> GARNER: I do not accept your apology.
>
> WEINER: It wasn't to you I was apologizing. It was to my parents.

Weiner even celebrates the moment with a reprise of "Look Over There," showing how well he has absorbed Barry's lesson.

In a way, *La Cage aux Folles* is about a happy family confronting an unhappy family because of a technicality. It's a classic premise for farce, perhaps most classically stated in Moss Hart and George S. Kaufman's *You Can't Take It With You* (1936). Still, *La Cage* stands out from other shows for the riotous nature of its drag-club setting, with its "notorious and dangerous Cagelles." So Barry calls them in the show's first moments, following a spectacular decorative effect in which the buildings around a square in Saint-Tropez seem to move toward us and then turn, as if indicating the way to the club itself, to honesty and liberation—to independence from bigots, a thematic preoccupation for the musical since the 1920s, in the Cinderella titles, a few of the operettas, and *Show Boat*.

Of course, the musical's aesthetic preoccupation is zany song and dance, and a backstager set in and around a drag club has that built in. Choreographer Salmon enjoyed the opportunity to bring costume changes into *La Cage*'s first number, "We Are What We Are." The twelve Cagelles appeared posed in elaborate gowns, then doffed the outer layer to tap in their pastel pajamas as the abandoned finery soared up on rigging into the flies. Salmon then created yet another change, to tunics and short skirts, using attire to invent a visual crescendo with which to build the number.

"A Little More Mascara" offered another surprise, beginning as George Hearn's character solo as he made up in his dressing room but then moving "onstage" to turn into a performance number for him and the Cagelles. The comic title song, extolling "the magic and the mood" while advising customers to "avoid the hustlers, and the men's room, and the food," presented Salmon with yet another great opportunity. The vamp preceding the verse tastes of taboo on the interval of a second in the minor—it has the sound of Oscar Wilde cruising Peter Pan—and the refrain eventually explodes in a crazed cancan for the Cagelles.

This was the kind of dance theatre that the musical *used* to excel in— not Dream Ballets or violence but sheer joy, getting more out of rhythm than the lyrics and music can by themselves. Yet the ensemble's neatest surprise lay not in a dance but during the Cagelles' curtain call. As a little white dumpster traveled from stage right to left, the twelve dancers discarded their wigs and dresses, dropped them into the bin, turned to face us: and, lo, two of them really were women, Linda Haberman and Deborah Phelan.

A high-powered entertainment that acceded to the spiraling capitalization costs of the big musical with a production of spendthrift command, *La Cage* came in at summer's end as a guaranteed hit. Its same-sex romance, complete with sentimental fadeout to reprise of love song in moonlit square, utterly failed to offend. Was it because its dangerous content was set into such old-fashioned packaging? At a time when hit musicals wore the New Look, *Company*-tight and *Chicago*-spare, *La Cage* was reassuringly old-hat.

Along with those hoary blackouts and the scene-change gallop music was an antique observance of autonomous comic shtick, the kind that perverts character for a laugh. Thus, sneaking past a news reporters' pile-on by joining the drag show in full kit, Jay Garner and Merle Louise presented not mortification but enthusiasm. Garner in particular betrayed his character's wary asceticism. So thoroughly "dragged" that he looked like Marie Dressler, he should have made a hasty exit. No: director Laurents had him enjoying himself and putting on a show. This is not how a homophobic hypocrite politician behaves when escaping from journalists in woman's attire. Even the show's technical shocker was old wave: when the club's stage was cinematically "moved" to the right to show action in the wings. This had already been pulled off in *Me and Juliet* (1953).

Nevertheless. *La Cage* had been playing so well in its Boston tryout that RCA Victor taped the album two and a half weeks before the New York opening, and the show held the Palace Theatre for 1,761 performances and became an international attraction, just as the French film based on Poiret's play had been. A disappointment in England and Australia, the musical attained repertory status in Germany and Austria, and played South America, Italy, and Hungary, among other places.

A smash: and any decent cast can play it. Masculine Georges and effeminate Albin are star parts, yet the hoardings have featured also-rans and understudies. Walter Charles and Keith Michell headed one national tour, and Keene Curtis and Peter Marshall the other: a fine serving of talent, with Michell in particular a dazzling Georges, shockingly conclusive on the line "And I'm young and in love" that closes "Song on the Sand." Michell shared his Georges also with his native Australia and Broadway, following Jamie Ross, who followed Gene Barry. Yet the secondary players can be anybody.

Indeed, the two kids, though representing the traditional Boy Gets Girl, have little to do. The girl does not even enter the story till halfway through the second act. However, this does not stop her from dancing out into the middle of the *first* act, summoned by the boy for a dance duet after the vocal on "With Anne On My Arm." She is not physically present in any real sense, just in that twenties-musical-comedy sense that similarly welcomed the Astaires to get up and strut: because they could. The lights were turned down on the rest of the stage, and Gene Barry, who had been listening to his son at the number's start, now turned stone-still, pretending that he was as invisible as the set. The girl whirled in, choreographer Salmon gave her and the boy an effervescent minute together, she vanished, the lights came back up, and the show had got away with a stunt so Jurassic it was almost avant-garde.

That song was also given to Hearn and Barry. As "With You On My Arm," it went a bit vaudevillian when Barry invited and Hearn declined and then gave in, with spoken interjections between the lines. Is this Herman's observation that gay coupling is "equal" to hetero coupling, as comfortably interchangeable as a song lyric? Certainly, Herman did not aggrandize the kids' romance with a big ballad. That spot goes to Albin and Georges, in "Song on the Sand." A spoof of love-song clichés, it conjures them up yet does not actually utter them, letting the melody—and Georges' feelings for Albin—supply the content. It's a cute way to write a traditional honeybunch number without honeybunching. But it's also a subversion of status quo, because it's exactly the sort of tune that the two kids might sing thirty years after the curtain call. In effect, the love that dare not speak its name doesn't need to: there is only one kind of love.

Some day we may get a true-gay revival of La Cage, with, say, English rootytoot Rupert Everett and pornmeister Jeff Stryker as Albin and Georges. (And, like Georges, Jeff actually has a son from a heterosexual fling, so he could bring Tony-baiting verisimilitude to his character portrait.) On the other hand, we are unlikely to see a revival of the aforementioned Dance a Little Closer, and not because of its handling of the gay couple. Here was a real bomb, with book, lyrics, and direction by Alan Jay Lerner and music by Charles Strouse, based on Robert E. Sherwood's play Idiot's Delight (1936).

This is the sort of show favored in the 1940s and 1950s, the musical play based on a more or less serious antecedent usually but not necessarily from the 1920s or 1930s—Rain, They Knew What They Wanted, Street Scene, Green Grow the Lilacs, The Little Foxes, O'Neill, Pagnol, Molnár. The form sometimes tilts toward opera, but more often it balances book and score with the Higher Dance, featuring where possible a Dream

Ballet in which dancers temporarily take over the lead actors' roles. Originated in *Oklahoma!*,* this genre reforms the musical, for instance in lyric writing that explores characters' individual voices. Then, too, happy-go-lucky fun is banned. The girl's energizing irruption into *La Cage aux Folles'* "With Anne On My Arm" is unthinkable in the musical play: characters can appear only where they actually *are*. (Apparitions are permitted. Rodgers and Hammerstein's *Allegro* [1947], a musical play without an adaptational source, fairly revels in them; and another original, *Follies* [1971], is thoroughly haunted. But these figures appear for a dramatic purpose, not because the boy wants to dance with the girl.)

Dance a Little Closer had a premise problem. "Let's do a musical with the Lunts" is an intriguing notion till one realizes that the musical has no Lunts. Alfred Lunt and Lynn Fontanne were exponentially glamorous stars during the Golden Age of American Drama (roughly 1919–59) and the only ones to combine a masterly grasp of the contemporary thespian virtues of style, surprise, and wit in one mated package. There had been great duos before, but never a duo like this. They jumped from Chekhof to Shakespeare to boulevard comedy, and they spent their youthful prime working for the Theatre Guild, which gave them (and their public) snob prestige. They liked "trick" roles, wherein Alfred could change his looks in some violent makeup job and Lynn could fool the playwright himself with an enigmatic smile for a sly twist ending.

Idiot's Delight gave them their trickiest roles ever. The setting is a hotel in the Italian Alps, where a diverse group of people anxiously awaits the outbreak of the next war. The well-made layout allows Sherwood to pass the first act introducing his characters—a French munitions tycoon, a German scientist, a hotheaded leftist, a honeymooning English couple, hotel staff, Italian soldiers. The second act develops them to a suspense climax, and the third act works it out, as war does come, in a spectacular air raid during which Sherwood drops his curtain.

However, all of this is mere background to the Luntplay of Alfred as a fourth-rate song-and-dance man with a sextet of cuties and Lynn as the

---

* Those who see *Show Boat* as the progenitor of the form mistake its epic grandeur for its essence. No: most of *Show Boat* inheres in the zany frivolity of musical comedy, though revisions have been stamping out much of the fun since 1946. Still, the comic nature of Captain Andy and other leads and the use of dance as decoration rather than interpretation place *Show Boat* in a category of its own.

tycoon's Russian girlfriend, in a bizarre blond wig and an accent thick as borshch. What makes the second act so suspenseful is not the threat of war so much as Alfred's insistence that Lynn is no Russian but an American adventuress with whom he spent a night years before in Omaha. Lynn's guttural laughter at this is the talk of Broadway. And at the end, when, alone with Lunt at the top of Europe on the point of possible death, she tells him that she *is* the floozy he met in Omaha, it's about sixteen enigmatic smiles too late for us to be sure that she means it. It defines the Lunts' unique brand of acting that one came out of their shows exhilarated and inspired—and knowing less about their characters than one did when the curtain went up.

Can *Idiot's Delight* be a musical at all? The play never really concludes its political argument, so aware, so responsible, so—to quote Lord Byron's joke about Poet Laureate Robert Southey—"quaint and mouthy." And the very concept of "the Lunts" is meaningless today—not those people, but what they meant to the public. *Idiot's Delight* is a stunt of a show, and it duly became a stunt of a movie, with Clark Gable and Norma Shearer. Sherwood wrote the screenplay, and in some ways the film is stuck in the play. *Gable Sings!*: his number is "Puttin' on the Ritz," as it had been Lunt's on stage; and Shearer is dressed as a replica of Fontanne. Shearer even does what Fontanne did—it is either Lynn Fontanne's worst performance or Norma Shearer's best. But a lengthy opening sequence spells out that Omaha backstory, now making it plain that the pair had met and loved and parted after all.

Unfortunately: because literalizing the Lunts' *fantasia* saps the work of its mystery, leaving nothing but Sherwood's arguing archetypes. Yet this is what Lerner and Strouse did. Besides updating the action to "the avoidable future," they included an Omaha flashback with Dream Pas de Deux midway through Act One for *their* Lunts, Len Cariou and Liz Robertson. Worse, Cariou had been in musicals before, which kills Lunt's trick of mastering fourth-rate hoofing and singing *especially for you tonight*; and Robertson was playing what she was, an Englishwoman, losing Sherwood's spicy Russian flavoring.

Some shows put a foot wrong early on and never recover, and *Dance a Little Closer* was one of those shows. Though its first visual presented a dimly glimpsed ensemble throwing themselves around the hotel lobby in a sort of end-of-the-world debauch, the show quickly moved to the disastrous first number, Len Cariou's act with his girls. "It Never Would've Worked," a tour through a womanizer's liaisons, found Cariou unbecomingly dressed in a blue-spangled tuxedo jacket and a derby, his footwork awkward and the song itself a witless mess. The audience was confused. It's probably supposed to be a terrible act: but surely not this terrible. Shouldn't Strouse and Lerner have found a clever way to style terrible instead of sinking into it, to put on the Ritz by having the wrong kind? The air-raid siren that went off during the song, announcing the seriousness of the narrative, should have disturbed one. Instead, it came as a relief.

In forties fashion, *Dance a Little Closer* proceeded through the original script, finding its music strictly within the limits of character and situation. However, except for Cariou's Harry, all the principal roles were altered from Sherwood. The French munitions tycoon became a German-accented but apparently cosmopolitan adviser to heads of state (George Rose). The honeymooning couple became the gay pair (Brent Barrett, Jeff Keller), who made the most of an appealing waltz, "Why Can't the World Go and Leave Us Alone?," while skating on a strip of imitation ice. George Rose, too, took a turn on it—not with Robertson, his designated partner, but with an alternate fair damsel. "He Always Comes Home To Me," another waltz, was Robertson's philosophical summation of their arrangement. But her establishing number was "No Man Is Worth It," a jazzy put-down of the entire gender.

Clearly, Strouse and Lerner saw something more than a stunt in *Idiot's Delight*. Attracted to Sherwood's confrontation of Lunt's realist and Fontanne's romancer, they must have thought that a good score would ignite the passion in the realist, tour the romancer's secrets. And *Dance a Little Closer*'s score is not bad. Robertson got better support than Cariou, but they came together most pleasurably in the title song, one that would have become a standard when this kind of show was in its heyday. George Rose (as Dr. Josef Winkler) even extended himself past his usual performance, aggrandizing the Rose Sprechstimme into a pseudo-operatic baritone for "A Woman Who Thinks I'm Wonderful" to match its quotation of *Lohengrin*.

However, updating from the 1930s to something like 1983, the year of *Dance a Little Closer*'s premiere, means upgrading the potential disaster from world war to nuclear suicide. Why not forget Sherwood and make a musical out of *Dr. Strangelove*? Then, too, following the play faithfully in forties–fifties fashion means that one's action, in this case, will be locked into a two-character play for one's final fifteen minutes. Surely Jerry Herman wouldn't let a libretto trap him into anything so naked, so . . . spoken play. The last quarter hour of *La Cage aux Folles* is energized by "The Best of Times," a joy number with a purpose: singing in his Mother disguise, George Hearn enchants the entire company, even the bigots, suggesting how gay art finds its employment in even a homophobic culture.

Next to that, Strouse and Lerner are left with nuclear war and no magical stars; some musical *that* is. It closed on opening night and all but marked the end of Alan Jay Lerner's career. An adherent of the forties–fifties musical play—which reached its climax, like it or not, with *Camelot* (1960)—Lerner adapted afterward to contemporary styles but even so couldn't pull off a hit, or even a succès d'estime. Of his seven titles after *Camelot*, all were flops or bombs save *Coco* (1969), a Big Lady Show that finally paid off on its tour.

The Big Lady Show is a genre of the 1960s and 1970s, when star vehicles did not so much exploit the star as exalt her (or, in certain cases, him). This was especially necessary when the work centered on a Novelty Star, unused to song and dance, but it held true even for full-fledged club members such as Carol Channing or Joel Grey. In older days, a Marilyn Miller or an Ed Wynn carried a show. The Big Lady Show carries the star, through a coordination of effects that, frankly, Miller and Wynn didn't need. They had the Entrance and their specialties, yes—but they never took part in a curtain call built with all the sensual crescendo of the famous crane shot of the Babylonian bacchanal in D. W. Griffith's *Intolerance*. Stage-managed bows exacting ovations from a dutifully over-whelmed public are Big Lady style in its essence.

Lauren Bacall made such a hit in *Applause* (1970) that *Woman of the Year* (1981) seemed a sensible follow-up: as another very public figure, in another contemporary musical comedy with a story drawn from the movies, with another set of first-division writers tailoring the piece to her talents. Hollywood's *Woman of the Year* (1942) introduced the team of Katharine Hepburn and Spencer Tracy; the two didn't at first know how well their partnership was to play, and it shows on screen. So there's a bit of extra friction for Bacall and her costar, Harry Guardino, to toy with.

The musical's updating will promote Bacall from Hepburn's international journalist to today's version, a television anchor diva. Guardino will trade in Tracy's job of sportswriter for something more colorful—cartoonist, creator of a feline smart alec named Katz. Here's a neat touch: an animated Katz will appear on a video monitor—and so will Tessie Cat, the cartoonist's spoof of the anchor diva after she denigrates his calling. Then they meet cute, love is sparked, marriage follows, and—as in the film—it seems doomed to failure because of . . . well, is it her lack of nesting skills or his distaste for her independence?

With a book by Peter Stone and a score by John Kander and Fred Ebb, *Woman of the Year* won mixed notices but played for two years, mainly because the star gave it a great send-off. She had one of those just-getting-away-with-it voices, and, a decade after *Applause*, she still couldn't dance. But she took stage with such verve that Frank Rich called her "a natural musical-comedy star." Note that the box-office take slowed up for an unexpectedly able Raquel Welch and then collapsed entirely for a nonetheless superb Debbie Reynolds.

But then, Bacall is one of the Biggest of Ladies in the sheer authority of her show biz, and director Robert Moore and choreographer Tony Charmoli made it look as though Bacall was in charge in the way that Ethel Merman and Robert Preston always were in their shows. Bacall enjoyed a Surprise Entrance, backstage at the ceremony in which she was to receive the eponymous award. As Madame Chairperson made the presentation, a stagehand walked by and picked up a life-size blowup of Bacall's photograph—and there was the real thing, who had been standing behind it. Charmoli could even center Bacall in a dance number, "One of the Boys," by having twelve chorus men handle all the actual dancing. Bacall mainly strutted and got up on a bar while charading such manly arts as boxing, playing baseball, and drinking. Amusingly, Guardino sat the whole thing out at a corner table.

"One of the Boys" is the typical Big Lady item in which the ensemble adores the star—"Mame," "Hello, Dolly!," "When Mabel Comes in the Room." That act of worship usually occurs in the title song. But "Woman of the Year," sung at that awards ceremony against the chorus women's repeated "chirp" of happy chatter, was in fact Bacall's establishing song. A zippy $\frac{4}{4}$ in the style once called "that Broadway rhythm," it got the evening off to a confident start, letting Bacall flourish in the kind of vocal line that they used to write for singers with belting hot power.*

Some of the score is minor Kander and Ebb, and little of it reaches their best. But the whole thing is pitched in their characteristic "can't wait to hear the cast album" style, always in narrative mode yet never forgetting to stir up the fun. Guardino's torch number, "Sometimes a Day Goes By," is, well, a torch number. But Bacall's torch number, "I Wrote the Book," is ragtime with a vocal backup by two cleaning women. "The Poker Game," for Guardino and his fellow artists to put over while complaining about Bacall's assault, is an antic waltz that stokes their anger only to dance with it. "It Isn't Working" is a breathless ensemble piece energized by a bass fiddle scale as Bacall and Guardino's friends and associates indulge in Schadenfreude over the marriage's gloomy prospects. And the much-praised comic duet, "The Grass Is Always Greener," was so strong a composition that its staging consisted entirely of Bacall and Marilyn Cooper sitting on kitchen stools.

With such an ingratiating score, it is worth noting that none of the six principals fielded a top-notch singing voice. Yet except for the solo lines in "The Poker Game" and some choral work, the score was divvied up among those six leads. Besides Bacall and Guardino, they were Roderick Cook, who Rex Harrisoned through the music as Bacall's secretary; Grace Keagy, who has a solid but not pretty voice, as Bacall's housekeeper; Marilyn Cooper, the fetching ingenue of *I Can Get It For You Wholesale* (1962) but now vocally worn; and Eivind Harum, who could sing just well enough, as a defecting Soviet dancer. And with Bacall's and Guardino's throaty delivery owning or sharing much of the twelve separate song titles, *Woman of the Year* was no operetta.

On the other hand, one doesn't particularly notice this when there is so much to listen to: when the lyrics are as telling as the music. Like all major Golden Age lyricists, Fred Ebb is smart, and he writes for a smart public. The allusions that one is expected to comprehend—in Ebb's lyrics

---

* For the national tour, the show underwent revision, including two new numbers. One replaced the main section of the title song with a more pointed defiance of gender discrimination. It doesn't work, because the new material itself isn't good but also because the Big Lady Show specializes in the perfecting of genre numbers. The original "Woman of the Year" is a Jerry Herman kind of thing, specifying person, place, and time within a standard framework: beads, feathers, and an idea. The second "Woman of the Year" is more exact, more careful, and a dud.

and Peter Stone's book—take in "Gertrude and Alice" and "the Scala walkout by Callas," Jean-Pauls Belmondo and Sartre, Khachaturian's ballet *Spartacus*, Plácido Domingo, "The Saga of Jenny," and a pride of references to the comics. (Pia Zadora is a running gag.) This sophisticated or even educational side of the musical, already mentioned, starts to disappear in writers making debuts after the 1970s.

Something else that disappears is the conventional view of gender division that *Woman of the Year* inherited from its source. Why should Katharine Hepburn be judged as unfit because she can't cook and clean? She has vastly more interesting things to do *and* the money to hire someone to manage her household. Spencer Tracy makes no attempt to accommodate Hepburn's world of current events and the arts; one wonders how many of the references *he* would get in the lyrics of, say, Ira Gershwin. And while we're at it, is writing about sports more admirable than writing about current events? In *From Reverence to Rape*, film critic Molly Haskell denounces Hollywood's attitude toward Hepburn's more self-willing characters as "the furtive revenge of mediocrity on excellence; she is being convicted merely for being a superior creature." Indeed, isn't it the height of irony when Tracy ditches Hepburn just before the awards dinner with "I've got an angle that would be sensational. The outstanding woman of the year isn't a woman at all"?

This line, very slightly altered, was retained in the musical's script. That proves how dated the *Woman of the Year* musical was even when new. And today such brazen selfishness from a leading man in an essentially happy show would be unthinkable. The 1999 revival of *Annie Get Your Gun* had to tiptoe around racial sensibilities: of course. But it also got *its* leading man to meet the self-sacrificing heroine halfway, to call a halt to the ego-defense war and try being a Man of the Year. And note that the revision was written by the same Peter Stone.

Meanwhile, what *is* a modern musical? And how much of the Great Tradition is still operating? The Big Lady Show is gone, for starters, improved upon—indeed, overwhelmed by—a piece such as Harvey Schmidt and Tom Jones' *Colette* (1982), on the life of the French writer, and less a vehicle for than a challenge to Novelty Star Diana Rigg. There is strong content here, taking the heroine from rustic teen to national sage, with some lesbian activity and interludes as a music-hall performer, and moving from an intimidating first husband who passed her work off as his own to a confrontation with the Nazis because her third husband is part-Jewish. Colette is impish, contrary, brilliant, excessive, delicate, tireless, immortal. The show's book writer—lyricist Jones—will have to be quite a wit to keep up with his subject and her capricious self-presentation. Let's taste an interview scene from late in the second act:

> REPORTER: Do you have any ideas about women's rights?
> COLETTE: No, I haven't. But when I do, they will be expressed with the utmost violence.

Colette was such a national treasure that she was the first woman in French history to be granted a state funeral. But *Colette* will not worship Diana Rigg. She'll have to work for her laurels. And note, too, that Colette's lifetime, from 1873 to 1954, somewhat coincided with the course of the direly history-filled Third Republic. The Big Lady Show is light in texture; *Colette* will be busy, exotic, and perilous.

Schmidt and Jones had already written a few songs and incidental music for an otherwise straight-play *Colette* (by Jones' wife, Elinor), in 1970. That sounds typical of this team, so often attracted to the miniature— *The Fantasticks* (1960), *The Bone Room* (1975), *Roadside* (2001). However, Diana Rigg's *Colette*—which took nothing from the earlier work—employs a massive score with a ton of numbers and lots of voice, even from Rigg. Not a birthright vocalist but a superb actress with great technical command, Rigg simply figured out who Colette was and sang *that*, giving a smashing performance in one of the most picturesque of all musicals.

The score is amazingly good, and the cast presented a combination of the sensible and the wild. John Reardon was Colette's duplicitous first husband, Martin Vidnovic her third;* eccentric English ballerino Robert Helpmann made his musical debut as a gay sidekick who takes Colette into the theatre world; glamorous Marti Stevens was the Marquise de Belboeuf ("Missy"), Colette's most notable woman lover and in real life a

---

* Ron Raines completed this trio of Broadway's outstanding baritones as Colette's second husband, Baron Henri de Jouvenel. But the huge show ran long in its dress rehearsal, so Raines' role was cut as an emergency measure. Raines went out of town with the production, covering the other two parts with the expectation of being reinserted into the narrative when time permitted.

kind of Attila the Nun in men's clothes, which made most people who met her extremely unhappy; and vanished operetta diva Marta Eggerth made a return as Colette's wonderful mother. Using Rigg as narrator and the chorus as commentators in the "concept" manner, rich in dance numbers and a visual feast, *Colette* was bound to make a splash and win Rigg a Tony. Yet it was perhaps too special a piece to be popular outside New York aficionado circles. Sure enough, after tryouts in Seattle, San Francisco, and Denver, the show closed down and never came in.

To this day, no one can explain exactly what went wrong. The staging team—director Dennis Rosa and choreographer Carl Jablonski—lacked experience in big musicals, and producer Harry Rigby was capping a career made of arresting ideas and no business sense whatsoever. It would appear that Rosa was fired before a replacement could be secured, leaving the two authors uncertainly in charge. Then, too, the West Coast and Denver may not have been appropriate venues for the tryout of a work imbued with French culture and the notion of a *tout Paris*, with its *crises* and *scandales*. Missy's seduction of Colette was alarmingly direct; one character was a devotee of cocaine; and did anyone in the audience understand what was going on in the *Claudine* sequence?

This charmingly bizarre combination of spoken dialogue, song, and dance treats one of those continental European abstractions of which Americans have no experience. In fact, we have no word in English for what Colette's *Claudine* novels represented in Parisian culture in their day, the very first years of the twentieth century. The closest we can come is with what worldly people used to mean by the word "naughty," something at once erotic and innocent, unclear but shocking. Claudine is a schoolgirl, sexually experimental, determined, adorable: Colette herself. Claudine's adventures became the rage of Paris; there were Claudine hats, Claudine chocolates, Claudine postcards. There was a *Claudine* play, and the lead actress and Colette roamed Paris dressed as Claudine twins, with Colette's husband—called simply Willy—fondly doting upon his charges like an older man with girls he introduces as his nieces. This is *very, very* naughty.

Indeed, is this even legal? What about that strange French penchant for becoming a public figure with only one name? Henri Gauthier-Villars—this same Willy—had a brilliant mind for the creating of ephemeral writing but could not bear writing himself. Instead, he directed a galley of scribes. He signed the *Claudine* books and became the most visible celebrity in town—and all this is covered in the musical's *Claudine* numbers. First comes a solo for Rigg, "Claudine," couched in the child-like style that Schmidt and Jones excel in. Next comes a swinging waltz, "Two Claudines (are better than one)," that expanded, Claudine by Claudine, till the stage was fairly dancing with *petites femmes*, including Rigg, who was regroomed into a schoolgirl right before our eyes. To top off the series, out came a preening John Reardon to sing "The Father of Claudine," whose lyric stops just short of pedophilia. It's as near as American art can get to sampling that European notion that everything found in nature is . . . okay, natural. But it's sure to make most American audiences wary.

Was Seattle the right place for this show's shakeout? The city was flattered by the visit, and local critic R. M. Campbell filed successive reports on the show's development. He noticed that *Colette*'s most shocking moment, the heroine's lesbian kiss during an Egyptian number at the music hall, had been scrapped, but he seemed more impressed by drop-ins from such out-of-town media as *Newsweek* and the London *Daily Mail*. Above all, Campbell praised Rigg's portrayal, with its "breadth, humor and pride. Rigg has transformed Colette's earthiness into an aristocratic sensibility."

Indeed, some transformation is essential in a show like this. The title role calls for a skilled performer; one cannot celeb one's way through a show like *Colette*, for it is no Big Lady valentine. Like *Gypsy* or *Kean*, *Man of La Mancha* or *Sweeney Todd*, *Colette* tests one's talent. From its very first moments, one heard the stirrings of big ideas, of Schmidt and Jones in an ambitious mood: woodwinds tapping out the interval of a second on high, then the bass instruments surging in like tidal undertow. *The Fantasticks* got away with a piano and harp; *Colette*'s pit, scored by Larry Wilcox, sounded like a symphony orchestra. After a bit of excited prelude, the curtain flew up on Rigg alone, ruminating in biting, classy tones:

COLETTE: It comes upon me suddenly, like an itch. . . . The need, the absolute need to put words upon a piece of paper. Why? I don't know why. Because it is my profession, I suppose. Because it is my hobby. Because it is my vice. Because when I write, the doorways open. And I have one more journey yet to make.

That journey was this show. Harp and muted strings had already cued in the first number, "There's Another World," a thrilling evocation in which life and work are staged as one: the principal figures in Colette's life put forth as if they were characters in her fiction. Rigg spoke over the music to introduce them to us, announcing the show as surely as ever a P. T. Barnum ever heralded his show biz. The flowing melody, on the other hand, invited us into the adventure of a character, not a star: not a Big Lady Show but a chronicle set to music.

As the number ended and the play took off, we followed the rise and rise of this inspiring woman, whose impish subordinates could have flourished only in France and whom only the French could have appreciated. As the protagonist makes this journey, from Colette Willy to gala Madame Colette, her own self, she runs a sizable show: four set-piece dance numbers, spicy jokes, staging surprises, a load of décor. Still, this is a work designed to hold true to its material.

Thus, in Act Two, when Colette falls in love with Maurice Goudeket (Martin Vidnovic's character, and in historical fact sixteen years younger than Colette), Rigg will not be allowed to indicate the older woman rejuvenated in romance. She must show us, in a series of duets with Vidnovic starting with the undulating "Riviera Nights." Set in a nightclub in *La Cage aux Folles'* Saint-Tropez, the number lets us see how Vidnovic uses dance and a sense of humor to tease the older woman's vanity. The worldly Colette of course knows what is going on. But she believes in such universal wisdoms as A Lady Enjoys Being Courted. At that, Rigg looked extra handsome in a white frock with a deep-cut bodice and a belt of hanging beads that sailed out as she twirled. Given the ease with which the modern musical can travel from place to place, *Colette* faded cinematically, out on the nightclub and in on Colette's bedroom, where Rigg and Vidnovic sang "Oo-La-La," a playful thirties fox-trot of flirting ironies. Because bad marriages have soured Colette on householding, the two agree to live apart and to take their affair lightly. It shall play a limited run, like all-star Corneille. But "Something For the Summer" is followed by "Something For the Winter" and then by Vidnovic's intense "Be My Lady."

Note that the ensemble has not vanished during this episode, for the influence of the concept musical of the 1970s freed the chorus of virtually any show to comment upon or take part in the action without being physically "present." A transitional number called "Madame Colette" allows them to detail the attentions paid to eminence—the honors and interviews, the feeling that all the nation waits upon one's opinion. Then, most daringly, the Nazi occupation is treated—by irony—in a ballad, "The Room Is Filled With You," which Colette addresses to Goudeket, on the run from the Gestapo. A Nazi officer appears during the music to try to get Colette to cooperate in a scheme to unmask partisans, using Goudeket's life as a threat.

As he did in life, Goudeket returns to Colette (though he spent much of the war in hiding). However, this is not the completion of the show's central throughline. In the much more conventional *Dance a Little Closer*, the return of the lover is more important than the possibility of war, but Schmidt and Jones still have Colette's final journey to conclude. They do this, first, with the sentimental "Growing Older," and, second, with a notion, an idea about Colette and the life that someone like her can lead. By now, Rigg's articulation is tense, the syllables cut off as soon as they are uttered. She is indeed old, and feeling it. She rounds off her opening introduction of the other principals by telling us what became of them. Then:

> COLETTE: It's getting colder. Get me a blanket.
> GOUDEKET: Colette! If you could look back on your entire life, and keep part of it and throw part of it away, what would you keep and what would you throw away?
> COLETTE: I'd keep it all! It's *my* property! My *goods*!

Whereupon she begins the finale, "Joy," the kind of life-affirming anthem that the musical has long made essential to its philosophy. What is greater than the sheer experience of *being*, in all its possibilities, the disasters as well as the victories, "such beauty and such pain"?

This is a native American view, and it is partly why such pessimistic European arguments as expressionism and absurdism have never taken root here. The classic life-affirming work is of course Thornton Wilder's *Our Town* (1938), written, however, from within a tragic outlook that believes man incapable of comprehending his joy. By coincidence, Schmidt and Jones were to set *Our Town* to music later on, as we'll see. But *Colette* offers the positive interpretation, because a writer like

Colette creates joy from beauty and pain alike. So, as "Joy" grew in redemptive power, the music filled the theatre while the entire cast crowded the stage in a hubbub of Colette—her loves and struggles and greatness. At the center of it stood Diana Rigg, an ecstatic Colette surrounded by her shadows, truly an immortal. "Joy!" the singers cried. "Joy!" Rigg threw out her arms to embrace the very theatre itself. And there the curtain fell.

An immense and beautiful show with one of the greatest of the musical theatre's unknown scores, *Colette* typifies state-of-the-art stagecraft in its turn-on-a-dime changes of scene and garrulously narrating chorus people who do everything with the action from gossiping about it to deconstructing it. The show is also typical in the honesty with which it tackled its adult subject matter.

Unfortunately, it is yet further typical in its employment of what we might call the Deflated Revision, a small-scale revival that tries to find a virtue in intimacy for its own sake. Deflation may alter the original considerably, as in *Ballad For a Firing Squad* (1968), an off-Broadway reduction of another out-of-town casualty, *Mata Hari* (1967), with great variation in the tunestack; or in a version of *Flora, the Red Menace* (1965; 1987) with a wholly new book writer. The 1965 *Flora*, a George Abbott show, suffered the usual Abbott inconsistencies but enjoyed the usual Abbott energy. The Deflation, stripped down to nine very busy people, has all the tang of a high-school show in the Girls' Gym.

Sometimes Deflation is less a revision than a frugal staging of the original; and what fun is that? *Colette*'s Deflation was bound to lose color and tone, the epic feeling of a natural force placed in cultural context. As *Colette Collage*, the Deflation went through two stages, first for the off-Broadway York Players in 1983, with Jana Robbins in the lead. "Remember music?" Marilyn Stasio's enthusiastic review began. Yes, but remember orchestras? Betsy Joslyn headed the cast of the second edition, for Musical Theatre Works, in 1991. Subtitled "*Two Musicals About Colette,*" the piece is divided into *Willy* and, after the intermission, *Maurice* (Goedeket). Most of the 1982 score remains, and a few new titles, are added. But "There's Another World," with its expansive conjuring up of Colette's imagination, doesn't fit this tiny *Colette*; and the rhapsodic finale gasps for breathing space. Most important, the role of Colette calls for an actress with theatre-filling glamour, and these do not often turn up in small-scale productions. Interestingly, the recording of *Colette Collage* uses two stars, Judy Blazer for *Willy* and Judy Kaye for *Maurice*. Still, this was not a project—or a life story—meant for the Matchbox School of Dramatic Art.

Colette is a dark piece, and darkness has become the hallmark of the modern musical of artistic ambition. *Colette* had the fun, too—a daffy cancan for a number about a bohemian bar, "Semiramis," the mischievous "Claudine" continuity, or Vidnovic's teaching Rigg to dance in "Riviera Nights." But *A Doll's Life* (1982) reveals how the fun is draining out of the dark musical, giving a new meaning to "musical play." That term used to denote a musical comedy with earnest subject matter—*Oklahoma!*, say. Or *Brigadoon, A Tree Grows in Brooklyn, Fanny, New Girl in Town*. However their producers billed them, they were of a musical-comedy type, even with a weighty theme. More recently, the musical play is just that: a beautiful piece of noir.

Characteristically, this musical play prefers unlikely subjects. Not *Green Grow the Lilacs* or *Idiot's Delight* unlikely—something impossible, such as what happens to Ibsen's Nora after she slams the famous door to walk into twentieth-century theatre at the end of *A Doll's House*. With music by Larry Grossman, book and lyrics by Betty Comden and Adolph Green, and direction by Harold Prince, *A Doll's Life* seemed an odd mating of the concept musical with musical comedy, for Comden and Green had generally worked in farce while Prince had spent the 1970s with Stephen Sondheim. (Grossman was caught mid-form, standing then just about halfway between the antic *Minnie's Boys* [1970] and the intense *Grind* [1985].)

In the event, Comden and Green met the challenge with startling ease, sounding quite unlike the team that wrote "Just in Time" and "Adventure" with Jule Styne. *A Doll's Life*'s lyrics have poetry and insight worthy of an important story; and Grossman outdid himself. Always a good melodist, he enlarged his sound to create a modern operetta—very dramatic but stuffed with music. Of course, this is one of those scores in which the ensemble will cut jaggedly into the narrative with emphases and questions, exhibiting an almost evil precision in pinning down a character. At such moments, the orchestration (by Bill Byers) has the radiance of high-tech lighting; some of these concept shows feel like a three-hour session with an angry psychiatrist. Still, "Letter To the

Children" and "Learn To Be Lonely" are achingly intimate, "Stay With Me, Nora" is the latest in the musical's endless line of irresistible come-ons, and "No More Mornings" explores the heroine's post-coital bliss in the sweeping waltz style known to the merriest operettas.

The plot, however, invents problems. The newly homeless Nora learns how difficult life is for an unpropertied woman without the protection of marriage. Work is scarce and, when found, exploitative. But Nora has charm and can use it to meet men on equal terms. One thinks of Jerry Herman's line from *Mame* about the successful combination of "sex and guts," for by the middle of the second act Nora is both a mistress and a perfume magnate, something of an exploiter herself. But it has always been her aim to return home to husband and children. Now that her husband can entertain accepting her—perhaps—as an equal, he says, "We must talk." As they sit down to do so, with an expectant ensemble looking on, the curtain falls.

The first problem is that this is physically possible but culturally unlikely. A perfume magnate? The second problem is a confusingly self-referential prologue in which the principals of *A Doll's Life* are seen in modern dress, as actors rehearsing *A Doll's House*, with the same romantic leads, Betsy Joslyn and George Hearn, in both. The third problem is The Door, an important (and mobile) part of Timothy O'Brien and Tazeena Firth's sets, but so omnipresent that it seemed less like the outstanding symbol of the Ibsen revolution and more like a prowler.*

A fourth problem lay not in the show itself but in the eyes of its beholders. The mixture of operetta and Ibsen, of feminism and Comden and Green, seemed absurdly incoherent, even pretentious—a word that mediocrity all too eagerly hurls at the ambitious. Were there interior contradictions in even the most artistic musical attempting to load a sequel atop Ibsen?† Or was Broadway simply in a mood to laugh at those in charge of the show? Comden and Green were essentially Rodgers and Hammerstein–era people who had Survived. They hadn't produced a hit since *Applause* (1970) or a genuinely *loved* title since *Bells Are Ringing*

---

* Coincidentally, *Colette* also made much of door symbolism, also as the entrée to the heroine's independence. As in Ibsen, the door was something heard—a slam in *A Doll's House*; a musical Leitmotiv in *Colette*—but not seen.

† In 1968, the Danish playwright Ernst Bruun Olsen had unveiled his own sequel to *A Doll's House, Hvor Gik Nora Hen, Da Hun Gik Ud?*, a frankly leftist propaganda piece.

(1956). Later, they attained National Treasure status, arousing ovations when sighted in the City Center lobby on Encores! nights. But in 1982, they were in eclipse, and show biz is wary of failure. Larry Grossman had no stylistic profile at this time, but Hal Prince was a duck in a barrel for what some saw as artist's arrogance. All those Concepts, that Presentation! Prince even had a hit with Andrew Lloyd Webber! So some were enjoying a revenge, now that the fast closing of *Merrily We Roll Along* (1981) had launched a series of Prince flops not to be broken, at least on Broadway, till yet another hit with Lloyd Webber.

Certainly, the atmosphere along The Street as *A Doll's Life* came in from an unsuccessful run in Los Angeles was at best Uninterested. The *nomyenklatura* would not be turning out for opening night; tickets were actually available at the half-price booth in Times Square.

Those who did see one of the show's previews or one of its 5 official performances might have been confused by the way the authors and Prince developed their proposition. "Rare Wines," a duet for Nora and a wealthy industrialist (Edmund Lyndeck, the wicked judge in *Sweeney Todd*), comes off as a combination of seduction and union negotiation. They are clearly headed for the boudoir, but she counters his growly endearments and heavy breathing with suggestions on how to improve working conditions for his women employees. Later, her crashing solo "Power," meant to reveal the intoxication of a woman who has had a taste of testosterone, is simply wrong. There are such women, but for two hours *A Doll's Life* has shown us that Nora isn't one of them. She's somewhere between the Girl whom Boy Meets and the independent women that Oscar Hammerstein liked to write about, Julie Jordan forced by extraordinary circumstances to be Anna Leonowens. "Shall I Tell You What I Think of You?" or even "Dat's Love" is about as "masculine" as this woman can be. "Power" endows her implausibly.

Having said this, one must also single out *A Doll's Life* as one of the most beautiful stagings of the era—intelligent, arresting, thematically consistent, and lit (by Ken Billington) to expunge the old blackout waits we noted in *La Cage aux Folles* so that the eye might travel along with the players while the background and stage pieces shifted imperceptibly. These period shows always give the costume designer (here, Florence Klotz) a main chance in the *Little Night Music* mode, especially when the ensemble poses in its commentative groupings, so old-fashioned in the clothing yet so new-wave in their concept plastique. Prince also employed something new to the musical, silent figures who maintained their own unit within the ensemble. Billed as Woman in White, Woman in Red, Woman in Black, and Man in Black, these mysterious exegetes enacted rather than sang their commentary, as when the Man and one of the Women swirled across the stage in a ballroom coupling, or when, during "Letter To the Children," the quartet appeared on an overhead catwalk, one of the females on her knees as a scrubwoman and a second moving in a Robert Wilson adagio toward the third.

Prince's use of his people often suggested ballet by other means, the music, stage pictures, and narrative blended into near-perpetual motion. For instance, the sequence that took "Nora" from the opening rehearsal of Ibsen's play into the new story created an unusual sort of musical scene, made not just of dialogue, arioso, and full-out song but of visuals as well. The famous *slam!* of Nora's walkout was timed to the very beat on which the music began, as Nora launched her adventure, now in antique costume: trapped in the narrow mores of the nineteenth century. She looked odd, as she was meant to, against the modern dress of the "actors" of the rehearsal—but now some of them were also in the dress of Ibsen's day. The four silent figures made their first appearance as the actors worried over Nora's curious behavior and as the rehearsal floor plan of desk, chairs, and so on rose to serve as a backdrop: something utterly basic now become utterly fantastical.

We speak of *Carousel's* Bench Scene as a summit of the musical's alchemy of words and music in shifting combinations; here was a combination of words and music and the sheer *sights* of theatre as well. It was how Prince led us from the Ibsen we know to the new story that he wanted to tell. And more: as the company went on questioning Nora's motivations and possibilities, we discovered that they had completed their change to the clothing of 1879; meanwhile, the lighting board began to erase everything but the train that would take Nora to the rest of her life. A young composer (Peter Gallagher) entered the car, and the penniless Nora played him for her fare, to the scolding of the chorus. The story proper had begun.

That the story is bizarre does not distract from the production's achievement. One of the libretto's episodes centered on *Loki and Baldur,* Gallagher's opera—"a Norwegian epic," he claims, "to make Wagner shake in his slippers." It surfaces first at a piano reading hosted by a diva (Barbara Lang) interested in Gallagher. Again, the costumes are an eyeful, but the lights dim out on everyone in a unique freeze-frame that somehow appeared to drain the color out of everyone but Betsy Joslyn and George Hearn. Now playing prosperous lawyer, Hearn is the energy that has emptied the stage of its fill, the appetite that has led lighting designer Billington to magic the world into black-and-white, except for the pair starring in this very new-minted Boy Meets Girl. "I've been studying your case," sings Hearn in "You Interest Me," over stabbing brass and worried strings. One might call it the musical's version of a movie close-up: but movies don't have this music, these voices. Then a gaffe from Joslyn affronts Lang, who brusquely breaks up the audition. Again the lights change the scene for us, instantly banish from view all but an apologizing Joslyn and a stone-cold Gallagher, who whirled around and slapped Joslyn *crack!* in the face.

The entire theatre jumped at this brutal effect; and of course the show meant from the start to explore man's inhumanity toward women. Yet the piece is as much about class as about gender, in something as small as the gifted young composer's having to work as a waiter and in something as large as the realization that the difference between the seductive Nora and a bordello prostitute is a middle-class education.

Maybe *A Doll's Life* had too much intellectual subject matter to succeed; and too much interesting music and too much Europe. Another aspect of the modern musical is the modern audience, which seems to be running out of concentration. It also doesn't know how to absorb irony anymore. *Loki and Baldur* reappeared after the audition scene as snippets of an actual performance, complete with Lang playing Baldur as a trouser role, Wagnerian touches, and little Nibelungs with pitchforks. It's a spoof, right? Or is that what opera is supposed to be?

"I took the old legend," boasts composer Gallagher at one point, "and gave it a hidden political, sociological meaning!" That's what Hal Prince and his writers did with Ibsen. It's a noble undertaking, but—like a number of the best shows we'll encounter in these pages—it may be too smart for its public.

But then, even Galt MacDermot and William Dumaresq's *The Human Comedy* (1983) proved too smart to run, with a sheaf of raves from the critics. Premiered at Joseph Papp's New York Shakespeare Festival,

The Human Comedy moved to the Royale Theatre and closed two weeks later, despite a superb cast and an astonishingly attractive score.

As so often with modern musical adaptations, the source is unexpected: William Saroyan's 1943 novel of the same name, itself drawn from an original film script. And the MacDermot-Dumaresq version is through-sung, another mark of the modern show: it's an opera. What, by the composer of *Hair* (1967)? Of *Dude* (1972)? But, remember, operas don't have to be *Loki and Baldur*. In fact, MacDermot's *Via Galactica* (1972) was also an opera. It was as well a crazy bomb, while *The Human Comedy* is an exhilarating folk piece.

Employing a battery of musical styles (including a few of his own invention), MacDermot slipped into the wartime 1940s of Saroyan's tale with music that seems to "feel" the period without having come from it. MacDermot's 1940s are timeless; so are Saroyan's. His story, set in Ithaca, California, focuses on the Macauley family and their friends and associates. The widowed Mrs. Macauley (Bonnie Koloc) has one son at the front, Marcus (Don Kehr). The teenage Homer (Stephen Geoffreys) finds work at the telegraph office, and four-year-old Ulysses (Josh Blake) wanders about town having charming adventures. There are also a sister (Mary Elizabeth Mastrantonio) and Marcus' girl friend (Caroline Peyton), and the two grown-ups at the telegraph office (Rex Smith, Gordon Connell). There are also the folk of Ithaca generally and even the spirit of the dead Mr. Macauley (also Don Kehr), for it is Saroyan's notion that all humankind—indeed, all life on earth—enjoys a mystical union, and that death is not an end but a transformation. Thus, Marcus can die yet not be mourned, for he sends on in his place his buddy Tobey (Joseph Kolinski), an orphan who will become the new Macauley.

Saroyan was a crackpot, a Pangloss; but it's a sweet idea even so. Really, it's another *Our Town*—though, like *Colette*'s "Joy," it thrills rather than depresses. *Colette* was about the individual, the genius; *The Human Comedy* tells how everyone helps everyone else in a utopia where genius is superfluous.

The Human Comedy's director, Wilford Leach, devised for the two-month run downtown an arena-style playing area, with the orchestra separated on either side and the entire cast in view throughout the action. There was virtually no division between the play and its public, making the spectator feel a part of Ithaca and of Saroyan's ecumenical conceit.

Uptown at the Royale, behind a proscenium, *The Human Comedy* lost that sentimental contact; but that isn't why it is one of the few musicals to close despite money notices. The title is perhaps too vague—and Saroyan, a presence in the middle and late 1930s, lost his audience over the years in a series of self-imitating failures. MacDermot was no one's idea of a Master; and who was William Dumaresq?

Alas. A beautiful piece was wasted, for the authors' faithful adaptation finds the wonder and exaltation that Saroyan's fans have always heard in his work. Amusingly, some of Dumaresq's odder constructions—surely, one thinks, duplicating Saroyan's whimsy—are in fact inventions. In the musical, the ever inquiring Ulysses asks his mother, "Where might Marcus be?," which suits the throbbing question-and-answer number MacDermot composed. But in the novel, the boy just says, "Where's Marcus?" Perhaps this was changed because some of Ulysses' exploits were unstageable and Dumaresq's lyrics had to work all the harder. An extended sequence in the novel in which Ulysses gets caught in a new kind of painless bear trap (and who but Saroyan would think to invent one?) unfortunately had to be reduced to one of those offstage events.

Still, the Saroyan Idea lights up the work in every number, even the *objets trouvés* such as "I Can Carry a Tune," Homer's assurance that he can deliver a singing telegram; or "Hi Ya, Kid," Ulysses' encounter with a black train worker, used as a binding element in three appearances. One number, "I Said, Oh No," juxtaposes two girls' singing of a "young love" pop tune with a Mexican woman's keening for her serviceman son, killed in action, all three reaching unison on the "oh no"s. Anything in Saroyan turns into music—a grammar-school lecture ("The Assyrians"), a salute to dessert ("Cocoanut Cream Pie"), even a robbery at the telegraph office ("Give Me All the Money"). Throughout, MacDermot pushes his singers into their upper registers, giving the thistledown Saroyan an intensity that his plays could have used.

Note that *The Human Comedy* employed some familiar names (Donna Murphy understudied two roles) but no one who was at the time a genuine theatre star—yet another characteristic of the new musical. Which did we lose first, the Ethel Mermans or the Ethel Merman roles? *Colette* was unthinkable without a star, but *A Doll's Life* imprisons its leading players within its dramatis personae, and *The Human Comedy* is so *ensemble* that it has no leading players. "Life makes all of us leading players" is how Saroyan might have put it.

One could call *Colette* a kind of show-biz backstager, *A Doll's Life* an intellectualized musical play, and *The Human Comedy* a show all about feelings. They nonetheless have one thing in common, and this, too, typifies the modern musical: they failed. Most of the interesting shows fail nowadays; what runs is shlock, dance pieces, and a few revivals.

Ah! Another sign of the age. The love of revivals became a craze in the 1980s. There were replica stagings—*Fiddler on the Roof* and *My Fair Lady* in 1981; *Mame* (with Angela Lansbury, Jane Connell, Willard Waterman, and Sab Shimono of the original cast) in 1983 for a shockingly short run; *The Wiz* and *Oliver!* (with Patti LuPone's Nancy, winning the hearts of young and old alike with her enchanting habit of falling headlong onto the stage floor at the slightest provocation) in 1984, both also fast flops.

Revivals in general seemed a history course, teaching works from virtually every decade of the century and one from way back in the First Age. Joseph Papp and director Wilford Leach gave us a triumphant staging of Gilbert and Sullivan's *The Pirates of Penzance*, a work premiered (for business reasons) not in London but in New York, in 1879. True, an impromptu matinée was given the day before in the English provinces by a *Pinafore* troupe, holding scripts and in their *Pinafore* costumes. But *Pirates'* true first night was given at our own Fifth Avenue Theatre; and now, in 1980, it started off in Central Park's Delacorte Theatre before moving to the Uris for an early 1981 opening for a bit short of two years.

Although the *Pirates* score was bolstered by two interpolations from other Gilbert and Sullivan works (including *Ruddigore*'s "My Eyes Are Fully Open," which also found its way into *Thoroughly Modern Millie* twenty years later), and although the already comic piece was filled with gags that would have startled the authors, this was almost a faithful resuscitation. By the 1980s, works in revival were routinely being rewritten to the point of mauling; *Pirates* wasn't rewritten. (One regret: Sullivan's orchestrations went quite bald in William Elliott's makeover, and they never sounded right at any time.) The critics were thrilled to a man, not least with Kevin Kline's Miles Gloriosus of a Pirate King, landing every lunge, every sword thrust, in the wrongest place possible—with what panache! "Younger patrons may think they're going in to catch Linda Ronstadt," wrote Douglas Watt of the *Daily News*, "but they'll come out whistling Kevin Kline."

The casting was mostly unexceptional—George Rose in the patter role, Estelle Parsons (replacing the Park run's Patricia Routledge) as the comic Older Dame, and Alexandra Korey (replacing Alice Playten) as Edith, the girls' chorus leader. Doubters may have worried over the participation of pop lady Ronstadt opposite Rex Smith in the romantic leads, and indeed they edged Sullivan into top 40 territory in their vocalism. But the whole thing worked very nicely, from the mobile little pirate ship to Graciela Daniele's choreography, one of the many ingredients that helped unify the old material (the writing) and the new material (the actual performance of it).*

If the quaint world of G&S can be so pleasingly modernized—and yet *not* modernized—why were native pieces so badly presented? George M. Cohan's *Little Johnny Jones* (1904) and Rudolf Friml's *The Three Musketeers* (1928) are basic American art in, respectively, crazy-plot musical comedy and costume operetta. The Cohan revival started out at the Goodspeed Opera House in 1980 in a dreary reduction by Alfred Uhry that gutted the score and left out the plot's climax on the trail of kidnappers in San Francisco's Chinatown. Of course, book revision is meant to rationalize a chaos and cut to the content. But these bizarre old shows are intricate bagatelles: they have no content, and cutting one sequence can weaken the entire structure. Goodspeed's uncharismatic Johnny, Eric Weitz, was succeeded on a national tour by Tom Hulce, David Cassidy, and finally Donny Osmond, who brought it into New York in 1982. By then, Goodspeed's physical production had been expanded and some of the score restored, but the critics savaged it, and it closed on opening night.

As a late-twenties operetta, *The Three Musketeers* needed no rationalizing: operettas were the most integrated shows of that era. So this

---

* With such critical and popular success, it seems odd that no other nineteenth-century work was given a rival airing—but few know that Theodore Mann, of Circle in the Square, sought his own *Pirates*. Your reporter himself advised Mann to try Offenbach's *La Vie Parisienne* (1866), the least dated of all so-called operettas, a play with songs about the Modern Babylon. What better suited the New York of Andy Warhol and the recent Studio 54 Case? But Mann was inexperienced in the musical, while Papp had worked with top talents. Mann's Offenbach got as far as a workshop, by which time the star, Madeline Kahn, had withdrawn. The project was not pursued.

one they spoofed, in a version by Mark Bramble that dropped much of the original score in favor of Friml interpolations. Or so one imagined. The program was silent on the derivation of the unfamiliar numbers, and it took a ready ear to detect *The White Eagle's* proud "Regimental Song" in the falsetto cock-a-doodles of a quartet with new lyrics called "The Actor's Life."

This show, too, had started elsewhere; so much does, nowadays. From Stamford, Connecticut it came, where Bramble had directed and Onna White choreographed, with David Garrison as D'Artagnan and Kim Criswell as the Queen. Tom O'Horgan was to have taken over for New York with an entirely new cast. But by opening night, in 1984, that new cast was working for director Joe Layton and choreographer Lester Wilson.

It hardly matters, as this was one of the worst revivals in memory, for no provision was made for the vocal allure that is operetta's key ingredient. The English Michael Praed and the American Liz Callaway were the romantic leads, with Queen Darlene Anders and title men Chuck Wagner, Brent Spiner, and Ron Taylor. Buckingham, the Queen's love interest, was Joseph Kolinski, Tobey in *The Human Comedy*. These people can sing, in the right venue. Operetta just isn't their venue. Only villainess Marianne Tatum broke through the hurdy-gurdy Friml, in a plump mezzo with a surprise high F sharp. Meanwhile, the bad guys camped and posed, everyone ran around in the auditorium (D'Artagnan led a horse up the stage-left aisle), and the one stylish note in the evening occurred in the first few seconds, when the French theatre's customary three blows of exhortation were heard, with the orchestra striking up on the third blow. This revival lasted 9 performances.

Where is the Great Tradition now? At least two thirties shows held up, in 1983, Rodgers and Hart's *On Your Toes* (1936) and Marc Blitzstein's *The Cradle Will Rock* (1937). The latter appeared on the bare stage and with the solo piano that are all but de rigueur today, even though the famously canceled original production had sets and an orchestra. John Houseman, who produced that unseen *Cradle*, now directed the show, for the Acting Company, at the American Place Theatre. His cast included Patti LuPone and America's great patriot Tim Robbins playing the opening scene of Moll and Gent; and the three-week limited engagement returned for an aggregate total of 64 performances. It's a good showing for this work, considering its stick-figure satire and kazoo-ready ditties. On the other hand, if a troupe but stick to what Blitzstein wrote, as the Company did here, it's hard to get this strangely elemental and consistent piece wrong.

On Your Toes is harder; a 1954 revival failed, even in a time that loved big-dance musical comedy. One reason why *On Your Toes* doesn't play itself, without curating, is the typical George Abbott book (written with Rodgers and Hart), filled with contrivance and bombastic song cues. Another is the story, which implausibly involves the schoolteacher hero with gangsters. Of course, story wasn't why musicals were conceived in the 1930s. *On Your Toes* was planned to feature a dance-off between ballet and hoofing, and to give the work's original choreographer, George Balanchine, a chance to jazz up *la danse* in "Slaughter on Tenth Avenue."

Balanchine's choreography was retained, with some new work by Donald Saddler (hoofing) and Peter Martins (ballet). Also retained, most unusually, was Hans Spialek's original orchestration, with its duo-piano glissandos, piquant woodwind trills, and swing-band percussion. In fact, this *On Your Toes* marked Broadway's first taste of the *riesumazione*: the archeological reclamation of the Golden Age through restagings striving for authenticity. *On Your Toes*' décor was new, yes. But the script and tunestack came right from 1936, and Abbott himself directed, for the third time.*

There was no updating. Any other director would have tossed out "The Three B's" for its many allusions to music no longer in the household repertory—"Poor Butterfly," Shostakovich's opera *Lady Macbeth of Mtsensk* (a headline scandal of the 1930s), Liszt's *Les Préludes*—and would have worried that a late-century public would be mystified by the vaudeville act that opens the show. Set changes were accomplished by the old-style blackout, or even by performers finishing a scene in front of the show curtain, a technique that went out in the 1960s.

Best of all, the show brought back something we'd sorely missed—the star. Protagonist Lara Teeter, ingenue Christine Andreas, ballerino George de la Peña, and oldsters Dina Merrill and George S. Irving were

---

* Direction of the 1936 *On Your Toes* was credited to Worthington Miner (who "staged") and producer Dwight Deere Wiman (who "supervised"). However, Rodgers states in his memoirs that while Abbott wasn't around for rehearsals, he rejoined the company during the tryout and completely took over.

straight out of the casting book, even the unexpected Merrill, whose singing was kinda sorta but who definitely supplied her role's wonted glamour.

Natalia Makarova, however, was something extra-special. From Soviet defector to American Ballet Theatre luminary to ... George Abbott–Rodgers and Hart leading lady? Tamara Geva and Vera Zorina played the part in the earlier stagings; it calls for a star ballerina. But who could have known that Makarova had been nourishing a penchant for explosive mischief? "To think I was faithful to that man ... *for two months!*" she cried, after having been two-timed by de la Peña, Giselle throwing a Paramount tantrum in Anna Sten's accent. It's a nonsinging role, except for her part in the full-cast rendering of "There's a Small Hotel" during the curtain calls, and the dancing is not comparable to the Decathlon that Gwen Verdon pulled off in *Redhead*. But Makarova had the dangerous charm seldom seen these days. Busy on Western stages for a decade, she had nevertheless not had the chance to be herself before, and enjoyed tremendous success, going on to lead London's *On Your Toes*, now opposite American Tim Flavin.

Did *On Your Toes* prove the efficacy of the faithful reclamation? Or should one favor the "revisal," clocking old work into new modes? A *Brigadoon* in 1980 was set in 1980, though updating is easy in a ghost town: it's always "today" in Brigadoon. This version made mention of the Susan B. Anthony dollar coin, but otherwise the many script alterations—presumably by director Vivian Matalon—seemed to want to emphasize what was already in the work rather than to add to or change it. Matalon brought out the tribal nature of the townsfolk earlier than the 1947 original had done, also ending the first act earlier, to show Brigadoon's men standing on a hilltop, looking balefully about themselves, as the set revolved. The unnecessary "Jeannie's Packin' Up" and "My Mother's Wedding Day" lost their vocal lines (the music itself was retained), and Fiona jumped into "From This Day On" without any orchestral lead-in, as if in a lover's outburst at parting.

There were two blunders: horrible new orchestrations ("The Heather on the Hill" lost its schottische accompaniment) and a bafflingly awful comic as Meg Brockie. But the Agnes de Mille choreography turned up, as always, and the critics generally enjoyed themselves, praising particularly the romantic leads, Martin Vidnovic and Meg Bussert. *The New*

Yorker's Brendan Gill noted that the miking varied "from High Tin Can to inaudible"—another aspect of the new musical, as technicians spent the 1970s and 1980s fumbling with a crackpot science.

The question of whether to revive in the most faithful sense (as with *On Your Toes*), slightly to reshuffle the original elements (as with *Brigadoon*), or to use an old work as a template for a new piece (as with *Little Johnny Jones* or *The Three Musketeers*) was perhaps to have been settled by the Houston Grand Opera's *Show Boat* in 1983. After all, this was the company that in 1976 gave *Porgy and Bess* an outstanding revival, with many cuts opened up. But Houston's *Show Boat*, directed by Michael Kahn and choreographed by Dorothy Danner, was not quite the reinstatement one hoped for. The score did return almost in its entirety, including "Hey, Feller," not heard for fifty years. ("Dahomey" was missing, and "Till Good Luck Comes My Way" was dropped during the tryout.) The tuba and banjo of Robert Russell Bennett's 1927 scoring, purged for the 1946 revival, came back along with most of the Bennett charts—though, strangely, the credits on the program's title page mentioned no orchestrator at all. As a keepsake for *Show Boat* buffs, a taste of the long-discarded jazz-up of "Why Do I Love You?" in the original's finale dance turned up in the exit music.

However, there was a personnel problem. First, there were simply too few people on stage for the big moments that this work counts on. Moreover, some of the leads were improperly cast. The Magnolia, Sheryl Woods, lacked the fluty *grandezza* of the twenties diva. The Ravenal, Ron Raines, is an outstanding operetta baritone—but Ravenal is a tenor, less a hero than a worthless gallant. Lonette McKee was a matchless Julie (as she would be again, for Harold Prince in 1994). But, like all modern Julies, she is not the soprano that Kern and Hammerstein wrote for but a bass. She sang "Bill" in D Major, a sixth lower than Helen Morgan's B Flat. The piece sounds like a dirge down there; it's supposed to be a *happy* song that, for plot reasons, is quavered out by a wraith in misery. The irony dramatizes Julie's tragedy.

Then there was Donald O'Connor. His Captain Andy, loaded with unbearable ad-lib "ha-ha"s, lacked the richness that this central role requires. O'Connor's added tap solo at the end of "Why Do I Love You?" might have shocked the purist; on the contrary, it's exactly the kind of specialty that any twenties musical would have indulged, *Show Boat* included. But in general, O'Connor brought a Freed Unit banality to the character of a pixilated philospher-king.

Clearly, the Great Tradition is in recession, and the musical will be new if only because it has lost its relationship with the past. We must look to the Sondheim-Prince party for our future, then: for here was the source of the most fervent preaching throughout the 1970s. But 1981 is when they have their bomb.

Merrily We Roll Along looks back to tradition in its source, the 1934 play by George S. Kaufman and Moss Hart. Their second collaboration, quite out of the comic line they had inaugurated with *Once in a Lifetime* (1930) and carried through in *You Can't Take It With You* (1936) and *The Man Who Came To Dinner* (1939), *Merrily We Roll Along* was a failure. Still, it remained a classic title because of its unique organization: it runs backward. Starting in 1934 and then making eight stops, in 1927, 1926, and so on back to 1916, it claims one of the biggest casts ever assembled for a straight play. There is a single lead role, that of playwright Richard Niles. He has two best friends, painter Jonathan Crale and a sort of Dorothy Parker named Julia Glenn. There is also Richard's first wife, a piece of brownstone trash; and his second, a glamorous actress. Various others come and go or appear in a single scene—Richard's producer, his latest leading lady (and adulterous girl friend), a pianist modeled on George Gershwin, the hideous in-laws of his first marriage.

The play demonstrates how the protagonist loses his self-belief as he strives for success, starting as a creator of art at the little Provincetown Playhouse and a man blissfully in love but ending as a purveyor of fashionable comedies with Somerset Maugham titles like *The Ostrich* and *Silver Spoon* and utterly miserable. So the action "begins" at his latest opening-night party, which climaxes when his wife throws iodine into the eyes of her rival. To cap the paradox of a man's trying to find happiness by giving it up, the final scene, at Richard's college graduation, shows him delivering the valedictorian address. He speaks in highest praise of the two things he most values: friendship and idealism. And those are the very things we have seen stripped from him in the eight preceding scenes.

Inverting the passage of time is not a stunt. The plan is to trade in conventional narrative suspense for ironic revelation. Thus, we don't see the deep bond between Richard and Jonathan gradually dissolve: we see Jonathan approach Richard in a restaurant after a quarrel and separation, see Jonathan say hello and offer his hand, and see Richard smash him in the face as the two slam into a brawl. *Thereafter* we see the two of them friendly but losing contact, and later see the two so incredibly close they might be lovers.

In fact, there's nothing Lurking About in this relationship. Though Kaufman and Hart dared to begin one scene with Jonathan wearing a woman's coat, it belongs to his date of the night before, and she promptly enters from the bedroom. Jonathan is a type of heterosexual popular in plays and films of the period, an eccentric and even irritating young bohemian who is all the same fiercely lovable: a kid brother. It is rather Julia who cultivates a pathetic hidden crush on Richard, Julia who has the intelligence that Richard's women lack but who cannot enchant him and who ends as a public humiliation, muttering, scandalizing, and openly coming on to unavailable men—in her own words, "a drunken whore."

Merrily We Roll Along was very cleverly put together. The authors gave enough script time to the secondary figures so that the leads could—as *Camelot's* Merlyn puts it—"youthen" in costume and makeup before their next entrance. With nine different locales, three to an act, the text allowed designer Jo Mielziner to move from a full-sized set to a small set to another full-sized set within each act, making for minimal waits between scenes.* The three leads were cast with names of small renown—Kenneth MacKenna (Mielziner's brother, by the way) as Richard, Walter Abel as Jonathan, and MacKenna's future wife, Mary Philips, as Julia. There was one star turn, by the prankish veteran Cecilia Loftus as Richard's outspoken second mother-in-law, who neatly skewers Richard's society dramas at the top of her lungs at a fancy party:

MRS. RILEY: (imitating a Park Avenue heroine) "There's no one here, Alfred. They've all gone into the garden. Shall we dawnce?" . . .

---

* Some historians have blamed Mielziner's design plan for *Merrily's* high operating costs and financial failure; one suggests that *Merrily's* producer, Sam H. Harris, chose not to hire him again. On the contrary, Mielziner was a technical innovator of great ingenuity. He would have tackled the *Merrily* commission as a challenge precisely to keep the play in motion with speedy set changes. It was more likely the gigantic cast that kept *Merrily* in the red—and note that only a year later, Harris (and Moss Hart, at that) asked Mielziner to design their Cole Porter musical *Jubilee* (1935).

"I can face anything, dearest, as long as I know that I have you. Shall we dawnce?" . . . "Edgar! Father has shot himself! Shall we dawnce?"

I've given extra time to the original play in order to emphasize what an excellent idea it was to musicalize it and how badly the idea at first turned out. The play Merrily is loaded with inarticulate passions—Richard's for his writing, Jonathan's and Mary's (in very different ways) for Richard, the ensemble's in general for success. What more can music ask for than something inchoate to bring to full term? The play is verbose, but it has tang and plenty of picturesque detail. Is there too much *there* in it? Because trying to boil it down to its essence led Prince, Sondheim, and book writer George Furth to make a number of bizarre errors.

Their Merrily would not be another forties–fifties musical play, for the Sondheim-Prince format is very post–Rodgers and Hammerstein, using the nonlinear elements of the concept show and the echo texture of the modern score with its Leitmotiven and their developments. Also, the musical play centers on strongly written characters, while the musical Merrily is especially vague about the protagonist, now called Franklin Shepard. The new Jonathan Crale, unfortunately renamed Charley Kringas, is fully drawn, but as a sanctimonious nag, completely lacking Jonathan's roguish sense of humor and his endearing need to please. It's hard to imagine anyone's forming a bond with this character, with his constant need to come kringasing in with a list of one's faults. As for Julia, now one Mary Flynn, she was not completely realized in the play and is no better realized in the musical. (She does, at least, have one of the few lines carried over from Kaufman and Hart, the very first words of their script: "Know what I'm having? . . . Not much fun.") The musical Merrily was a concept show for characters who don't deserve one.

Another error lay in the updating. The musical opens in 1980 and closes in 1955. Because "fashionable playwrights" didn't really exist by 1980, the protagonist became a composer who gives up creating to produce Hollywood movies. Isn't this implausible? Yes, it has happened—Arthur Freed, for instance. But Freed was not the uniquely gifted talent that Franklin Shepard is supposed to be. Freed was good second-division, unenterprisingly tuneful in tonic-dominant harmony. Moreover, as a producer he was in charge of some of the best-loved films in movie history. We never learn what kind of producer Franklin Shepard is: the authors envisioned him so tenuously that in the musical as played in 1981 every-one thinks his latest release is a dud, and in the final revision played today everyone thinks it's a sure thing.

Another error was dropping all the incidental coloring in the show-biz scenes that enriched the play—the backstage of it all, with Gershwin at the keyboard and a recklessly earthy mother-in-law wrecking your soirée; but also the ghastly in-laws of the young playwright when money means not luxury but independence. (In the musical, these in-laws are only referred to, in a line of "It's a Hit!") Even the first wife, a strong presence in the play, is a cipher in the musical. We don't see why the marriage broke up, as we do in Kaufman and Hart—better, why the authors believed the marriage deserved to. They use the wife to discover their hero. The musical doesn't know who its hero is.

A more crushing error lay in casting the musical with kids. Apparently, Prince wanted a company unseasoned and raw but with the energy and infectious idealism that the three leads have at the evening's end. While following the action, the public could at length relate in a personal and perhaps doting way to the actors as well as the characters in their blindly joyous anthem, "Our Time." In effect, Frank, Charley, and Mary would become what their impersonators had been all along: innocent kids who have no idea how hard it's going to be. Thus, the musical might twist Kaufman and Hart's old Broadway legend of a piece into something modern and moving.

But it wasn't moving. It was amateur night. Only Jason Alexander and Terry Finn, as the producer and his wife, upheld professional capability. The Frank, Jim Walton, was an understudy promoted during previews when James Weissenbach proved inept. The Mary, Ann Morrison, was too young to play a woman who makes her first contact with the public as a jaded wreck. The Charley, Lonny Price, was Lonny Price. The first wife, Sally Klein, had nothing to play, especially when she lost her ballad, "Not a Day Goes By."

Choreographer Ron Field was flabbergasted. Under Prince, Field had made history with Cabaret (1966). Now he was trying to give what little dance the show had some protection from the bungling performers. Tony Charmoli could stage Woman of the Year's "One of the Boys" around Lauren Bacall by framing her charisma with the dancing corps, but Field had nobody to stage around and no dancing corps in any real sense. The big dance breaks were so carefully calibrated to the company's modest abilities that they were like euphemisms. Prince simply wouldn't admit how bad the show looked, and Sondheim even thought Weissenbach was valid. When Prince fired Field, he said thanks.

There was still another error: the décor. Because the musical moved the play's high-school graduation idea from the last to the first scene, the permanent set was a high-school gymnasium lined with lockers. The costuming was dominated by sweatshirts bearing the characters' identities—"Best Pal," "Talk Show Host," and so on. It must have sounded like a workable program, as the young place and the young clothes would support the young cast. Still, it looked terrible. Not unusual: accidental. Like a train wreck.

But why don't we pause to consider the errors made by *Merrily's* audiences? Many professed to be "confused" by the chronology. Some apparently were expecting a flashback structure—a contemporary prologue followed by a linear narrative starting somewhere in the past and taking us up to the present day again. Others just could not keep track of the way events that occurred later *in the running time* had created events that had already occurred before *in the action.* And a few probably could have followed the action but didn't want to bother. It's so much easier to wave it all away and claim to be "confused."

So let me digress with a personal note. When I was very young and eager to get old and sophisticated, I got into the matter of theatre and begged grown-ups to give me books on the subject. So I learned about Broadway, and about people like Sam H. Harris and Kaufman and Hart. I wanted to be Moss Hart, partly because he had directed *My Fair Lady*; partly because I saw him on television being sophisticated with his wife, Kitty Carlisle, who sang the heroine on my then favorite show album, a studio reading of *The Desert Song*; and partly because he had co-written *Merrily We Roll Along.* I fostered a mild obsession with this work, because playing a story backward seemed the most sophisticated theatrical event since Aeschylus introduced the Second Actor. At the age of eight, I understood how *Merrily We Roll Along* ran backward, and I was not "confused." And if an eight-year-old gets it, who are these jackasses in 1981 who say they don't? Sondheim has told us that at one preview, two enraged queens gleefully chased him up the theatre aisle, pretending they didn't know he was right in front of them as they tore his work apart. And let us consider also the many walkouts during *Merrily's* six weeks of previews and 16 performances. Did these people really have something better to do in the succeeding hour or so than to hear the rest of the latest Sondheim score? Whom are you contentless loons trying to impress?

Boys and girls, I say that what we have here is another of those Broadway pile-ons, just as with *A Doll's Life*. Not that *Merrily* was a good show. When it started previewing, it was terrible but the music was very, very good. When it opened, it was terrible but the music was very, very good. Yes, it was by then less terrible, even a lot less terrible: for an astonishing amount of clarifying and cleaning had been performed. But even so *Merrily We Roll Along* was an embarrassingly feeble reduction of a play that, whatever its faults, keeps its major themes in smart order from finish to start while giving us an intricate comparison between living life in the midst of everything and living life in nowhere. It has an *idea*. The musical has nothing but a score.

So *Merrily* became the *Candide* of the younger generation, the beloved score that keeps a show alive. And, too, the recording sounded good enough—kid voices and all—to persuade some that the original production must have been vastly undervalued. Now came the book revisions, to give the music a surer setting; but the music was revised as well. Frank got the introspective "Growing Up," and the producer's wife opens Act Two with an edgily jazzed-up "Good Thing Going," which at first seems like her character song sent out from the usual concept-show limbo but turns out to be a performance spot in Franklin's first Broadway show, an amusingly jarring surprise. "The Hills of Tomorrow," originally the first of the Frank-Charley collaborations, has vanished along with the graduation scene, and the first big plot number is now an exposition number, "That Frank," a revision of "Rich and Happy."

As with *Candide*, it is the book that has most changed. But the current *Candide* book—the 1988 Scottish Opera version, sanctioned by the composer—is a successful reclamation. *Merrily* the musical still has no lead characters but, rather, descendants of Kaufman and Hart's people, denuded of all identifying features save their rubric sweatshirts. The latter, of course, are no longer used in the physical sense; metaphorically, they're still there, captioning figures who undergo little development.

The score, at least, is not only popular but something special in the Sondheim oeuvre in its use of the ur-theme. *Sweeney Todd* uses and reuses themes, but Sondheim's organization of *Merrily* derives mainly from "The Hills of Tomorrow." This is logical: the hills of tomorrow are what Kaufman and Hart were telling of, the dream of who you thought you'd still be when you finally reach them. That notion, as a musical theme, creates the show's music in various ways (most notably in "Good Thing Going"). But we notice also how Frank sings a snatch of the climactic "Our Time" in the first story number, while the "Dreams don't die" melody cell occupies the orchestra in snazzy brass riffs throughout the scene; or how the title song and "Our Time" crash together during the first-act finale; or how the hush of wonder in the main strain of "Our Time" later (that is, earlier in the show's playing order) becomes the smug release to "Rich and Happy." The program implies that destiny lies entirely in one's character: the elements of *you* are always available, even before you know how they work. Thus Sondheim finds a musical equivalent of Kaufman and Hart's view of the world.

The verbal perceptions are similarly telling. One line asks, "Why don't you turn around and go back?," which is what the show itself does. The phrase "movers and shapers" in the last scene is uttered optimistically, as suggesting a group worth joining; in the first scene, it is Mary's rejection of Frank's society, a group worth loathing. She hasn't simply changed her mind: she has at length become discouraged, the characteristic state of some of Sondheim's most intriguing people—Ben Stone, Countess Charlotte, George (in Act Two of *Sunday in the Park With*), most of those in *Assassins*, Fosca. But these are rather gaudy folk, even the apparently quiet ones—as we learn when mandarin and socialite Ben breaks out in his top-hat-and-cane folly. Mary isn't gaudy. She's like someone you might have known in high school. Her demoralization is one of *Merrily*'s most powerful messages, because it isn't only the haunted who lose their way in life. It could happen to you.

Most interesting is the audition of "Who Wants To Live In New York?," an early up-tune version of "Good Thing Going." The producer they perform it for will eventually put on the aforementioned Broadway show, but at this point he's distant and impedient. The number itself is odd, a sort of comic thing that is just about to turn into a love song, on the line "But since I've met you"—and *just then* the producer cuts in with his dismissal. That is, at exactly the point at which the material arrests the ear, the producer reveals that he doesn't listen to new music. He wants "Some Enchanted Evening": something one can enjoy without having to concentrate. Something that isn't "confusing."

That producer was *Merrily*'s audience, and that is the modern audience, the curse of the modern musical. This audience has become restless, exhausted, and stupid. It has had its show biz miked and voice-overed and misspelled till it no longer knows how to listen or watch. If the musical, America's smart form, no longer has a smart audience, what can its future hold but degradation?

At least *Merrily We Roll Along* isn't "confusing" any more. A 2002 mounting in Washington, D. C. went over especially well, partly because director Christopher Ashley cast—as directors rarely do—an extremely charismatic Frank in Michael Hayden. He's supposed to be something beautiful that everyone uses for personal validation, available anew for each pilgrim's salvation fantasy. Also, Raúl Esparza's Charley brought the character back to Jonathan Crale—to the dear little nut that you have to forgive because he didn't mean it for the thousandth time. Esparza sang an intense "Franklin Shepard, Inc." entirely in his television-interview chair, a daring staging for a number that is a dancing avalanche of accusations and regrets.

The Washington staging was imaginative in general, opening with the entire cast (except Hayden) amid a crowd of upright pianos, emphasizing that at the core of this piece stand two best friends who believe they are going to write the greatest songs the world will ever hear. Somewhere in the number, Hayden simply materialized, as the Franklin Shepards do in one's life. One minute they don't exist, and the next they're the star of your show.

One of the pleasures of following the many *Merrily* revivals is noting the difference in both text and approach. There was the 1985 La Jolla version, offering the work's first overhaul, with John Rubinstein, Chip Zien, and Heather MacRae, directed by James Lapine. The Kaufman-Hart iodine incident, missing in 1981, was reinstated, though now the victim was Frank. At Arena Stage in 1990, with Victor Garber, David Garrison, and Becky Ann Baker, the iodine was aimed at Frank's starlet girl friend, following 1934. Each revival seems to make more changes, though stagings in Leicester, England, in 1992 and at the York Theatre Company in 1994 appeared to present Final *Merrily*. Then, at the Donmar Warehouse in 2000, a great deal of the original book sneaked back in and the mounting won a Best Musical Olivier for its trouble.

What other two-week failure has been running so long? Or enjoys a twenty-first-anniversary reunion concert of almost all the original cast, performed in an atmosphere of tearful delight? It's a *hit*! And isn't its Broadway return the most ineluctably invited of guests in our twenty-first-century revival party? At once the most traditional and most modern of shows, it has a *Chorus Line* appeal, a universality—few of us aren't discouraged after grand hopes. The old-time musical sings "Ridin' High." The modern musical—this one—sings, "I want it the way that it was." It can't be: that is what "modern" means.

2

The aficionado prefers a crazy bomb to a mediocrity, because the musical as a form has such potential as entertainment that the merely adequate can fatigue the spirit while the disaster can amuse with its drastic misjudgments and desperation gambles. Also, crazy bombs often contain attractive music or a collectible performance.

Onward Victoria (1980), which closed on opening night after a withering blast from the critics, was certainly not doomed by its subject, the revolutionary nineteenth-century feminist Victoria Woodhull. People who want to change the world make excellent protagonists—one thinks immediately of *The King and I*'s Anna, *Camelot*'s Arthur, *Man of La Mancha*'s Cervantes, perhaps Sweeney Todd. Earlier attempts to build a musical around Woodhull include a *Vicky For President* with Carol Channing, which actually got as far as an official announcement but never materialized. *Winner Take All* (1976) played Los Angeles, with Patricia Morison and, as Victoria's sister Tennessee Claflin, Janet Blair.

It was Jill Eikenberry and Beth Austin who brought the girls to Broadway—but *Onward Victoria* was a cheap-looking, gaggy debasement of important social history. The first woman to run for U.S. president, Woodhull advocated not only gender equality but sexual freedom. Yet the book and lyrics, by Charlotte Anker and Irene Rosenberg, reduced all this to slogans and smutty puns. Worse, they portrayed the public censor Anthony Comstock as a comic figure: his briefcase hid the coiled whip of the bondage buff, and his character song, "Everyday [sic] I Do a Little Something For the Lord," giggled over his hypocrisy. However, censors are not comic figures. They are book burners, and—as Heinrich

Heine famously pointed out—book burners eventually become people burners.

The Anker-Rosenberg story line twists chronicle with an invented love affair between Woodhull and the eminent Congregationalist minister Henry Ward Beecher (Michael Zaslow). This concludes in Beecher's trial for adultery, in which the alienated Woodhull testifies against Beecher to destroy him. As it happens, the real-life Beecher was charged with adultery, and—as in the show—acquitted. Still, the whole episode was played so implausibly that the show might have been set in Oz, even if the cast included such other real-life figures as Cornelius Vanderbilt and restaurateur Charlie Delmonico. Doug Johnson's lavish poster art seemed to promise an operetta-sized production, with its parade of feminists and top-hatted financiers, drumming soldier and child rolling a hoop, all surmounted by a billowing American flag. In fact, the show was sparsely decorated and tried to get by with too small a cast for its grandiose theme.

So it was a terrible evening *except*. Keith Herrmann's music was sometimes tuneful. The opening number, "The Age of Brass," was one of those gala pieces of crowd control introducing each of the principals while setting the scene. "In New York, the only sin is being timid," the chorus warns, preparing for a battle of big egos. One can see why Woodhull and her times have inspired writers of musicals, but Anker and Rosenberg lacked vision. "Magnetic Healing," a number recalling the two sisters' background in carnival side-show quackery, is intriguing. But most of the score strikes typical poses. The first-act finale, "Unescorted Women," in which the sisters have to take their coachman into Delmonico's in order to be seated, is classic floppo: so terrible it's inspired. Yet this was topped in Act Two by "Beecher's Defense," in which Woodhull, in court, lets fly with a horde of shameless double meanings. Her ex-lover's "divine uplift," for example, must make his congregation "proud to have a preacher so well endowed." What, in the 1870s?

Onward Victoria was a good idea badly executed. *Bring Back Birdie* (1981) was a bad idea; sequels of musicals always are. Apparently, this "twenty years on" by *Bye Bye Birdie*'s authors, Charles Strouse, Lee Adams, and Michael Stewart, was meant not for Broadway but for stock and amateur marketing: the sequel would suit the high-school or community group that had enjoyed putting on the 1960 show and wanted more of it. Somehow or other, a quartet of producers thought it suitable for Broadway as well, with a Joe Layton staging and a cast headed by the original Rose, Chita Rivera, opposite Donald O'Connor in Dick Van Dyke's old role, with Maria Karnilova as O'Connor's comically abusive mother. The plot premise found O'Connor trying to locate the vanished Conrad Birdie for a TV special while O'Connor's family implodes on such temptations of modern life as rock stardom and religious cultism.

The premise itself has potential as social satire, but everything is in the execution, and the execution was the worst musical ever written by people you'd heard of. Stewart's script recalled the excesses of brainless twenties musicals in its reality-defying plotting and lumpy proportions, and very little of Strouse and Adams here was even slightly listenable. The original *Birdie*'s charm inhered in its consistency: it was entirely about how rock and roll affects the generation war. *Bring Back Birdie* treated that and so much else that the satire never found a place to land. David Mitchell's concept set of TV screens of varying sizes moving in and out conveyed something, but the show itself didn't. Now it had Rivera going country-western in "A Man Worth Fightin' For," then it revealed that Karnilova was a long-lost show-biz star so that she could make a return on that TV show performing a vampy charleston called "I Love 'Em All." Some unexpected fun was generated during previews when Rivera's bodice slipped open while she was dancing; at another performance, O'Connor went up in his lyrics and suddenly told the audience that he'd never liked the song in the first place. *Bring Back Birdie* lasted 4 performances.

Some crazy bombs are less crazy than futile, even if more or less enjoyable. Early audiences were taking well to *Copperfield* (1981), the latest Dickens adaptation, entirely by Al Kasha and Joel Hirschhorn. Still, no show so old-fashioned as this, with such a derivative score, was going to get past the critics. Perhaps producers Don Gregory and Mike Merrick hoped to luck into a second *Oliver!*. But then they shouldn't have cast Carmen Mathews as Aunt Betsey Trotwood, for Mathews had flop convection displacement of such electric power that she closed not only her own shows but everything playing within a three-block radius. Besides, there cannot be a second *Oliver!*, an apparently easy-to-make piece that on the contrary breaks every rule in the handbook.

Copperfield followed the handbook slavishly, from its emptily bouncy character song for George S. Irving's Mr. Micawber, "Something Will

Turn Up," to "I Wish He Knew," the tortured ballad of Agnes Wickfield when David becomes engaged to Dora Spenlow. True, Leslie Denniston sang "I Wish He Knew" most beautifully, and it is a pleasing sort of number—as it had been in countless earlier shows.

Copperfield wasn't a bad evening, just a familiar one. There were two songs painfully reminiscent of *Oliver!*, young David's tearful "Anyone" (very similar to "Where Is Love?") and a taunting by other boys that, like that scene in *Oliver!*, was *Copperfield*'s title number. The script, inevitably losing much of Dickens' plot and even major characters, emphasized David's romances with Dora and then Agnes and also the scheming of Uriah Heep (Barrie Ingham). Rob Iscove's direction and choreography did not win him many devotees, perhaps, but Tony Straiges' scenery was an eyeful and there was even a dashing ensemble number, "The Lights of London," in celebration of David and Dora's wedding. Beginning with psalmlike reverence, it soon opened up into a full-scale "everyone onstage for the Church Number" rouser, something that had all but disappeared from the musical by then. There was one cute trick, too, during "Here's a Book," when young David (Evan Richards, understudied by Christian Slater) disappeared behind furniture and came back into view ten years older (Brian Matthews) to get the main action into gear. *Copperfield* ran only 13 performances, yet it still got a Tony nomination for Best Score. (It had been a sluggish season for new music, with *42nd Street*, *The Pirates of Penzance*, *Sophisticated Ladies*, and *Tintypes* all employing old material.)

Some bombs are neither crazy nor futile. Their flaw is that no one wants to see them. *Do Black Patent Leather Shoes Really Reflect Up?* (1982) has a charming program: a gentle spoof of parochial education, taking its class from second grade to high-school graduation in a revue with one throughline, the courtship of Becky (Maureen Moore) by Eddie (Russ Thacker). John R. Powers' book, based on his autobiographical novel, amusingly blended the comic with the simple reality of Catholic school— the nuns forever clicking those little metal gizmos for silence, the priest blandly whacking boys' heads with his missal as he walks the classroom aisle, the confessions ("Bless me, Father . . . this week I lied twice and had 2,738 impure thoughts"), the ignorance of the outside world ("Nat Nizer, that public-school kid . . . he said that, instead of legs, nuns have wheels under them"). James Quinn and Alaric Jans' score is more functional than inspiring, but it ably supports Powers' panorama; and director Mike

Nussbaum and choreographer Thommie Walsh kept the piece in motion even without plot suspense. It was a great chance for non-Catholics to learn about something else in the world. But like so many other mildly pleasing titles in this era, the show was gone within a week.

Merlin (1983), however, lasted 199 performances after some two months of previews. The previews might easily have run longer, but a few critics charged in on their own nickel to review a work they had sensed must be too terrible to live. Three actors shared the title role: once again little Christian Slater, along with magician Doug Henning and George Lee Andrews. Henning of course was the evening's central figure, as in *The Magic Show* (1974), showing up between the show's story and music segments to dazzle with his stunts. Everyone was amazed when Henning got onto a white pony and vanished at stage right to reappear, exulting, at stage left.

The rest of *Merlin* had less to exult about. Six names claimed authorship (including the by now standard "concept" credit), and the piece was still a dreadful mess. It did at least present Chita Rivera as the villainous Queen without name, in a lamé poncho with stick arms so she could spread her evil wings. The Queen wants to set her son (Nathan Lane) on the English throne; Merlin opposes her. He favors Arthur. Yet there was no flavor of Olde England in any of this, no atmosphere. The Elmer Bernstein–Don Black score was modern and the references were modern, despite the participation of Philomena the Unicorn (Rebecca Wright) and other "Creatures of the Glade." One of the show's special effects involved the chorus' assembling of a wicked Black Knight, a robot with glowing green eyes. At one performance, the Knight was imperfectly assembled, and when it moved its metal shorts fell down. "Show-off!" cried that naughty Nathan Lane.

Reports on *Merlin's* financial losses varied from four million to six million dollars, and this was extremely worrying news. *Merlin's* older theatregoers who had started seeing musicals as children had once attended a Broadway whose biggest musicals capitalized at something like forty thousand dollars. And this at a time when The Road so teemed with waiting theatres that Broadway flops could pay off in the provinces. In their lifetimes, these older theatregoers saw spontaneous walk-in business almost entirely vanish; people walked into movies now. Higher risk meant tighter budgets, but every economy compromises the form. Pit orchestras lack a solid string section (or any strings at all) not because the modern sound is made of winds and keyboards but because producers can't afford a full-size band. Worse, the giddy gloom of the synthesizer is becoming acculturated, while the harp, once essential to the very sound of a musical, is seldom heard except in revivals.

Budget shortcutting has also dignified the tawdry unit set, with its bits and things sliding on to imitate a change in locale where once the whole show moved and the locale was literally changed. The unit set has in fact become so intrinsic to production that some think of it as a kind of breakthrough, a thing in itself. *Dance a Little Closer* spent a fortune on its unit set and it still looked cheap. Every time someone came down the hotel lobby stairway, the Alps shook.

Ironically, it may be the interesting shows that don't get on, for it seems that no money problems can stop a crazy bomb from showing up. They keep coming: like *Marlowe* (1981). Zounds, the thrill of the title character, described as "a sixteenth-century man with a twentieth-century mind"! The allure of the hard-rock score, so useful in establishing the Elizabethan timeplace! The excitement of the set, made of tin foil and the Con-Tact adhesive trimming with which your aunt lines her pantry shelves! The grave dignity of the historical figures, as when Will Shakespeare tells a reluctant damsel, "I've sweated sonnets for you!," or when Queen Elizabeth I dismisses a certain Captain Townsend from her bed chamber with "Don't forget your codpiece!" Then the climax: Marlowe rises from death in a Day-Glo jumpsuit on a cloud of dry ice as the front-row spectators run out of the auditorium because of all the smoke.

Incredibly, *Marlowe* lasted six weeks, in that strange little Rialto Theatre, on the west side of Broadway just above Forty-second Street. (The place hosted so many flops that Carmen Mathews asked to have her ashes scattered backstage.) With a cast headed by Patrick Jude and Lisa Mordente, and otherwise played and staged by unknowns, *Marlowe* made one contribution, in further debunking that old factoid about Victor Herbert and Kurt Weill being the only composers to score their own shows. *Marlowe*'s composer, Jimmy Horowitz, made his own orchestrations.

Into the Light (1986) was not only crazy but offensive to Christians. Its tale of a believer in science who becomes converted to faith most outrageously based its action on that obsession of fools the Shroud of

Turin. This artifact allegedly "proves" the Resurrection, or at any rate adduces material evidence to support it. But attempts to materialize Christian Revelation can only dwarf it, cheapen it. This is the belief system that created the civilization of Dante, Goethe, and Beethoven. It does not need some carbon-dating technician to affirm it.

It was especially unhappy to see Dean Jones, the original Robert of *Company*, mixed up in this trashy auto-da-fé. Jones played the aforementioned scientist, arrogantly agnostic, who tries to prove the Shroud a fake. He fails to, finds God, and is rewarded when his troubled son suddenly gets untroubled. The show's composer, Lee Holdridge, called it "a combination of lyrical opera and space odyssey." I could have some fun with that, but I don't think I'm going to.

Marilyn: An American Fable (1983) was like a combination of *Marlowe* and *Into the Light*, using a historical figure to promote a grand theme on the workings of the American religion, which is show-biz fame. And of course Marilyn Monroe has always fascinated, for the insane tragedy she insisted on making of her life. Indeed, the show, with a book by Patricia Michaels and a score by five people (not counting those unbilled in the program), accords with the standard view of Marilyn as the typical American in her belief that stardom is the cure. And it quite coherently demonstrates how she cultivated a neurosis that wrecked her career.

Unfortunately, that demonstration was the sole coherent element in this big and busy event, one of the most spectacularly idiotic shows of all time. It was no insane tragedy, however. For one thing, it had a happy ending, as the heroine (Alyson Reed) walked upstage with her younger self (Kristi Coombs) after singing a reprise of "A Single Dream," one of *Marilyn*'s many soft-rock anthems of the kind later associated with Celine Dion. It is not too much to say that one could almost hear our entire tradition of theatre music falling apart as *Marilyn* unfolded.

It was an enjoyable evening all the same, so relentlessly atrocious that one wondered if it was trying to catch on as a failure fou. Consider this taste of Monroe's Actors Studio period—using, of course, a slight misquotation of the most obvious single line of classic theatre to establish Monroe's Striving For Art:

MONROE: "I long to be in Moscow!" (glum reaction from class)
MONROE: (as before) "I long to be in Moscow!"

BOY: (scornfully) She's acting!

GIRL: Yes, no reality!

SECOND BOY: I didn't believe it!

Lee Strasberg gets her to pretend she's on a sinking ship and can't reach the lifeboat. Now:

MONROE: (exactly as before, but louder) "I long to be in Moscow!"

ALL: (while cheering) *Breakthrough!*

Yes, Lee Strasberg (Steve Schoket) was in it, along with Monroe's three husbands, Jim Dougherty (George Dvorsky), Joe DiMaggio (Scott Bakula), and Arthur Miller (Will Gerard). Hedda Hopper (Mary Testa) and Louella Parsons (Melissa Bailey) punctuated the chronicle with helpings of the gleefully destructive "Gossip." There were also two young Monroe fans (Lise Lang, Willy Falk) and a singing trio called Destiny that sprinkled gold dust on the stage and generally hung around as symbolically as possible.

All this took place on a soundstage in "Hollywoodland," as the authors rounded up the usual clichés and, once in a while, did something interesting. Perhaps mistaking the rowdy preview response—hooting and giggling but also cheering, if with a certain ironic intent—for support, the show's thirteen producers decided to bring in fixers. These included songwriters Wally Harper and David Zippel and stagers Thommie Walsh and Baayork Lee, all uncredited. The changes were so many that the opening-night program did not list some of the numbers or identify the actress playing Paula Strasberg.

In the end, *Marilyn's* few good moments only underlined how frivolous the rest of the show was. Never was one so sorry for actors, especially Alyson Reed, who gave a titanic performance, complete with the Monroe voice. A few lines threw her the chance to limn that odd Monroe charm:

AGENT: (ushering Marilyn into a producer's office) Here she is—Norma Jean Baker.

PRODUCER: Sounds like a loaf of bread. It's a terrible name.

MONROE: (amiably, Hollywood's tabula rasa) Change it.

PRODUCER: (suddenly interested) What have you done?

MONROE: About what?

Willy Falk also got a major opportunity, with his hymn to his idol, "You Are So Beyond." The lyrics are not only the worst in all of *Marilyn* but the worst ever heard. Still, the melody is valid. Falk didn't care; he sang the song as if it were "You'll Never Walk Alone." As he reached the final A of the refrain, the orchestra jumped the key signature a step up and Falk soared into the vocal inflections of rock so dazzlingly that an audience that had been jeering all night gave him an ovation *during* the music. The applause following the number briefly stopped the show, and—after a very short book scene—Falk got another ovation.

What *Marilyn*'s public best remembered, however, was not "You Are So Beyond" but the Worst Number Even Seen On A Broadway Stage: the one in the bathtub. Don't speak of "Puka Puka Pants" or "Garlic" or even the Morgue Number cut after a single airing in *Thou Shalt Not*. *Marilyn*'s contribution to this singular sweepstakes was cued in when the heroine's search for meaningful roles was once again thwarted by a cheesecake part. Suddenly, someone called out, " 'Miss Bubbles,' Take One!," and the chorus boys ran in waving plungers as Reed appeared in a champagne bubble bath. The rest of the number is beyond description, but it's worth noting that this was the show's one episode that bore no relation to Monroe's life's events. It was, unexpectedly, just there, historically incorrect and incorrigibly dumbo.

But after that, what is one to say of *Legs Diamond* (1988)? Nominally based on Budd Boetticher's 1960 film *The Rise and Fall of Legs Diamond*, the musical actually culled little from the screen. The plan had been to star singer and songwriter Peter Allen as a kind of comic dancer–cum–gangster in Prohibition New York, romancing many a babe as Ray Danton had done in the film. This plan seemed irresistible to the usual host of producers, and indeed the public was keen, for the show began what was to become eight weeks of previews to a sizable advance.

Naturally, Allen would write the score: and that was part of the problem. An acceptable melodist, Allen was a terrible lyricist, a yammerer who couldn't rhyme and who would take mildly interesting concepts absolutely nowhere. Oddly, his *Legs Diamond* songs were generally enjoyable—the Hero's Wanting Song, "When I Get My Name in Lights"; the mysterious establish-the-nightclub number, haunting to a fault, "Speakeasy"; the gold digger's onstage character number, "I Was Made For Champagne." In fact, the score was theatrical in the way Allen's work had never been before.

A few of the numbers—"Now You See Me, Now You Don't" and a trio for women fed up with the hero's flaws, "The Man Nobody Could Love"— could have come right off the cast album of a semi-forgotten fifties hit. The critics noted how surprisingly acceptable the music was, after so much had been printed about the problems the show had in pulling itself together.

But then, the story itself had no real drive. Charles Suppon wrote the show's initial book, with Harvey Fierstein eventually devising an almost entirely new one, to no avail. The film is cheap crime, but it has presence, even in Diamond's off-the-rack motivation to avenge his brother's murder. The brother (played in the show by Bob Stillman) was dropped during previews, losing one of the new work's few links to the film—to a source, at any rate, of character content. The second woman lead, played by Christine Andreas, was also dropped, along with Allen's opening number, "Ain't I Something?" (which survived vestigially in the score), because it was obvious that audiences didn't think so.

They can't have been much persuaded by the other characters, either: the worldly older woman who runs a saloon, of course named Flo (Julie Wilson, classing up an unworthy joint with the late-in-Act-Two-torch-spot, "The Music Went Out of My Life"); that gold digger who was made for champagne (Randall Edwards), who of course speaks Fluent Bad Grammar; the ugly crime boss (Joe Silver) with the unbelievably deep voice. Of course.

Allen himself was the main problem. It never was clear if he really had a fan base large enough to support a Broadway run. Was he even a wonderful singer? For vocalism of highest order, Broadway and its concomitant recording culture counts on such names as Brent Barrett, Davis Gaines, Norm Lewis, Howard McGillin, Brian Stokes Mitchell, Hugh Panaro, Ron Raines; and The Street still remembered playing host to Sammy Davis Jr. But Allen? He looked good in the period costumes, but he couldn't read lines—and the voice, finally, was more a curiosity than a pleasure and completely lacked *espressivo*. Worst of all was the blissfully puerile worldview. Like *Marilyn*, *Legs Diamond* saw a story in the American hunger for celebrity. However, as with *Marilyn*'s vapidly strident ballads, *Legs Diamond* furthered the "popping" of Broadway with such attempted matings as "Catskills" with "act kills" and a line such as "We should have gave [sic] up yesterday."

What a relief to turn to flops with craftsmanlike scores, whatever else went wrong. *Oh, Brother!* (1981) is another title with an irresistible opening number, "We Love an Old Story." Quasi-ragtime on the usefulness of renewing old tales with new tweaks, it serves as an apologia for the show, the second Broadway adaptation of Shakespeare's *The Comedy of Errors.* Following the original plotline very much as did the first adaptation, *The Boys From Syracuse* (1938), *Oh, Brother!* made two important changes. The scene was moved from Ephesus to an unnamed country in the Persian Gulf, and the action, running without an intermission, was devoted to a trainload of physical fun played at breakneck speed.

Some may think of *A Funny Thing Happened On the Way To the Forum* (1962), but *Forum* is largely verbal. *Oh, Brother!* pulled endless chains of sight gags, stacking and twisting them. It must have been exhausting to play, yet its principals had plenty to sing as well. A lovely ballad drawn in part from Shakespeare, "I To the World (am like a drop of water)," and the pleading "How Do You Want Me?" vied with the jazzy "Everybody Calls Me By My Name" and a spoof of *The Boys From Syracuse*'s "Sing For Your Supper," similarly a close-harmony girls' trio, called "A Loud and Funny Song." David-James Carroll and Harry Groener were the (former) Antipholuses, Joe Morton and Alan Weeks their servants, and Judy Kaye and Mary (Elizabeth) Mastrantonio the women. Two men played a comic camel, in burnoose, sunglasses, and sneakers.

Michael Valenti and Donald Driver wrote the mostly appealing score—but why did librettist Driver (who also directed) want to set his fun in the politically explosive Middle East? Why not Pol Pot's Cambodia, scenic North Korea? The critics almost entirely damned the piece, and more than one noted how injudiciously Driver had chosen his milieu. True, he made very little reference to current events. However, at one point, one of the long-lost brothers explained his past to his father as "We were raised by a kindly old Arab terrorist." Even the Boca Raton Broadway Tonite! Dinner Theatre Featuring Our Exclusive Broadway Tonite! Take All You Want Buffet won't be getting to this one in the imaginable future.

Is There Life After High School? (1982) deals with even more explosive territory, gathering nine men and women to look back on those days of friendships and feuds and minor triumphs. It may remind one of *Do Black Patent Leather Shoes Really Reflect Up?*, but that show was about a form of education. This show is about people. As the opening number, "The Kid Inside," explains it, one is never truly graduated from high school. One gets out of but never gets over it, and the show's revue format suggested alumni at a reunion helplessly going over old events. Craig Carnelia's score and Jeffrey Kindley's script (again suggested by a book, this one by Ralph Keyes) touched on many universal themes, yet the show ran only 12 performances. Is it too universal? Too vaguely general? One seldom felt that one's own experience had been enhanced, and little else in the score had the ecstatic ring of "The Kid Inside." Harry Groener enjoyed a pleasant solo in "Things I Learned in High School," and Maureen Silliman made the most of the first-act finale, "Diary of a Homecoming Queen," the autobiography of a popular girl whose life peaked on a single thrilling day in her senior year. Act Two started with a real rouser, "Thousands of Trumpets," on the glory of the marching band. Still, the show may have suffered from too much day-to-day reality and too few surprises, just like high school itself.

Raggedy Ann (1986) has a very poor reputation that I wish to reassess. Made, obviously, on the Johnny Gruelle characters, the show tried to tell a grown-ups' tale with children's materials. Sooner or later, someone was going to get a musical out of Gruelle,* but it most likely should have been a children's cartoon. Actually, that's how this project got started, in 1977, with songs by Joe Raposo. For some reason, when Raposo expanded his score to fill out a stage version with a book by William Gibson, the story turned extraordinarily dark, raving with symbolism and an uncomfortable blend of bourgeois family life and the supernatural.

This "musical adventure" takes the customary quest format: Raggedy Ann and Andy, a panda who speaks in "Confucius say" dialect, and yet another comic camel escort Raggedy Ann's dying owner, Marcella, through Grisly Woods National Park to the Doll Doctor. Flying on Marcella's bed on a tight deadline, they are pursued by General Doom, a gleefully baleful "gwaaah-ha-ha!" villain. "The *cause* is silence!" he roars. "The *silence* is total! The *total* is nothing! The *nothing* is *eternity*!"

---

* Connoisseurs of the early Third Age will be aware of "Raggedy Ann," from Jerome Kern's *Stepping Stones* (1923), in which Fred and daughter Dorothy Stone impersonated Gruelle's doll siblings. It was an insert number, plopped into the action as an extramural interlude, but it so encapsulated the show's spirit that Gruelle himself designed the *Stepping Stones* poster, a drawing of Ann and Andy in full kit.

Parts of the script seemed like eternity, too, though Gibson is one of our more accomplished playwrights, with some experience in the musical. Other parts of the book were a Freudian *guignol*, as Marcella's runaway (even suicidal) mother and inept father (who doubled as the Doll Doctor) turned up on the quest, while General Doom tried to seduce Raggedy Ann. John Simon called it "a kind of cross between *The Wizard of Oz* and *Die Frau Ohne Schatten*": L. Frank Baum's quest party of hero-ine and physical grotesques menaced by Richard Strauss' all-powerful father-god of the spirit realm, who is defeated by self-sacrifice. For this is what ultimately saves Marcella: Raggedy Ann must give up her heart.

The cast was undistinguished, except for Ivy Austin in the title role, with a genuine doll's voice, girlishly plaintive yet at times piercing in a singsong delivery. What was truly distinguished was Raposo's score, a captivating miscellany of twentieth-century pop styles breaking through the narrative gloom. There was rag, swing, tango, a Flying Number, a Wedding Number. Best of all was "A Little Music," sheer melody on a strolling vamp that climaxes as Raggedy Ann and the Camel do some challenge opera on *Lucia di Lammermoor* Mad Scene riffs. The number proposed to lull General Doom into sleep with a tune "like Crosby used to croon": but that was the *Raggedy Ann* score in general. Here's a first in this book: the serious modern musical with a the-way-we-used-to musical-comedy score, all in an arresting presentation by Gerry Hariton and Vicki Baral (sets), Carrie Robbins (costumes), and Patricia Birch (direction and choreography). Yes, the bed really flew; and the second act began with the curtain not rising but falling, vacuumed up into a hole in the middle of the apron. Still, the show was too gnarly for kids and too enchanted for parents, and it folded inside of a week.

It often happens that unusual shows with flaws—like *Raggedy Ann*—are more interesting to sit through than slick hits. Still, if *Teddy & Alice* (1987) gave pleasure in part, it suffered from an unforgivable drawback: no story whatsoever. *Raggedy Ann* was crowded with event, even if a quest provides more throughline than actual plot. *Teddy & Alice* barely had a throughline, which was that Theodore Roosevelt won't consent to the marriage of his daughter Alice to Nicholas Longworth; then he does. There was a small subplot concerning whether or not T.R. will win the nomination for election in 1904 and maintain the White House, but there was no narrative suspense, because history tells us that T.R. served till 1909 and that Nicholas and Alice Longworth were a prominent Washington couple. Better, the widow Longworth was for many years D.C.'s classiest scamp; her famous line was "If you don't have something pleasant to say about someone, come sit next to me."

The thinking behind *Teddy & Alice* was that there must be a show itself in a president who can run the country but can't control his nonconformist daughter. But Alice (Nancy Hume) was never dramatized. She was just another bright-eyed heroine with a Wanting Song in the second slot of the tunestack, "But Not Right Now." T.R. (Len Cariou, in a role intended for Robert Preston) was the usual T.R. stereotype, though Nick (Ron Raines) at least got something to play while contending with T.R. for Alice.

But that, too, was a problem. Why was this father trying to keep his daughter from the man she loved—a highly eligible catch at that? Presumably, we were to see T.R. as a lovable tyrant, but what's lovable about a tyrant? I thought his obsessive interest in his daughter's romance disquieting, and it didn't help that it took a visitation from the ghost of his first wife—who died shortly after bearing Alice—to get him to give in.

The famous and near-famous thronged the view, from statesmen Henry Cabot Lodge and William Howard Taft to labor leader Samuel Gompers and muckraker Ida Tarbell. Yet the production was pretty rather than atmospheric. Book writer Jerome Alden knew his subject, having created the one-man show *Bully* (1977) for James Whitmore to tour in, but this was history by charades. One thing worked besides the capable performances, and that—as so often in a flop—was the score. Ironically, its composer had been dead for half a century.

What happened was that a living composer, Richard Kapp, teamed up with the legacy of John Philip Sousa for *Teddy & Alice*, arranging Sousa's melodies and composing a great deal on his own, to Hal Hackady's lyrics. Here lay the show's attraction, for the result was nothing like the cranked-up antique one might anticipate. Nor was the evening burdened with marches, the Sousa specialty. Only in the overture and entr'acte, the opening ("This House") and its finale reprise, and the first-act finale, "Wave the Flag" (set to "The Stars and Stripes Forever," at the 1904 Republican National Convention), were marches heard. On the contrary, *Teddy & Alice* had an up-to-date, if very pre-rock, score. The Sousa gave it a peculiar ring, a kind of echo of operettas that charmed the ear in Kapp's versions of the originals and the ingenious ways that orchestrator Jim Tyler toyed with them. Alice's coming-out party in the White House Rose Garden called of course for an old-style coming-out-party dance. But then irrepressible Alice led everyone into ragtime with "Leg o' Mutton," and her launching vocal brought in a *concertante* group of solo violin, banjo, and celesta over the orchestra, the 1901 equivalent of "It has a beat you can dance to it."

Some songs were too old-style, especially those for the politicians. And when Cariou insisted that the score allot him a number with his children, the best that Kapp could offer was "Charge," the sort of piece they used to cut in Boston because whole sections of the audience were going out for Sno-Kones during it. We must also rebuke "Can I Let Her Go?," T.R.'s pensive solo drawn from a dashing melody in Sousa's "The Thunderer" but used at snail's pace. The joke was to let the audience gradually catch on with amused noises of recognition, but the number caught lyricist Hackady in an uncharacteristically uninspired mood. Lyricists, beware! If they hear one lame line, those quick to quarrel will use it to characterize your entire evening's work.

Still, much of *Teddy & Alice*'s score had the piquant flavor of rediscovered old music rather than the more usual pastiche re-creation of it. The lovers' duets, "Perfect For Each Other" and "Nothing To Lose," stood among the season's most tuneful items. Was it Sousa or Kapp (or both) who composed "Battlelines," for the second Mrs. Roosevelt (Beth Fowler), with the running-gag age joke that even the great Sondheim has not scorned (in *Forum*)? It ended with her own cry of "Charge!" The show must have seemed like a wonderful sell even without Robert Preston, because after blistering reviews it still ran for ten weeks at a time when many flops died in two.

Smile (1986) lasted six weeks, though it's by far this chapter's best title yet, our first failure that was a consistently entertaining and intelligent piece. Michael Ritchie's 1975 film of the same name, a spoof of beauty pageants, is scathing; early versions of the musical *Smile*, always to Marvin Hamlisch's music, veered close to Ritchie's tone or sought instead to sympathize with at least some of the characters. The version that made it to Broadway teamed Hamlisch with Howard Ashman for both book and lyrics; and Ashman staged, with choreographer Mary Kyte, a somewhat cinematic backstager, forever mooching around behind the scenes to learn what lies behind those smiles. Ashman's tone was less than scathing but not entirely sympathetic in an extremely fast-moving piece, set on a revolving stage almost constantly working as Ashman "cut" to another part of the action.

The Young American Miss pageant, in Santa Rosa, California, was clearly an aspect of American culture that many theatregoers know nothing about—the rural or small-town Americana of Garth Brooks fans, the Jaycees, baton twirling, and big games. The pageant's manager couple are square (Jeff McCarthy) and ruthless (Marsha Waterbury), their choreographer (Michael O'Gorman) a cynical third-rater. Among the sixteen contestants, two in particular caught the authors' attention. One is a somewhat independent girl (Anne Marie Bobby) too smart for all the hypocrisy. The other is an appealing piece of trailer trash (Jodi Benson) obsessed with beauty contests and the Walt Disney view of the world. Her establishing song is, in fact, "Disneyland."

As the three days of rehearsals, pre-judging, and the pageant itself unfold, we are brought close to these people. McCarthy is not the confident bluffer he seems but a sensitive guy with an inattentive, ambitious wife. Benson at length adopts Bobby, teaching her winner's stratagems though Benson herself is a born loser, with no source of self-esteem except these contests. She has the knowledge but not the power; Bobby has the power but not the need. Nothing in the movie anticipates what Hamlisch and Ashman made of this strange friendship, which reaches its natural end not sixty seconds before the final curtain: Benson comes out to urge Bobby to affirm their alliance by joining her in a Miss Sunbelt contest, only to see Bobby embraced by her mother, who troubled to drive a great distance to bring her home. It's a devastating moment for the virtual orphan Benson, one in which the show's entire contents have been sublimated without the use of either song or dance.

That may be why *Smile* didn't get a single good notice. Its score might actually be too well integrated, caught up in the excitement of leaving for ("Typical High School Senior"), rehearsing a number in ("Shine"), having an anxiety attack about ("Until Tomorrow Night"), and appearing in ("Smile") the pageant. Dialogue inserts were cut into almost all the songs, so that even the irresistible "Smile" failed to land. It should perhaps have been a Michael Bennett moment; too much of the score skittered in and

CLOSE A LITTLE FASTER

out of book scenes in a kind of whirlwind. And isn't it also true that, except for the seen-it-all choreographer, these are people that New Yorkers generally don't care about?

Closer to their hearts are the characters of *The Rink* (1984), Chita Rivera and Liza Minnelli: or, rather, Anna Antonelli (Rivera) and her daughter, Angel (Minnelli). Returning home after a fifteen-year absence, Angel is outraged to learn that her mother is having the family roller-drome demolished. In a clever stunt, the six-man demolition crew play all the subsidiary roles—women included—while mother and daughter dispute the past in flashbacks and blame each other for their estrangement. It takes a whole evening, but they make their peace, Angel tells the wreckers to get to work, and set designer Peter Larkin then pulled off a spectacular coup, raising the entire unit set—the rink itself—high in the air as Anna, Angel, and Angel's young daughter enjoyed an apotheosis.

Note that a full-scale story could thus be played by a cast of nine; note, too, that instead of the usual romance, *The Rink* treated a mother-daughter relationship. No, don't think of *Gypsy*, because that show isn't about the relationship: it's about the mother. *The Rink* explored the difficulties in maintaining good feelings when the family is split (Rivera's husband abandons them) and drugagonzo times (the 1960s) draw Minnelli into dangerous enthusiasms.

Directed by A. J. Antoon and choreographed by Graciela Daniele, *The Rink* was one of those shows making the best of a tight economy, keeping its two stars and the six wreckers very busy; Scott Ellis played six roles *besides* Lucky, the cutest of the wreckers. Terrence McNally's book took advantage of the rule laid down by the seventies concept show: Do several things simultaneously. Flashbacks. Visitations. Commentary by the ensemble.

And of course it was *The Rink*'s songwriters, John Kander and Fred Ebb, who restarted the concept musical (after some at first inimitable tries in the 1940s) with *Cabaret*. Here, their score was largely character songs, getting off to a very direct start in the first number: the curtain rose on someone facing upstage in one, Liza Minnelli turned to face us, and she went right into "Colored Lights." Alternating between a confessional verse in $\frac{4}{4}$ and a nostalgic waltz with a hint of Nino Rota's Fellini music, the song instantly places the character: sensitive, romantic, and much clearer about who she was as a child than who she has been ever since.

Rivera's establishing number, not long after, was "Chief Cook and Bottle Washer," a charleston in its music and sarcastic honesty in its lyrics. So the show is set. Grudge match: the dreamer versus the realist.

There were some lovely incidentals—the courting solo of the deserted Rivera's admirer, "Marry Me," a Schubertian melody with the added ache of diminished and major seventh chords, beautifully sung by Jason Alexander. Or another of those Kander and Ebb revue numbers that erupt out of nowhere yet feel impeccably integrated—"Without Me," "No Boom Boom," "See the Light." *The Rink*'s example was the title song, wherein the six wreckers, idle while Minnelli holds up the demolition, key on their own roller skates and try a run around the place. "I made a date with Sue to hear Sinatra sing" is a typical line, site-specific yet something that anyone might utter in anecdote. This is the eternal musical comedy in Kander and Ebb, even in a dark show. (Rivera is mugged at one point; and who can forget Jason Alexander, in another cameo, as squalid Uncle Fausto, adjusting the hang of his genitals before a family photograph with a deadpan look of hetero solipsism?)

There was one mistake and one giant gaffe. The mistake was "The Apple Doesn't Fall," a comic number for Rivera and Minnelli after they get stoned together (it's Rivera's first joint) and compare preferences in implausible topics. Worse was "All the Children in a Row," Minnelli's eleven o'clocker, on sixties activism and drug taking. "Proudly marching arm in arm, singing Dylan's songs" may be the silliest instant-image lyric of the eighties not from *Marlowe* or *Marilyn*. It certainly doesn't typify this very enjoyable and at times adventurous score; but the show ran only 204 performances.

And the beautiful *Rags* (1986) had to give up in less than a week. Like *The Rink*, this one was flunked for unimportant errors and despite a glowing, dramatic, one-of-a-kind score built of native ragtime crossed with immigrant street music. Orchestrated by Michael Starobin to isolate the historical moment when "jazz" first squealed out of who knows how many different sources, *Rags* dealt with the Jewish immigrant experience in the New York of 1910. Joseph Stein wrote an unusually tight book to accommodate Charles Strouse and Stephen Schwartz's giant score. Telescoping events in various places into musical scenes, it also employs Leitmotiven, a few of which swell with the kind of nationalistic euphoria associated with American symphony during the 1930s and 1940s. *Rags* is something of a pageant, the great and small thrust together, "jumbled up in strange harmonies," as one of the lyrics puts it. It is a compliment to say that one simply cannot hear in this epic the man who composed *Applause* and *Annie*.

The unimportant errors include the floppo number "Yankee Boy," Larry Kert's declaration of intent to assimilate, a fiercely embarrassing song, embarrassingly staged. Then, too, the elements of comedy and grim historical reality chafed against each other at times, as when the young Bella (Judy Kuhn) had to display a fun-loving side (in "Penny a Tune") but also a sociocultural commentative side (in "Rags"), and then disappear for large amounts of book time and finally get killed in a sweatshop fire. Her boy friend (Lonny Price), on the other hand, got stuck with little to do but sell gramophones while everyone else was chewing up hunks of plot. The main strain followed Rebecca (opera soprano Teresa Stratas) and her young son (Josh Blake, Ulysses in *The Human Comedy*) arriving at Ellis Island to find husband Kert. A codicil involved Stratas with a leftist radical (Terrence Mann). Bella's father (Dick Latessa) and a widow (Marcia Lewis) as willing as Barkis filled out the scene. Unbalanced and groaning with principals (though this did suggest the clutter of urban immigrant life), *Rags* really was too big for its own size.

An experienced director of musicals might have resculpted its proportions, but *Rags*' producers hired Joan Micklin Silver. The writer and director of the 1975 movie *Hester Street*, Silver had already thus "done" the *Rags* premise—an Eastern European Jewish woman and her child uncomfortably uniting with her Americanized husband. But *Hester Street* is a tidy little piece, not a panorama with politics, tragedy, and fizzy tidbits. More to the point, *Hester Street* is a movie, not a musical. Where is the disciplinary association?

Why do producers think like this? When I was in high school, the Religious Activities Committee ran a clothing drive for the Blackfeet Indian reservation. Brand-new clothing was preferred, of course. But used clothing was accepted, and no doubt some of what was offered to the committee—and, one hopes, not forwarded to the tribe—could have been called "rags." Is that an association? Why wasn't Friends Academy's Religious Activities Committee hired to direct *Rags*? Would they have been inferior to Silver, who was fired during rehearsals, leading the show to play a Boston tryout without a director billed in the program?

What looks worse, a house without walls? The authors ran things till Gene Saks took over, with Ron Field handling the dancing. Though a musical-comedy talent, Field did a masterly job in musical-play style in the title song, in which Kuhn went wandering uptown to a realer—an *established*—America. The song itself eloquently dramatizes the plight of an innocent tossed into an alien culture at its lowest and least promising level. Field illustrated this as Kuhn sadly watched a ballroom couple in their immaculate waltz, their aplomb, their beauty. Set designer Beni Montresor had laid out a series of visuals to be switched at will from crowded to open; this moment was all open, as the downtown Kuhn gazed upon the cultural perfection of American culture: as Irving Berlin might have gazed upon Vernon and Irene Castle. But Berlin made the culture his; the Castles danced to his tune, in *Watch Your Step* (1914). And Stratas and her son, we sense, will prosper. But Kuhn's is the unfortunate version of the paradigm.

Rags was a cornucopia, and its treasure was the amazing Stratas, with her strangely masculine speaking voice, her maestra's command of song, and her utterly habilitated acting honesty, even in her Broadway debut. In a solo called "Blame It on the Summer Night," sung as she realizes that she is falling in love with Terrence Mann, she let the woodwinds flirt with her, the brass schmoozing knowingly, in Starobin's beguiling blues. Strouse wrote for a character glowing in carefree guilt, but the orchestra disputes that, equating klezmer with sex. Old-time theatregoers who now attend less or not at all complain that today's musicals are poor in the sheer musical excitement that was once the hallmark of the form—the matching of Ethel Merman with "I Got Rhythm," say. But "Blame It on the Summer Night" was one such moment. These days, our flops are sometimes more musical than our hits.

The character that Stratas played was an odd one, with a terribly dramatic backstory of fleeing oppression and begging for sea-liner passage money yet ever ready with a foolish homily. At a *Hamlet* performed in Yiddish, she observes, "In second marriages, it's always the children who suffer." Starting as a wife seeking comfort in her man's arms, Rebecca grows to be suspicious of his easy-money accommodations. America, to her, is not a business. America is freedom. True, it is compromised by the disciples of scam and by pitiless employers; and we know that Bella would have got out of the burning factory if the merest commonsense safety rules had been in force. *Rags* sees the inherent contradictions: it is not a naïve work. It is, however, an emotionally powerful one. We hear Strouse define Rebecca's flight from oppression in "Children of the Wind," its refrain built of great blocks of diatonic power in the anthem style that so many distrust as the corruption of pop opera. On the line "Take us to the day," Rebecca soars from a B natural (in B Major) to a high B Flat (on a B *Flat* Major seventh chord with a suspended fourth), a truly hair-raising effect. *Rags*, is a show whose audience wasn't mustered because some critics cannot take in that much music at once, or dismiss an inspiring score because of the book's problems. Does it have to be *My Fair Lady* to be worth seeing?

Our last flop could be thought of as the dumbest show of all, or as an arresting notion whose occasional brilliance was obscured by clownish mistakes. At its final performance, half the audience was cheering and the other half making low noises; but it's socially dangerous to defend this title, which has become the identifying term for the bomb of bombs. Nowadays, when they want to convey a musical's sheer wanton grandeur of terribleness, they call it "a train wreck." In 1988, they called it *Carrie*.

The crazy bomb as art. Drawn from Stephen King's novel, *Carrie* had a book by Lawrence D. Cohen, music by Michael Gore, and lyrics by Dean Pitchford (the romantic lead in the Public Theater's staging of *The Umbrellas of Cherbourg*, in 1979). Terry Hands of the Royal Shakespeare Company directed, and the work indeed began in England as an RSC production, seen in Stratford only, and for only three weeks, with a part-American cast headed by seventeen-year-old Brit Linzi Hateley as the beleaguered heroine, Carrie White, and our own Barbara Cook as her religion-Nazi mother. Cook felt that Hands and choreographer Debbie Allen were ignoring outstanding problems, and she left the show. Betty Buckley replaced Cook for Broadway, alongside Hateley's Carrie, Charlotte d'Amboise as Carrie's relentless nemesis, Darlene Love as the Carrie-friendly gym teacher, and Sally Ann Triplett and Paul Gyngell as the nice couple trying to give Carrie support.

King's novel—and Brian De Palma's movie version, with Sissy Spacek and Piper Laurie as daughter and mother—challenge any stage version with mission impossible. A few of the musical's people had been involved in the film—Lawrence Cohen wrote the screenplay, and Betty Buckley played the gym teacher. But how to *stage* the movie's many special effects?

Carrie is so unhappy at her mother's domineering puritanism and her coevals' brutal teasing that she unwittingly pulls off telekinetic stunts, expressions of her long-pent-up anger. These supranormal exhibits aren't what she wants: they're how she feels. They can be the merest stirring in the pantry or the trashing of a high-school prom, the exit doors jammed shut as the place and all in it are destroyed.

Carrietta—as Mrs. White named her and insists on calling her—is otherwise a girl like any other. But though she wants to be part of whatever's going on, she is so ill prepared for teenage socialization that she doesn't know about menstruation. She goes to pieces with a lightning bolt of a scream when she begins to bleed in the showers.

That occurs in the first of the musical *Carrie*'s sequences, a series of separated scenes, each with its own style in look and sound. *Carrie*'s creators planned a unique show—an *abstraction* of King's tale in every way. As a composition, it could be called another of those rock operas. But it did have a book, if a short one, and the music veered from rock to traditional theatre writing.

This variety may have been the first of *Carrie*'s mistakes. For while all the scenes between mother and daughter were finely wrought, much of the kids' music was automatic rhythm—not bad but not interesting, just more of that stuff you can dance to. "In," for the girls' gym class that opens the show, was a placeholder, gym music. "Don't Waste the Moon," at the drive-in, was considerably better. "Out For Blood," at the hog farm where d'Amboise collects the blood with which to douse Carrie at the prom (the event that triggers the climactic slaughter), utilized taped sounds of pig grunts in a number so floppo, so egregiously bad, they haven't yet coined a term for it. "Wotta Night!," at the prom, is, again, functional. Prom music.

However, none of these numbers took place in anything looking *like* those places. This was the abstraction, then, of *Carrie:* to take it out of Musical Comedyland into the big white box of modern theatre. One recalls how Peter Brook's Royal Shakespeare A *Midsummer Night's Dream* essentialized this scenic instrument of modern drama, or how the Scottish Opera's *Candide*, directed by Jonathan Miller and John Wells, adapted it for use by musicals. The look is ideal for gestural theatre, epic theatre, concept theatre, many theatres. But doesn't *Carrie*'s angry magic need to be seen in an everyday—a *realistic*—context? Otherwise, she's no weirder than anyone else in the story. They were all weird: the girls in ironic strip-per white with red trim for the gym scene (with real showers and apparent nudity behind befogged Plexiglas), and the boys in spaceman white for the drive-in, which consisted of a geometric pile of little metal car fronts.

Set designer Ralph Koltai and costumer Alexander Reid clearly had some new ideas about the potential of physical production in commercial theatre. There was a vision behind all this—but it was one better suited to the kind of musical that Eugène Ionesco might have written with Johnny Rotten for direction by Tristan Tzara. Late in Act One, at The Nightspot (thus billed), everyone had changed into colorfully studded jumpsuits, the girls in red fright wigs, in a dark space boxed in by mirrors.

And by then *Carrie* was lost, its look overly rococo and its storytelling specious. The turning of the heroine's inarticulate furies into a power that she herself controls not only corrupted King's psychology but showed a complete lack of common sense. If Carrie can command her powers, wouldn't she employ them to improve her social situation, if only by intimidating her tormentors? A scene in which Carrie dressed for the prom with the aid of floating comb, mirror, and so on (worked, in an ancient theatrical trick, by stage staff in black, invisible against a black background) suggested Walt Disney's Cinderella and her mice. Worse, the first act ended as Carrie defied her mother with a fire show: her fingers turned into flames, the stage broke apart as more flames licked up into view, and Carrie's mother, in a chair, was levitated ten feet above the stage.*

Another aspect of disaster for this show—and for this era's musical theatre in general—was a complete lack of humor. By 1988 we were used to dark shows. But most of them could at least affect a little sarcasm here and there. *Kiss of the Spider Woman* treats a grisly subject, but it collects many an amusement and one outstanding jab of camp, when Chita Rivera is impersonating a Russian cabaret star in some movie. The day before her marriage to a count, her maid, Lisette, brings her an anonymous letter: the count has betrayed her and her lover, "the student revolutionary Bolshevik anarchist." Chita responds like lightning, as if

---

* The chair effect proved stubborn and, rumor told, worked at only one performance. Off the top of my head, I can name ninety thousand gay men who apparently were there that night.

she has known many such counts, many such student revolutionary Bolshevik anarchist lovers:

CHITA: I must save him. (To Lisette) Summon my troika.

Carrie ushers in the period of absolutely humorless shows—the European pop operas, *Passion, Side Show, Jekyll & Hyde, The Capeman, Parade, Jane Eyre*. Some of *Carrie's* public found things to laugh at, true; but the work was seriously intended.

Rock with strings, vision without perspective, and its own gaudy funeral, *Carrie* marked an attempt to find some new *thing* in musicals between Rodgers and Hammerstein and stupid pop. *Carrie* played 5 performances after the by now customary pans, because, as I've said, a number like "Out For Blood" means that there would be no credit given to the superb mother-daughter numbers. The psalmlike "Open Your Heart"; the driving "And Eve Was Weak," almost murderously enraged; and the deeply psychosexual "I Remember How Those Boys Could Dance" stand among the best numbers the era heard. One would never know it from *Carrie's* reviews.

Critics are tougher on shows than they used to be. It is not that their standards are higher today, but that some of them reflect the public's lack of interest in following a narrative work in all its beseeching detail. The audience has become exhausted, too dim to follow those elaborate musical scenes and that jagged choral commentary and those concept-show leaps in time and space and all the rest of the kit that demands a spectator who is fit and intelligent and alert. Someone, say, who responds with discrimination to each next thing that the show throws at him. Someone who can *listen*.

There is a moment, early in *Carrie*, when the girls taunt the hapless Carrietta with their standard assault of "Scary White!" This leads to Carrie's plangently defiant singing of "That's . . . not . . . my . . . *name!*," the last word of which cues in the pounding vamp of the title song and our feeling that the authors have, at least for the moment, become one with the character and her world, and one with us. This is the musical's certain talent: isolating a moment in someone's story so eloquently that we become the story's whore. The art makes us as avid as helpless; we cannot be anywhere but inside that point of view. It steers us, inspires us.

It is all but impossible to praise this side of *Carrie* to anyone who didn't see the show. There's no other flop like it; there's no other *show* like it. *Carrie* is unique. As an eight-million-dollar casualty, the piece will never outlive "Out For Blood" or its avant-garde abstractions or its failure to read King's tale correctly. For some, it was an exciting evening, gaffes and all. It was unpredictable; and that is the best theatre possible.

3

THE MUSIC OF THE NIGHT

The strange thing about pop opera is that because the format is so strait, the good ones are not all that different from the bad ones. In other types of musical, we find great variation within genres. Operetta takes in *The Student Prince* but also *Titanic*. Musical plays count *The Cradle Will Rock* and *Paint Your Wagon*. Musical comedies move from *Anything Goes* to *She Loves Me*.

Unfortunately, certain weaknesses inherent in pop opera's origin and development have limited it as a genre. The through-sung music drama using a "popular" rather than "classical" sound could perhaps be dated back to *Porgy and Bess* (1935), *The Golden Apple* (1954), or *The Most Happy Fella* (1956). Critic Ken Mandelbaum, however, points to the Jacques Demy–Michel Legrand film *Les Parapluies de Cherbourg* (*The Umbrellas of Cherbourg*, 1964) as the first pop opera, because of its singing of every line of dialogue, no matter how mundane, in a somewhat formless *arioso* that sometimes expands into a structured number; and because of the Big Tune that repeatedly crashes into the orchestral texture.

Pop opera's index of weaknesses starts with those Big Tunes, as they sometimes seem to return less for dramatic emphasis than to sell albums and singles. The lyrics, too, do not attract the craftsman, which explains the resolute use of couplets with one-syllable end rhymes and no enjambment. It's the opposite of Cole Porter: cleverness without fun, and rhyme without wit. So many short, flat statements accumulate the feeling of doggerel.

Then there's the often unvarying musical texture. Pop opera emphasizes the romantic, leaving out the discordantly prankish feeling supplied by numbers like "Hernando's Hideaway" or "Get Me To the Church On Time." But such music lacks the intensity demanded for pop opera's outsized characters and tumultuous story lines. In pop opera, the grotesque is preferred—the Phantom, Norma Desmond, Inspector Javert, les Thénardier, the Engineer—and everyone else in the narrative is, if not a scary clown monster, a terribly earnest young person. So, again, whether the show hits or fails, its people are the same people we heard being grotesque or earnest the last time.

And what of the all but indispensable "overproduction"? The chandelier, the helicopter, the *Starlight Express* rollerdrome? To be fair, pop operas aren't overproduced. Pop operas are spectacles, the way operetta was in the late 1920s. The public likes a big show, with big music and big singing. This, really, is what the word "opera" means to most people.

Why do so many opinion makers hate pop opera? Their dragonnade often reaches apocalyptic utterances, no less worrisome for being comically hyperbolic. One person prominent in New York publishing circles told me that he hated Andrew Lloyd Webber more than he hated Hitler. Then he added, "And I'm not joking."

In some cases, this may simply reveal a distaste for opera that these detractors didn't know they had. They probably wouldn't like *La Traviata* or *Fidelio* any more than they like *Les Misérables*, but social context keeps them from admitting it. Detesting—more precisely, disestablishing—*Les Misérables* is a prerequisite for intellectual probity; to scoff at Verdi or Beethoven makes one look stupid.

Is it the form's vast and supposedly undiscriminating audience that irritates, theatregoing as if making a tourist stop and blithely refusing to be told what it's allowed to enjoy? Is it a crisis of hip, the brain trust reacting to pop opera the way rockers react to *Carousel*? Does pop opera's international rootlessness cause worry, perhaps in some dim way? For though the genre is basically English with some French truffling, it goes around the world as no national artwork can. Pop opera tears down the ethnic categories within which reside, for example, *On the Town* on the one hand and *Half a Sixpence* on the other; or *Hans le Joueur de Flûte* and *Gigantes y Cabezudos*. These works sound like the places they were made in; pop opera comes from nowhere. What counts is where it's going: usually on a worldwide tour that will busy six or seven companies for a generation.

Pop opera established its foothold on Broadway in the 1970s with two Lloyd Webber titles, *Jesus Christ Superstar* (1971) and *Evita* (1979). The first was, like it or not, an Event—even, most thought at the time, a one-off. *Evita* proved otherwise. Even so, it was during the next two decades that the genre asserted itself on The Street, in Lloyd Webber's dance revue *Cats* (1982), *Song & Dance* (1985), *Starlight Express* (1987), *The Phantom of the Opera* (1988), *Aspects of Love* (1990), *Sunset Boulevard* (1994). There was as well one Broadway-bound Lloyd Webber piece, the incoherent *Whistle Down the Wind* (1996), which closed in Washington, D.C.

Meanwhile, the two French guys had joined the movement. After *La Révolution Française*, which played Paris in 1973 but was never performed anywhere in English, composer Claude-Michel Schönberg and lyricist Alain Boublil gave us *Les Misérables* (1987), *Miss Saigon* (1991), and their own out-of-town closing, *Martin Guerre*, whose American production, bound for the Plymouth Theatre, gave up in Los Angeles in 1999.*

Oddly, another Lloyd Webber work, seen here at first before *Evita*, employs elements that other pop operas avoid by policy: not only comedy but spoof, and an intimacy that reduces an Important Saga to the size of a schoolkids' holiday show. As with *Superstar* and *Evita*, Tim Rice wrote the lyrics to Lloyd Webber's *Joseph and the Amazing Technicolor Dreamcoat*, seen at the Brooklyn Academy of Music at Christmas time in 1976 and 1977 with David-James Carroll in a staging by Frank Dunlop and Graciela Daniele. Tony Tanner's production for Ford's Theatre in D.C. played off-Broadway and then in 1982 The Street itself, with Bill Hutton and, inaugurating a now unshakable tradition of women Narrators, Laurie Beechman; and there was a 1993 revival as well.

A silly mooch-about on a unit set or something close to it is anything but pop opera. Indeed, *Joseph*—a commission for a London boys' prep

* Yet another problem of pop opera is the confused nature of its authorship, as both Lloyd Webber and Schönberg run through an anthology of word men. *The Phantom of the Opera*'s title song claims three lyricists—Mike Batt and the show's credited writers, Charles Hart and Richard Stilgoe. It would appear that no writer after Tim Rice has earned Lloyd Webber's trust entirely. Schönberg is even more collaborative: *The French Revolution* has not only two lyricists (Alain Boublil and Jean-Marc Rivière) but a composer besides Schönberg, Raymond Jeannot. The text of *Les Misérables* is the work of Jean-Marc Natel as well as Boublil along with the two English adapters, and *Martin Guerre* has its Anglophone adapters, Edward Hardy and Stephen Clark, though Hardy's name was expunged from the billing for the 1998 revision. As we have seen with *Marilyn*, roomfuls of authors don't tend to create works of integrity.

school in 1968—started out as a shortish piano-accompanied cantata and underwent periodic expansion as it traveled to disc and the stage. "Sha la la Joseph" is a typical refrain, and the Pharaoh of Egypt is played as Elvis in a well-observed symmetry: the true king of pop as the king of a pop opera. *Joseph* is whimsical; what other pop opera is? Its mock swing, mock-Oriental riffs, and mock country (with harmonica and piano boogie) remind us how little pastiche turns up in Lloyd Webber's big works, aside from some fake opera in *Phantom* and a French pop tune heard in *Aspects of Love*'s café scene. "Quoting" music obviously cites a reference, and that can lure the listener out of the romantic spell that pop opera seeks to cast.

Joseph reveals little of pop opera's power (both to move and to outrage), though it does remind us of the form's verbal puerility in Rice's bad ear for rhyme and his crazy stunting ("biscuit" placed to mate with "district," perhaps the most obtuse failure to hear the sound of English in all pop opera).

This of course is not a vexation in *Cats*, whose lyrics are drawn from T. S. Eliot's *Old Possum's Book of Practical Cats*.* At 7,485 performances the longest-running attraction in Broadway history, *Cats* was revised for its New York stand on its way from London so successfully that the Broadway edition is now Standard *Cats*: with a bouncy new melody for Mungojerrie and Rumpelteaser,† and a lavish Puccini takeoff for the Growltiger sequence, to replace "The Ballad of Billy McCaw."

Pop opera's critics may discern an irony at the notion of a revision: they believe that all pop operas are contrived of more or less equal parts hype, marketing, and scenery. Even more baffling, to them, must be the insanely intricate revision of *Starlight Express* in London in 1993 during the ninth year of the original run. This was instituted not to correct flaws but simply to encourage, with new fun, the return of enthusiasts.

---

* Eliot knows rhyme. But in reordering "The Rum Tum Tugger" so that Paul Nicholas could impersonate a rock star and brag in the first person (from Eliot's third), *Cats*' director, Trevor Nunn, invented the illiterate misalliance of "sneer" and "ears." (The original mates "ears" with "shears.") This may seem a tiny point, but it reminds us how much the uneducated sloppiness of contemporary pop infects pop opera generally, despite the latter's occasional links with important literature and High Maestro cinema in its source material.

† Thus in Eliot and the published music. *Cats* programs spell it as "Rumpleteazer." Note, too, that *Cats*, merry rather than romantic, allows for some pastiche.

*Starlight Express** is the train show, with the entire cast on roller skates, running races along a track and across a moving trestle. Like *Cats*, it's more revue than narrative, though *Starlight Express* deals heavily in character relationships and, unlike *Cats*, enjoys sung conversations between the set pieces.

More important, the two shows are separated by their music, for the *Cats* sound style begins in Lloyd Webber's impish reading of Eliot and gradually rises to pop opera's typical massed choirs of singers and orchestra players, as in the almost ecstatic finale, "The Ad-dressing of Cats." *Starlight Express* is rock and roll with spots of blues, gospel, rap, and even country. The last is "U.N.C.O.U.P.L.E.D.," something that Connie Smith or Melba Montgomery might easily chart on without having to change a single syllable. (The model, of course, is Tammy Wynette's hit "D-I-V-O-R-C-E.") The American diesel locomotive, a preening muscle-hunk (with pneumatic biceps built into his costume) called Greaseball, gets a piano rave-up entitled "Pumping Iron," and a treacherous caboose, C.B., enjoys one of the score's few non-rock numbers, "There's Me." The cast also includes a bisexual engine, Electra, who enjoys Eurotrash electro-pop in "AC/DC," written in the suitably unstable meter of $\frac{7}{8}$.

On the other hand, the boxcars are given the amusingly monotonous "Freight," in which they identify themselves as Rocky, Rocky II, and Rocky III. (All three films had been released by this time.) For the 1993 revision, the authors have the girl train cars ragging on the boys' low I.Q., the Rockys themselves now communicating in heavy Cockney accents.

Of course, there must be the Big Tune, on the order of "Don't Cry For Me, Argentina" or "Memory." "Starlight Express" is the least imposing of the genre, with especially lame lyrics. As it happens, its use in the show turns on an ultra-American concept: the true hero already *is* the person

* The musical is entirely unrelated to Algernon Blackwood and Violet Pearn's 1915 play *The Starlight Express*, about children contacting the spirit world to cure their parents of depression. The play would be forgot but for its incidental score and songs, composed by Edward Elgar. The music is still popular in Britain and was surely known to Lloyd Webber, who grew up in a musical family. One listens for a recollection of Elgar in *Starlight Express*, if only for discreet homage, in vain. Amusingly, there is a "recollection" of a piece from *Show Boat*, "It's Getting Hotter in the North," in the main strain of "Rolling Stock." As the *Show Boat* number was dropped during rehearsals in 1927 and not performed till 1988, four years after Lloyd Webber wrote "Rolling Stock," he could not possibly have recollected it in any real sense. Still, it's fun to hear Jerome Kern rocked after all these years.

he seeks to become (as in *The Wizard of Oz* or *The Great Gatsby*). "I am the starlight!" exults the protagonist, Rusty the steam engine. "I can achieve!" Neither the story line nor the score has led us to this point, however; it is simply presented to us. *Starlight Express* is thus a solution without the clues—and I hear that chorus of pop-opera haters crying, "So are they all!" They aren't; this is the weakest of the group. For anyone who resists—who, to be candid, doesn't want that gaudy Andrew Lloyd Webber to succeed even at writing knockoffs of America's easiest music—*Starlight Express* is like a line written for the 1993 revision: "Forty tons of empty chrome."

Worse, the race courses used in London, extending around the auditorium's side and rear and upstairs as well, could not be duplicated for Broadway. Not that the races were interesting in themselves: they involved too many characters we hardly knew, and could be followed in toto only on a giant video screen. But at least it was all . . . well, racy. Broadway's *Starlight* could not of course drop the races, but they were less elaborately run. Even so, the production cost eight million dollars, by far the biggest capitalization The Street had known to that time.

The show ran 761 performances in New York: a flop next to the Big Event that was *Jesus Christ Superstar*, or the star power exercised by *Evita*'s Patti Lu and Mandy Patinkin, or the striding *Cats*. *Starlight* didn't even get a Broadway cast album, though the work's only value lies in the score. It's not important theatre writing, but it charms.

The lack of story in *Cats* and *Starlight Express* is not typical; pop opera usually treats a great deal of plot. Doubters love to claim that they can't follow the second acts of *Les Mis* and *The Phantom of the Opera*. But the former is, after all, the reduction of an extremely long novel. The latter, admittedly, gets a bit cockeyed in the second-act churchyard scene built around "Wishing You Were Somehow Here Again." This is because *Phantom*'s adaptation of Gaston Leroux's novel omits the book's crucial earlier scene in the cemetery at Perros, where the heroine's father is buried. Still, what pop opera's critics never want to credit is the form's occasional proficiency in laying out the rhythms of a big dramatic story made largely of big dramatic music.

Miss Saigon, for instance, is very clever in its use of the libretto of Puccini's *Madama Butterfly* to create a new story, set during and after the

Vietnam War. Unlike *Rent*, which updates and relocates *La Bohème* while faithfully absorbing its action, *Miss Saigon* expands and finesses. It builds up Kate Pinkerton; changes Butterfly's uncle, a bonsō, from a religious ideologue to a political one—in fact a murderous fanatic; and reinvents a bustling, cynical marriage broker as the flamboyant Engineer, the show's one star part. It's Jonathan Pryce as Goro, casting too gala even for Salzburg when Herbert von Karajan was running European music.

To be fair, Butterfly herself, called Kim, loses stature in this version. A teenager who accepts tragedy with the bitter welcome of an Oedipus, she retains nobility but now lacks epic irony. Butterfly's tale is especially troubling because she has no way of knowing that Pinkerton plans to betray her right from the start. Hers is a truly Greek doom: accidentally chosen. But *Miss Saigon*'s Pinkerton, Chris, genuinely loves his Butterfly and has no intention of losing her—as we learn in another of those pop-opera spectacles, the Helicopter Scene.

Actually, while Nicholas Hytner's original London *Miss Saigon* used every bit of Drury Lane's gigantic stage, the show had less pure spectacle than is usual in the form. It was a big but not beautiful production. The helicopter sequence, however, was ingeniously presented, in John Napier's design and David Hersey's lighting. Set during the last minutes of the Fall of Saigon, the episode shows the heroine and her American marine separated by unexpected history.

At first, we see it all as if from within the American embassy compound. While the Vietnamese, terrified of the coming Communists, besiege the fence upstage, crouching American soldiers with their backs to us aim their machine guns at the mob. Then the perspective is physically reversed, in a conceit typical of Asian theatre. (Some may recall its use at the very start of the "Pretty Lady" scene in *Pacific Overtures*.) Now the Americans are far upstage, and the Vietnamese are right in front of us. The switch in viewpoint heightens the drama, pulling us from the American position to that of the Vietnamese—from the determined but useless Pinkerton to the determined but ill-starred Butterfly, trapped on the wrong side of the fence, of the war, of life. Every person in the crowd with her has his own reason to need a place on that helicopter, but we concentrate on Chris, desperately shouting for and failing to find Kim as technical sorcery embodies the airship. The crowd cowers under the force of the whirling blades as it lands. Kim signals to Chris. But he cannot see her, someone drags him inside, and the last ship of Kim's hope takes off without her.

It is the show's central episode. Helicopter whirrings are the first thing we hear as the work begins, and the show's logo art combined a woman's face and a whirlybird in a stylization of Asian calligraphy. Unfortunately, the helicopter scene seems misplaced. We reach it long after the narrative chronology has passed it, in the form of Kim's nightmare three years later. "They needed something big in the second act," say the doubters. This may be so. It is just as likely that the authors hoped to tighten audience interest with a jump cut, from Kim and Chris' honeymoon, the ballad-with-saxophone "The Last Night of the World," to the Communist takeover of South Vietnam, "The Morning of the Dragon." It's an arresting leap, for, immediately after, juxtaposed with Kim's belief in her American, is a look at his new life with his new American bride. What on earth has happened?, we wonder, as, thousands of miles apart, the two women duet in "I Still Believe."

So the questionable placement of the Helicopter Scene may be sharp dramaturgy rather than—as the skeptics would have it—"marketing." *Miss Saigon*'s score may in any case be, on certain technical grounds, the best of all the pop operas. For one thing, lyricist Boublil collaborated with one of the few craftsmen to venture into this arena, Richard Maltby Jr. More usually composer David Shire's partner, Maltby enforced a ban on that idiotic assonance masquerading as rhyme (though a few did inject themselves even so), and characterized the tone of the Engineer with a precision that pop lyricists generally lack. Still, there remained the usual plethora of sweaty declarations—such as "I am the guilt inside your head!"—with which pop opera's characters so often go *thud!* in those relentless end rhymes.

Schönberg, also, is a more consistent composer than Lloyd Webber. He develops his Leitmotiven conscientiously, and has never committed anything like Lloyd Webber's attempt to fold the raucous disco of *Phantom*'s title number into an otherwise traditional lyric-dramatic score. *Miss Saigon* even has a comic spot—rare in the form—for the Engineer, "The American Dream." A savage indictment of the Engineer's materialism, the piece brings onstage a vast white Cadillac, whose hood the Engineer humps in

THE MUSIC OF THE NIGHT

anticipation of becoming one of America's leading pimp-capitalists. For authenticity, the Statue of Liberty rides in the front seat.*

Miss Saigon also stands out for Jonathan Pryce's participation, which producer Cameron Mackintosh thought so crucial to the work's New York stand that he threatened to cancel the production if a resistant Equity didn't back down. Pop operas don't usually have star parts the way *The Music Man* and *Gypsy* do. True, Michael Crawford's Phantom and Colm Wilkinson's Jean Valjean are famous assumptions. But other stars enjoy success in these roles—Davis Gaines, for instance, as the Phantom—and even anybodies play them. To be sure, Bernadette Peters made a very personal impression in the first half of *Song & Dance*. (The second half is almost entirely danced.) But that is, after all, a one-woman show.

So it was notable that Pryce left the Engineer somewhat vacated after his stint. Of the other titles, only *Sunset Boulevard* centers on an above all charismatic talent, as diva collectors ponder the contributions of Patti Lu (too human for Norma Desmond, but with much *voce*) in London or Glenn Close (just insane enough, but husbanding the *voce*) in New York.

Sunset played least problematically among the cognoscenti, but then this was a slavish adaptation of a popular film. Acres of the screenplay are spoken and even sung, and the content did not undergo the revising that nagged *Cats, Song & Dance, Starlight Express, Miss Saigon*, and especially *Martin Guerre*. Altering shows in revival has become so routine that one speaks of the "revisal." But you're supposed to be a superannuated classic like *No, No, Nanette* or *Annie Get Your Gun* when suffering alterations, not two or three years old.

Those hostile to pop opera could adduce this endless retooling to their charges of insubstantial composition. They might decry the canny positioning of Norma's three grand solos, "With One Look," "New Ways To Dream," and "As If We Never Said Goodbye," as more of that pop-opera marketing: the diva commands, then yearns, then bangs out the anthem. They might denounce the visuals as more scenery substituting for music. Again, John Napier turned the tricks, showing us, first of all, the

---

* One wonders if Schönberg and Boublil will ever write "The French Dream": a savage indictment of the entire French army oinking and squealing as they run from the foe to pack Nazi death trains with Jewish French citizens (even before the Nazis told them to) and then rat up Europe's most heartless black market while awaiting liberation by the United States.

murdered Joe Gillis floating in the pool; then a video account of the car chase that takes Joe to Norma's mansion; then the mansion itself, a fifi cathedral of such tonnage that the public must gasp when it rises at the end of Act One to reveal an inset scene of a bohemian New Year's party; and then, for Act Two, a taste of Cecil B. DeMille when Norma returns to Paramount during the shooting of *Samson and Delilah*. No one seems to have commented on the best trick of all, the very last thing one sees: a projection of Norma Desmond in youth, innocent of fame and wealth and murder. Not a star: a human being.

The Norma we experience is so star that pop opera's love of a poster logo consisting of one or two simple pictorial elements against a solid color background was subverted, from the New York production on, with the addition of a photograph of the Norma, turbanned, kohl-eyed, crazed. *Cats*' two eyes, *Les Mis*'s waif against a burning banner, and the original *Sunset* street sign over the shadow of palm fronds emphasize the genre's consistency, its immiscible uniqueness in theatre history. After all, the traditional Broadway logo was a varying art form, usually a fully delin-eated drawing—*My Fair Lady*'s inside-joke Hirschfeld of Shaw animating a puppet of Higgins animating a puppet of Eliza; Tom Morrow's color painting of Berlin club life for *Cabaret*; Tony Walton's *Chicago* showgirls. David Merrick's *42nd Street* pretty lady helped engender the pop-opera logo of a lone eyeful to travel unchanged through world cultures. But it was pop opera that introduced (in *Jesus Christ Superstar*'s facing angels) and insistently affirmed in subsequent productions this stingy use of art. For what purpose? *Marketing!*, cry the infidels. Marketing again? This is judging a cover by its book. More fairly, this logo question illustrates the central problem of pop opera's very nature that I cited at the start of this chapter: the shows are too much alike in the way they function.

At that, Broadway has been spared the odder entries in this line. Consider *Metropolis* (1989), seen only in London. Based on Fritz Lang's famous sci-fi silent, *Metropolis* enjoys pop opera's strong points: an odd story, a ton of décor, and a boombox of a score. But *Metropolis* also suffers from pop opera's weak points: an odd story, a ton of décor, and a boombox of a score.

There is, first of all, that questionable authorship, that "extra man" that this form cannot seem to do without. Composer Joe Brooks co-wrote the book and lyrics with Dusty Hughes; but why do we hear of "additional material" by David Firman? Then there is the inconsistency of the writing, now dramatic and even inspiring and now simply demented. The music varies from "theatre" through rock to electrosynthotech babble, often in operatic structures. "Hold Back the Night"—note the pop-flavored title—is built from a trio into a chorus the size of Mahler's Eighth. Keep in mind that *Metropolis* offers a futuristic *Romeo and Juliet* with workers slaving underground for a sunlit drones' society and that the scenario assigns two roles to the heroine: as Maria and as an evil robot. The musical christens her "Futura," a comic-book reduction, and "Futura's Dance" sounds like something that Yma Sumac would request at a Nazi Sunday-afternoon Wish Concert, with gossiping mynah birds and wailing coconut. Even worse are Futura's lines. "Pretty children," she says, of the pupils of the real Maria. "I love my pretty, pretty, pretty, pretty, pretty children."

The inconsistency extends to the performances. American Judy Kuhn, the Maria, functioned in straight Broadway, while Brits Graham Bickley (the Romeo) and Brian Blessed (a Montague obsessed with machines) delivered their English in international BBC. Others in the cast defiantly trumpeted their regional English accents, a trendy leftist-liberation touch now afflicting the English theatre in general. Kuhn had the dirty work of trying to make Futura viable—one can't—and Bickley got the Lloyd Webber Big Tune, "If It's Only Love." It starts well, but then it dithers, proving that what Lloyd Webber does is not as easy as it may appear.

To be fair, *Metropolis* was a hoot even with its flaws. Yes, it's deranged; Lang's celebrated film is even more so. Pop opera can let us down with its overwrought people screaming out the secrets of love and war, but to view this as a formal defect is like derogating the western for its shoot-outs. Pop opera can accomplish wonderful things that merely life-sized musicals can't—in the lyrical magnificence of *Phantom*'s love duet, "All I Ask Of You," the voices flying high on the Big Tune, then falling back to the tonic as the orchestra soars in its own rendition; in the *trompe l'oeil* magic of the journey to the Phantom's lair, as doubles and triples of the leads race down Maria Björnson's hallways-tipping-into-stairways to the candlelit grotto; as the authors stun us with a quaint surprise at the very start of the show: it begins in spoken dialogue without a note of music.

This form can be smart, too. Gaston Leroux's novel speaks in passing of an opera that the Phantom has written; Lloyd Webber makes it a part of his show. His joke is that as the Phantom is advanced in scientific expertise, his music, too, will be far beyond what 1861 was used to.

Composed in a kind of atonal tonality, *Don Juan Triumphant* stumps and angers the singers at a Sitzprobe till the rehearsal keyboard suddenly breaks into the music by itself and the spellbound singers perform the score like robots ready for *Metropolis*. There is, too, that extra shocking moment when, onstage during this opera-within-an-opera, the heroine interrupts a duet with the Phantom to reach up and calmly unmask the monster before the public.

No question, *Phantom* had the ideal story for pop-opera treatment, with the form's grotesquerie built in. It is also the biggest of the scores, written in anticipation of an opera-sized pit. Sixty-three instrumentalists made the first recording, and thirty-seven played the show in New York, most unusual for the time. (*Camelot*, with the biggest orchestra of *its* era, had only thirty-three.) One might expect productions to swell with opera singers, but that has happened only here and there—in ex-Wagnerian Peter Hofmann's Hamburg Phantom, for instance. Director Prince may feel that actors who sing give better theatre; opera singers are too obsessive about The Voice. The original London leads, Michael Crawford, Sarah Brightman (then Mrs. Lloyd Webber), and Steve Barton, opened also the New York run, with Opéra managers Cris Groenendaal and Nicholas Wyman, eerie ballet mistress Leila Martin, and company principals Judy Kaye and David Romano: not a professional opera person in the lot. Sooner or later, there's bound to be a crossover recording, perhaps even a production by one of the major opera companies. But pop opera is not a pop version of opera. It's an opera version of pop: building opera's intensity out of the vernacular musical idiom.

So *Chess* may be the most typical of the pop operas. *Phantom* is arguably the most impressive, or at any rate a shockingly good show. *Miss Saigon* is the most consistent, first for its juxtaposition of the two Vietnamese leads in a comedy of humors, Kim so noble and the Engineer so debased; and second for its throughline of cultures at war, as the bar girls envision America as a movie with a happy ending, Chris sees it as the world's savior, and his friend John denounces it as a clumsy giant accidentally squashing little people. *Miss Saigon* also boasts the best set of orchestrations in the entire series, by William D. Brohn. All this even though *Les Mis* remains the one with the best lyrics.

But *Chess* cuts in with the most pop-based of the musical sources, Benny Andersson and Björn Ulvaeus of the Swedish group ABBA; with the genre's founding lyricist, Tim Rice; with the ultra-basic ontogeny of concept album leading to London smash directed by another of the form's essential names, Trevor Nunn. The LPs appeared in 1984, the show began a three-year run in London in 1986, and the Broadway version—in a revision and a new staging—closed after a two-month struggle in 1988. Chess did not therefore take off on the usual global conquest. Still, a work of such high quality must rebound, especially after the success of Mamma Mia!, whose score recycles ABBA hits.

What hurt Chess in New York is something that would seem to be irrelevant, at least to the pop-opera movement: Michael Bennett was diagnosed with AIDS. Here Chess becomes the least typical of the set. Pop operas tend to be put in the care of theatre directors—Trevor Nunn, Hal Prince, Nicholas Hytner—not choreographer-magicians like Bennett. But Bennett had enjoyed a sensational triumph with Dreamgirls (1981), a book musical so constantly sung that some think of it as America's pop opera.

So Bennett was ready for Chess, a through-sung piece treating the politicization of the game in international tournaments. The apolitical Bennett was uninterested in the Cold War shoving match embedded in Chess' story line; rather, he instinctively fastened on the media coverage that tarts for statesmanship. Set designer Robin Wagner gave Bennett a wall of video monitors overlooking a huge chessboard—Chess' "stage"—that could be hydraulically raised, lowered, or tilted. The album's three leads repeated their roles: Russian champ Tommy Korberg, American champ Murray Head, and the latter's coach, Elaine Paige. When Bennett abandoned the production to fight his illness, Trevor Nunn stepped in despite a lack of sympathy with the design and the ensemble casting, which suited a Michael Bennett fantasia rather than the character-conscious musical plays that Nunn preferred.

On the other hand, Nunn had staged Cats, as empty of character as a show can be. Cats is a vaudeville, so what was Nunn's problem? Hating the London Chess, Nunn resolved that the New York production would be as different as possible in every way. He commissioned book material (by Richard Nelson); he organized the visuals around a bunch of pillars in constant motion, a real distraction because they were operated by stagehands hidden inside and one kept expecting them to have a crash; and he literalized. In London, "The Story of Chess" opened the show as a ballet of chess figures on that game board stage, a striking and elegant way to conceptualize a work's first minutes. In New York, "The Story of Chess" was confusing backstory, a father explaining the game to his very young daughter. Yes, she'll grow to be the American champ's coach, and the father figures in the plot, and the backstory occurs during the 1956 Hungarian uprising against Soviet oppression, a useful adduction to the show's political background. Yet the old man and the little girl, strangers to us, proved irritating instead of touching; and one wondered how these two found the chance to chat while Soviet tanks were banging up Budapest. Even with David Carroll, Philip Casnoff, and Judy Kuhn in the leads, this *Chess* never recovered from Trevor Nunn's having had to appropriate Michael Bennett's production in London.

Too bad: for this is a surprisingly good score, something more than what the word "pop" means in even its widest sense. There are touches of rock in the "Terrace Duet," and rather a dose of it in "No Control." Yet the Russian champ's establishing number, "Where I Want To Be," uses classical technique to describe this extremely lonely man's vertigo at the summit of world affairs. One actually hears a terror of heights in the accompaniment, which starts as a little keyboard waltz, intruded on by the summons of a drum and the lying of woodwinds: East-West politics. When the singer reaches the main strain ("Where I want to be . . ."), he stays repetitively on one tone and then another, as if barely maintaining his balance while the orchestra suggests the crazy swaying of his supports.

Much of *Chess* is like that, not least in Anders Eljas' orchestrations, which sound like those for no other show, with undulating melodic lines over the carousing of the xylophone—music for a war without battles— then self-effacing, listening to the singers, gleefully deadpan on the line "No one can deny that these are difficult times."

Even Tim Rice is on his best behavior, suddenly aware and intolerant of pop's false rhymes. It was apparently Rice's idea to use the game of chess as a metaphor for the contest of democracy and totalitarianism. *Chess'* plot *is* a game of chess, made of ploys and deceptions. The real power lies in the American and Russian operatives, especially our Walter (Dennis Parlato) and their Molokov (Harry Goz). They "play" the three lead characters as if they were game pieces—though Casnoff's ugly American is himself a player. He may be based on Bobby Fischer, the American champ famed for childish stunts and provocative statements.

Casnoff's role was the hardest for the authors to pin down; he has the hit tune, "One Night in Bangkok," and a venting autobiography, "Pity the Child," the show's sole number to employ the stridulous one-mike, one-mouth, eighty-thousand-listeners vocalism that pop opera is famous for. Yet he is in the end only exasperating. We know the other two better, for though they are victims of the playing, they are never pawns. No, the pawn is the Russian's wife (Marcia Mitzman), who has another hit, with Kuhn, "I Know Him So Well." What Kuhn and Carroll are is knights, played in sacrifice for a checkmate.

In fact, Chess functions without the characterological stability of the typical pop opera, with its monumentally saintly Jean Valjean and Kim; its morally besmirched figure redeemed by love who must neverthe-less die doom-laden in the gentle Paris rain to trickling guitar, Les Mis' Eponine; its psychotic Javert and Norma Desmond; its Phantom, its Evita; its Christ. These people have the obsolete clarity of story leads in a D. W. Griffith silent. But note that the Chess album never concluded its plot action: a synopsis stated that more games were to come. The stagings necessarily gave the public completions—yet in New York David Carroll was the protagonist at first and Judy Kuhn the protagonist at last. Whom is Chess about?

And is the pop-opera era over? The tryout failures of a Lloyd Webber (with Hal Prince directing) and a Schönberg-Boublil suggest as much, though the factional hysteria continues, because that penetrating vocal style has infected innocent scores as well. Not Thoroughly Modern Millie or The Producers, no; one cannot oversing musical comedy. But the leads of Side Show (1997), Alice Ripley and Emily Skinner, went Three Tenors on the big act endings, "Who Will Love Me As I Am?" and "I Will Never Leave You," while singing with charming and subtle musicality elsewhere in that score. Ripley can even venture into Lloyd Webber (she created Sunset Boulevard's Betty Schaefer in New York) without screaming; and Skinner's second-act opening of My Life With Albertine (2003), "I Want You," was cabaret of matchless intimacy.

So, clearly, pop opera has left a mark on the performing of musicals. And the more-song-but-less-or-no-book approach of the serious musical may observe further influence. But one of the earliest of these modern Broadway operas was Galt MacDermot's The Human Comedy, and MacDermot has surely heard no Lloyd Webber. He may not have heard Carousel.

It is bemusing to consider other London importations, which by comparison to pop opera come off as scripts with the merest doodad of a score. Pam Gems' *Piaf* (1981) won its star, Jane Lapotaire, a Tony for Best Actress in a Play. Yet the evening included more than a sampling of Edith Piaf standards, sung by Lapotaire to piano, accordion, and bass. The musicians were permanently fixed on a nearly bare raked platform, as were the actors playing various people in Piaf's life. As they prepared to switch from, for example, German Soldier #2 to Lucien, they changed clothes upstage while the play went on.

This is a very English sort of idea for theatre, and indeed *Piaf* was performed here in Howard Davies' London production, with Lapotaire and Zoë Wanamaker joining a new American cast. Also typically English was the rendering of the French characters in a selection of those regional British accents, preferring Cockney for the mean-streets Parisian milieu. True, there is something silly about American actors using French accents to portray the French. The French themselves do not have French accents: they just speak French. But presenting French people in a jumble of British accents at the Plymouth Theatre on West Forty-fifth Street in Manhattan strains the suspension of disbelief. Let's see: a dope pusher from the Marais sounds as if he were about to burst into "The Lambeth Walk"? Then, too, some found the expletive-rich dialogue and the generally coarse behavior jarring. Freer souls found the piece exhilarating.

"The Lambeth Walk" itself reached Broadway in *Me and My Girl*, Lupino Lane's 1937 vehicle about a Cockney coming into the nobility. No one would argue that the show was not a musical, but the original in fact had more book than score by far, and this 1985 London hit, directed by Mike Ockrent, was very much a revisal, with a new book by Stephen Fry and six interpolations. These were all by the show's original composer, Noel Gay (with various lyricists), and while their composition spanned two decades, they worked beautifully together and thoroughly suited the situations they were plopped into. "Leaning on a Lamppost" seemed so at one with the show's spirit that it inspired the artwork for the poster. But it was in fact one of the six guests. Such finesse is rare in a revival filled with extra numbers, but this new *Me and My Girl* was produced by Richard Armitage, Gay's son, in loving but also accurate celebration.

Like *Piaf*, *Me and My Girl* came to Broadway (in 1986) with its original lead, Robert Lindsay. One of the added numbers, a sentimental duet for an old couple, "If Only You Had Cared For Me," was dropped as being too senile; and yet another Gay title, "Hold My Hand," came in to firm up the central romance. Where London audiences may dote, New Yorkers say, "Prove it!," so Ockrent had choreographer Gillian Gregory pep up the corps.

The New York principals, too, seemed chosen for spunk—heroine Maryann Plunkett, old grandees Jane Connell and George S. Irving, and fortune hunter Jane Summerhays. They all gave a punchier version of the staging that would play London for almost eight years, to New York's still quite satisfying three years and four months.

What is notable about this ebulliently empty musical comedy is that it opposes the pop-opera style in every respect. It is a jest rather than a romance, it uses performers rather than singers, and its every expression finds voice in The Music They Don't Write Any More. At that, what has the score to express but that musical-comedy joy in being alive? This is pop music *as* pop music, devoid of expansion and innocent of rock. Only once does the evening venture into the emotional, in "Once You Lose Your Heart," which combined the defiant and the rueful in Maryann Plunkett's powerful rendition.

Like all English musicals, Me and My Girl is extremely English, and the subject of social class fills a well of laughs and plot points. Yet this new version of it visited not only New York but Mexico City, Budapest, Tokyo. Odder yet is the comparable global tour made by Blood Brothers, a play with songs—often unexpected ones. It is a rule of composition that even the best numbers won't land if they're sung by the wrong character, or at the wrong time. Yet that happens constantly in this piece. But then, its sole author, Willy Russell, is a playwright rather than a technician of the musical; he wrote his own handbook for this dark tale of twins parted at birth, one to grow up in comfort and the other in poverty. Of course they find each other—and here the subject of class creates not Me and My Girl banter and a contagious outbreak of "The Lambeth Walk" but tragedy.

Premiered in 1983, Blood Brothers was revived in 1988, and it was this staging that came to Broadway (in 1993), with three Brits, Stephanie Lawrence in the central role of the mother, Warwick Evans as the perfervid Narrator, and Con O'Neill repeating his London triumph as the twin raised in sorrow. Blood Brothers totted up a solid two-year run on The

Street, a remarkable showing for a work so out of genre, any genre. Perhaps it attracted theatregoers alienated by standard fare.

One might have expected visits from European shows generally in the wake of the English and French successes. There were few. The Polish *A Chorus Line*, *Metro* (1992), whose English translation was largely the work of an American actress, Mary Bracken Phillips, was actually performed by a Polish cast, but the run lasted two weeks. A Dutch hit tried Broadway as *Cyrano: The Musical* in 1993. Like *Metro*, it came over in its original production, this directed by Eddy Habbema. An elaborate unfolding of Rostand's classic tale in designer Paul Gallis' protean stage of sliding screens and backdrops, *Cyrano* was certainly a high-tech eyeful.

But another *Cyrano* musical? It was another pop opera, at that, with a few spoken lines but music that never turns off. Composed by Ad Van Dijk to Koen Van Dijk's lyrics (in the English of Peter Reeves and Sheldon Harnick), *Cyrano* made no attempt to contain all of Rostand. The reduction made a simple throughline of the hero (Bill Van Dijk); his love, Roxane (Anne Runolfsson); his "face," Christian (Paul Anthony Stewart); his friends; and his enemies. The show moved in blocks of sound—"Opera, Opera" as *le tout Paris* gathers for the performance that Cyrano will interrupt; then "Aria" from the tenor whom Cyrano has sworn to drive from the stage; then "One Fragment of a Moment" for Roxane and Christian; then "The Duel" as Cyrano tosses off verse while humiliating an antagonist in swordplay; and so on. Director Habbema kept the full ensemble in play as much as possible: "Opera, Opera" was a costume parade as Gallis created a miniature proscenium and fluty set for the freakishly overcostumed tenor; and "One Fragment of a Moment," though sung as a duet, was presented as the reflections of a couple who haven't yet spoken, sighting each other amid a teeming crowd.

The score, too, was very appealing at times; but there were stretches that as book scenes would have tightened the action. There were as well the usual pop-opera reprises, though no ringing out of the Big Tune in the orchestra and no gaffes in the lyrics. The usual complainers were able to isolate one questionable line during the convent sequence, in the nuns' "He Loves To Make Us Laugh": "tremendous fun for every nun." If Homer nods, why can't Koen Van Dijk? Truth to tell, his lyrics—in Dutch or the quite faithful English rendering—are seldom more than functional. This is fair cause for complaint, for Rostand's text is besotted with language, and his message tells that the very meaning of love is a poetry not of face but of soul.

Still, the musical is not without invention, especially in that opera episode, changed from Rostand's original scene in the Hôtel de Bourgogne, host to *spoken* drama. After all, this really is *Cyrano: The Opera*, so a little satire on the Baroque vocal style is suitable. Then, too, the folks singing "Opera, Opera" are busily intoning that notion about the physical nature of romance that *Cyrano* is going to disprove. The breakthough arrives in the show's outstanding number, Roxane's "(If you weren't handsome at all) Even Then." It worries Christian, because all he has is handsomeness: Roxane has fallen in love with Cyrano, the author of all Christian's sublime letters, all his extemporaneous lovemaking, all his soul. And then of course Christian dies in battle, and Roxane goes into that cloister—and now, again, the musical alters Rostand. Cyrano's burlesques have offended every heavyweight in Paris; only his swordsmanship protects him. But a great log fells him in a suspicious accident; his head wound will kill him for the final curtain.

In the play, this is discussed, not seen; in the musical, designer Gallis prepared a row of smallish lights along the length of the stage; before it, Cyrano was attacked by thugs. Then the lights glittered as the "Opera, Opera" crowd—including the humiliated tenor—applauded and jeered as if they were an audience behind the footlights, watching a comedy. A wonderful touch.

Even better was the climax of the redefining of the nature of beauty, in a scene drawn very closely from Rostand. As in the original, Cyrano read aloud Christian's last letter, supposedly for the first time. The darkening sky told Roxane that he could not possibly see to read. She turned: to see him reciting from memory. In a flash of realization and despair, she knew whom she had really loved all along, even as she lost him for a second time: for now the real Cyrano died.

Though the simplest five minutes in a busy staging, this last scene was the show's highlight, if only because Rostand wrote one of the great can't-fail finales. Like Jane Lapotaire and Robert Lindsay, Bill Van Dijk had to come over with the show, because his English is excellent and his austerely played Cyrano contrasted well with the production's "Opera, Opera" flamboyance. The typical Cyrano revels in *gasconnade*, playing puppeteer to the text, but here it was Anne Runolfsson who decorated the scene. A superb singer given all the work's best melodies, she now got the best of the few spoken lines when she turned to see Cyrano as he really is. At first alarmed, she became almost savage with self-knowledge. "*Your own letter!*" she shouted. The music calmed her, and they spoke:

ROXANE: So it was you.
CYRANO: (fervently) It was Christian.
ROXANE: (so sadly) No, you . . .

Rostand follows this with a ten-minute set piece of a death scene. In the musical, barely a minute remained, and the effect was overwhelming.

Few enjoyed *Cyrano: The Musical* as much as they did *Piaf, Me and My Girl,* or *Blood Brothers.* But there is something to be said for a show that inspires us emotionally. *Piaf* is too dry a stunt, and *Me and My Girl* is there to delight, not inspire. *Blood Brothers* is a very moving piece, but its curiously innovative construction makes watching it—at least up to its drastic final scenes—a somewhat intellectual experience. One may be as much bemused by Willy Russell's "Fooled you!" narrative as involved in it.

Pop opera, on the other hand, is where the big-emotion shows like *Show Boat* and *South Pacific* went to when the musical got sophisticated—*Candide, Company, Follies, Pippin, Chicago, Barnum, Nine, The Mystery of Edwin Drood.* Yet the pop-opera era seems to be over, just as the era of that other big-emotions form, operetta, ended at about 1930. But operetta ended on a technicality: huge budgets and running costs cut the genre down virtually the day the Depression started. If pop opera is over, it is because the two major bylines, Lloyd Webber and Schönberg-Boublil, both suffered the aforementioned failures.

However, the musical in general was absorbing some of operetta's traits during the 1920s, and pop opera in its turn has left its mark. The nonstop musical structure and hyper vocal delivery can be heard every year on The Street, along with the free recycling of musical passages that in the craftsman's hands unifies a work but otherwise disintegrates one. Then, too, any musical with powerful feelings and a mainstream pop style can be denigrated as a "pop opera"—*Aida,* for example, another title of wide appeal that appalls the status-conscious.

What better characterizes as eccentric an age in which the form that has produced some of the biggest hits in history is so insistently vilified? This is another of the many reasons why the Golden Age—the musical's Era of Good Feelings—gave out in the 1970s, when only a few pop operas had appeared, and when *Evita* could win the Tony and the New York Drama Critics Circle Award for Best Musical. Back in the 1920s, when the Golden Age was new, the genre of musical that some theatregoers resented in a kind of hysteria did not exist.

Of course, in those days one bought tickets because of the star, or the composer, or the producer (if a Ziegfeld, Dillingham, or Cohan), or even because one liked the photographs posted outside the theatre. One would never have thought of going to a show because of the guy who staged it.

4

BIG DEALS

The permanent set was a portion of a spa, all in white bathhouse title, and the cast—one man, twenty-one women, and four little boys—wore black. The narrative source was Federico Fellini's 1963 film *Otto e Mezzo* (Eight and a Half), a plotless and at times surreal piece about a movie director who can't make a movie. *That* one.

The book was by Arthur Kopit, the score by Maury Yeston; and of course the show is *Nine* (1982).* One cannot truly base a theatrical work on something as diffuse as $8\frac{1}{2}$, but significant episodes of it informed *Nine*'s writing and staging: the color codes in the costuming (though the women of the film are usually in white against the black of the protagonist, Guido Anselmi, planned for Laurence Olivier but reassigned to Marcello Mastroianni); the scenes in parochial school; the Saraghina episode; even the familiar scene in the bathhouse, which suggested *Nine*'s set. In all, the musical was an ideal adaptation, for while the film may be extra-familiar to some as, arguably, the masterpiece of one of cinema's handful of genius directors, the new work transforms it. As we'll see, the

---

* Fellini stressed his protagonist's inability to function artistically by withholding even a title, giving the film a number only. It was in fact the *tenth* Fellini work, but he counted as halves one piece that he co-directed and two short pieces included in anthology releases. *Nine*, as the name of the musical version of $8\frac{1}{2}$, makes no sense, though it does relate to the age of the protagonist's younger self, back when life consisted simply of trying not to sin, as opposed to the adult world of trying not to be consumed by one's ambition, lust, anomie, and fame. While we're pausing, we should note that Fellini was originally going to give the film a title: *La Bella Confusione*, which is, roughly, *A Fine Mess I've Made For Myself*.

years after *Nine* swell with movies turned musical by the simple addition of songs and a functional staging. They are burgled; $8\frac{1}{2}$ was enriched.

It was so, first of all, by Yeston's marvelous score, an odd combination of character numbers and revue-like specialties that served as plot songs. One item, "The Germans at the Spa," was arguably unnecessary, but it contains some of Yeston's best lyrics and adds a harmlessly antic touch to a show that is, after all, a nervous breakdown played as a farce. Certain numbers—"Guido's Song," "My Husband Makes Movies," "Only With You," and the mordantly touching "The Bells of St. Sebastian"—were embedded in the action. But "A Call From the Vatican" was really a physical showpiece for Anita Morris as she deftly pretzled up into *Guinness Book*–level contortions. "Folies Bergeres," Liliane Montevecchi's salute to the sheer intoxication of song-dance-and-beauty entertainment, was irrelevant to the story, as Guido (with a new surname, Contini) doesn't make musicals. Still, it could be thought of as the show's closest link with the movie: as an explanation of what it is going to be transformed into. For one of the cleverest things about *Nine* is how its director makes something enjoyable—a song-dance-and-beauty show, really—out of something serious. The hybrid work can thus relax its tension for "The Grand Canal." This sequence of ten short pieces, in which Guido visualizes a film about Casanova, feels like something designed to fill out the second act, always a danger zone for plot-starved musicals. But, again, the medley does give us a taste of the director on the set, so to speak.*

Nine's cast, whether leads or featured players, remains matchless in many a memory. Not only wife Karen Akers, lady loves Anita Morris and Shelly Burch, mother Taina Elg, movie producer Montevecchi, and whore on the beach Kathi Moss. But even the smaller roles—Stephanie Cotsirilos' pertly acerbic critic, say—came off splendidly, uniquely. Morris' black outfit, a peekaboo body stocking articulated in black curlicues, emphasized her mere honeypot role in Guido's life, and "A Call

---

* Another of the now famous alumni of Lehman Engel's B.M.I. workshop for apprentice writers of musical theatre, Yeston used the class to pursue the notion of a Casanova musical. He may have recycled some of the material in *Nine*; this can be defended on the grounds that $8\frac{1}{2}$ is about Fellini and Fellini himself released a *Casanova*, with Donald Sutherland, six years before *Nine* appeared. We appreciate Yeston's discretion, too, in not using what he regarded as his outstanding *Casanova* number, "In the Middle of the Eighteenth Century," though the harpsichord in its accompaniment did find its way into Jonathan Tunick's *Nine* orchestration. Incidentally, it's Folies Bergère, not Bergeres.

From the Vatican" was of course a comic tease. But Morris' singing of her torch song, "Simple," ached with despair.

So these were rich impersonations, none more so than Raul Julia's Guido. The music vexed him on the high notes, but otherwise he embodied what the show says he is: the most interesting man in the world. Equating Guido Contini with Federico Fellini (which we are clearly meant to do), we find so much content in his movies, and some of it so ambiguously presented, that everyone can find a place in him. His audience becomes his subject matter, and the people in his life become his lead players. This explains the large assortment of women surrounding one man: he is the ultimate alpha male, leaving no room for rivals.

The real alpha male of *Nine* was its director, who gets his salute at last: Tommy Tune. Who really does the heavy lifting in a show that is as much an experience as a composition of words and music?

So the alpha male (or female) of the modern musical is the director-choreographer. There actually had been some way back in the Second Age—Julian Mitchell was thus in charge of Ziegfeld's first seven *Follies* revues. But the job as such did not alter the musical's history till the prominence of the choreographer in the 1940s gave rise to the reigns of Agnes de Mille, Jerome Robbins, Michael Kidd, Bob Fosse, and Joe Layton as creative participants in the making of musicals.

Tommy Tune joined this group in the 1970s, but *Nine* was his break-through title, with a style entirely of its own category. Folks still speak of certain moments, such as the flashbulb that went off in Karen Akers' face on the tonic button of "My Husband Makes Movies," causing her to flinch. Or the young Guido's presentation to Montevecchi, during "Folies Bergeres," of a gift box that gave up a feather boa, unfurled to its full length till Montevecchi cried, "Oh, I *love* it!" Or the way the women—now changed into white with splashes of color—were strung out in a line for "Every Girl in Venice (is in love with Casanova)," as if rowing a giant gondola down a canal. Or Akers' determined exit after "Be On Your Own," right up the stage-left aisle of the 46th Street Theatre, as if walking out of the play itself.

One would think that these High Maestro productions make the works themselves unrevivable except in replica resuscitation. But *Nine* returned to Broadway in 2003, directed by David Leveaux and choreographed by Jonathan Butterell. It was welcomed, even acclaimed, but it was nothing like the whirling festival that Tune had held. It was fun to see, as Guido's mother, the sternly loving "Grams" of television's *Dawson's Creek*, Mary Beth Peil, now entirely loving. And another TV star, Jane Krakowski, of *Ally McBeal*, reinvented "A Call From the Vatican" by launching and finishing it on a wire from above. But the portrayals did not quite challenge the originals, and Antonio Banderas failed to suggest the man onto whom the West has temporarily projected a load of hungry voodoo. He sang with stunning force for a Novelty Star. But this Guido lacked variety and surprise.

Perhaps the director-choreographer is more than a mere showman, then: some of them know how to talk to actors, to bring the narrative conflicts to a persuasive authenticity. Still, we love the dazzle of musical comedy in high tech, and this Tune can do as well, most unexpectedly in *My One and Only* (1983)—unexpectedly because, when the show first opened, in Boston, Tune wasn't its director. He was its star.

So was Twiggy, as the pair reunited for the first time since Ken Russell's film of *The Boy Friend* (1971). They were supposedly doing a revisal of a Fred and Adele Astaire Gershwin show of 1927, *Funny Face*. However, the old piece, a forgotten show with a famous title (at that only because of the Fred Astaire–Audrey Hepburn Paramount musical of 1957, with a completely new story) was no more than a jumping-off place. The book, by Timothy S. Mayer, told its own completely new story, with Tune an aviator and Twiggy a swimmer: Charles Lindbergh loves Florence Chadwick. The score contained eight *Funny Face* songs (including three dropped during the 1927 tryouts), along with the usual Gershwin flotsam and "The Cuban Overture" for a dance number.

The director was Peter Sellars, known for fashionably peculiar opera stagings, and the sets, by Adrianne Lobel, recalled the primary colors and odd shapes of the constructivist movement. Not long after the disastrous Boston premiere, Sellars, Mayer, and Lobel were all gone, and Mike Nichols had stepped in for emergency surgery. Nichols turned a tedious chaotic mess into a fast-moving chaotic mess; and Michael Bennett was briefly involved. But it was Tune who then remade the show, during four weeks of further rehearsals before the New York previews began.

What can one do in four weeks? One can't write a new show. Yet that seems to be what happened, as new book writer Peter Stone and Tune (with his co-director, Thommie Walsh) worked around Lobel's sets and the aviator-swimmer romance to concoct a new piece. Six *Funny Face* numbers remained, now in a sea of Gershwin from here and there, and although there was a new plot—centered on aquacade impresario Bruce McGill's attempt to keep Tune from McGill's star attraction, Twiggy—Tune's mission now was not to authenticate character conflict but to unleash the high-strung sociability of musical comedy.

Coincidentally, the original *Funny Face* itself suffered radical overhauling in tryouts. But all one had to do in those days was to reapply the musical-comedy handbook. When presenting "the new Gershwin musical" in 1983, however, one is already in collision with what the public expects—an old Gershwin musical—and one must break rules. One might even defy the most important of them all: Thou shalt tell the public what the show is within the first five minutes. *My One and Only*'s curtain went up on a line of doors, out of which stepped three black guys to scat in counterpoint. The door piece went up as the guys charlestoned and went into "I Can't Be Bothered Now." Posters of Tommy Tune, aviator, and Twiggy, swimmer, appeared. So we knew who those two were. What is the *show*?

Now it was raining. The chorus—black guys, white girls—danced in yellow slickers with electric-blue umbrellas. Now Tommy Tune came down from the flies in a parachute, sensibly taking the section of "I Can't Be Bothered Now" that begins with "I'm up among the stars." As he landed, a train flat appeared. "Hello, America!" boomed the Georgian Prince Nicolai—the villain, though we didn't know that yet. In white suit and fur coat, he introduced his aquacade girls in their black-and-white water suits. "Are being lovely, yes?" purred Prince Nicky. Everyone charlestoned. Now for the star of the aquacade—"Third woman to swim English Channel, but first attractive one!" This was Twiggy. Tune and she fell in love at first sight, to the strains of "Blah, Blah, Blah." The song (first heard in the 1931 film *Delicious*) mocks the clichés of ballad, so we sense that this show will evince and comment upon style rather than simply have it. A knowing musical from an unknowing time. When Twiggy doffed her coat, she was in a silver lamé swimsuit, and Tune ran off to prepare for the first book scene, set in his airplane hangar, while everyone finished off a last bit of "I Can't Be Bothered Now" with more charleston.

Eventually, we learned what the show was: the new Gershwin musical. Doesn't that say it all? That rule about prepping the public at the start was written into the handbook relatively late in the Third Age, when musicals started telling unexpected stories and acting odd, so the audience needed help in absorbing it all. A Scots village does *what* every hundred years? The life of a *doctor*? The *Iliad* and the *Odyssey* set *where*? It became important to substantiate the entertainment in some helpful way, so that the coming novelty did not overwhelm.

But Tune's Gershwin show returned us to before that revolution. One doesn't need to substantiate anything if one's work is song, dance, and comedy about Boy Meets Girl in what's left of Adrianne Lobel's constructivist sets. These, by the way, included a wonderful quarter-moon chair in which Twiggy reclined while singing "Boy Wanted" in response to an interviewer's questions; a long, thin strip of real water in which Twiggy and Tommy danced after singing "'S Wonderful," having crash-landed in the tropics (which turn out to be Staten Island); and even a cinema in which Twiggy and Tommy sang "He Loves and She Loves" during a showing of a silent film entitled *White Baggage of the Casbah*.

The show was an ingenious romp, which made it easy to take the reuse of old music, a desperation gambit that would later become an obsession along The Street. It was really Tune's reinstituting of the first principle of twenties musical comedy—to give everybody a good time—that made *My One and Only* unique. *Nine* had to be unique by the very nature of the writing. But *My One and Only* could easily have been . . . well, a tedious chaotic mess.

Of course, the super-director with a background in dance, like Tune, has a credibility advantage in that his choreography establishes his style, and thus makes his stagings stylistically intelligible as wholes. For instance, if Twyla Tharp were to direct a musical that for some reason didn't contain any dancing, one would still recognize the Tharp style simply by the way she moves her people around.

The director who is not a former choreographer has a disadvantage, then, for it would be difficult for most spectators to observe a style in his work. The one exception is Hal Prince, because his background in the concept musical (from *Cabaret* through the five Sondheim collaborations of the 1970s) has given his work a look and spirit. However, Prince gravitates toward tricky-idea shows, so his work is vulnerable if its dramatic content is not perfectly integrated. No one could have come out of *My One and Only* complaining about the implausible story line; implausibility is a virtue of the form that *My One and Only* was reviving.

But *Grind* (1985)—one of the shows that Prince staged while he was in his flop period, from *Merrily We Roll Along* to his reaccession with *The*

Phantom of the Opera—must be thematically coherent and narratively persuasive. It wasn't. As in *Cabaret*, a house of entertainment was made metaphor, but the burlesque "grind" house was used as much to preach racial tolerance as to denounce a place where escapist fun promotes false values. The two metaphors did not play well together, the theatre-is-illusion unneccesary after *Cabaret* and the racial text too bluntly plopped in. There was an awful lot going on in *Grind*—backstage life, romantic triangle (among Ben Vereen, Leilani Jones, and Timothy Nolen), and plenty of concept. In all this material, the throughline of an aging comic (Stubby Kaye) losing his sight and finally dying seemed distracting, the kind of subplot that used to get written out in Boston. *Grind* actually played its tryout in Baltimore, where its messy layout was firmed up. But it came to New York still overfreighted with people and ideas.

Grind did not properly take its place in the line of Prince's epochal seventies stagings. The show looked fine, with its nightmarishly stylized theatre façade and small runway into the orchestra seats. The score, by Larry Grossman and Ellen Fitzhugh, made for interesting listening; what Prince show score doesn't?* Still, except for a climactic assault by racist thugs on the burlesque company during a performance, in which the attackers rose up out of the Mark Hellinger auditorium, *Grind* ran short of conflict, of a need for a second act. Concept isn't story. For all the show's themey distillations, its most intense moment came during Fay Kanin's book, when the burlesque impresario (Lee Wallace) upbraided his wife (Sharon Murray) simply for having entered one of the "black" dressing rooms:

WALLACE: For God's sake, Romaine, can't you use your head for once insteada your ass?
MURRAY: (after a long pause, extremely hurt) You shouldn't talk to me like that, Harry.

If *Grind* had too much content, Prince's next American work, *Roza* (1987), had almost none. The score, by Gilbert Bécaud and Julian More,

---

* There's *Baker Street* (1965), true. But it is characteristic of Prince that he not only works with the best but inspires the best in his writers.

was wonderful, even if the synthesizer-dominated orchestra occasionally sounded like a vast tin can. But the show, based on Romain Gary's novel *La Vie Devant Soi* (the source of the Oscar-winning French film *Madame Rosa*), had no story. Georgia Brown played a survivor of the Jewish Holocaust raising prostitutes' kids in an immigrant quarter of Paris. So Bécaud filled his music with the sounds of the stranger, primarily Arab, in a series of vividly rhythmic numbers.

The opening, "Don't Even Think About Tomorrow," and the follow-ing "(You don't know what) Happiness (is)" bear the stamp of fine the-atre music, composed for a particular space in a narrative but also to cajole the ear. (Unfortunately, Prince discovered that the pair were both first numbers of the concept sort, announcing a work's belief system. One can't have two first numbers, so the more densely argued "Happiness" forced out "Tomorrow.") Amusingly, Brown's recollections of her days in a bordello were aired in a genre we very seldom hear from any more, the acerbic tango, in "House in Algiers." "Different" was even more unusual, as Brown and three neighbors dished and joked over cards while, between these quartets, a transsexual Brazilian (Bob Gunton) reflected on his past.

One can see why Prince wanted to do the show, wanted this music heard. And there was, at least, a powerful relationship between Brown and one of her charges, an Arab boy named Momo. The last number in Act One, "Moon Like a Silver Window," was used to advance time by switching from Young Momo to an older actor in the same role, all the while elaborating Brown's alarming dependence. Roza is the champion survivor, yet in the end she is as helpless as the rest of us. It made for an arresting first curtain; but Act Two had nowhere to go.

Brown herself was a problem. More's script made her a spouter of hom-ilies and repetitive exclamations. "There's an old Polish saying" ran one typical line. "When you have money, save it. When you don't, spend it." Most of the rest of Brown's spoken part consisted of calling people "meshuggah" and cackling often enough to outfit a thousand perform-ances of *Hansel and Gretel*.

Worst of all, the paucity of interesting secondary characters and that plotless second act left Prince without the foundation on which produc-tion is made. There was nothing to delineate in those sudden illustrative touches, as when the black chorus men singing "Ol' Man River" in

Prince's 1994 *Show Boat* furiously tore down a curtain painted with a tranquil scene of cotton fields; or even in the gala arrival of the principals at the start of Prince's 1997 *Candide* in a "horse"-drawn wagon, to underline the presentational style in which Prince has consistently presented his work.

Roza lasted 12 performances; and of course failure is as much a part of an interesting theatre career as success is. It's a truism—but can you tell me which of the following Golden Age composers never wrote a show that closed out of town? Here's the list: Jerome Kern, George Gershwin, Vincent Youmans, Cole Porter, Vernon Duke, Richard Rodgers, Harold Rome, Marc Blitzstein, Frederick Loewe, Jimmy McHugh, Jule Styne, Frank Loesser, Bob Merrill, Cy Coleman, Richard Adler, Mitch Leigh, Harvey Schmidt, Stephen Schwartz, Stephen Sondheim. And here's the answer: only Rodgers.

One should try to pack the failures in with the successes; don't end with a disaster, as Bob Fosse did. By now, Fosse may be the most appreciated of all director-choreographers, because he did some of his best work after de Mille and Robbins abandoned Broadway and others of that generation fell into uninteresting patterns. But Fosse's *Big Deal* (1986) was worse even than its bad reviews and 70 performances suggest.

The source was Mario Monicelli's 1958 comedy *I Soliti Ignoti* (roughly, *The Usual Suspects*, released in the United States as *Big Deal on Madonna Street*). Centered on a bumbling gang of safecrackers, the film had been beckoning to Fosse as far back as the 1960s. Somehow, having written his own script, he could never find the right songwriters. Then he was assembling a pool of collaborators. At length, he decided to use twenties and thirties standards for a Depression-era Chicago setting with all black principals.

It was one of the few musicals with a genuine auteur, an all-Fosse production. The songs were well chosen—Loretta Devine opened the evening in a spotlight performing "Life Is Just a Bowl of Cherries," which will prove to be an ironic comment on the action; and in a court scene a judge sang "I've Got a Feeling You're Fooling." But "Pick Yourself Up," a useful number, appeared in a fast and tuneless arrangement, "I'm Just Wild About Harry" suffered a musical hook that overwhelmed the melody with fifties jive, and "Button Up Your Overcoat" was slow and draggy. Worse, Fosse met his public with an all but empty stage: scaffolding and stairs leading up to a platform at stage left. It was good dancing room, but an evening-long eyesore. Fosse's book, outlined by white (Wayne Cilento) and black (Bruce Anthony Davis) narrators, was insanely dreary. The few Fosse showstoppers thus could do nothing for a show that had never started.

Fosse did virtually no work on *Big Deal* during its Boston tryout, though many people told him that, if nothing else, the score needed brightening. The old Gershwin used in *My One and Only* was made radiant and saucy, but *Big Deal*'s dark lighting seemed to depress even its music. The performance lacked joy; one came out humming the concept. Yet *Big Deal* was not just any bomb. It was a Fosse bomb, a high-energy bomb, a bomb that, like its characters, took a lot of trouble to go nowhere.

But why? *Big Deal* was the opposite of everything that the word "Fosse" stood for: "Steam Heat" and "Rich Man's Frug" and "Hot Honey Rag." Numbers that *land*. What odd world was Fosse trying to discover by sapping the musical of its juice?

Meanwhile, the prominence of High Maestro super-production led to a comparable treatment of old shows. With so many revivals coming in each season, Broadway now got a taste of the typical modern opera staging that draws a work out of its traditional packaging. Two of these arrived in the 1993–94 season, Howard Davies' *My Fair Lady* and Nicholas Hytner's *Carousel*. With Richard Chamberlain and Melissa Errico, Davies had exactly what Moss Hart worked with when *My Fair Lady* was new—an established "classy" personality as Higgins and an unseasoned Eliza. Davies also got the first opportunity to bring this classic show back to Broadway without duplicating Hart's classic production, and exploited this especially in his set designers, Ralph Koltai and an unbilled Heidi Landesman. There was a feeling of Magritte about the Ascot scene, whose choristers were ranged upstage at heights varying from five to twenty feet above the stage floor; and Higgins' study was dominated by a vast white head; and Errico's rendering of "I Could Have Danced All Night" (as a comic spot) was played in no more than a bed, a window, and sky. As befit the first new staging since 1956 (and with both the authors dead), Davies ventured some ideas about text, such as ending Act One *before* the Embassy Ball, which is now common practice.

The Davies My Fair Lady did not do great business, but Carousel was a hit, as it had already been at England's National Theatre. Where Davies changed the look and to a slight extent the characterological tone of My Fair Lady, Hytner gave the whole of Carousel a new feeling, that of a humanistic parable. Bob Crowley's sets and costumes were extremely mannered in a dark "box" that seemed to have no back wall—placing the Bench Scene, for instance, on a crescent bordering a hill surmounted by a church façade that clearly had no structure behind it, all this overlooked by a great yellow ball of a moon.

The moon was an *idée fixe* in Crowley's design; the National used it as a decoration on the souvenir sweatshirts. But Hytner did more than stylize Carousel: he retold it. When a Rodgers and Hammerstein well-wisher ran into Mary Rodgers in London the morning after Mary saw the production and asked her, "How was it?," Mary simply—and most informatively—replied, "It starts in the mill."

Carousel as written starts in an amusement park. But Hytner wanted to explore the social structures on which Carousel turns. So, as the music started, the moon in view was a giant clock about to strike six, as the mill girls neared the end of their workday. "Miss *Jordan!*" boomed the boss at one lost in reverie on the end, in a new line of text introducing the heroine's moony nature. Julie Jordan, "I like to watch the river meet the sea": remember?

Only the theatre of the millennium can accommodate the changes that Hytner and Crowley rang into "The Carousel Waltz"—following the girls out through the mill's front gates (made to look like those of a prison) to meet their boy friends, thence to the park, whose freestanding pieces eventually turned into the whirling carousel itself.

Throughout, one felt that the more Hytner and his choreographer, Kenneth MacMillan of the Royal Ballet, dug into the characters and situations, the more Carousel they found. That is, theirs was a liberated and authentic Carousel, not one adscititiously embellished. For once, Billy (Michael Hayden) was not just a ne'er-do-well but an angry, rootless, inarticulate guy who has never had a break, and Julie (Sally Murphy) a dreamer from such a drably narrow background that she's not sure which dreams she is permitted to have. Carrie (Audra Ann McDonald) was the least changed from the traditional, but her Mr. Snow (Eddie Korbich) gave us a pompous little nobody who can't wait till he's somebody so he can arrange to have his enemies list run out of town. Most interesting, the heaven sequence was played as a Sabbath Meeting of some arcane Protestant sect, the ensemble dressed in blue greatcoats or robes with white collars and hats.

It is sometimes suggested that the super-director has been so to say summoned, to fill the void created by the depletion of the writing pool. When there are no, or fewer, Rodgerses and Hammersteins, there must instead be Hal Princes, Nicholas Hytners, Bob Fosses, Tommy Tunes. But the super-director appeared simultaneously with Rodgers and Hammerstein.* Great writing made necessary great directing, so that the performers could keep up with the innovatively dramatic tales and their subtextual concepts.

Sometimes it takes a great director to put disorderly or simply non-dramatic material into theatre, as Prince did with *Evita*, and as Des McAnuff did with *The Who's Tommy* (1993). True, *Tommy* has been staged here and there, and prominently filmed, by Ken Russell. But few if any New York theatregoers ever saw a *Tommy* staging, and the film is more a set of illustrations than a dramatization. In effect, McAnuff was conjuring up a *Tommy* for a public that had greatly heard but never seen it: Tommy watching the murder in a mirror's reflection, drooling Uncle Ernie and sadistic Cousin Kevin, the pinball machine, Sally Simpson. There were three Tommys (at different ages), including Michael Cerveris as the grown hero, along with a host of folk similarly destined for lead roles on Broadway, including Alice Ripley, Sherie (later René) Scott, Norm Lewis, Jonathan Dokuchitz, and Michael McElroy.

Oddly, while the work had always seemed fully developed in its original two-LP form, it was now felt that something was missing. Specifically, Tommy's parents, more fully realized in McAnuff's scenario than on disc, needed a duet to lead them to Mrs. Walker's smashing of the

---

* Even before, in a way. Discounting Julian Mitchell (and Edward Royce, George M. Cohan, and certain other directors of the Second Age), referred to earlier in this chapter, one still finds evidence that, somewhat before *Oklahoma!*, at least Hassard Short was viewed by the knowing public as a major director with some "control" over composition. And the extraordinary Rouben Mamoulian won highest honors by staging (with Agnes de Mille) *Oklahoma!* itself. De Mille and Jerome Robbins made important contributions to Rodgers and Hammerstein as directors (though Robbins was billed on *The King and I* as choreographer only), and Fosse made director-choreographer status before Rodgers and Hammerstein had produced their last show.

mirror that symbolically holds Tommy in thrall. As originally written, this central moment, which frees Tommy of his "sight" of the murder and thus cures his disabilities, arrives arbitrarily. McAnuff wanted to show the Walkers losing patience with their son, who has thus far been nothing more than a human guilt trip. So The Who's central artist, Pete Townshend, wrote "I Believe My Own Eyes," the only case in which a "track," so to say, has been added to a classic work of sixties rock a generation later.

Welcomed to Broadway with tremendous notices, *Tommy* was a smash. Wasn't it also a pop opera? Did The Who get a pass while Lloyd Webber and the French guys get ritually clobbered?

Actually, though *Tommy* is an opera, it is not properly of the pop-opera genre, because it is a satiric rather than a romantic work. Or, using Friedrich Schiller's terms, it is sentimental and not naïve. It considers its material intellectually and at a remove, whereas a work like *The Phantom of the Opera* operates strictly within the natural limits of its narrative. Rock really has been a satiric form ever since the day *Sgt. Pepper* was released, when it became the music that observes itself. This gives *Tommy* an independence of spirit that pop operas never have. They all resemble each other; there is nothing like *Tommy* in all the rest of music.

Of all the era's super-productions, the prime one, surely, is Michael Bennett's *Dreamgirls* (1981). This is a complex show on a simple theme: the rise and breakup of the Supremes. Actually, the characters created by composer Henry Krieger and librettist Tom Eyen are original, even if Diana Ross considered taking legal action. Indeed, the average show-biz buff learns a great deal more about lead singer Effie Melody White (Jennifer Holliday) and backups Deena Jones (Sheryl Lee Ralph) and Lorrell Robinson (Loretta Devine) than he knew of the Supremes. This is part of the show's complexity: its specificity of character, illuminating six principals in considerable though sometimes necessarily ephemeral detail.

Eyen and Krieger focus on the three girls; their manager, Curtis Taylor Jr. (Ben Harney); Effie's composer brother C.C. (Obba Babatunde); and soul meister Jimmy "Thunder" Early (Cleavant Derricks), not only as individuals but as individual talents. *Dreamgirls* is a backstager with a formidable volume of information on the music that these people believe in and the music that they perform—which, the show hastens to tell us, are not always the same thing. And more: we know at least some of the six in the way they look at the world. The eventual Curtis-Deena marriage falls apart because of Deena's character (as an idealist) and Curtis' character (as a businessman): Curtis believes in success, and Deena wants to fulfill herself. Again, it's not the same thing. When we learn that Deena is considering taking the lead in a biographical film and that Curtis opposes the project—"the woman wasn't glamorous," he insists—Eyen does not need to tell us who the woman is. That detail is unimportant. What matters is how little use Curtis has for something Deena sees as vital, noble. No wonder he has to give her up.

There's yet more. Because after all the politicized black shows like *Aint Supposed To Die a Natural Death* (1971) and *Raisin* (1973), *Dreamgirls* looks at race relations in terms of art and capitalism. This is the real relationship—black music versus the white charts, for instance, or the Vic Damone soul that blacks must adopt for conservative white audiences. And none of it is sloganized; it's all part of the story. It would have been easy to make Curtis another cadgy hustler. But Curtis isn't just shrewd: he's smart enough to know "concepts," as he himself says. So he's the only character who comprehends the cultural programs that pattern American culture. Yes, Curtis is willing to be crooked in a crooked world. But—this is important—he is not an opportunist. The reason he doesn't understand Deena's vision is not that he himself lacks one. He has a *different* one, in which art has dignity and style. He scorns Jimmy Early's R&B not because it's black but because it's noisy and unpredictable. Ironically, Curtis and Deena share a flaw: neither of them knows how to have fun.

All this creates so much *there* that *Dreamgirls* would have had to move like lightning even if Michael Bennett hadn't been its main producer and director-choreographer (with co-choreographer Michael Peters). Bennett knew that a well-paced musical navigates through book scenes to get to songs—but, also, that a brilliantly paced musical navigates through movement. Not just dance: entrances, exits, crowds changing shape, the sudden appearance of new design elements and the way they vanish, the narration of lighting. And, of course, the famous five towers that moved on their own to define and constantly reorder the playing spaces.

At a cost of three and a half million dollars, *Dreamgirls* was Broadway's most expensive musical yet, but not because of a load of scenery. The bulk of the money went toward the computerization of the towers' ballet. Like so many modern musicals, *Dreamgirls* didn't have all that much dance; but the evening as a whole was filled with kinetic art. The show itself was dancing.

For instance, the opening sequence, at a talent contest in Harlem's Apollo Theatre, moves us back and forth between the onstage acts and the backstage events, and between song and dialogue, to start the exposition and introduce all six of the principals. Bennett did this by using the towers to "edit" the action as if in cinema. There was no overture. After four beats of percussion, the Imperial Theatre's curtain rose on the first of the talent-show acts, the Stepp Sisters in "I'm Looking for Something (baby)." They have hardly started when the first backstage scene erupts in front of the Stepp Sisters (who are playing to the "audience" upstage). Two backup singers are walking out on a lead singer, and as the Stepps keep up a nonverbal vocal presence, the first of our Dreamettes comes in, Deena. A late train has locked them out of the talent show's lineup, but Curtis intercedes for them. Lorrell and C.C. and then Effie arrive, and some more dialogue—always over the music—does a bit of establishing. The Stepps conclude, the announcer invokes the name of headliner James Early, and now Little Albert and the Tru-Tones have appeared for "Goin' Downtown."

It was a famous curiosity of the Apollo sing-offs that despite the democratically open admission, virtually all the acts were extremely good. This allows Krieger and Eyen to create numbers that could easily have charted in real life, without straining the show's own reality. By the time Jimmy himself enters, we learn that it is *his* act that the two previous walkouts have abandoned. This gives Curtis the opportunity to agent the Dreamettes in in their place—their first professional job. Meanwhile, more spoken dialogue over the "onstage" vocals gives us, fleetingly, a crucial insight: the Dreamettes come from an extended family, not only a shared background but, we infer, a group of people who have sacrificed to give these girls a shot at success. Just now, we get only the information that Deena's mother has painstakingly made their costumes. But there is the feeling that more than three hopes are wrapped in the Dreamettes package.

We also get a fast look at the three women themselves. Deena is resourceful, Lorrell amiable, and Effie a problem. Obstructive and suspicious, she is another of those ego-poor souls who compensate with a big front. After Tiny Joe Dixon goes into his slow-strolling "Takin' the Long Way Home," the towers turn as if gazing right at the Dreamettes, and the Apollo stage now faces us for the girls' number, "Move (You're Steppin' On My Heart)," pulling us right into their career for their First Big Night.

They are of course wonderful, and the towers move again to jump-cut us backstage as Curtis negotiates a contract for them to back up Jimmy on a tour. The Dreamettes don't win the contest. Tiny Joe Dixon takes it— in a fix, by the way—and offstage voices intone "Show biz, just show biz," a refrain that runs through the evening. The high-powered music of the talent show is gone, but music continues under the book as it did in so much of *A Chorus Line*. We hear the odd laden line, such as Curtis' "I work for no one," a casually revolutionary remark in *Dreamgirls*' world of racial show biz, where every black person works for someone.

But the story never stops moving: Effie doesn't want to sing backup. She will, finally, because she is already in love with Curtis, and he knows it. He has chosen Deena—yes, already; he confesses as much later. But remember, he knows concepts. And the present concept is that Effie is helpless in his hands. Jimmy teaches the girls "Fake Your Way To the Top" as the towers reshape the storytelling area to become the performance itself, on the Apollo stage that very night.

There, as elsewhere in American show biz *at that time*, it was impossible to fake one's way to anything. Jimmy's number, an inchoate piece about the musical life and its "game of hits," is the kind of thing a Jimmy Early would regard as a mere performance piece, not a credo. Because Jimmy doesn't fake. His style is slow-build rave-up soul; the music, not the lyrics, relates the message. Curtis, whose destiny is already inextricably intertwined with that of the Dreamettes, and of Jimmy as well, resents this kind of performance. *His* style is so utopian that it defies existing categories. He knows what the music is, but the music hasn't been written yet. And Effie will be his victim and Deena his lost horizon—and all this has been placed in the shadow of those towers within *Dreamgirls*' first fifteen minutes.

Of course, none of this would have been possible without Krieger and Eyen's composition, atonishingly confident for unseasoned writers. Eyen had come out of the off–off alternative stage as a completely non-Broadway character. His one brush with The Street, *Rachael Lily Rosenbloom and Don't You Ever Forget It!* (1973), a piece of Nance: Ten, Looks: Three camp, closed in previews just days from the intended premiere. Eyen does commit the sin of failing to rhyme not only in *Dreamgirls'* Top 40 set pieces (where it is appropriate) but in the connecting music dialogues that give *Dreamgirls* so much of its character.

Still, Eyen suppressed his mania for gay vaudeville to put his imagination at the service of his characters. Few musicals have offered such variety and consistency simply in the way their people express themselves. Hearing one of the Dreamettes—or, as they are restyled, Dreams—speak, one immediately knows which of the three it is. Most *Dreamgirls* buffs may at once fasten on Effie's line when, in Act Two, she comes crashing back into the lives of her by then former friends, introducing with resentful triumph a Mr. Morgan, her lawyer: "and he wants to *talk* to you!"

The best of this score may well lie in such scenes, in that connecting tissue just mentioned. Many of the show's admirers felt betrayed when the cast album, foolishly limited to one LP, contained very little of the character-conflict ensembles that made the show unique. This is not a score that reduces well to the titles listed in the program; the music runs through the story like a camera through a movie.

Thus, Act One ends not with Effie's being fired from the Dreams and her spectacular torch song in soul bel canto, "And I Am Telling You I'm Not Going," but with a mere snippet of something else that follows it. This last bit is almost the equivalent of the fade-out ending of a 45 side. That is, until one hears how it was staged: Effie and her personal tragedy were "wiped away," as the backstage dressing table she was sitting at moved off and the newly reconstituted act, with Deena as lead and a fourth Dream (Deborah Burrell) replacing Effie, came hurtling out for their Las Vegas debut. It's the Big Time, with all the vexing Effieness of their past put by. This striking visual observation was all that the story needed. The rest of this new song didn't matter. Effie didn't matter. The entrance onto the Vegas stage was all that mattered. And there, at that moment, the curtain fell on Act One.

Michael Bennett fashioned many such moments, now simply to excite the tale, now going into close-up or pulling back for Whole Idea. The man knew how closely allied American happiness and show-biz success are. There are other happinesses, true: Deena goes off to make her movie, not because it will be a hit but because it should be made. Whose vision wins out in the end? The authors can do no more than reunite the Dreams and C.C. with Effie: restoring, in short, the extended family that they represented in the first scene. A last song and goodnight.

But Bennett had the very last word. He didn't on *Follies*, whose book he thought a deglamorizing garage sale of show-biz lies. So for *Dreamgirls* he devised a curtain call to satisfy Curtis Taylor Jr.'s idea of show biz: the entire cast in evening clothes. That's glamour.

Glamorous to a fault was the 2001 Actors' Fund benefit *Dreamgirls* concert, a thrilling all-star reading. The *minor* roles went to such leading persons as Alice Ripley, Emily Skinner, Brian Stokes Mitchell, Malcolm Gets, John Bolton, Brad Oscar, Patrick Wilson, and Orfeh. The leads were almost completely miscast. Norm Lewis caught hold of the fascinating businessman-artist-dreamboy that is Curtis Taylor Jr. But Audra McDonald, Heather Headley, and Lillias White are too diva to *start* the narrative. Yes: to end it, when the Dreams have seen so much that they have to part. Show biz, just show biz. But Audra has Deena Jones' range with too much knowledge. Deena, in the 1960s, when *Dreamgirls* begins, could not possibly know what Audra knows today. And Lillias White is too secure for the agonized Effie, so absurdly eager to invent excuses for not having to risk failure. Audra, Heather, and Lillias walk out on stage and the audience erupts. There is no risk. The way *Dreamgirls* has to start is with three black girls who haven't the slightest idea that they are about to change the history of American music.

5

That's right. Tell me the musical is still vital when in fact it is overrun with old music, old movies, revivals, dance pieces, and nights of solo cabaret. *Lena Horne: The Lady and Her Music* (1981)! *Herman Van Veen: All Of Him* (1982)! *Peg[gy Lee]* (1983)! And Shirley MacLaine, Barbara Cook, Mandy Patinkin, Patti LuPone, Charles Aznavour. They're fine performers, but doesn't this sort of thing belong in the Persian Room?

And the films! *Seven Brides For Seven Brothers* (1982), *Singin' in the Rain* (1985), *Meet Me in St. Louis* (1989), *State Fair* (1996), *High Society* (1998), all already musicals when they were movies, and all flops on stage. New York porn-talk host Al Goldstein thought that *High Society* needed not a script doctor but Jack Kevorkian "to put this play out of its misery."

Is it even worth dissecting the respective tunestacks to learn how the Hollywood program was enlarged, and by whom? The problem with these cinema classics is that once they're filmed their cast becomes their character content, and thus eternally reproach any new thespian grouping. What's that suave David-James Carroll doing in the Howard Keel role in burly *Seven Brides*? And why is Melissa Errico singing Lilo's "I Love Paris" and Ethel Merman's "He's a Right Guy" in *High Society*? Melissa Errico is not the person Cole Porter had in mind when he wrote those songs. For that matter, why did they hire the dance-world genius Twyla Tharp to stage *Singin' in the Rain* on the condition that she counterfeit the film, right down to the walk over the couch in "Good Morning" and those idiot grins in "Fit as a Fiddle"?

The Disney people—amid terror cries of "The Mouse is encroaching!"—got huge hits out of *Beauty and the Beast* (1994) and *The Lion King* (1997), possibly doing more to help cultivate a future theatregoing generation than any native New Yorker has done. For further cultural fertilization, *The Lion King* opened the refurbished New Amsterdam Theatre, home of *The Ziegfeld Follies*, *Sally*, and *The Band Wagon*, but a Tenderloin nickelodeon after the Walter Huston–Brian Aherne *Othello* in 1937. And note that while *Beauty and the Beast* was essentially a flat staging of the cartoon, *The Lion King* was a cartoon by different means, reconceived by Julie Taymor to bring theatrical enterprise to familiar material.

Big (1996) made the mistake of literalizing the film, losing all its touching confusions for a "remember this scene?" replica. At least this one had to be turned into a musical, with its own new score, by David Shire and Richard Maltby Jr. They, too, replicated the film's content. With Mike Ockrent directing and Susan Stroman choreographing, one expected a more inventive piece. And why were the kids so unattractive? The lead character, little Patrick Levis, was fine; but his best friend was the singularly charmless Brett Tabisel. In the film, the best friend was an eager little guy with the wonderful ability to have no problem believing that his pal had magically become a grown-up with a job and a suit and a girl friend. Yet the point of view was clearly that of kids over *here* and grown-ups over *there;* that's the film's agon. The musical correctly observed this in the first number, "Can't Wait." But most of the rest of the show, especially in John Weidman's book, was dutiful and uninspired.

Maybe Maltby and Shire are better equipped to create revues, as in their popular *Starting Here, Starting Now* (1977) and *Closer Than Ever* (1989). The revue form allows them to write whole shows in a single song—*Closer*'s "You Want To Be My Friend?" (the angry retort of a steady girl who has just been dropped) or the raving "What Am I Doin'?" (the confessions of a stalker). Certainly, the three expectant couples of *Baby* (1983) gave Maltby and Shire nothing to work with but six dreary people. And in *Big*, even the weird story didn't call up a weird song. As the bewitched hero, Daniel Jenkins sang "This Isn't Me," "I Want To Go Home," "Fun" (the F.A.O. Schwarz number), and "Cross the Line" (for a dance sequence and his first kiss). All of this placed him as a character but told us nothing we didn't already know about the sort of people who show up in musicals.

"Stop, Time," a mother's lament about how fast they get away from you, is lovely, and was fervently sung by Barbara Walsh. "Coffee, Black" showed Jenkins taking command of his impossible reality as a toy-business genius. (Of course: he still plays with them.) It's a vital number, showing him finally enjoying the grown-up's power that till now has only puzzled him. But there was too little of this altogether.

And *The Red Shoes* (1993)? As with *Big*, the 1948 movie at least had to be turned into a musical, though it came with its Big Number built in, the eponymous ballet, from Hans Christian Andersen, about the girl whose dancing slippers kill her. One of the film's many brilliant strokes is that this is also the story of the film itself: ballerina Moira Shearer is caught between her composer boy friend (Marius Goring) and her over-bearing impresario (Anton Walbrook). Directed by Michael Powell and Emeric Pressburger, the movie is celebrated as the great ballet backstager, unmatched for its theatrical atmosphere, its sly continental flavor, its fantastical naturalism.

How, then, can it possibly work on stage? *Big* might have been some-how redefined. But *The Red Shoes*, a work of the most spirited content, cannot go anywhere: the film has conclusively defined it. True, there is all that dancing; and Broadway can sample happy bits of *Coppélia*, *The Sleeping Beauty*, *Les Sylphides*. In fact, the curtain will rise on the famous a minor theme from *Swan Lake*, so dramatic in itself that Universal used it under the credits of the Bela Lugosi *Dracula*. And we have Marsha Norman's book and lyrics (to Jule Styne's music) and Susan H. Schulman's direction, in a return after this pair's success with *The Secret Garden*; and *The Red Shoes* is another woman's story.

Still, the impresario is a problem. He is a man without a romance—or, let us say, with an abstract one. He calls ballet his "religion," but ballet is really his lover, and his love is control. Thwarted, he becomes intensely vindictive, even murderous: for it is he far more than the clueless com-poser who sends the distraught Shearer literally dancing out of the theatre to throw herself in front of a train.

The musical smoothed the impresario down with an establishing song, "Impresario"; a pitch-the-new-ballet-to-the-dancers number, "It's a Fairy Tale"; even a disgruntled-lover number, "Am I To Wish Her Love." It humanizes him; that's the problem. This simply isn't the greenroom Frankenstein that Walbrook played. In the show, when his current prima donna announces her engagement, the impresario blandly rises above this lack of professional dedication. In the movie, he vanishes without having made an exit, as if a sorcerer; and somehow the place where he had been standing looks very, very angry.

Roger Rees was cast as the impresario, and Hugh Panaro, deglamorized as an earnest weed, played the composer. Leslie Browne and Jon Marshall Sharp were the lead dancers and George de la Peña the ballet master so memorably played in the film by our *Colette* gay guy, Robert Helpmann. This was all fine; and so was Margaret Illmann's heroine, though she couldn't sing all that well. She had nice little tones for the notes but no legato, and her solos largely disappeared during previews. So did Roger Rees, whose courtly impresario lacked Walbrook's menace. It was the writing that was at fault, not Rees, but the production team brought in the saturnine Steve Barton and cut some of the character's numbers.

It still didn't work, though Jule Styne's music was his best for Broadway since *Sugar*, twenty-one years earlier. Styne struggled to give a story set in the European dance world of the early 1920s some scenic traction—in a dashing waltz, "Corps de Ballet"; in ballads with lilt rather than the typical Stynean flip, such as Panaro's "When It Happens To You" or even Barton's "Am I To Wish Her Love," lifted from "I! Yes, Me! That's Who!" in *Look To the Lilies* (1970).

Perhaps Styne saw *The Red Shoes* as another of those Last Operettas; it certainly had a dated feeling. The overture began with a *molto fortissimo* tympani blow—the first moment of countless fifties shows—then built through a few tunes while heading for the big ballad as trembling strings sounded the warning . . . wait for it . . . and . . . "When It Happens To You" broke out in the clarinet in a steady fox-trot to the snare brushes and the muted brass choirs. I love this kind of thing, but everyone else is tired of it.

Meanwhile, Bob Merrill, under the name Paul Stryker, was assisting on the lyrics, and Stanley Donen, not one of the newer names, had replaced director Schulman, working with the show's original choreographer, Lar Lubovitch; and the show still ran 5 performances. It was a sad end to Jule Styne's great career, a *Big Deal* end. Styne died nine months after the show closed, just short of ninety, having never tired of composing, having never met a promising talent he wouldn't help, and having left behind the unique style of the Jule Styne Swing Ballad. It's cruel to say that he lived too long, but he did last into an age that lacks curiosity, a real requiem for a theatre man as enthusiastic as Styne. You have to be curious. One of Marsha Norman's exchanges in *The Red Shoes*' script fixes it for us:

BARTON: Do you know why this new ballet of ours is going to be successful? . . . Because it is a *modern* ballet, so *completely* new.

DE LA PEÑA: Ballets are by definition old. How can the audience follow the story if they don't already know it?

If one can't find a movie to stage, one can always agglomerate old songs under some unifying theme. A partial list: *Blues in the Night* (1982), in which Leslie Uggams, Debbie Shapiro, and Jean Du Shon sang Bessie Smith, Harold Arlen, and the like, each unaware of the other two in their Chicago hotel in 1938, though at one point all three poured a drink at exactly the same time; *Rock 'N Roll!: The First 5,000 Years* (1982); *Jerry's Girls* (1985), featuring Herman with Dorothy Loudon, Chita Rivera, and Leslie Uggams, lost in the vast St. James Theatre; *Jerome Kern Goes To Hollywood* (1986); *Uptown . . . It's Hot!* (1986), a cheap Vegas-style tour through black show biz, with imitations of John W. Bubbles, the Nicholas Brothers, Cab Calloway, Ella Fitzgerald, Pigmeat Markham, and so on up to the present day; *Black and Blue* (1989), comparable but extremely lavish at a cost of five million dollars; *Smokey Joe's Cafe* (1995), a salute to historic rock and rollers Jerry Leiber and Mike Stoller whose five-year run ensured that this largely worthless format would go on for another generation; *Swinging on a Star* (1995), on the lyrics of Johnny Burke, broken into one-acters, each with its own setting, from a U.S.O. show to Paramount Studio; *Putting It Together* (1993, 1999), two different versions of a salute to Sondheim using the numbers narratively and featuring the musical returns of, respectively, Julie Andrews and Carol Burnett; *It Ain't Nothin' But the Blues* (1999), three of whose seven performers, with two others, were cited as the authors of a book that didn't exist save for the odd "Hit it, boys!" before the next song. So of course it got a Tony nod for Best Book of a Musical.

Most promising of all was *Jerome Robbins' Broadway* (1989), a compendium, this time, of not music but stagings: his *West Side Story*, his *Fiddler*, his *King and I* "Small House of Uncle Thomas." There were a few curiosities, such as the "Charleston" from *Billion Dollar Baby* (1945) and "Mr. Monotony," dropped from two shows. There was a huge cast reproducing the original choreography (where possible; sometimes Robbins couldn't recall the combinations), and even the original décor was reclaimed. But first one must legalize permission. So all Broadway buzzed when the famously difficult Robbins approached Peter Larkin, *Peter Pan*'s set designer in 1954. Said Larkin to Robbins, "I've been waiting thirty-five years to tell you to fuck yourself."

Then there's the old dodge of writing new shows using defenseless old music by dead writers who can't stop you. At least for the posthumous *pasticcii* made of Johann Strauss' less well known tunes, someone had to write a set of lyrics. *Crazy For You* (1992) simply used Gershwin songs arranged as character and action numbers in a story borrowed from *Girl Crazy* (1930). With much smarter material to work with than they would have in *Big*, director Mike Ockrent and choreographer Susan Stroman came up with something Broadway had been missing without knowing it, the good old-fashioned musical-comedy hit. With the silly old jokes that have lasted this long because they're *funny*. With the stereotypes whose irritations come off as endearments when they're well played, as for instance by Jane Connell's Rich Old Scold. With the first-act curtain falling as punctuation to a giant plot twist. With the chorus people we've met as the rustics of Deadrock, Nevada blithely reappearing in society finery when the action moves to Manhattan.

In a time when, to many ears, all the new story shows seemed to be gloomy tales set to the "Theme from *Jaws*," *Crazy For You* was what the musical was supposed to be back when the nation fell in love with the form: entertainment. No, something more than that. Something infectious, seductive. It makes you wish you could be in a musical comedy, too. Not performing in one: living there.

Ken Ludwig's *Crazy For You* book, mapped out by Ockrent, retained only the outline of *Girl Crazy*: eastern bon vivant getting acclimated in the Wild West while enlivening the place with show biz. Ludwig's main additions counted an opening New York sequence to firm up the protagonist's backstory; a New York producer, Bela Zangler (Bruce Adler), whom the hero impersonates but who turns up out west himself for that twist at the first curtain; and a subplot for the hero's eastern fiancée (Michele Pawk) and the hero-hating saloonkeeper (John Hillner). Ludwig's main deletions from *Girl Crazy* included a host of dated conventions, including the unassimilated Jewish comic and the reality-defying second-act plotting that makes so many twenties and thirties musicals hard to revive.

So the book was fresh, not a warmed-up hash. But the music, mixed of chestnuts and rarities, was not fresh. "Someone To Watch Over Me," for heroine Jodi Benson, simply did not work; it forced Benson to borrow information we've already had from Gertrude Lawrence and countless other singers. And that typical second-act moment, The Lovers' Sad Parting, was vitiated by giving hero Harry Groener "They Can't Take That Away From Me" and Benson "But Not For Me." True, the latter is from the original *Girl Crazy* and has no particular associations. But it's too familiar a piece to move us in *Crazy For You*—and shouldn't we leave "They Can't Take That Away From Me" to Fred Astaire to sing to Ginger Rogers, as he is still doing today, in the movie *Shall We Dance?*

The more unusual numbers worked better, for the obvious reason: we didn't already know what they were going to say. And isn't that partly how the score to a book musical is supposed to work, by informing rather than reminding us? Or is George de la Peña right, in *The Red Shoes*, when he says the public cannot absorb new material?

Certainly, the rare numbers were the best part of *Crazy For You*'s score. "I Can't Be Bothered Now" revived the guy-and-his-girls number, as Groener soared up out of a taxicab crowded with Fiancée and Mother to dream up a show-biz specialty, with twelve girls then climbing out of the taxi in pink fluff and carrying telephones to notify callers that Groener's too busy enjoying himself to do anything important.

This reinstitution of old music needs expertise especially in the dance arrangements and orchestrations, and Peter Howard and William D. Brohn, respectively, proved indispensable in bringing back the very sound of having fun, as when Groener and Benson's first love duet turned out to be a pas de deux to "Shall We Dance" while the Deadrock set slid out of sight and the music jumped out of $\frac{4}{4}$ to a pounding waltz. Clever indeed was the use of "I'll Build a Stairway To Paradise" for the arrival of showgirls in Deadrock, styled as a dangerous invasion of burlesque tootsies and taking in not only *Crazy For You*'s title song but the verse of a forgotten *Girl Crazy* number, "Bronco Busters."

Another bygone title, "What Causes That?," sent aficionados scurrying to their reference books. Written for but dropped from *Treasure Girl* (1928), it was given to Groener (in his Zangler getup and accent) and the real Zangler, and was not only the best integrated number in the score but the best integrated number in the whole season. This is what once gave the musical its pacing: a situation developed in a book scene till nothing less than the heightening of music can define it. With the modern musical so often flooded with music, that sense of sublimation was being lost.

This explains why so many of the biggest hits today are old-fashioned musical comedies. However, unlike *Crazy For You* (and Mike Ockrent's English new-old show, *Me and My Girl*), these works lack Ockrent's stylistic acumen. They can be clever; but he had wit. His untimely death has been a tragic loss to the musical-comedy revival.

Not all these new shows with old scores enjoy the Big Run and international impact of *Crazy For You*. An adaptation of Shakespeare's *Twelfth Night* updated to Golden Age Harlem, *Play On!* (1997), used the songs of Duke Ellington—an arresting idea, if old songs are to be recycled. Ellington's book shows never succeeded, and they contained precious few of the melodies he is best known for. *Play On!* featured them—"Take the 'A' Train," "I Let a Song Go Out Of My Heart," "Mood Indigo," "Love You Madly," "It Don't Mean a Thing (if it ain't got that swing)."

Cheryl L. West's book relied too much on the old stereotypical jokes. But her use of Shakespeare, under Sheldon Epps' direction, was clever. Music—an important subject in Ellington's songs, as in "Hit Me With a Hot Note and Watch Me Bounce"—was the key. Viola is now a composer, Vy (Cheryl Freeman), forced into masculine attire because women musicians aren't taken seriously. Duke Orsino becomes the Duke (Carl Anderson), a band leader. Olivia is a blues singer called Lady Liv (Tonya Pinkins), and as Viola has no brother in this retelling, her opposite is Malvolio, a club manager, Rev (Lawrence Hamilton). Set on a revolve for lots of mobility and enlivened by matching chorus costumes for each number, as in a twenties, thirties, or forties show, *Play On!* really got the most out of Ellington. Luther Henderson's arrangements found the makings of a quartet in "Solitude," and "I'm Beginning To See the Light" turned into a plot number as the pompous Rev was redeemed by music. To woo appropriately, one must first learn jive.

But the show failed, perhaps because twenty-two months of audiences had heard virtually the same score in *Sophisticated Ladies* (1981), an eye-filling revue that starred Gregory Hines just as he was breaking through to stardom. Elaborate where *Play On!* was unobtrusive, *Sophisticated Ladies* had terrific tryout pains, much firing and screaming. Yet it got to the Ellington songbook first in fine Ellington style, with the composer's son Mercer leading the twenty-one-man onstage band.

Another way to offer a new show without having to hunt down a new score was the show-biz bio using the subject's signature tunes, or some of those along with new ones—or even with a *completely* new score that could at least derive its inspiration from old styles. Although both his fans begged him not to, Larry Kert proposed to make his Broadway return in *Jolson, Tonight*, which began in a dinner theatre in Glen Cove, Long Island in 1979. A 1980 summer-stock tour followed, though money problems dogged the production. Suddenly, the show's producer decided to put on a different Jolson piece, with Bert Convy making *his* return. At one point, Nicholas Dante was the book writer, and at another point, couturier Pierre Cardin was the producer. *Jolson, Tonight* never made it to Broadway, and neither did *Chaplin* (1983), with Anthony Newley and an entirely new score; or *Satchmo: America's Musical Legend* (1987), with a new and old score; and *Durante* (1989), with Lonny Price in the title role and Joel Blum and Evan Pappas as Durante's partners, Clayton and Jackson, with an old score and one new number.

There will be other Jolson shows—Stephen Mo Hanan played a *Jolson & Company* for the York Theatre in 1999—and they won't stop coming till some idiot takes the concept to Broadway and bombs at a loss of ten million dollars. The Jolson Thing is an aberrant and unexplainable piece of show-biz history that refuses to go away long after the retirement of its performing style and repertory. No one can tell us why a pesky egomaniac won cultural prominence by hamming his way through songs like "Mammy" and "Sonny Boy." So why should anyone want to bring that Monstro back from the deep?

This is desperation show biz. So is *Harrigan 'n Hart* (1985), a look at two famous gents of late-nineteenth-century musical-comedy history, unfortunately with no sense of period or place and with extremely incorrect historical details. Michael Stewart's book and Max Showalter and Peter Walker's score enjoyed some interpolations from the Harrigan-Hart shows. Both "musics" were tuneful and engaging. And Joe Layton's direction kept the evening spry and colorful. But where Layton's Cohan musical, *George M!* (1968), generally respected the styles of its time (except for Joel Grey's overexcited Cohan), *Harrigan 'n Hart*, confounded history.

The outline of the chronicle is the teaming of Edward Harrigan (busy Harry Groener) and Tony Hart (Mark Hamill) to mount shows treating Irish immigrant life with a groundbreaking honesty. Sensitive about whispers that he is queer, Hart is bullied into marrying an Englishwoman (Christine Ebersole, as usual the most interesting player in the piece), who then turns into the Yoko Ono of the 1880s and breaks up the act. Tragically, Hart dies not only young but insane, though the musical jumps over this to close in a Hollywoodish apotheosis of Harrigan and Hart in their prime.

It's a valid story, but Stewart did not do his homework. He misspelled Harrigan and Hart perennial Annie Yeamans' name and apparently thought she was black. Perhaps Stewart was misled by historians' notations that Harrigan and Hart, most unusually for the day, used racially integrated casts. In fact, Annie Yeamans was not black; the lead black Harrigan and Hart character Rebecca Allup was played by Hart in blackface; and blacks were used only as a separate ensemble in Harrigan and Hart shows. Color-blind casting is sound democratic policy, but assigning white Annie Yeamans to black Armelia McQueen promotes the notion that racial integration pervaded nineteenth-century American theatre, or even that it inhabited a small corner of it. This simply is not true.

Then, too, Stewart's version of old comic shtick seems to stem from thirties burlesque, not from Harrigan and Hart's Theatre Comique. So unprepared was Stewart for the idiom of Old Broadway that he mistakes "Dutch" comedy for scenes involving characters from the Netherlands. No. "Dutch," a corruption of the German *deutsch,* means "German," and it pertained indiscriminately to comics using fake German or Yiddish accents.

Worst of all, Stewart characterizes Harrigan and Hart as the inventors of musical comedy. In a Showalter-Walker number, "Something New, Something Different," Harrigan and then Hart, while rehearsing, are seized with the realization that by adding songs and dances to a play, they can . . . no! *yes!*: Create Musical Comedy!

Where's my revolver? This scene takes place sometime in the late 1870s, decades after operas, ballad operas, minstrel shows, and things very like what we today call "musicals" had not only appeared but become acculturated. The official "first" American musical, *The Black Crook,* appeared in 1866 and was seen everywhere there was a good-size theatre.

Such other founding entries as *Humpty Dumpty* (1868) and *Evangeline* (1874) had already been produced, with resounding impact. Furthermore, these Harrigan and Hart shows were not musicals, but rather plays with a few songs and a dance or two. *Harrigan 'n Hart* presents "Something New, Something Different" as if the Gershwins had just been inspired to write *Lady, Be Good!*.

Harrigan 'n Hart was a fast failure, and *The Will Rogers Follies* (1991) was a hit, even a smash, at 963 performances. This was not because it was more faithful to the show biz of *its* day (roughly, the Ziegfeld era), but because *Harrigan 'n Hart* was a silly little valentine and *Will Rogers* was a spectacle put together by confident pros—Cy Coleman and Betty Comden and Adolph Green supplying the wholly new score, Peter Stone writing the book, and Tommy Tune staging it. No replica of old fashions, *Will Rogers* at least did not misguise its subject. The idea was to present the Will Rogers story as a *modern-day* Ziegfeldian revue, complete with directions from Flo himself, in voice-overs taped by Gregory Peck.

Tune wisely made no homage to the Ziegfeld touch per se, with the undulating showgirl parades, the fastidiously painted Joseph Urban backdrops, the comic sketches, the many major and minor headliners. Novelty Star Keith Carradine played a Rogers of great charm with an agreeable singing voice; Dee Hoty was his wife and Cady Huffman a showgirl billed as "Ziegfeld's Favorite." Dick Latessa as Rogers' father completed the circle of principals; Ziegfeld couldn't have got through an opening chorus with so few leads. But, again, this really was a show in present-day showspeak.

It did lack narrative content, even if aviator Wiley Post (Paul Ukena Jr.) kept jumping up from the stage-left box to shout, "Let's go flying, Will!"—a reminder that Rogers' life will end in the crash of Post's aircraft. What kept the show entertaining was the one thing that Tune has in common with Florenz Ziegfeld: style. It was Tune's guidance of the look and motion of the revue that held it together, even in the particular choice of dog act (The Mad Cap Mutts) or the way in which the Rogerses introduced their four boys in "Big Time." A catchy tune detailing the pecking order of the vaudeville community (the lowest rank is held by accordion players, a quintessential Comden-Green joke), it peaked when the entire family, in identical cowboy getups, waved while the five males spun lariats.

If *Harrigan 'n Hart* had old songs to preserve and *Will Rogers* an old tradition to uphold in counterpart rather than replica, *Ain't Broadway Grand* (1993) had nothing but an unimportant saga to recount, at that in a risibly fraudulent version. The musical's long-term history claims a number of adaptable legends. Some of my readers may know of the film *Cradle Will Rock*, though it treats far more than the fabled premiere of Marc Blitzstein's first show. But who would have thought that composer Mitch Leigh (with lyricist Lee Adams) would base his return on a show recalling how showman Mike Todd turned *As the Girls Go* from a flop to a hit?

Hands up: who never heard of *As the Girls Go*? One of the last of the big-scale star-comic shambles musicals made of burlesque and, for respectability, a clean-cut juvenile and ingenue, *As the Girls Go* was the fourth-longest-running book musical of the extremely prosperous 1948–49 season. Ironically, producer Todd spent so much money on it that it finally banked red. This is the only thing worth knowing about it, so *Ain't Broadway Grand* had to invent a story where none existed. In this version, *As the Girls Go* starts out as *Of the People*, a socially aware show. This is nonsense, as was Thomas Meehan and Lee Adams' book in general; and their Mike Todd, Mike Burstyn, made a charmless hero. Aren't these con-men producers supposed to be played by guys one can't help liking, as when James Caan impersonates Billy Rose in the movie *Funny Lady*? At least we got Debbie Shapiro Gravitte as Gypsy Rose Lee.

That's an advantage of the flops in this era—if Christine Ebersole isn't in them, Debbie will be, not to mention Alix Korey, who played Todd's secretary in *Ain't Broadway Grand*. But this flop was so terrible that even Debbie and Alix could not mollify the house. Nor could composer Leigh, who had gone out of his way to give delight, throwing off his customary screwy ostinatos for straightforward fox-trots, waltzes, and Latin rhythm. There's even a ragtime number, as comic Bobby Clark (Gerry Vichi) explains his art in "Tall Dames and Low Comedy."

Clark was *As the Girls Go*'s star, eager for burlesque fun while *Ain't Broadway Grand*'s Mike Todd schemes to win admiration from "that Theatre Guild crowd." *What?* This is akin to Sylvester Stallone's scheming to win admiration from Tom Stoppard. *It never happened. Ain't Broadway Grand* was so unknowing that its every attempt to make remark came off as implausible, false, or irrelevant, as when Todd is pitching

Of the People to a prospective backer:

TODD: You heard of Rodgers and Hammerstein?
BACKER: They wrote it?
TODD: No, better—Fischbein and Klein.

The script so deadened the house during the 25-performance run that presumptive laugh lines reached people planning next season's wardrobe, rehearsing a confrontation with their boss, or dozing:

BOBBY CLARK: I read *Of the People*. Where are the laughs?
TODD: There are no laughs. It's a satire.
AUDIENCE IN LUNT-FONTANNE THEATRE: (vast silence)

Easiest of all in this remaindered show biz is the revival, whether from a tour or a museum house like Goodspeed, or special for Broadway: *The King and I* (in 1985), *Take Me Along* (1985), *Cabaret* (1987), *Shenandoah* (1989), *Ain't Misbehavin'* (1988), *Gypsy* (1989), *Fiddler on the Roof* (1990), *Guys and Dolls* (1992), *Camelot* (1993), *Grease* (1994), *Company* (1995), another *King and I* (1996), *Once Upon a Mattress* (1996), *Annie* (1997), another *Cabaret* (1998), *On the Town* (1997).

Some were faithful, such as the first *Cabaret*. Some were fiddled, such as the second, Sam Mendes' scorching production. Some featured an original lead—Yul Brynner's King, John Cullum's *Shenandoah* patriarch, or even Robert Goulet, graduated in a kind of theatre-world "social promotion" from Lancelot to King Arthur. Some were very successful, such as the cartooned *Guys and Dolls*. Some were built around stars so beautifully suited to their role that their revival had the authenticity of new work, as with Tyne Daly's *Gypsy*. And one was so cleverly staged that a piece that was cheesily retro even before the notion of retro existed now came off as sharply observed satire.

Richard O'Brien's *The Rocky Horror Show* had first visited Broadway in 1975 in its original London staging, by Jim Sharman and with lighting by the suitably macabre Chipmonck. But its faux-tawdry inversions of sane playmaking seemed merely tawdry, at least to Broadway theatregoers. Now that everyone has got O'Brien's joke, the piece can play Broadway, and in 2000 director Christopher Ashley gave it a starry cast, with Dick

Cavett as the Narrator, Lea DeLaria in Meat Loaf's old double role, Jarrod Emick and Alice Ripley as the squares, ageless Joan Jett and *Rent's* Daphne Rubin-Vega assisting Tom Hewitt's mad doctor, Raúl Esparza in O'Brien's old role, and Sebastian LaCause as the fabricated dreamboy. The show is no longer dangerous; but this artfully playful revival argued strongly in favor of thinking these old shows through instead of automatically rewriting them.

The Most Happy Fella (1992) was not rewritten, but it was done to the accompaniment of two pianos—at that, only five months after the New York City Opera had given it with a full-size orchestra. The cover story for this travesty held that the composer himself had commissioned the two-piano version, thus giving it imprimatur.

No. When *The Most Happy Fella* was released for stock and amateur production in the late 1950s, Frank Loesser—whose business firm not only published his work but licensed the stagings—foresaw Don Walker's scoring of his opera-sized music reduced to keyboard tiddley-pom in high schools, summer theatres, and the like. Hoping to mitigate such disaster, he made the duo-piano edition available so that piano-only performances might be musically strengthened, that more of his polyphony be heard. Loesser never had it in mind that this most musical of musicals be presented on Broadway with nothing but two pianos in the pit, as if it were *Salad Days*. The City Opera's Tony, Louis Quilico, was much more persuasive than the two-piano team's Spiro Malas; but that's beside the point. Only in a doomed theatre culture trying to survive on the makeweights of the Sheridan Square Playhouse would this *Most Happy Fella* be accepted, much less praised.

The Gershwins' *Oh, Kay!* turned up in 1990 in an all-black version, still set in the original's 1926 but moved to Harlem. A revisal with a dull new book, it did program eight of the eleven 1926 songs, two of the numbers dropped during the 1926 tryout ("When Our Ship Comes Sailing In" and "Show Me the Town," the latter reused in 1928 in *Rosalie*), and two rediscoveries, the very seldom heard concert piece "Sleepless Nights" and a new ballad, "Ask Me Again," which Ira had lyricked as recently as 1981.

In fact, with only two interpolations from other Gershwin shows, there was some admirable fidelity at work here. *Sincerity*, I call it. The "concept" was credited to director-choreographer Dan Siretta, a Goodspeed stalwart—and the production had been seen there (and in Michigan) first. However, few Goodspeed revivals have the locomotive dash of this *Oh, Kay!*. Brian (later Stokes) Mitchell played the romantic lead opposite Angela Teek, but the real stars were Stanley Wayne Mathis, Gregg Burge, the enchanting Kyme (pronounced "Ky-mee"), and the brilliant dancing corps, who tore up the stage in one big number after another.

Unappreciative reviews closed it after two months, thoroughly dismaying Kyme, who had prepared for the occasion in vocal coaching with Ramona and Orfeh; in ethnic dance with Bhaskar, Morocco, Asia, Trini, and Ahi; in *je ne sais quoi* with Sylvie, Lilo, Patachou, and Geneviève; in existential critical detachment with *Variety*'s Hobe; in lighting-gel strategy with Chipmonck; in comic *brío* with Cantinflas; and in millennium coiffure philosophy with Pinky Babajian. Lo, Kyme's spirits lifted when David Merrick reopened the production three months later, with Ron Richardson and Rae Dawn Chong in the leads. It collapsed during previews.

Two Roundabout revivals of the 1990s explain why revivals aren't very good for the musical despite its obsession with them: today's directors don't understand how old "business" (as they used to call "shtick") works, they mistake decorations for throughlines, and they don't understand that a song they don't happen to like is necessary to narrative flow. Director Scott Ellis completely mistook the purpose of "Twelve Days To Christmas," the last number in *She Loves Me*, which Ellis staged in 1993. The number actually isn't "Twelve Days To Christmas." The number is a series of short book scenes developing the growing intimacy between the show's leads, formerly feuding mailbox romantics. Book writer Joe Masteroff wants to establish their delicate bonding over the passage of time leading up to Christmas, and Jerry Bock and Sheldon Harnick oblige with throwaway musical bits in which the chorus rampages through the *She Loves Me* boutique counting off the days till boy reveals secret plot twist to girl, followed by kiss panel and final curtain. The music is merely punctuation; it's the *dialogue* that matters. But Ellis put all the emphasis on Rob Marshall's athletic staging of the choral interjections, leaving boy Boyd Gaines and girl Judy Kuhn as excrescent interruptions of an ensemble number.

Rob Marshall's *Little Me* in 1998 didn't get it, either. The comic who is playing all those roles isn't supposed to *play* those roles. The joke, as introduced by Sid Caesar in the 1962 original, is that the clown makes no attempt to portray the Ivy League hunk, miserly grouch, movie director, and so on. He changes costume and puts on crazy accents, but he is always The Same Funny Man Being Very Silly. He doesn't act; he times. And the heroine is not a comic. She's a broad, because *Little Me* is a musical comedy based on a central trope of thirties–forties burlesque: a hot trick playing straight to the quips of a jester. Tall dames and low comedy.

My readers may recall that moment in *Gypsy* when Tessie Tura refuses to go on as the broad: "You ever hear of a strip woman playing scenes?" Tessie observes the conventions. But Marshall had Faith Prince japing and Martin Short acting. It took *Little Me* far from its inspiration in the world of fifties television gag writers, where Neil Simon dreamed up this raggy spoof. Out of context, the show doesn't play well. Marshall didn't make the mistake of breaking the comic's tour de force into a team act, the enfeebling novelty of the 1982 *Little Me* revival (with James Coco and Victor Garber). Still, Marshall kept trying to get more out of two leads that are meant to be nothing more than stereotypes. "Poor Little Hollywood Star," in the original, found Belle singing a lament in front of neon titles of her idiotic semi-porn films, such as *Moses Goes To Town*. Marshall spent money to create pictorial window cards for her movie career, such as *The Lizard of Oz*, replicating the famous shot of a thrilled little Judy. What does this have to do with a heroine whose name virtually means "Big Tits" and whose endowment defines her life?

Not the best of the 1990s revivals—nor, at 536 performances, the most successful—but possibly the most representative is the 1994 *Damn Yankees*, directed and revised by Jack O'Brien with choreography by Rob Marshall. Imported from the Old Globe Theatre in San Diego, this *Damn Yankees* starred Victor Garber and Bebe Neuwirth as the infernal pair, with Jarrod Emick as the younger Joe and Vicki Lewis as the nosy sportswriter, Gloria Thorpe. Counting Dick Latessa as the manager of the Washington Senators and a players lineup including Gregory Jbara, Scott Wise, and Michael Berresse, the production was already spending lavishly in the talent shop; and there was a spare-no-expense feeling about Douglas W. Schmidt's scenery. True, the revival's stadium was a miniature compared with the 1955 original, and the somewhat lingering blackouts for a few of the set changes had been outdated for a decade.

Still, there was a feeling that O'Brien wanted to stage *Damn Yankees* as if it had just been written and deserved a genuine premiere. Most revivals economize. One thinks of those two pianos chirping away for *The Most Happy Fella*, or the cheap wigs in the Roundabout's *1776* in 1997. Or the perfunctory spectacle of the onstage scenes in the 1999 *Kiss Me, Kate* revival; the original blinded the eye with an explosion of Renaissance patterns. Or the tidy little *Bells Are Ringing* in 2001.

Some things in this *Damn Yankees* were akin to 1955 but developed in high-tech, so the locker room had running-water showers and a nude shot from Jbara (backal only). "Shoeless Joe From Hannibal, Mo." used much of Roger Adams' 1955 dance arrangements yet with extremely new-style choreography topped by Scott Wise's series of cartwheels, two quick ones followed by a third in slow motion, a real tour de force. And "Who's Got the Pain?," originally for Gwen Verdon and chorus boy Eddie Phillips, was now a bigger number for Neuwirth and the Senators in toto. And "Near To You," in 1955 a duet, was here expanded into a trio as both older and younger Joes sang to their wife while she tossed restlessly in bed.

Other things were completely new, such as a number following "Shoeless Joe" as the new hero is seen making headlines and delivering celebrity endorsements, to a fifties vocal backup sound and some spoken continuity from Gloria. There were some anchoring fifties allusions that the original obviously hadn't needed, to J. Edgar Hoover and Clyde Tolson and to "Milton" (Berle). Most important, there was a great deal more in the book scenes setting up and developing the Shifty McCoy subplot that in the original George Abbott–Douglass Wallop book seemed to fall into Act Two out of nowhere.

O'Brien's restructuring of the script improved on the narrative used in 1955, even clarifying the collapse of the Devil's pact with Joe. O'Brien showed us (as the original did not) young Joe shouting, "Let me go!" to exercise his escape clause. He then vanished through a trapdoor as old Joe suddenly appeared in his place to sock out a homer and win the Senators their pennant after all.

Of course, it's not difficult to improve on a George Abbott book, because Abbott was a sloppy storyteller; audiences were more indulgent of musical comedy's inconsistencies in the 1950s.

However, it is very difficult to improve on a George Abbott musical as a whole, because he was superb at casting and directing his casts. Consider Lola and the devil in 1955: Gwen Verdon's sunburst of wanton talent playing against Ray Walston's high-speed deadpan. Any production without Gwen Verdon is going to be less wonderful than a production *with* Gwen Verdon, so Bebe Neuwirth was at a disadvantage from the start; and Victor Garber's doofus Satan lacked both menace and comic grasp. Nor did the situation get better when, a year into the run, Jerry Lewis and Charlotte d'Amboise took over.

In all, this *Damn Yankees* was an attempt to make a new show out of an old one while respecting the old one's strengths—such as keeping the original tunestack intact, without a single interpolation. The seventies and eighties revival tended to mash old shows up as if bingeing on infidelity; the nineties revival is less reckless. But it does lack some of the old frivolous brilliance of style that tells us why it didn't matter that George Abbott's story lines got messy in Act Two: his shows played *really* well. This *Damn Yankees* played acceptably, peaking in the numbers with the ballplayers. It did a solid job in bringing back a piece worth a second look, but it lacked the delight produced in 1955.

Possibly the best revival of the 1990s has turned out to be the most successful of all revivals, still running (in its eighth year) as I write. This is *Chicago*, directed by Walter Bobbie and choreographed by Ann Reinking "in the style of Bob Fosse."

Originally given by Encores!, the Bobbie-Reinking rendition naturally takes the original's physical presence down to the minimum. However, Fosse's *Chicago* was itself a kind of spectacle gone minimalist, grand and gaudy but with little visual distraction. A circus with actors instead of animals. Nothing but performances. Or even: *Allegro* perfected, Fosse bringing forth the art that Rodgers and Hammerstein invented in 1947, in which the musical would be freed of all impediments to the flow of dialogue, song, and dance as one energy.

So the Encores! *Chicago* was virtually a purification of a clarity. This, ironically, only emphasized what Fosse had done in the first place. Reinking, the last of the original 1975 production's Roxies, reclaimed her role to Bebe Neuwirth's Velma, with James Naughton as the lawyer, Joel Grey as Roxie's husband, and Marcia Lewis as the prison matron, all fine. But it's notable that almost anyone seems able to step into these roles with success. The leads from London's version of the production, Ruthie Henshall and Ute Lemper, changed the tenor of the roles without damaging the evening. For while Henshall brings a maidenly flavor to even her most scandalous moments, thereby underlining Roxie's sociopathy, the highly inflected Lemper style idealizes the Epic Theatre nature of the show—that air of intellectual presentation disguised as fun. Lemper played with such knowing bravado that one half expected Bertolt Brecht and Erwin Piscator to take a bow after her numbers.

The lead roles vary so easily that Naughton's lawyer could unfurl his material from entirely within the tuxedo he wore, so that a touch of dance in "We Both Reached for the Gun"—a shimmy, actually—seemed to embarrass the actor rather than the character. Whereas Michael Berresse, promoted from Roxie's murder victim to the lawyer later in the run, salted *his* formality with a rakish savor, and was happy to expand his dancing quotient; and Brent Barrett played the lawyer as if in a sardonic version of *The Desert Song*, big and gala and happy with the hoax. It may be that the "concert" presentation, preserved when *Chicago* moved to Broadway, re-creates Fosse's characters as archetypes. Thus, they are open to any actor's specific personal revision while retaining a permanent symbolic identity.

Is this *Chicago* the most faithful of the nineties revivals? The book is lightly cut, and the cast in erotic uniform rather than realistic costumes, as they had been in 1975. Still: the orchestrations have not been remastered, so to say, by some new man, much less newly written from scratch. The choreography tries to recall the original dancing as loyally as possible. And the spirit, above all, is Fosse. The *Damn Yankees* revival retired the original's spirit for something less idiosyncratic, less jumpily propulsive. It naturalized fantasy. *Chicago*—another Verdon show performed without Verdon, not to mention a Chita show without Chita—could almost be a touring version of the original paying a call on Broadway at the end of its line but with a brand-new set of leads for extra pep. It fully deserves its great success.

Chicago's origin at Encores! brings us to another reason why people think the musical is in great health when it is breaking apart. The revival has become institutionalized as a Great New York Thing at City Center's annual three Encores! concerts of old shows. But this is only because new shows aren't filling the ear with the melody that aficionados dote on and Encores! is. Its own reason for being is not to bring back forgotten works, as some think, but to give another airing to the listenable score, forgotten or not. This explains the choice of such classic titles as *Pal Joey* and *Wonderful Town* along with oddities like *Sweet Adeline* and *Bloomer Girl*.

Actually, Encores! is by now a Great *American* Thing, having inspired copies such as Los Angeles' Reprises!. So it may be worth looking back on the struggle to create in New York this kind of alternative "listening room" for old works, with little or no décor. The first such attempt was made by John Bowab, who programmed *She Loves Me*, *Knickerbocker Holiday*, and that paragon of the unknown classic *The Golden Apple* in Town Hall. Bowab cast nobly, with Madeline Kahn and Rita Moreno heading *She Loves Me* and Richard Kiley as Pieter Stuyvesant in the Weill. But this was the early 1970s, the musical was still in its Golden Age, and the public had no need for supplementary diversion. Bowab had to cancel in midseason without having attempted *The Golden Apple*.

Next came Bill Tynes' New Amsterdam Theatre Company, also head-quartered in Town Hall, and devoted more to operetta and old musical comedy than Encores! would be. Indeed, Bill put on four titles from the Second Age (*The Firefly*, *Sweethearts*, *Eileen*, *Leave It To Jane*), and concentrated on the 1920s and 1930s. He did big shows, too. So where John Bowab's more intimate fare could thrive in staged readings, Bill had to strategize. Works such as *The New Moon*—his first offering, in 1981—or *Rosalie* or *Music in the Air* or *Jubilee* called for big choruses and a lot of dance. How much of these originally elaborate productions could be left out or "suggested"? And should modern audiences sit through the verbose librettos favored in once upon a time?

At first, Bill used narrators to set scenes and condense some dialogue to synopses. For *Eileen*, Victor Herbert's saga of Irish freedom fighters against the English, Maureen O'Sullivan and E. G. Marshall read out the continuity in opposing "characters," Marshall as belligerent and O'Sullivan as peacemaker. Soon enough, Bill dispensed with the narrators and tried to avoid shows with overlong books so he could perform them complete. His casting was excellent, featuring singers like Judy Kaye and John Reardon, letting Paula Laurence retrieve her original role in *One Touch of Venus*, discovering talents such as Davis Gaines and Rebecca Luker, and assigning comic roles to people like Christopher Hewett and Alix Korey, who know how to play corn.

Bill started hiring choreographers, too. He was to find himself giving full-out stagings, just managing at the last to get up a modest *Sally* at the Academy Theatre in 1988 before his death at the age of thirty.

Bill was purist to a fault: a wonderful one, because it guided him toward an enlightening archeology rather than the misleading reinventions we get in revisals. Bill really loved The Old Ways, too. At his *Sweet Adeline*, making the customary intermission pitch, he informed his public that while all New Amsterdam shows were performed with the original orchestrations, the pit on that night was not only playing the original Robert Russell Bennett scoring but had on their music stands the copyist's parts used in 1929 during the show's original run.*

One can hear the thrill in Bill's voice as he says this. Had he lived, I believe he would have taken over the old Hammerstein's Theatre (today the Ed Sullivan) in lieu of the demolished Ziegfeld, and produced a reconstruction of the complete 1927 *Show Boat* with the *entire original cast*.

No less purist than Bill, musician John McGlinn took over much of Bill's stock company, moving the concerts to Weill Recital Hall, and emphasizing Kern. McGlinn even programmed a show that had closed out of town (Kern's *Zip! Goes a Million*), a feat of disinterment never equaled elsewhere in the major venues of the concert revival movement. Because Weill Hall's tiny stage can just accommodate the cast and orchestra players, there was no staging. For dance sections, the performers turned to McGlinn to beam as unidiotically as possible while he conducted the rest of the music.

I would guess that without all this preparation, particularly from Bill Tynes, the Encores! series would not have existed. Encores! is faithful to the scores but cuts and even shreds the librettos and prefers relatively recent work. It has never offered anything from earlier than the Third Age. It scants the 1920s, prefers to it the 1930s and 1940s, is more comfortable in the 1950s, and most likes the 1960s. No wonder: its public is

---

* This use of archival material was made possible by the discovery of old T. B. Harms-Chappell material in the Warner Bros. warehouse in Secaucus, New Jersey, in 1982. While some shows were vaulted with complete orchestra and vocal parts, cut numbers, script revisions, and the like, others are missing odd pieces here and there, and *Jubilee*'s orchestration, also by Bennett, had vanished. Bill thought this title too significant to neglect, so he commissioned a new scoring from Larry Moore. All was well till someone claimed to have found the Bennett parts at the St. Louis Muni, which mounted revivals of virtually every famous musical and kept *Jubilee* in rotation into the 1950s. In the event, the Bennett charts had been ravished, with little left but the odd woodwind line, and Moore's *Jubilee* is the one in current use. We heard it at Carnegie Hall in 1998 with the all-star lineup of Beatrice Arthur, Tyne Daly, Sandy Duncan, Alice Ripley, Michael Jeter, Stephen Spinella, and Bob Paris.

leery of unfamiliar titles. One senses a chill as the lights dim for a *Strike Up the Band* or *Tenderloin*.

Encores! also takes the risk of programming a work requiring a star turn—even a work written for a specific kind of star—then trolling around to see who's game. This is not the way a *DuBarry Was a Lady* or *On a Clear Day You Can See Forever* was put together when new, and it has led to trouble, including in those two works. Sometimes a merely valid cast mixes surprisingly fine chemistry, as in *Out Of This World*, which was entirely delightful. Sometimes a good cast goes dud, as in *Li'l Abner*. Sometimes a long-lost score of immense appeal is given to us as a present—in the *Ziegfeld Follies of 1936*, with some of the best performers around. Sometimes James Naughton seems so unprepared in *No Strings* that one wonders what they are carrying around in those black looseleaf notebooks.*

We're all glad that Encores! is there, but it must be said that if the musical were still in its Golden Age we wouldn't need encores: we'd have new shows. I mean, good ones. The reason that Encores! had to be invented to bring good old ones back is that many of the new ones blow dead rats in hell. Would Broadway host cabaret, stagings of movies, and revues of old music if something worthy—such as a book show with a new score—could take stage instead?

There are, of course, new writers coming along all the time. But they are fewer in number than of old, and they have a harder time getting their shows on. Worse, they seem to have a harder time getting second or third shows on after a hit.

That could be a problem, later on.

---

* There was a superb inside joke in a generally excellent *Carnival!* directed by Kathleen Marshall and starring Brian Stokes Mitchell, newcomer Anne Hathaway, Debbie Gravitte, and Douglas Sills. At one point, two of the carnival puppets in their little theatre were seen to be reading from tiny cutdowns of those black notebooks. Horrible Henry lost his place and had to thumb through the script, just like James Naughton.

6

A curiosity of the musical's beginnings is that the essentials of success involved performers and staging technique but not writers. The First Age, running up to 1900, was a time when all the good writing originated in Europe—Gilbert and Sullivan, Offenbach, Johann Strauss. American shows, more thinly derived, depended on star clowns, les girls, and grab-bag scores made of old tunes rekitted with new lyrics and the chance contributions of freelancers. Not till late in the First Age did native composers such as Reginald De Koven and John Philip Sousa and librettist and lyricist Harry B. Smith impose upon the scene the ideal of a full set of original words and music by a single team as the language of American musical theatre—and of course by then a host of writers were already launching the Second Age.

This lasted from 1900 to about 1920, when the reigns of Rodgers and Hart, Cole Porter, the Gershwins, Oscar Hammerstein, and their fellows create the Third—the Golden—Age, whose first Essential demands a first-rate score.

Thus, since about 1950, historians have centered chronicle on how the vocabulary of composers, and to an extent of lyricists, reflects or deviates from tradition. Typically, unusual music likes unusual subject matter: so composer and lyricist William Finn treats AIDS, life in a Depression-era soup kitchen, and his own experience battling a brain tumor. Finn is best known for the *Falsettos* trilogy, starting with *In Trousers* (1979), which introduced the professional neurotic Marvin. The real action occurs in *March of the Falsettos* (1981), when Marvin becomes a professional neurotic gay man, juggling relationships with male lover, ex-wife, and son. In

Falsettoland (1990), the lover succumbs to AIDS surrounded by an extended cultural family.

There is some unity here, for all three were premiered at Playwrights Horizons, and some of the casting was consistent. Chip Zien originated Marvin, then shared with Lonny Price the role of a pleasantly quack psychiatrist while Michael Rupert succeeded as Marvin and Stephen Bogardus played his lover, Whizzer. Alison Fraser played the wife in the first two titles, replaced by Faith Prince in the last. Moreover, while Finn himself staged *In Trousers*, James Lapine directed (and apparently helped structure) the two later shows. Most important, these unblinkingly off-Broadway looks at the urban homosexual cosmos moved to Broadway, in 1992, as *Falsettos*—a billing of the second and third of the trio only—and ran for fourteen months. There had of course been gay characters on Broadway—Bert Savoy's hissy, lisping drag figure in the 1920s; Danny Kaye's flaming photographer in *Lady in the Dark* (1941), and many comparable sterotypes of the day; Lee Roy Reams' hairdresser in *Applause* (1970). We've seen gay couples in this very volume. But not till *Falsettos* was The Street let so far into the world according to gay that Marvin's love song in bed to his dozing boy friend, "What More Can I Say," climaxed with Marvin's peek under the covers, followed by a voluptuary's grin at the public.

It is the world according to Finn: for so idiosyncratic is his voice that it creates characters and feelings that have not previously existed. His titles alone conjure up new places—"Four Jews in a Room Bitching," "My Father's a Homo," "Everyone Hates His Parents," or "Jason's Bar Mitzvah," which sounds ordinary till one finds it taking place in Whizzer's hospital room. Finn's music narrates amply because he lets a ready rhyme lead his lyrics, the words piling up ideas and the melody keeping up as best it can. This makes for tumultuous structures, intricate characterizations, a kind of chatty hysteria. In the 1980s, this very personal style appeared to offer an alternative voice to the ubiquitous Sondheimism that some felt had come to dominate the younger generation.

In fact, no one was imitating Sondheim (except in cabaret spoofs), and Finn was no more an "alternative" to anything than Cole Porter, say, had been an alternative to Jerome Kern. There will always be different voices sounding off in any given era. What mattered was Finn's enthusiasm, the onrush of the music as it chased the crazy notions in the lyrics. It was a notably off-Broadway style, made for the "teeny tiny band" invoked in the opening of *Falsettoland*: eccentric, obsessive, experimental, a more focused and naturalistic complement to what Al Carmines and Maria Irene Fornes tried out in the pseudo-fantasy *Promenade* (1969).

Still, Finn knew success on Broadway with the binding of Final Falsettoworld as *Falsettos*, and his following work included an adaptation of George S. Kaufman and Edna Ferber's play about a theatrical dynasty rather like that of the Drews and Barrymores, *The Royal Family* (1927). This is mainstream material. Jerry Herman himself considered it, visualizing an apotheosistic finale in which three generations of musical-comedy divas would amaze the public with a terminal eleven o'clock number, a "Leave 'Em Wanting More," say, a "Then You Put It Over."

That's the problem. There were no musical-comedy dynasties, because there is no way to pass on expertise in song and dance biologically. Someone in the gene pool will sing flat or tread on toes. Worse, Finn's style is too modern-sounding for the Kaufman-Ferber contents, imbued with a way of life vastly outmoded by the 1920s in the first place. Matriarch Fanny Cavendish, so memorably delivered by Eva Le Gallienne in the 1975 revival, is a nineteenth-century figure—as was Le Gallienne, for that matter, with her actor-manager repertory companies, her dedication to the Higher Drama, her gala feuds. She was dedicated to these, too, and refused to utter the words "Helen Hayes" even though *The Royal Family* played the theatre bearing Hayes' name and Le Gallienne was often in taxis trying to get there. Now try to imagine that personage leading a daughter and granddaughter in the eleven o'clock number of a musical by William Finn.

The Royal Family of Broadway, the working title, found Finn extending himself, trying to write Finn For Broadway. Listen to these suddenly "normal" song titles, so ready for the tunestack in *Playbill*: "How I Wanted To Be There Tonight," "I Don't Know Why You Love Me," "Listen To the Beat," "The Girl I'll Never Be," "Just Another Opening Night," and that eleven o'clocker, "Sing and Rejoice." There's even a hint of period pastiche tucked into Finn's signature sound; and "(There's) Too Much Drama (in my life)," for the figure based on John Barrymore, updates period in a superb character number. But the Kaufman estate* voiced

* The Kaufman estate comprises his daughter, Anne Kaufman Schneider, affectionately known to intimates as Kiss of the Schneider Woman. She does not understand why her wonderful father's plays have to be turned into musicals. Aren't they already good theatre?

misgivings. The world according to Finn doesn't relate to Barrymores. But what does, today?

The team of Stephen Flaherty and Lynn Ahrens also came forth on off-Broadway at Playwrights Horizons, in *Lucky Stiff* (1988). But their work stands squarely in the Great Tradition, as befits graduates of Lehman Engel's B.M.I. workshop. *Lucky Stiff* is not untypical of the kinds of shows written for the class, but it seems out of place at Playwrights Horizons, so associated with the artistic oddity—*Assassins, Floyd Collins, My Life With Albertine*. *Lucky Stiff*, drawn from Michael Butterworth's novel *The Man Who Broke the Bank at Monte Carlo*, is a farce on the ancient legacy-with-a-catch plot: hero (Stephen Stout) must wheel the corpse of his dead uncle around Monaco while being shadowed by his nemesis (Julie White), determined to break the will and get the money for an animal fanatics' charity.

This is a tasteless idea, even if the uncle turns out to be alive after all; and both the writing and staging (by Thommie Walsh) were shrill and busy. Perhaps the project was simply wrong for Flaherty and Ahrens. For while they prefer adaptations to original ideas—a hallmark of the B.M.I. alumni, by the way—this team in particular seems most inspired when given a specific place and time to turn into music. The French Antilles, ragtime America, sixties Dublin, and even a children's fantasyland are places they have visited with unique aplomb.

So *Once On This Island* (1990), a Playwrights Horizons production successfully moved to Broadway, reveals a truer Flaherty and Ahrens, in an irresistible Caribbean accent. Such rhythmic ensembles as "Some Say" and "Why We Tell the Story" fill the show, leaving little room for ballads. It is all atmosphere, ethnicity. Just the vowel-rich pronunciation of the heroine's name, Ti Moune, is a zephyr of delight in these parts, and while the plot itself is sad, its dependence on the protective frame of a village storytelling session and on elements of fantasy give it the reassuring character of a fable.

Graciela Daniele's direction and choreography of a lively cast honored this realization of Rosa Guy's novel *My Love, My Love*. It's a Cinderella tale in which Cinderella dies; but almost all the other characters are fairy godmothers of one kind or another. Besides, the captivating La Chanze—another lovely name—gave Ti Moune an innocence that forgives all oppression: redeems it with her purity of resolution. She loves so well that she may die but love will not, and we hear it in the music. "We Dance" is a characteristic title, as the villagers explain a lifestyle based on avoiding contact with the lordly "grands hommes" and staying on the good side of the gods. "Papa Gé, don't come around me," they plead. He is death, ever present, sardonically shrugging. But the restless music urges the grimness out of the tale, as when Ti Moune sets out on a journey to claim her grand homme and Asaka (Kecia Lewis-Evans), the goddess of the earth, directs a chorus of animals, trees, and breezes in the exuberant "Mama Will Provide."

As if to prove that only an exotic setting can stir them, Flaherty and Ahrens wrote a partly dull score for My Favorite Year (1992), based on Richard Benjamin's film about an Errol Flynn sort guesting on something like Sid Caesar's television show in 1954. The 1950s give one little to draw on musically, unless one is doing rock and roll. And the many eccentrics filling out the character sheet—every lead but the protagonist, Benjy Stone (Evan Pappas)—pushed the piece into the realm of the comedy musical, a hard form to bring off these days, without interesting crazies in the roles.

My Favorite Year is a stageful of uninteresting crazies—the Caesar figure (Tom Mardirosian), the Flynn figure (Tim Curry), the protagonist's stupid, naggy mother (Lainie Kazan), her Filipino husband, a former boxer (Thomas Ikeda), the TV writers, the Brooklyn relatives. There are uninteresting sane people as well, which unfortunately includes Benjy and the girl he dotes on (Lannyl Stephens). Only Andrea Martin, playing one of the TV writers, was able to score.

It was a by-the-numbers adaptation of a movie, so popular—really, so undiscourageable—in this era. Like Big, My Favorite Year dutifully musicalized its subject till it was still the movie, without its atmosphere, charm, or excellent performances. The movie offered Peter O'Toole as the Errol Flynn character, quite living up to the exposé of him, found in ex-wife Siân Phillips' memoirs, as disgracefully impossible and utterly marvelous; one mustn't make a musical on that person if one hasn't the tunes ready for him, the lyrics set.

Was there anything that Flaherty and Ahrens could bring to the material to lift it, thrill it? "The Duck Joke," in which Andrea Martin patiently took the clueless ingenue through a course in comedy, greatly amuses with its rendering of a perfectly amiable human being without a shred of humor. ("Use your hands," Martin urges.) And the boy-girl plot took a melodious turn in "Shut Up and Dance," a comfort-food number in which two awkward kids do Astaire and Rogers with an offstage Hollywood chorus. There was one floppo piece, "Rookie in the Ring," for Kazan's mother character. Yet even the duller titles did hit the right accents, so to say. And the evening took off outstandingly, with "Twenty Million People," one of those anticipatory introductions of the lead players that simultaneously supply background on the timeplace. For its first five minutes, My Favorite Year was a hit.

Of course, Flaherty and Ahrens went on to greater things. Some other new voices never managed to fill out a curriculum vitae, perhaps seeing their projects languishing in workshop purgatory. What other reason can there be for Broadway to have failed to give us a second musical by Rupert Holmes after his spectacular debut as composer, lyricist, book writer, and orchestrator of The Mystery of Edwin Drood (1985)? The third Central Park Public Theater musical (after Two Gentlemen of Verona and The Pirates of Penzance), this had the most original concept of the three, though based on Charles Dickens' last, unfinished novel. As if acknowledging the prominence of the gloomy musical while wishing to preserve the merry musical, Holmes adapted Dickens as a play-within-a-play. Drood wasn't being performed by the New York Shakespeare Festival but by the resident troupe of the Music Hall Royale in London in 1873. We were always to be aware of the actors portraying Dickens' people, through byplay to us and among themselves—ad-libs, conferences with the Chairman (George Rose), even a prima donna walkout through the theatre aisle by the "principal boy" (Betty Buckley as the title character in manly drag), complete with Trophy Dog on Leash.

Dickens' novel is dark even for Dickens; its first scene is laid in an opium den, and Edwin Drood is murdered early on. Or is he? No corpse is found, and a peculiar detective turns up in Drood's cathedral town of Cloisterham. Is the detective Drood in disguise, investigating his own "murder"? Dickens died halfway through composition and left not a clue about what he had in mind. The tale has an apparent culprit, Drood's uncle John Jasper (Howard McGillin), who lusts after Drood's betrothed, Rosa Bud (Patti Cohenour). But isn't the obviously guilty party bound by rules of genre to be innocent?

With a set of characters designed to unmask England as a society of Pecksniffs, the novel is not only dark but argumentative. Holmes used the music-hall frame to bring in the fun. Here's the Chairman announcing a change in casting:

> CHAIRMAN: It will come as no surprise to our regulars that Mr. Hitchens is once again Massively Indisposed, due to injuries he received while fighting for a lady's honour. (Pause) Apparently the lady wished to keep it.

So *The Mystery of Edwin Drood* is a musical play surrounded by a musical comedy, a superb way to utilize the former's dramatic vitality and "extra" music while taking advantage of the latter's "let's step out" delight. Holmes kept the lyrics Dickensian even as he let the music rove about in time. There is no pastiche in any real sense, yet the sound fits the setting. A constant use of seconds, fourths, and major sevenths in the harmony builds an evocative score, so energetic in the march duet for uncle and nephew, "Two Kinsmen," so eerie in Rosa's worried ballad "Moonfall," and so operatically dimensioned in "No Good Can Come From Bad," a confrontation ensemble on the night of the supposed murder.

Some of this is delivered in the musical-play style we have been hearing since the 1970s, vivid and impassioned. But Holmes doesn't let the serious music overwhelm the entertainment. Remember, the fun surrounds the mystery. So Jasper's furtively murderous, almost gleefully tortured "A Man Could Go Quite Mad" takes off on a vamp that could very nearly be the musical equivalent of the cartoon sight gag of the villain stalking his prey by zipping from tree to tree. However dire the *Drood* plot gets, it is nevertheless being performed on the stage of a music hall.

Princess Puffer (Cleo Laine), the proprietress of the opium den, is the role most tuned to music-hall usage: Laine actually brought the public in on the last line of her establishing number, "The Wages of Sin." But the entire company gave a splendid send-off to the staging concept in "An English Music Hall," the opening number used in Central Park. The accuracy of Holmes' ear for language took a rich turn here, when the Chairman, considering Western Civilization's forms of musical entertainment, confessed a respectable interest in chamber music. "I take some every week," he assured us. Right: it's medicine. *Music hall* is art. The slight revision for Broadway replaced this number with "There You Are," apparently because director Wilford Leach wanted an introduction to the individuals of the Royale's troupe, disporting themselves throughout the Imperial Theatre's auditorium with couplets betokening their character essentials.

This players-in-the-house opening and Rose's role as emcee supported *Drood*'s unique surprise: the audience was to vote on the outcome of the plot.* First, the actors themselves voted on whether or not Drood was dead. He was (which occasioned Buckley's angry walkout). Then: Who was that detective really? and Who killed Drood? and Please choose one male and one female principal to make a happy-ending couple.

Holmes and Leach worked out endings for every possible vote, so *Drood* became Broadway's first aleatory musical, gently postmodern in period candy-box sets and costumes by, respectively, Bob Shaw and Lindsay W. Davis. *Drood* won the Tony and ran 608 performances, though a London staging at the Savoy in 1987 was a fast failure. This is odd, considering how constantly the English pour Dickens into musicals—not only *Oliver!* (1960) but *Pickwick* (1963), *Two Cities* (1969), and *Nickleby and Me* (1975) in London, and many other drawings from the well in the provinces.

Also odd was *Drood*'s London revision, awkward and unnecessary. True, the New York *Drood* softened Dickens' exposé of racism in Cloisterham's suspicion of the Ceylonese siblings Neville and Helena Landless. Their New York number, "Ceylon," was a bit of fluff with finger cymbals; a new number for London turned into a biting ensemble on how the English regard colonials. Another new number, "A Private Investigation," introduced *Drood*'s one effect of near-rock, and sat badly with the rest of the score. But some of the script changes partook happily of the traditional English jokebook, as when the Princess Puffer (Lulu) and the old churchyard caretaker Durdles (Phil Rose) were voted as the happy couple:

PUFFER: (with virginal excitement) Will it be a white wedding?
DURDLES: Only if there's a blizzard!

* At least I believe it unique to the Broadway musical. It was tried at least once in a straight play. The courtroom drama *Night of January 16* (1935), on a murder case, culled its jury from each night's audience. At show's end, the jury would vote guilty or not guilty; the cast rehearsed different endings to cover the eventualities. The play was written by the objectivist philosopher Ayn Rand.

Now I have another delightful and beautifully staged show, also based on an English novel. Lucy Simon and Marsha Norman's *The Secret Garden* (1991), from Frances Hodgson Burnett's novel of 1909, tells of an orphaned little girl whose defiant spirit cures a lamed little boy. He, too, is an orphan: because his mother is dead and his father withdrawn. Unlike *Drood*, *The Secret Garden* could set no comic frame around the gloomy stuff, for it is a tale made of gloom, living on it—or, better, dying of it. Only at length does it come into the light, working through the symbol of the garden, locked up to grow wild till the young heroine, Mary Lennox, learns to put herself into harmony with nature and saves garden, boy, family, all.

The book is a classic, and a very English one, with the wuthering on the Yorkshire moors about the manor house, with the starchy house servants and the unpredictable groundskeepers, with beautiful dead sisters haunting the living, and with a shady doctor figure. It's Hitchcockian. How surprising to learn that Burnett emigrated from England as a teen to Tennessee more than forty years before she wrote *The Secret Garden*. A woman's novel about the spiritual growth of a young woman might well attract women as a work for musical adaptation, and *The Secret Garden* did so even before Simon and Norman. The earlier work, with a score by Sharon Burgett, Susan Beckwith-Smith, and Diana Matterson, demonstrates through its lack of interest how imaginative the Simon-Norman version is. Recorded by an astonishingly top-line cast headed by Barbara Cook, Judy Kaye, and John Cullum, this secret *Secret Garden* sounds like a sixties cult flop with too many waltzes and a gigantic pit. What can you do with a show that starts with an "any minute now" sort of chorus of bustling servants carefully filling one in on the backstory? Indeed, it's called "Any Minute Now," just as "Dickon Is My Name" and "My Mother" and the class-war chorus "The Likes of You and Me" and the two villains' ironic comic spot "How We Love Children" are called what they are and do what such songs have been doing for far too long.

Simon and Norman keep investigating the edge of things to find their center. Allotting intimately dramatic music to Mary Lennox and her adopted family and a folkish sound to the help, the authors avoid bustling choruses and ironic comic spots. Servant Martha (Alison Fraser), Mary's confidante, speeds the plot along with the impishly cajoling "If I Had a Fine White Horse" and the urgent "Hold On." Gardener Ben (Tom

Toner) offers the wonderful "It's a Maze," which Susan H. Schulman staged as a tour through the park of Misselthwaite Manor while Mary (Daisy Eagan) sang twee nonsense verse and shrubbery and other fixtures danced past her. Dickon (John Cameron Mitchell), Martha's brother, has the show's key number, "(When a thing is) Wick (it has a life about it)." He is telling Mary of the possibility of reviving the ruined garden. More truly, his observations advise Mary on how she can bring her uncle and his son, the crippled boy, out of darkness into day.

The word "wick" comes from the Old English "wíc," denoting a place where life is found, and surviving in such names as Warwick and Ipswich. The song "Wick" is about life—finding it where it seems over. As a hammered dulcimer plays a toccata and the brass build the sound, Dickon's voice rides over a kind of folklore-rock, a climax to the show's central conflict: Mary's vitality challenging the moribundity of her uncle Archie (Mandy Patinkin). It needs little more than "How Could I Ever Know?," the farewell duet of Archie and the ghost of his dead beloved, Lily (Rebecca Luker), for the story to find conclusion.

So, yes, there's a ghost, and a commentative chorus, and a synoptic musical scene covering the story's opening, during a cholera outbreak in Bombay. That other, old-fashioned *Secret Garden* presumably lacked the technique to treat an epidemic in foreign parts. It doesn't have a ghost, either, and leaves out important parts of the story. This may explain why that version has been seen in provincial England only. It's too simple and merry, whereas the story is about the eradication of merriment. Uncle Archie's mourning has so consumed him that his dead wife is more real to him than his living son:

MARY: Does everyone who dies become a ghost?
ARCHIE: Only in concept musicals like this one.

No, he doesn't say that, boys and girls; but I'll bet he's thinking it. What he says is:

ARCHIE: They're only a ghost if someone alive is still holding on to them.

A taste of India in the music (not only in Bombay but later, in the reclaimed garden) and Heidi Landesman's brilliant set, modeled on a Victorian toy theatre, helped give the production a certain idea of

Imperial England, all the while preserving Burnett's flirtation with fantasy. After all, it is a robin that leads Mary to the lost key to the garden and then to the locked door itself. An ordinary adaptation might have buried this all-important point of plot movement in the middle of Act One—as that other *Secret Garden* does. To Simon and Norman, Mary's moment of contact with the garden is the great creative event in her life, her entrance into womanhood, into wisdom, into the power to heal. It *must* conclude the first act, as the most attractive suspense since Marian Paroo tore out the page of data that would have unmasked the music man and thus lets him take the town. It's one piece of the Great Tradition that lives on, an arresting first-act curtain: *Brigadoon, Guys and Dolls, Me and Juliet, Gypsy, La Cage aux Folles, Dreamgirls*. For *The Secret Garden*'s act finale, designer Landesman showed us the garden's outer wall, as Mary inserts key in lock and pushes the door open. We are eager for the wall to vanish, letting us, too, into the garden that changes lives. Not yet: as Mary peers inside in wonder, the first-act curtain falls.

Astonishingly, we have not heard a second Holmes or Simon-Norman score on Broadway. But then, writing in the Tradition is increasingly difficult in the commercial sense, for the successful new scores are more often anti-Tradition—gimmicky pastiche pop tunes, say, or a tour through rock styles. Another solution is to set a country subject to the country sound while bending the music to serve the interests of theatre. Three such works have enriched the repertory in different ways—on The Street or at Playwrights Horizons; by a man unused to theatre work, a newcomer with interesting genetic entitlement, and a woman with some theatre experience in the regions; using classic Americana, a tale drawn from old headlines, and an existential quandary.

Only one of these three country writers really was a country writer. He was Roger Miller, author of the music and lyrics to *Big River: The Adventures of Huckleberry Finn* (1985), to William Hauptman's book. Using a few of the major episodes and much of the actual language of Mark Twain, *Big River* owes some of its success to its appearance near the end of Broadway's worst musical season ever. (Illustratively, the Tony nominations for Best Musical could challenge *Big River* only with the unpopular concept show *Grind*; *Quilters*, about pioneer women and almost as exciting as one of their sewing bees; and the decisively horrible *Leader of the Pack*.) *Big River* was warmed-over Twain, perhaps, for all its fidelity. But Miller's score really did paint a unique *tinta* with its hymns and curios.

It even started with something one would hardly expect from a country balladeer like Miller: an old-fashioned post–Rodgers and Hammerstein opening-number exposition, with spoken lines in between the vocal sections, to set the scene and designate those of importance to the action. "Do Ya Wanna Go To Heaven?" presents the townsfolk of St. Petersburg, Missouri with an admirable sophistication of talent but creating the utmost simplicity of feeling. And that is the Twain style for certain.

Other numbers were more traditional pop sing-outs, such as the lively "Muddy Water," a duet for Huck (Daniel Jenkins) and Jim (Ron Richardson), the runaway slave Huck befriends. But much of Miller's treatment explored a Twainian musical theatre never heard before— especially in the various *Huckleberry Finn* adaptations preceding this one. "Guv'ment," a character number for Huck's evil Pap (John Goodman), is one of the most individual songs ever heard on Broadway, a blast of near-Dada from a drunken idiot.

Adam Guettel's *Floyd Collins* (1996) is the headline musical, by Richard Rodgers' grandson, to Tina Landau's book. Collins was a Kentucky man who got trapped in a cave in 1925 and became a national obsession for eighteen days, till his lifeless body was recovered. Befitting a show of the 1990s, the first number is not expository but thematic. The full cast is on stage, more or less standing there in half-tone lighting—*Big River*'s cast was posed and bright and eager—as one player begins, "Deep in the land of the hollows and creeks," over a country accompaniment in broken chords in e minor. "If'n you git lost." he continues, "you git lost fer weeks." It's an incantation, a threat, a moral. What land? The caves? One's personal life? The America of media shows, where the truth parties with show biz?

As in any country tale, there is a family and a place you came from. But Floyd (Christopher Innvar) is *going* to a place, he thinks, that legendary American place of fame and riches. He is the opposite of a Mark Twain hero, for whom success is usually a chore. In *Floyd Collins*, success is paradise. You don't have to know what exactly is in it to believe in it. So, even after he is trapped, Floyd can sing a lengthy duet with his visiting younger brother, Homer (Jason Danieley), "The Riddle Song," which characterizes Floyd with an exuberant love of life. He's Going There, surely. But the number is a brilliant and terrible heads-up to the audience, at least to those who already know what the last headline will be. In the musicals of Guettel's grandfather's day, one had to be a varmint or retrogressive on social issues or just Billy Bigelow to die in a musical. Today, even the most life-affirming souls may be selected to go nowhere.

The heroine of *Violet* (1997) is going to Tulsa, Oklahoma, where she hopes a faith healer will rid her of a scar from a childhood accident that runs across half her face. Like Adam Guettel, *Violet*'s composer and lyricist, Jeanine Tesori and Brian Crawley, use a "busier" country sound than does Roger Miller. *Big River*, with its large, open melodies and simple orchestrations, often sounds like a score played on a giant guitar. *Floyd Collins* runs on a series of surprising vamps and twisty developments, giving its principals the powerful longings of Sondheim characters, and characterizing the invading reporters, in "Is That Remarkable?," with hot little close-harmony blips in the high tenor range.

But *Violet* is the liveliest of these three scores, and claims the most interesting story line. *Huckleberry Finn* is really another of those human comedies in which civilization battles nature. Civilization loses, for *Big River* ends as the novel does, with Huck lighting out for the west and freedom. "I can't stand it," he says, of town life, heading for the last line of both book and play: "I been there before."

Huck does learn something on his trip, about the natural equality of human beings. But Violet (Lauren Ward) makes quite some personal voyage. The cast includes her father (Stephen Lee Anderson), two soldiers (Michael Park, Michael McElroy), various strangers, and the preacher (Robert Westenberg), who of course can do nothing for her. Note that he is played by the actor also playing the bus driver who conducts, so to say, Violet's quest. And the preacher is suddenly replaced in the scene of her failed healing by her father, the actual cause of her disfigurement.

Brian Crawley also wrote the show's book, from Doris Betts' story "The Ugliest Pilgrim." Crawley comes most alive in his lyrics. He makes poetry out of the vernacular, so that we receive these characters as if we're right on the bus or in chapel with them. And Tesori's ready ear sets them singing in what may be the best of all our theatre country scores. *Big River*, again, is very basic and *Floyd Collins* a sophistication. *Violet*, crafted to make simplicities eloquent, gets into the space between.

Above all, *Violet* presents an extremely sympathetic heroine. She is in anguish over her handicap, yet she refuses to let it interfere with her day-to-day. "All To Pieces," her catalogue of movie-star body parts she'd like to borrow, builds to a wonderful breakout section ("Oh, with lips like those . . ."), and Park, the ladies' man of the two soldiers, has a "Shall I Tell You What I Think Of You?" number, "You're Different," that tells us how far under her spell he has been pulled.

Susan H. Schulman's staging gave us a Violet without a cosmetic scar. It was up to Lauren Ward to tell us of it: in her complicated relationship with her culpable father; in her endearing wish to have the same kinds of friendships everyone else has; in her finally ending up with McElroy, the other of the two soldiers, the sensitive one, so that we could feel blessed by her redemption.

Roger Miller did not live to write a follow-up piece to *Big River*. But Tesori has been industrious, all the while refitting her vision to specific musical styles, as in her ingeniously liquid incidental score to Nicholas Hytner's watery Lincoln Center *Twelfth Night* in 1998. The orchestration, by Rick Bassett, takes in mandolin, recorder, celesta, Tibetan bowls, bansuri, ocarina, shakuhachi, Daxophone, dumbek, tabla, djembe, and even a violin. More conventionally, Tesori saw her *Starcrossed: The Trial of Galileo* (1994) produced at Goodspeed and *Thoroughly Modern Millie* (2002) make a splash on The Street. Guettel is less ambitious. Even so, he is invariably cited as one of the archons of new talent on Broadway though, at this writing, his sole musical per se played just 25 performances for a subscription audience in a small house. Surely Tesori should be on that list, too.

The writers of music and lyrics have formed the content of historians' charts, though obviously there is a need for specialists in book writing. It's handy when lyricists write their own books; but not all can. So there are crucial talents who own a dim history. Yet the prolific Harry B. Smith in effect invented the early-twentieth-century musical book. Herbert Fields took over the concern in the Third Age, to be joined by George Abbott, Abe Burrows, Joseph Stein, and . . . who?

By the years covered in the present volume, the librettist no longer claims an arcane creativity in between the fun parts, because there is no longer any between in musicals: they are that integrated. Still, James Lapine's tour de force as book writer and director of Stephen Sondheim's two eighties shows after *Merrily We Roll Along* has to be counted an important debut because of the confidence with which these unique projects were executed. *Sunday in the Park With George* (1984) infers its action from Georges Seurat's painting *A Sunday Afternoon on the Island of La Grande Jatte*, and *Into the Woods* (1987) utilizes elements of fairy tales. Still, both works are originals, which is more and more unusual today. And while the two exploit the customary Sondheim virtues and expansions of those virtues with new inventions, the books are unlike those of the seventies Sondheim shows. In effect, Lapine created new Sondheim.

Sunday may be the richest book in Sondheim's oeuvre to that point. Only *Follies'* script juggles as many different notions at once, and those are somewhat diffuse because of the work's epic nature. *Sunday* is tight: art (but really *artists*), love (but really emotional *generosity*), light (but really color but also darkness). It develops many a surprise along the way, such as the gradual revelation that while artists are supposedly crazy, the painting on whose figures Act One is made depicts folk far more eccentric than the ruthlessly professional Seurat. Only Louis the baker is an ordinary person. ("That's the trouble, nothing's wrong with him": probably the greatest character damnation in all Sondheim.)

Lapine's most ingenious turn is his variation on Boy Gets Girl. George (Mandy Patinkin) is too obsessed with his work to *give* to Dot (Bernadette Peters). She goes to America with Louis. But the second act, set mostly a century later, allots its last major book scene and climactic vocal to a touching George-Dot reunion, though George is now a modern-day artist and Dot his great-grandmother, in full first-act Grande Jatte kit.

Her advice to him, in the number "Move On," is another of the seemingly autobiographical explications that Sondheim placed in this study of how art is conceived: "Color and Light," "Finishing the Hat," "Beautiful." In Act Two, "Putting It Together" tells of the marketing of art—and here Sondheim breaks away into someone else's idea of art, because the song is given to someone who specializes in illuminating old masters and splatting them onto museum walls. This is art the way *Saturday Night Fever* is a musical. Patinkin and Peters played descendants of the first-act characters in the second act, suggesting a parallel between the two Georges. But the revolutionary George of Act One was taking Western art to a place it needed to reach. The fashionable George of Act Two is like the guy who mans the slide projector in Art History 101. This is not moving on. Yet surely Lapine and Sondheim see the two Georges as part of a continuity.

If *Sunday* makes a great deal out of very little plot, *Into the Woods* has more synopsis than Dickens. Frank Rich called *Sunday* "perhaps the first truly modernist work of musical theater that Broadway has produced," and *Sunday*'s Lapine is indeed the contemporary alchemist, pouring out his beakers of bubbling themes. But *Into the Woods*' Lapine finds him doing what Harry B. Smith used to do, which was: invent a lot of plot. In this show, all themes conduce to a single symbol—the woods—in which all activity after the exposition takes place. The woods are inviting but dangerous, a place of transformation where the self dares everything to expand the security of the ego structure. There is no Happy Ever After without a visit to the woods.

Starting with three tales—Cinderella, Jack and the Beanstalk, and Lapine's own The Baker and His Wife—Lapine adds in Rapunzel and Little Red Ridinghood. (Snow White and Sleeping Beauty make *bonne bouche* appearances at the finale.) We have moved as far as possible from *Sunday*'s real-life model, Seurat; and though Bernadette Peters and some of the other *Sunday* cast ensured their Sondheim cred by reappearing in *Into the Woods*, the new show employs a very different thespian layout, with ten principals instead of two.

Moreover, while *Into the Woods* has a bigger book than *Sunday*, it also has a bigger score, with an immense amount of musical scenes and under-scoring. There were times in *Sunday* when the music stopped—really stopped, so the audience could enjoy the contrast of the spoken lines as if at a performance of an old Cohan show, or something by Cole Porter for Ethel Merman. *Into the Woods* has few such moments; the music stops only to start again not very long after.

This makes *Into the Woods* as modernist as *Sunday*: not in making old art into new art by crossing genres (as *Sunday* does), but in the symbiotic relationship of book and score. Lapine has in effect eviscerated the book without going into opera—or, to use his own terms, he has sent the book on its own quest into the woods to come back singing. No book show before this one so fills its musical scenes with dialogue or keeps vocaliz-ing its spoken pages.

Consider the opening sequence, which begins with a chop of logic. The Narrator utters the indispensable "Once upon a time," and at once the orchestra jumps in with the Sondheim repeated chords, $C^{maj.7}$ moving to b^7 and back. As the Narrator continues, characters in all three of the major story sets have stated primary objectives—within thirty seconds. Duping us in our familiarity with Cinderella's horrible family and Jack's poverty, Lapine allows us to assume that we know the Baker and his Wife from somewhere, too, slyly adding in Little Red Ridinghood before Sondheim breaks into the title song. The repeated chords are again on hand, now with a hesitant inner voice and an eerie version of it on high.

The authors must add something special to keep the fascination hard; sure enough, there's a knock on the Baker's door. To his casually comic line "It's the witch from next door," Peters made her entrance, in faithful Grimm aspect, crook and all. Topping Lapine, Sondheim gives her a rap number, complete with homeboy percussion, and at the height of it her chair levitates.

The content of her rap lyrics has completely changed the narrative's goal, for another of the show's quirks is a volatile plotline. Finally, all six of the good guys—Cinderella, Jack, Jack's Mother, the Baker, his Wife, and Ridinghood—have returned to the title strain. The décor has changed to the woods, and, for punctuation, the company hesitates in fear at something. No—it's only Cinderella's family, dressing the stage on their way to the Prince's castle. They can swell the vocal weight of the climax of this fourteen-minute sequence, the most eventful exposition in musical-theatre history.

The show moves speedily through all its recombinations of characters and quests, as when the Baker's Wife has a quickie with Cinderella's Prince. "What is it about the woods?" she sings, trying to piece it together with one of Sondheim's most laden lines. However, if director Lapine's *Sunday* seemed unimprovably superb, the 1990 London *Into the Woods*, directed by Richard Jones, gave a better rendering. Not that the cast was better, even given Julia McKenzie's extraordinary Witch. But in New York one never quite left Broadway for Storybookland. New York's Princes, Chuck Wagner and Robert Westenberg, were the usual handsome guys with swords and brushes, and Baker and Wife (Chip Zien, Joanna Gleason) looked like waggish Upper West Siders heading for a Halloween party. In London, Sue Blane costumed the entire cast to look like those things that come dipping and clacking out of a cuckoo clock on the hour. Set designer Richard Hudson's woods were not a forest but a hallway of doors, emphasizing the abstract nature of the woods as a series of choices and a Place of Destiny.

Composer and lyricist Michael John LaChiusa writes his own books, putting him in rare company, rarer yet considering the advanced musical style he writes in. Varying his *colorito* from piece to piece, he started on the small side and then expanded, with the chamber work *First Lady Suite* (1993) and the tidy but intricate *Hello Again* (1994). Moving into super-director territory in collaboration with Harold Prince at the Public Theater on *The Petrified Prince* (1994), LaChiusa put "off-Broadway" behind him in one of the grandest and most powerful of modern scores, *Marie Christine* (1999). His source material is an extensive miscellany: bizarre fictions about Eleanor Roosevelt, Mamie Eisenhower, and Jacqueline Kennedy; Arthur Schnitzler's *Reigen* (*Round Dance*, generally called *La Ronde*) reset in the American twentieth century from decade to decade; an unfilmed Ingmar Bergman screenplay; and *Medea* in New Orleans and Chicago.

LaChiusa is ingenious in musical pastiche, mirroring the wit of his lyrics. *Hello Again* contains recollections of silent-movie upright-piano-and-solo-violin, German operetta, thirties "Dance with me!" tango, swing, wartime close-harmony girl group, early-middle fifties rock and roll, and disco, brought in as scene-setters or as part of the actual fabric of the sound of a particular episode. But LaChiusa's main concern is to for-mulate a distinct musical style for each show, deriving it out of the nature of the material. Thus, Schnitzler's cycle of two-character playlets, each centering on the sexual act and carrying over one character from the last sketch into the next, is restless, mercurial. So LaChiusa sets it to an evening-long rubato of quick movements pushing into expansive dia-logues, hurrying them along, tearing off to the next date.

Amusingly, *Hello Again* doesn't merely borrow Schnitzler's concept but discovers precise American equivalents for Schnitzler's Viennese stereo-types, including one gay and one bisexual character. A short-lived off-Broadway musical from the same source, Hal Jordan and Jerry Douglas' *Rondelay* (1969), retained Schnitzler's turn-of-the-century Vienna setting in a book musical filled with story and character numbers: "Tonight You Dance With Me," "The Days of My Youth," "Reidhof's," "A Castle in India," "Opera Star," and—inevitably, given an evening of rendezvous— "Auf Wiedersehen." But *Hello Again* sings almost entirely through each scene. Schnitzler called *Reigen* "Ten Dialogues," and though LaChiusa brings in outside voices—on the radio, from patrons in a cinema, in a *Titanic* lifeboat, which coincidentally has its own opera star—he closes in on each new pairing. *Rondelay's* program listed thirty-four separate titles; *Hello Again* counters with ten musical dialogues. These are not songs but an atmosphere of music, a place the characters live in.

This is an elaboration of the *First Lady Suite* structure: *Hello Again* is a suite with coordinated parts. But of course, the earlier work is dominated by its three titular divas, while *Hello Again's* cast is a democratic ensemble. Then, too, one knows generally what will occur in each scene of *Hello. Again*, whereas one could hardly have anticipated Mamie Eisenhower's encounter with black contralto Marian Anderson in Little Rock at the time of the racial crisis or that pair's subsequent Atlantic voyage to drop in on Ike, back in time, fighting World War II.

However, none of these early works alerted the ear to the coming eloquence of *Marie Christine*. By now, LaChiusa had so to say moved from Lincoln Center's basement (the Newhouse, where *Hello Again* played) to the Beaumont, the main stage upstairs. He was in cahoots with the top talents—Graciela Daniele, the director-choreographer of both *Hello Again* and *Marie Christine*, and *Hello Again's* leading ladies. Judy Blazer, Carolee Carmello, Donna Murphy, and Michele Pawk held assignations with soldier and senator, with senator and writer, making the show an actor's holiday of exhibition-level cameos. And now two of Broadway's finest singing actors, Audra McDonald and Anthony Crivello, played the Medea and Jason of *Marie Christine*.

In the days of the ancient Greeks, playwrights chose familiar stories to spin them, to reinform the audience about their meaning. So it is in *Marie Christine*, as LaChiusa gives us his own *Medea*. We know the outline of the myth and how it must end. We even already know what it means. LaChiusa must retell it with such artistry that he claims it as new work, his own.

He does this most of all in a structure that breaks even the newest, most revised rules in the handbook, as in Medea's first encounter with Jason, a sea captain named Dante Keyes. He finds her by the shore of Lake Pontchartrain, awaiting customers for magical assistance in their love lives: like the Medea of old, Marie Christine is a sorceress. The two begin a giddy courtship in a sequence of numbers centering on him.

Marie Christine has an important solo, but she doesn't share a note of duet with Dante, for the intention is to put on display Dante's alpha maleness so that Marie Christine—and we—will see in him the agent of her destiny.

So "Storm" (published as "The Adventure Never Ends") gives us Dante the resourceful hero. "Nothing Beats Chicago" reveals the ultra-contemporary hero who seizes opportunity. "Ocean Is Different" is the poetic hero, the romantic who not only sires the brood and protects the nest but enlightens his own little alpha males with the necessary wisdom. What is left, then, but the comic hero, in "Danced With a Girl," the tricky solo violin and lurching rhythm suggesting a drunken *Appalachian Spring*.

Marie Christine's only part in this is "To Find a Lover," a catalogue of her witchcraft and a wholly contrasting piece of music. This suite of five solos, her one to his four, delineates the sheer animal wonder of two vital personalities feeling their way through a speedy wooing; but they are of course a spectacularly bad fit. We've known this since Euripides, and LaChiusa reminds us not only in that Dante is a white from the north and Marie Christine a southern black but in their music. His is often diatonic (or, at least, as diatonic as this fiendishly chromatic score gets), delivered in steady rhythms, and conservatively scored. Hers is simply wild. The most syncopated lines ever written for Broadway and set to a cautionary alarm of drums and worries from some unknown place, Marie Christine's vocals are all the omen we need that the very purpose of the tale is terror. Hear the tumultuous choral and orchestral tutti that crashes out at the climax of her "To Find a Lover," as if at the unveiling of a fetish at a *vaudou* ceremony.

The scene was a tour de force for McDonald and Crivello, she so graceful in that glorious timbre and he perfectly styling the shamelessly lovable male who has never in his life lacked for devotees. The two are both aligned and separated by a musical cell, three notes setting the word "beautiful" and enclosing a perfect fifth. When Dante calls something "beautiful," it is in the major key. When Marie Christine calls something "beautiful," the three notes slip into the minor. And he calls Chicago beautiful: strength and hunger. And she calls him beautiful: love. "We were thrown out of Eden," she tells us, in the show's central number, "Way Back To Paradise," "for knowing too much." Her "we" is not humankind but the gender of women: another retelling of an old myth. Women were free till God realized that their independence assaults Divinity. "Way Back To Paradise" purports to be another of Marie Christine's cures for life's challenges. She wants to teach, but she hasn't learned the key lesson, though it is the eternal message of Euripides and LaChiusa alike: women are ruled by love, and that's why men rule women.

Like most of the best scores today, that to *Marie Christine* was too rich for the critics. They want *Contact, The Producers, Hairspray*. LaChiusa is now where Sondheim was in the early 1970s. But *Marie Christine* was recorded, and discerning ears will hear it. By the next generation or so, it will be in the repertory of every major opera company in the Western world.

7

What Exactly Is an Off-Broadway Musical?

It's small, like Larry Grossman and Hal Hackady's *Snoopy!!!* (1982), a sequel to Clark Gesner's even smaller *You're a Good Man, Charlie Brown* (1967). Or it's small and spoofy cute, like *Trixie True, Teen Detective* (1980), set in the look, sound, and attitudes of the 1940s. Or it's a small revival, as of *Pacific Overtures* in 1984, *The Rothschilds* in 1990, *I Do! I Do!* in 1996, or *As Thousands Cheer* in 1998.

What if it's small and sophisticated, but spoofy all the same, like *Tallulah* (1983)? It has Broadway leads, such as Helen Gallagher as Bankhead and Russell Nype as her senator father; but it has music by Arthur Siegel, who spent decades vainly trying to persuade The Street that he was good for something besides contributing to *New Faces* revues.

Very often, they are too small and wiggy to play Broadway, like *Just So* (1985), an updating of Rudyard Kipling in soft rock. Has there ever been anything less susceptible to modernization than this mythic zoology? In *The Village Voice*, Julius Novick adopted Kipling's tone: "In the days, O Best Beloved, when the secret of writing good musical comedies had been lost . . . the Julianne Boyd flew down upon Rudyard Kipling's *Just So Stories* and bore them off in her talons . . . and knocked nearly all of the magic and nearly all of the wonder straight out of every one of them." (Boyd, the director, was given equal blame along with book writer Mark St. Germain, composer Doug Katsaros, and lyricist David Zippel. Katsaros is presumably the model for Bobby, the egregiously pop songwriter in *A Class Act*.)

Sometimes they are not only small and wiggy but Very Something Else or perhaps just Too What They Are for uptown—like *Goblin Market*

(1986), a diaphanous concoction in which a chamber quartet saws away while two girls in lacy white sing the words of Christina Rossetti. It is all very Druidic and quixotic, repressed yet erotic. La. Or they can be extremely not repressed, such as *Hedwig and the Angry Inch* (1998), the inch being what remained of the transsexual rocker Hedwig's dick after a botched operation. Or they can be simply *Bat Boy* (2001), because he *is* a bat, though I increasingly think that the farther we get from shows with a valid role for Barbara Cook, the farther we get from what is enjoyable. This may be an insufferably eccentric opinion, but I don't want to see a musical treating Christina Rossetti, a transsexual rocker, or a bat.

Clouding the definition of the off-Broadway musical is the increasing appearance in its geography of works that could have been Broadway fare. Peter Nichols' play with songs (composed by Denis King) *Privates on Parade* was first given, in 1977, by the Royal Shakespeare Company on their main stages in England. A look at the British equivalent of our U.S.O. on duty in the late 1940s in the Far East, the show is comic in general and campy in particular (Denis Quilley played a spiky drag entertainer). And yet it climaxes in hideous bloodshed. Too offbeat for Broadway, it made it to the Roundabout's old home off Union Square in 1989. The cast was headed by Simon Jones (of the original English company), Jim Dale in Quilley's part, and ex-skater John Curry, Gregory Jbara, and Donna Murphy among the support.

It isn't very off-Broadway, though: it's West End in the wrong country. And why was the Kander and Ebb revue *And the World Goes 'Round* (1991) not on Broadway? Here was the very era of the big songwriter revue. This one used only five performers and a band of six, but Kander and Ebb are not off-Broadway writers. Kander's vamps alone fill theatres. Then, too, was it really wise to assign numbers introduced by such large talents as Barbra Streisand, Liza Minnelli, Chita Rivera, and even Robert Goulet to a cast of limited charisma? But the show ran a year, and also seemed to mark a turning point in how the Kander and Ebb partnership was perceived. From the Harold Arlen and E. Y. Harburg status of hidden treasures, they seemed suddenly to be graduated to household names.

The English mishmash *Return To the Forbidden Planet* (1991) had also played the West End, at the Cambridge Theatre: so what was it doing at the little Variety Arts on lower Third Avenue? In any case, this was scarcely a musical, or even an act of theatre. It was like something one puts on as a child in the garage, and even Aunt Agnes walks out on it. Author and director Bob Carlton apparently wished to salute kid sci-fi movies, using old rock and roll from "Good Golly Miss Molly" to "Pretty Woman." But the doings were gamy.

This hazy sense of what kind of show properly belongs where further broke down the very notion of an off-Broadway musical. The classic instance of promotion from modest venues keyed to a venturesome public to The Street is *Rent*, one of America's great success stories. And *Rent*'s East Village Otherness does celebrate the "atmosphere" of an off-Broadway: there's a place for us. But this show also deserves full access to the media infrastructure, playing to as big a public as possible, not only because of its high quality but because it turned out to have wide appeal even on the international level.

So it can't be thought odd that a little country piece written and staged by its six performers (including Debra Monk) started on off off, moved to off, and thence to Broadway, where it got a Tony nomination as Best Musical. *Pump Boys and Dinettes* (1981) is an all but bookless piece, an amiable menu of songs for the two diner girls and the four gas-stop boys across the road. They accompany themselves, joke around, and utter a few rustic wisdoms.

This is Broadway? Perhaps the best way to define the off-Broadway musical is: something that David Merrick wouldn't have produced. That is, a show whose *apparent* potential for commercial success and glamorous or at least bourgeois esteem is limited. Isn't that what *Rent* achieved? But it's hard to imagine David Merrick producing *Rent*, even aside from their belonging to different eras.

Merrick certainly wouldn't have produced *A New Brain* (1998), either: William Finn, brain surgery, a screamy bag lady, all that . . . that real stuff. Given downstairs at Lincoln Center, *A New Brain* is based on an incident in Finn's life, when he was (falsely) diagnosed with a brain tumor. It's a comically ghoulish piece filled with comic or ghoulish people, including the protagonist's predatory employer (Chip Zien), host of a children's television show as Mr. Bungee; the protagonist's bossy mother (Penny Fuller); and that bag lady, the sort of role that Mary Testa unfortunately tends to find irresistible, as here. The protagonist himself, Malcolm Gets, got the chance to show off his piano playing; and Finn of course found ways to do what musicals have always done (in the lovely "Sailing," one

of the newest of love songs), while going where no musical has gone
before ("Sitting Becalmed in the Lee of Cuttyhunk," another sailing
number, this one set to a dance rhythm and accompanying an MRI
procedure).

A *New Brain* is one of Finn's best scores, and that's odd, because a defining trait of the off-Broadway musical when it *could* be defined is Little
Music: jingle melodies in do-re-mi harmony. One thinks of those adaptations of classic plays during the 1960s that sounded as if they had been
composed by a toy poodle. Finn is one of our most questing songwriters,
and he can fill even a small-scale piece like *A New Brain* with music too
interesting to be little. And note that *A New Brain*'s cast was typical
Lincoln Center first division, nothing like the old off-Broadway ragbag
troupe of losers, has-beens, and hat-check girls. Indeed, *A New Brain*
isn't off-Broadway in any of the traditional characteristics, except that
it isn't what David Merrick called prestigious. So what *is* this show?

Naturally, the flowering of influential theatre companies such as
Playwrights Horizons has created opportunities for the reinstitution of an
off-Broadway musical. The result, however, remains ambiguous of genre.
Do these companies seek out work of a certain kind, or do they confer
"certain kind" status on any work they present? If *Floyd Collins* or *Violet*
had been produced not at Playwrights Horizons but at, say, the Lucille
Lortel, would they have been less . . . horizoned?

The Public Theater, at least, has always been ready to transfer indicated productions in the *Chorus Line* manner—though of course
A Chorus Line was a Michael Bennett show, by its nature designed to
travel show biz in first class. Did Joe Papp have such hopes for the *La
Bohème* that he presented in 1984? David Spencer put the libretto into
singable colloquial English (Musetta's Waltz Song began with "What
good is fame?"), and Wilford Leach directed a varying quartet of leads
that mainly included Linda Ronstadt, Cass Morgan, David Carroll, and
Howard McGillin. It's not as perilous as it sounds, for all four had the
vocal range for Puccini and they were young and cute and most of them
could act. True, opera singing is more than simply fielding the notes.
With "O soave fanciulla" (or, in the Spencer version, "There are days
when I'm weary") taken down a half step, Ronstadt had no trouble
hitting the final high B. But her sound lacked body and her line was poor
in legato, which in this case could be translated as "confidence."

The more able Patti Cohenour and Caroline Peyton rotated with Ronstadt, so that the Mimì wasn't really a problem. What doomed this *Bohème* was the attempt to play it without a string section. There were no violins, just a cello and bass in a pit of twelve; at times it sounded like a concerto for xylophone, and the music was completely destroyed.

Only Broadway can afford Puccini. Of course it was Baz Luhrmann's 2002 production (with even more alternate leads than Papp had, and the four acts similarly broken into two) that persuasively put *La Bohème* forward on the non-operatic New York stage. Some seemed to find this a breakthrough for opera in general, as a highly dramatic rendering with the romantic roles cast with comely youth. But this view is the old "fat lady sings" calumny against opera, out of touch with the art of today. At that, Broadway itself hosted works from opera-world composers Benjamin Britten and Gian Carlo Menotti in the postwar years, and, as with Luhrmann's *Bohème*, audiences were treated to intently dramatic presentations featuring nice-looking singers. What these shows didn't have was a director fresh from a Hollywood triumph with another opera plot (that of *La Traviata*) also set in Paris, *Moulin Rouge*. The subject of Luhrmann's *La Bohème* was Opera but the atmosphere was Glamour, so it went over very well, if without commercial success.

Luhrmann's cast sang in Italian to English surtitles, a happy solution to the translation problem (though it must be said that the Public Theater cast sang with excellent diction). Luhrmann also offered his audience a fascinating exhibition of the original Act Two—the crowd scene— teeming with activity and detail that even the best opera-house *Bohèmes* never manage. Resetting the story in the 1950s, Luhrmann did have to finagle the plot a bit to explain why the women at the start of Puccini's third act endure a customs inspection: Paris in the 1830s, when the opera actually takes place, was a protected city, with *douaniers* at the ports of entry. But in the 1950s, Paris was an open city, so Luhrmann moved that act to the Belgian border, a far cry from Paris and a fiction in any case, because there are no cities right on the border between France and Belgium.

Is there simply no such thing as an off-Broadway musical any more? They are still, if nothing else, smaller than uptown shows. Stephen Sondheim's *Saturday Night* (2000) had in fact been written (to Julius J. Epstein's book) for Broadway, for production in the 1955–56 season. The producer, Lemuel Ayers, died while the show was picking up its financing, so the title went into limbo. However, that unbearably familiar little tale never explains why no one else wanted to give *Saturday Night* an airing. True, the piece, covering events in the lives of seven young men and the girls they hook up with on three successive Saturday nights in 1929 Brooklyn, was not an easy sell. It lacks the quirky diversions typical of the mid-fifties musical, and is atypically small-scale, apparently not even calling for a chorus. It's generically esoteric.

But 1955–56 was the season in which Cheryl Crawford, producer of *One Touch of Venus*, *Brigadoon*, and *Paint Your Wagon*, put on Marc Blitzstein's *Reuben Reuben*, one of the most esoteric items ever to close in Boston. If *Reuben Reuben* was dareable, why not the far more ingratiating *Saturday Night*? Besides, very little was going up that season—one minor revue, a *New Faces*, and only six book musicals, an unprecedented dry spell even if one of the six was *My Fair Lady*. So no one else wanted to give *Saturday Night* a try?

It's amusing to shop *Saturday Night*'s score for Sondheimisms. His musical style was still in formation, but the lyrics are already observing twisty wisdoms, and convention is simply missing. Another of the 1955–56 story shows, *Mr. Wonderful*, opened with "1617 Broadway," the chorus with solos that sets timeplace with bromides and ends with everyone in a line with his arms stretched out. *Saturday Night* opens with a piano riff, played by one of the boys as some of the others contemplate another dateless weekend. The show's title song, conversational and eternally nagged by that piano, the number seems to belong in the middle of the act, *after* the introductory stuff. It turns out that *Saturday Night* skips the introductory stuff, so its first number is suddenly *there*. It's not a character piece that inveigles us in with tough love, like "Ooh! My Feet!," from another 1955–56 show, *The Most Happy Fella*. Nor yet is it the Announcement of Theme that we get, after a short book scene, in "All Kinds of People," from 1955–56's *Pipe Dream*. No, *Saturday Night* starts where the story starts, with a fresh eagerness that belies its age. We note, too, that the ballad "So Many People" anticipates the mature Sondheim. It plays with one musical theme almost exclusively through the refrain— and so, in a way, does "I Could Have Danced All Night," again from that season. Yes. True. Still, one wonders if critics and public would have been ready for this show, especially because it does little to suggest the 1920s in the usual ways, beyond simply mentioning folks like Theda Bara and Johnny Mack Brown.

Lola (1982) is similarly a Broadway show seen on off-Broadway. *Saturday Night* was a victim of fate. *Lola*, I suspect, couldn't raise the money for a venue grander than the York Players. The subject is Lola Montez, the Irish adventuress whose picaresque takes one from the courts of Europe (especially Bavaria, where her influence over Ludwig I led to a coup d'état) through gold-rush California to Ethel Merman's future hometown of Astoria, Queens, where Lola died, in 1861. She apparently visited Australia, too, for the National Australian Musical, *Lola Montez* (1958), is set entirely in Ballarat. This version of the saga is sentimental and raucous, with numbers like "(Be my) Saturday Girl" and Lola's "Let Me Sing! Let Me Dance!"

The version that Claibe Richardson and Kenward Elmslie wrote for the York Players is sophisticated, reflective, and blessed with one of those brilliant scores that live their life on disc. Elmslie's book presents us with two Lolas in a kind of dream play in which the heroine's many men friends in her California episode help her revisit key events in her past. Lola today (Jane White), haunted by her younger self (Leigh Beery), enchants a young man (Bob Stillman) who has come from the bank to foreclose on her jewels. However, *Lola* is not a narrative work but rather a dramatic song cycle, imagistic and intellectually elaborate. Not small: tragic. Not cute: sexual. "Naked in the night" is the first line of the pleading "Beauty Secrets," and many of the songs take a risqué turn. "Hooked!" "The Palace of Pleasure." "Staying In." The Tarot-reading "Shuffle the Cards." "The Whores Behind the Doors." "Mirrors and Shadows." It all suggests a Hal Prince concept musical with a Cole Porter score, though the songs are of course extremely modern, jumping off the Richardson-Elmslie *Grass Harp* lyricism into something more knowing and sly.

Maybe the question is not what is off-Broadway but how can it best serve the public: and that would be by giving pieces such as *Lola* an airing. This at least can lead to a recording, and *Lola*'s claims three of our best singers, Judy Kaye, Christine Andreas, and David Carroll. As with Lola Montez herself, the show's past may be shady; but there is always more future. The work simply hasn't come into its inheritance yet.

Not long after the York Players gave *Lola*, the WPA Theatre tried out Alan Menken and Howard Ashman's *Little Shop of Horrors* (1982), which moved to the Orpheum Theatre for 2,209 performances. Here is another work to confound our taxonomy: small and offbeat, yes, but played with an uptown sarcasm. Genuinely offbeat off-Broadway—*Promenade*, again, is the prototype—inhabits its screwy cosmos. *Little Shop* goes there to comment on it, and like *Hairspray* is a highly mainstream package.

So its girls' backup trio now fills in with doo-wah and now holds firm opinions about the goings-on, even trying to shove the bad guy off the stage. And in the heroine's establishing song, "Somewhere That's Green," the authors laid their rock-and-roll fun aside for an intricately evolved theatre piece. It continues the spoof, as it must; yet it actually sympathizes with the character's helplessly putrid ideas of suburban happiness— Pine-Sol, frozen dinners, plastic seat covers. Ellen Greene gave it such an apt reading, as a cartoon with a soul, that she was carried over for the 1986 film.

Note, too, that the authors went on to influential work with the Disney people, and that, for the move to the Orpheum, the WPA took on partners David Geffen, Cameron Mackintosh, and the Shubert Organization. This is not off-Broadway any more; this is almost David Merrick. On top of all that, the 2003 revival held a Broadway house—all but saying that the work's fine polish overrules the rough workings of its Roger Corman origin as the grunge that was filmed in two days.

Of all the Wrong-Way Corrigans, landing in incorrect territory, the most ridiculous was *Annie Warbucks* (1993), because it should never have existed in any form. Another of those sequels, it sought to exploit the fond reception that Dorothy Loudon got for her Miss Hannigan in the 1977 original. Why not give her her own Hannigan vehicle, I say, and leave out the rest of the *Little Orphan Annie* crowd?

No. *Annie 2: Miss Hannigan's Revenge* (1990), written by the original *Annie* trio of Charles Strouse, Martin Charnin, and Thomas Meehan and bringing back some others of the original production entourage, was one of the classic train wrecks. Elaborately implausible and incoherent, it seemed even to forget that what made the original *Annie* so popular was its heart and happiness. *Annie 2* had neither. There were momentary pleasures, such as the first number, "1934," which managed to allude to seven of the original show's songs, and a big tap number called "Coney Island." One of Loudon's spots, "Beautiful," would be heard again as "Everybody Wants To Do a Musical," Christine Baranski's big solo in

Nick & Nora (1991). And "When You Smile" did revive some of the original *Annie*'s convivial spirit. Punjab and the Asp, included in the *Annie* movie only, suddenly joined the dramatis personae; and two songs added during the frantic D.C. tryout, "Changes" and "But You Go On," were worthy. "But You Go On" is almost the opposite of *Follies'* "I'm Still Here": downtrodden and secretly resentful where the Sondheim exults in the crazy banality of survival.

Annie 2 never made it out of D.C., but it resurfaced in 1990 at Goodspeed's smaller stage. The authors were still tinkering, and one has to ask why. Why this little fish-fry version of a show intended to be a Big Broadway Hit? Not least when the reason for it in the first place—Dorothy Loudon's Miss Hannigan—was now written out of the action. A line from *Dreamgirls* nudges us, because Harold Gray's tyke, in the Martin Charnin edition, was turning into "a second-rate diva who can't sustain"—and indeed, this insistent refusal to give up on a stupid idea reflected badly on the participants. Why didn't the authors of *Show Boat, Anything Goes,* and *Lady in the Dark* write sequels of those shows? Doesn't this obsession with pulling off a second success in the same place impeach the quality of the original success?

But show go on: to the Variety Arts Theatre, at Third Avenue just below Fourteenth Street. Are you happy now, Charnin? The *Annie Warbucks* there revealed was simply a Broadway show cut down, unable to project the glad gala that the very word "Broadway" means. At least *Goblin Market* is a "chamber" idea; and *Tallulah* really is a celebrity imitation extended for hours. These two *are* small. The original *Annie* was the last of the great old-fashioned musical-comedy smash hits with a nationally popular hit tune. To see its debris shunted to a little place downtown was not glad.

Further confusing the idea of an off-Broadway musical, *Annie Warbucks* had a Broadway cast—Harve Presnell and Raymond Thorne in their familiar roles of Daddy Warbucks (as replacement) and FDR, with Donna McKechnie, Harvey Evans, and a cute new kid, Kathryn Zaremba. There was one little zinger of a joke, in which a White House subaltern of some kind made an exit to the question "Who was that?" The reply was "John Nance Garner" (Roosevelt's first vice president).

Only five of the fifteen *Annie Warbucks* numbers had been heard in D.C. (One, "Above the Law," had had different lyrics as "You, You,

You!") This suggests the almost deranged nature of the crusade to get a new show out of an old one. If the sequel had had any integrity, would its authors have had to tear it apart and put it back together with such different contents? Ironically, like another Strouse sequel, *Bring Back Birdie*, *Annie Warbucks* would have been fine for amateur groups that had found fulfillment in the engendering title and wanted to extend the experience with its offspring. It just shouldn't have been offered to real-life theatregoers.

Trying to get a fix on the off-Broadway musical through its roots, we can at least discern some patterns, and even a throughline: off-Broadway hosts work that cannot be done on Broadway under prevailing conditions. That is, it isn't an alternative theatre. It is the *only* theatre for certain kinds of shows. And, remember, conditions change.

So three indisputably characterizing off-Broadway musicals of the early years would surely be the Theatre de Lys *Threepenny Opera* (1954), *Little Mary Sunshine* (1959), and *The Fantasticks* (1960): because the first was offbeat, the second a camp, and the third tiny. When conditions change, *The Threepenny Opera* can be welcomed uptown, at least until it opens.* And camp goes to Broadway, especially in *Urinetown*.

Tiny will never go to Broadway. But certain projects demand intimate production, for instance *My Life With Albertine* (2003), from a section of Proust. Once again, it was that all but central "alternative" place, Playwrights Horizons, that gave the premiere. With a score by Ricky Ian Gordon and Richard Nelson and book and direction by Nelson, *Albertine* followed Marcel's destructively impulsive courtship of the title character, their troubled union, and her sudden early death. Set designer Thomas Lynch provided a mini-proscenium not unlike the one later unveiled in the Bernadette Peters *Gypsy*. In the bigger show, its purpose was naturalistically functional, to frame real-life performance in vaudeville and burlesque. In *Albertine*, where the stage-within-the-stage represents the older Marcel's private theatre, it reflected the airy Proustian world with period depictions—a bathing scene by the beach, a Pre-Raphaelite dance in the green world—not meant for the "public" to view.

* In fact, the de Lys *Threepenny Opera* was a revival of a *Broadway* show, for the piece was first given in New York at a major house, the Empire (at Broadway and Fortieth Street, across from the old Met), in 1933. It failed then, as it did again on Broadway in 1989. More about that presently.

Albertine's action is Marcel's retrospective of his young love, as he considers with sorry wisdom the miscalculations of youth. If the script seemed at times verbose even with too little story, the score is an entrancing suite on life and love. It is not integrated in the usual sense. Rather, it explores hidden corners of the tale, now delving into the lover's fondly duplicitous language in "But What I Say," now surprising three young women in a children's chanting game in "Ferret Song," that dance in the wood mentioned above. Or the little private stage fills with the ensemble for what looks almost like an operetta's opening, for "Balbec-by-the-Sea," on the delights of the Brittany shore, also as above. But instead of lyrics on the usual vapid geography, we get a structure almost entirely musical, as the singers go over the title line so obsessively they might be making love to it. Even the central number, the older Marcel's keening "Song of Solitude," caresses its sorrows as if there were no other way to experience being human. Extremely sensual at all times, the score loves to tease the abusively possessive Marcel, luring Albertine into public view for the at first vaguely bisexual "I Need Me a Girl." This music-hall waltz, crowing with Sappho triumphant at its close, fairly crowds Marcel, as he in turn crowds Albertine in his numbers. He doesn't merely love her: he climbs inside her and feasts like a parasite devouring the host.

What music would suit this tale? Gordon finds a place somewhere between classical and Broadway—better, between Messager and Poulenc. Genre is overthrown in this score, not only in the song forms and their lyrics but in the music as well. There is no other score even slightly comparable.

Casting in a Proust musical especially is crucial, and luckily that twilit world of off-Broadway's *soliti ignoti* is over. Off-Broadway and Broadway share the talent pool today. The so-billed Narrator (Brent Carver) and the Albertine (Kelli O'Hara) had distinguished themselves in, respectively, *Kiss of the Spider Woman* and *Sweet Smell of Success*. But who would play the central role of young Marcel?

Apparently, it was felt that a Sondheim stylist was needed, perhaps because Ricky Ian Gordon had been thrown out of Sondheim's Turtle Bay manse for a well-meant but seemingly impertinent question about the failure of *Merrily We Roll Along*: so there was a critical historical link. And Chad Kimball had played Milky White in the 2002 revival of *Into the Woods*. Sondheim purists complained that Kimball had failed to score in, or even attempt, the other two major Sondheim cow roles, *Gypsy*'s Caroline and the touching bovine cameo during the finale of Hal Prince's 1973 Brooklyn *Candide*, the one with the death scene. (To be fair, though Sondheim joined the club of *Candide* lyricists for this edition, the words sung in the cow's episode are by Richard Wilbur.)

Kimball was engaged as Marcel nonetheless. But his portrayal failed to match Carver's; the Narrator seemed an older version of someone else. Nor did Kimball suit the French atmosphere that suffused the piece. *Albertine* is not only European but sophisticated, in the old sense of "not for kids," and Kimball's Marcel came off as callow amid the aroused and heady wit of the rest of the show.

The sophisticated musical is not, however, an off-Broadway form. *Little Mary Sunshine*'s burlesque is far more typical—though the trick is for the actors never to seem in on the joke: only the authors and audience are. Generally, when people write spoofs for off-Broadway, they are called "spoofs." When gay people write spoofs for off-Broadway, they are called "camp." But they aren't always camp precisely. Camp invariably turns on a derogation of its subject, and Rick Besoyan wrote *Little Mary Sunshine* to express his love and admiration of old musicals.

Comparably, the authors of *The IT Girl* (2001) used the plot of the Clara Bow silent film *It* to express their fondness for old styles, re-creating for the York Theatre Company the sixties off-Broadway musical that spends its time "doing" some antique genre in antique melody with a cast of, here, six, singing dense vocal harmony to make up for underpopulation with the sheer authority of their thirds and fourths.

It was Elinor Glyn, that professional sage of Hollywood folkways, who coined the term "it" by naming the only four beings that possessed it. One was a doorman at the Ambassador Hotel and another Rex the Wild Stallion. But the other two were Clara Bow and Antonio Moreno, so Paramount teamed their rising new star Bow and their former contractee Moreno to make the ultimate romantic comedy, because "it" was all about sex. At least, so it was generally thought. Glyn insisted that "it" was more like what we now call "charisma." But no one needed a hot little *logos* for charisma. Once Glyn launched her notion, it sailed on its own terms.

So *The IT Girl* is a time machine. With a book by Michael Small and BT McNicholl and a score by Paul McKibbins and McNicholl, the show takes us back to Cinderella stories, to the Prince Charming boss' son

(Jonathan Dokuchitz), the true-blue shopgirl (Jean Louisa Kelly), the jaunts to Coney Island, and syncopation creating the New Music. There is no attempt to parody old songs as in, say, *Curley McDimple* and *Dames at Sea*. Except for *The IT Girl's* first number, "Black and White World," the tunestack offers no overriding perceptions of the timeplace. There's an "It" number, of course. But the rest is simple storytelling: the Prince Charming's "Stand Straight and Tall," "What To Wear?," the ragtimey "Step Into Their Shoes," on having compassion for the other guy, and the climactic ballad, "You're the Best Thing That Ever Happened To Me." This isn't camp. To camp the sixties off-Broadway musical, one would have to spoof a spoof.

After the miniature *Albertine* and the pastiche of *The IT Girl*, we need only cite a solid bite of the offbeat, and that must be *Radiant Baby* (2003). The Public Theater produced this look at the life of Keith Haring, the fumbling, intense graffito artist who saw the whole world as his canvas. It was probably a mistake, in the number "Taggin'," to liken Haring's singular stick-figure visions to the stupid defacing of walls and subway cars with messes of paint. But the bulk of the show properly treated Haring's work as the invocations of an artist.

Radiant Baby was not, however, a show about art, as *Sunday in the Park With George* is. This piece was more like the bio of a gay man, and director George C. Wolfe paced it at top speed as Haring made the typical gay man's trek, from small-town Pennsylvania to no-rules Manhattan. A trio entitled "New York Makes Me (hard)" found Haring and—so the program billed them—Two Incredibly Hot and Sleazy New York Men all but copulating to Debra Barsha's music. Haring's New York was that of the 1980s, so his story ended as many a gay man's did, with the cast all in white for "(I want to) Stay." A gaggle of synthesizers locked Barsha in technodrone, as so often happens now, both on Broadway and off. Is everything going to sound like this from now on?

Perhaps *Radiant Baby's* best moment came not in the music but in Stuart Ross' book, when Haring—in Daniel Reichard's very impressive portrayal—came face-to-face with one of art's gods, Andy Warhol, played in drag by Julee Cruise. In this dreamlike episode (Warhol had died before the scene took place), Haring feverishly quizzes Warhol on the importance of the creation of art, while Warhol answers only on the importance of the creation of a fortune. Perhaps Cruise brought too much of the actor's intelligence to her Warhol, enlivening a character who, in life, deliberately faked a vacuous façade. Or maybe Wolfe wanted to emphasize that Warhol was blithely in control of his state of existence, to show how superbly driven Haring was in his.

Offbeat both in subject and execution, *Radiant Baby* joins the small and the spoofy as the surviving modes of the off-Broadway musical. And yet. Hasn't Broadway itself absorbed the offbeat? What's more offbeat than *Sunday in the Park With George*? Or *The Wild Party* or *Amour*? Off-Broadway isn't even that small any more—the prestige stages can be quite resourceful in physical production, as in *My Life With Albertine*.

Perhaps there really is no off-Broadway musical: no type. The cultural geography demarcated by the "off" was settled by a certain public at a certain time, and that public is dispersed because that time is over. The Broadways have merged, as have the talent pools and the rules of authorship that expected Rodgers and Hammerstein to define one place and Al Carmines the other. Once, off-Broadway was the forbidden planet, the angry inch. Now it's the it girl: it has everything.

THE ERA IN PICTURES:
A PHOTO ESSAY

Hugh Jackman has so dazzled as Peter Allen in *The Boy From Oz* that we thought you might like a glimpse of Allen himself, in *Legs Diamond*. It's New Year's Eve at Julie Wilson's speakeasy; Allen's at center, dancing with Brenda Braxton. We're seconds from the end of Act One, when a suspenseful plot twist in the Great Tradition will see Allen shot, apparently fatally. Act Two opens with his funeral, but he sits up in his coffin to explain that the bullet was deflected by a deck of cards in his vest pocket.

Photo by Martha Swope.

More *Legs Diamond*: Randall Edwards delivers a combination character song and floor number, "I Was Made For Champagne." Note the art deco in Willa Kim's costumes, not only in the girls' skyline headgear but the chorus boys' suits as well. By the bye, those who enjoy *The Boy From Oz* might want to give a thought to Nick Enright, the author of the show's original book, who died relatively young in 2003, too soon to see all his ambitions fulfilled.

Photo by Martha Swope.

From the high-concept look of *Legs Diamond*, we come to the main reason why *Merrily We Roll Along* failed in 1981: an ugly staging. This shot offers another first-act finale, but Jim Walton (center) is not about to be shot. No one's "about to" do anything in *Merrily* because of its reverse narrative chronology. In the famous story, Michael Bennett runs into Ron Field during previews and asks how the show's doing. "It's *still* backwards," says Field. Note a young Tonya Pinkins in the striped jersey left of center.

Photo by Martha Swope.

Now for a show that really looked like something, especially after the original staging team was fired in Boston and Tommy Tune took over: *My One and Only*. Tommy's at center, leading the boys in the kind of dancing that was rendered frivolous by dark shows like *A Doll's Life* and *Sunday in the Park With George*. *My One and Only* reminded Broadway of the Great Tradition's most happy invention, the silly crazy show, in which hoofing is not only permitted but compulsory. Its joy redeems us.

Photo by Kenn Duncan.

What honors the Great Tradition more than a salute to the forms of Florenz Ziegfeld? *The Will Rogers Follies*, subtitled "A Life in Revue," referred to rather than revived Ziegfeld. Here's Dee Hoty, Keith Carradine, and the Rogers kids in "Big Time," spinning the trademark Rogers lariat before the once ubiquitous "olio" drop. A staple of vaudeville and burlesque, the olio (meaning "hodgepodge" or "anthology") was a curtain decorated with ads for local businesses, but this is a show-biz olio, announcing coming acts. Fink's Mules call out to us behind Carradine's head.

Photo by Martha Swope.

More *Will Rogers Follies*: Pow-Wow the Indian Boy (Jerry Mitchell) and squaws pause for a rare contemplative moment in this dashing production. This reminds us that Rogers may have been the first nationally beloved show-biz figure who was part Indian, of Cherokee blood. Eddie Cantor brought this up near the end of a genuine Ziegfeld show, *Whoopee*, in 1928, adducing also to his argument for racial tolerance the heritage of Herbert Hoover's Vice-President, Charles Curtis, elected barely a month before *Whoopee* opened.

Photo by Martha Swope.

None of our typical Fun With Captions here: just views of the brilliant Bob Crowley's sets and costumes for *Aida*.

Photos by Joan Marcus.

The show that reinstated the Great Tradition most elementally was
Crazy For You: a planned revival of *Girl Crazy* that, early on, decided
instead to revive oldtime musical comedy in toto. Boy Meets Girl was
never so sheerly *rescued* as here. Robin Wagner's scenery for the town of
Deadrock has backed away from the playing area so that the uncertain
Jodi Benson and the confident Harry Groener can open up that Meeting
from a could-you-use-me? Flirtation to a shall-we-dance? Courtship; and
Boy Gets Girl. Stay tuned for a Ziegfeldian finale.

Photo by Joan Marcus.

8

It has happened in all the arts: a loss of the individualistic power of personality that came into American society at just about the time that show-biz celebrity did, when the movies and, to a lesser extent, recordings became acculturated. It was what Al Jolson and Bette Davis had. It was Bert Lahr but also Fred Astaire, the Barrymores and the Marx Brothers, Marilyn Miller and Marilyn Monroe. It explains why Greta Garbo had a career and Andrea Leeds didn't. It was eccentricity; and now it's gone.

In the musical, we see this most immediately in the closing out of the historic lines of Singing Stars, Dancing Stars, Comedy Stars. Most stars today are yearbook-formal versions of themselves, airbrushed, smoothed out, available to all. Stars used to delight with their gaga originality, dividing the public into those who "got" them and those exasperated by them.

Even the supporting talent has been growing thin. The Saucy Ingenue, such as Pat Stanley. The Belting Broad, such as Susan Johnson. Curmudgeon David Burns, Tumultuous Zany Charles Nelson Reilly, Craze-Voiced Hausfrau Jean Stapleton, Bedeviled Schnook Nathaniel Frey. The moment they appeared, the house filled with that Something— and which came first, a paucity of such performers or a lack of opportunities for their kind? Where would a David Burns or a Susan Johnson fit into a *Tommy* or *Beauty and the Beast* or *Jane Eyre*? Back in the 1920s, if a producer caught an act somewhere in the huge show-biz infrastructure that he thought his public might enjoy, he'd snap it up and put it into his next show.

Where? Anywhere.

Say Florenz Ziegfeld got a tip about a bubble-dance act in vaudeville. Yes, it was a genre: a cutie wearing the legal minimum in Grecian silk dances around with a big fake floating bubble. Ziegfeld likes the cutie, and her name—Beth Beri—will read well on the hoardings. Ziegfeld buys out Beri's vaudeville contract to put her in . . . well, his next show is *Kid Boots* (1923), an Eddie Cantor vehicle with a country-club setting. Beri can bubble-dance while the stagehands are changing sets. And when Beri comes delectably out in one with her bubble, the audience won't think, Who's this interfering stranger? They'll think, Great, a bubble dance.

This sort of thing is so not on Broadway any more that I can cite the last time I saw it: in 1981, when the Goodspeed revival of Bert Kalmar and Harry Ruby's *The Five O'Clock Girl* (1927) visited The Street. One character, played by Timothy Wallace, figured here and there in the plot but was really on hand to play the musical saw, in an interpolation pulled from *The Passing Show of 1921*, "My Sunny Tennessee." The song has nothing to do with *The Five O'Clock Girl*, or even with *The Passing Show of 1921*. The song is just another of those old Dixie Numbers, so Wallace laid claims to a southern birthplace, slipped into the vocal, then started playing his saw. Yes, it's an instrument, and it looks exactly like a saw. The audience laughed and clapped with pleasure at this esoteric turn, and it cheered Wallace's falsetto high B at the close.

But note the problem: only in one of those ancient musical comedies could Wallace's parlor trick be accommodated. At that, even the specialties that were organically built into old shows seem beyond today's performers. When Encores! got to *Babes in Arms* (1937) in 1999, director-choreographer Kathleen Marshall had to fill slots originally occupied by the Nicholas Brothers, black juvenile adepts of the hoofing arts who were among the masters of their time. Once, there were countless Nicholas imitators, and many an adolescent black duo profited by the engagements that the Nicholases were too busy to accept.

That age is so bygone that there may be no Nicholases left. Their *Babes in Arms* roles can't properly be cut, because the villain of the piece is a white racist, and without targets his villainy becomes an abstraction. Encores! could do no better than to hire two black kids of whom one could sing and the other could dance only in a minimal tap-class way. The Nicholases were amazing talents, but Encores! turned their number,

"All Dark People," into amateur night (besides renaming it "Light on Their Feet," expurgating its verse and dropping its chorus). This is not how shows like *Babes in Arms* worked in 1937: they wrote for self-starting talent then.

Now they write for portrayal. So *Nick & Nora* (1991), though based on work from the 1930s, will not use charmers and eccentrics and clowns in its large cast of principals. It will prepare roles for actors who will then *portray* charmers, eccentrics, and clowns.

But doesn't that distract us from the point of the enterprise, which is to revisit the fun and glamour of the movie series launched by MGM in 1934 using Dashiell Hammett's Nick and Nora Charles? Nick is a detective living on his rich wife's money (and drinking so constantly that modern critics never fail to remark on it). Nora is amused at Nick's raffish friends and the odd manners of the suspects in each of his murder cases: because what juiced up *The Thin Man* was its mating of the mystery genre with what in 1934 was just beginning to emerge as screwball comedy.

Can an actor lacking in idiosyncrasy play a screwball? Yes, but. Because it won't be as much fun that way. Faith Prince can do it, nonetheless. She got *Nick & Nora*'s most vital role, that of the murder victim, already dead when the show starts. But *yes*, vital, for Prince kept turning up in various suspects' contradictory flashback narrations. As Lorraine Bixby, Prince utilized a bargain-basement twang and the personal habits of someone just begging to be shot. Debra Monk, another actress who can affect lunacy (as in *Assassins*), was here a lethally prim society matron with an excellent establishing number—and note the pun—"People Get Hurt."

But the other suspects lacked the droll menace that the *Thin Man* series doted on. Then, too, while retaining the thirties setting, the show modernized the view somewhat, giving Lorraine a bisexual orientation and studying the Charles marriage as an organism in need of some restorative therapy. Nora could no longer be the blithely supplementary darling in her husband's escapades, but a detective herself. As songwriters Charles Strouse and Richard Maltby Jr. and book writer Arthur Laurents wrote it, *Nick & Nora* was not only a murder mystery but a pair of dueling investigations in which Nick (Barry Bostwick) and Nora (Joanna Gleason) competed for leads.

It sounds a bit like *Annie Get Your Gun*. But the sleuthing details proved tiresome, and the score was cut up into scenes, bits, and tags, so the largely agreeable music never landed. Late in Act One, when the title characters reviewed the clues in "May the Best Man Win" and the insinuating follow-up for the ensemble, "Detectiveland," the authors were scissoring their way through the possibilities with brilliance, but the public was not keen any more. They didn't care who killed Lorraine, and they didn't even care about the Charleses' marriage.

The production dropped well over four million dollars while staggering through nine weeks of previews, including two postponed openings and the expressed irritation of the New York City Department of Consumer Affairs that a work in progress was charging the ticket prices of a finished piece. Laurents, also directing, got advice on the mystery form from Anthony Shaffer (the author of *Sleuth*), on having a hit from Jerry Herman, and on the Higher Integration from Stephen Sondheim. But *Nick & Nora* ran a week.

It can't be because of the current lack of screwball performers, though, because *City of Angels* (1989), like *Nick & Nora* a mystery set in Hollywood, was a hit. Larry Gelbart's book made none of Laurents' errors. First, he spoofed the well-known format of Raymond Chandler's forties detective stories. (The title was originally *Death Is For Suckers*.) By contrast, the relatively humorless *Nick & Nora* used less a format than two famous characters cut off from their habitual format. Further, Gelbart gave us two sets of people to follow, a real-life screenwriter (Gregg Edelman) and his folk, and the screenwriter's invention, the Chandleresque seen-it-all detective (James Naughton) and *his* folk, who appear in black-and-white sets and costumes.

Eventually, the two worlds merged as Edelman and Naughton flew up on a camera crane over a crowd of folk, but to that point Gelbart had spun out an authentically Chandleresque plot, unrecountably complex.* What helped audiences through the maze was Cy Coleman and David Zippel's score, witty in both music and words as it created variations on themes familiar from pulp fiction—"What You Don't Know About

---

* Chandler himself couldn't always follow his own plotting. When Howard Hawks was filming *The Big Sleep* in 1944, he suddenly realized that neither he nor his three writers (who included William Faulkner) knew who killed a minor character, Charles Waldron's chauffeur. In those days, they had telegrams instead of e-mail, and Hawks cabled Chandler asking who the murderer was. Chandler answered in two words only: "NO IDEA."

Women"; double-meaning sexplay in "The Tennis Song"; an old standby with innovative instrumentation in what from now on may be called the Vindictive Mariachi Number, "All Ya Have To Do Is Wait"; the two leads' challenge number, "You're Nothing Without Me." *Nick & Nora's* score failed to guide the public through the plot's complications because it kept emphasizing the complications. *City of Angels'* score kept emphasizing the characters while a highly amusing book kept us genuinely curious.

The tone was always right: "Three million people in the City of Angels," ran one line, "easily half of them up to something they don't want the other half to know." Coleman's styling of the noise of L.A. started the show off with vocal scatting over a piano-driven running bass, the very music of Chandler: a search for meaning in the rich, criminal lifestyle, the atheist looking for God. *City of Angels* was one of those rare shows in which every element matched.

The cast was excellent but functional—and that's a compliment, because in the 1920s a Broadway cast couldn't have functioned in these parts. To produce a *Lady, Be Good!*, you gather specialists. There's the ukelele comic, the silly-billy Brit, the shyster, the lover boy, the duo-pianists in the pit, and, in the spotlight, the Astaires, a show in themselves. The specialists each do one thing well, and the Astaires do everything with that clarity of personal charm that creates the content of stardom. The music and dancing have to go well, but the story doesn't; and there isn't any acting in the modern sense. The ukelele comic doesn't "act." He plays the uke and comes on to the chorus girls. The lover boy doesn't "act." He fills out his coat.

Where would one put such people in a *Nick & Nora* or a *City of Angels*? On the other hand, *Victor/Victoria* (1995) could have used some specialists, for very little of it functioned except in a dreadfully derivative sense. Julie Andrews' first book show since *Camelot*, thirty-five years before, this was another staged movie that, like all the others, was physically unable to reproduce what had been filmed—the panic in the restaurant, for instance, out of which Blake Edwards' camera cuts away for a silent long shot of deadpan bedlam. If ever a performer could revive the charm content of the Astaires' Broadway, it is Julie Andrews—but in something worthy. The sole moment of pleasure in this pile of santorum was one moment when the musical did something the movie didn't. Very late in the evening, the bodyguard (Gregory Jbara) who we had assumed had a nonsinging part suddenly opened up and chirped out a lyric. A crypto-specialist.

Perhaps a classic comedy might empower nature's clowns. Pierre Carlet de Chamblain de Marivaux might seem a far-fetched source, but this very major French playwright—fourth in number of performances at the Comédie-Française, after Molière, Corneille, and Racine—incorporated some of the "improvisational" Italian style into his scripts. Only some: for even in the eighteenth century the improvising tended to be frozen before the premiere, as in television's *Saturday Night Live* sketches. Still, Marivaux's plays employ crazy clown parts.

When James Magruder translated Marivaux's *Le Triomphe de l'Amour* into English, the play had not been seen on Broadway in our language since one special matinée at the Criterion Theatre, in 1904.* The translator of that production, Martha Morton Conheim, had won a contest run by the magazine *The Theatre*, and this production was the result. But the play is no stranger to American stages, just those of Broadway. Magruder's version was used in the 1993–94 season by Baltimore's Center Stage and, in New York, by the Classic Stage Company (with a cast including Daniel Jenkins and *The Practice*'s Camryn Manheim). Another translation, by Paul Schmidt, was performed at the Guthrie Theater in Minneapolis. For that matter, *Le Triomphe de l'Amour* had made it to The Street once more before Magruder, in a 1958 visit to the Broadway Theatre by Jean Vilar's Théâtre National Populaire.

Now for *Triumph of Love*, the musical, which brought Marivaux back to The Street one block west of that 1904 performance, in 1997. The songs were mostly by Jeffrey Stock and Susan Birkenhead, to Magruder's book, and the cast of seven included three comics, Nancy Opel, Roger Bart, and Kevin Chamberlin. Of course, nowadays all actors in musicals

---

* The Criterion was the new name of the former Lyric Theatre, one of four auditoriums housed in Oscar Hammerstein's Olympia complex, on the east side of Broadway between Forty-fourth and Forty-fifth streets. Opened in 1895, when Times Square was still called Longacre Square, and when the theatre district was still located between Herald Square and Fortieth Street, the Olympia was the first playhouse to settle the area north of Forty-second Street. (The American, despite a front entrance on Forty-second Street, actually sat on the north side of Forty-first Street.) The Olympia was pulled down in 1935, but a movie theatre erected on the site was called the Criterion, and much more recently the Roundabout Theatre performed on the same terrain in what was called the Criterion Center, in perhaps the sole link between *Old* Old Broadway and today.

with comedy have to be at least part comics, even the romantic leads, here Susan Egan and Christopher Sieber, and the dramatic leads, Betty Buckley and F. Murray Abraham. The very idea of belting champ Buckley and the nonsinging Abraham playing opposite each other (as siblings) in a musical reminds us how far we've come from the theatre of Martha Morton Conheim, where specialists supported stars. There are no stars now of that old kind; or everyone's a star and show biz is one vast reality show: because *everyone* in the cast of *Triumph of Love* plays leads on The Street. This could not have been said of the twenty-six players in Martha Morton Conheim's *Triumph of Love*, when stars Maclyn Arbuckle, Carlotta Nillson, and Douglas J. Wood did not head an ensemble so much as subdue it.

Today, the ensemble *blends*. It's versatile, too. Nancy Opel, whose dry delivery of the jazzily frolicking "Have a Little Faith (in me)" was the show's best three minutes, turned dour and drastic for *Urinetown*. Buckley and Abraham played delicately here; we have also seen them aggressive, demanding. Bart and Chamberlin certainly gave eccentric performances, as the masks of comedy (in Bart's ecstatic grins) and tragedy (Chamberlin's tiny yet dejectedly rebellious shrugs). Still, no one *was* an eccentric; who is, anymore? Authors write personality quirks into text— lyricist Birkenhead is especially good at this, with such rhymes as "until I've kissed you" up against "you botanist, you"—and the actors then perform it.

Where does that leave *The Goodbye Girl* (1993), which surely needed a solid heroine opposite a flamboyant cutup? It got them; but because Bernadette Peters and Martin Short had a romance to play, Short was forced to compromise his mad *buffo* with some manly dignity. Short's television career, from *SCTV* to Jiminy Glick, is the work of genuine inspiration, but it doesn't go well into a Neil Simon book show with a Marvin Hamlisch and David Zippel score.

The musical in general lost much of the fun in the source, Herbert Ross' 1977 film. There the male star was Richard Dreyfuss, neither a clown nor a romantic hero. Dreyfuss brought some naturalism to Simon's screenplay, written to heroinize his then wife, Marsha Mason, with an "odd couple" romantic comedy. The film gets into odd places, as when Dreyfuss ends up leading an off-Broadway *Richard III* as a wildly flaming queen. The rehearsals with the earnestly peculiar director (Paul Benedict, an off-Broadway fixture himself) and the ghastly performance caught something seldom seen in a big Hollywood movie, the actor's nightmare. The sight of Dreyfuss taking Shakespeare to the Planet Mary won him the Oscar, but in the musical the sequence lost its zany terror. It became a number, "Richard Interred," and got smoothed into the overall texture.

Oddly, the London *Goodbye Girl*, in 1997, featured a largely new score, by Hamlisch with Don Black, as if something had gone wrong in Zippel's verses. What was wrong was the recasting of the movie's off-kilter guy, with his own strange allure, into a musical-comedy hero played by a nut with his hands tied behind him. London's lead, the amiable Gary Wilmot, took the piece even farther from its own truth.

It is not only that the self-creating talent of Old Broadway has few successors. No one thinks of the 1960s as a time of Old anything, yet its classic shows have trouble assembling correct casts in revival. A *How To Succeed in Business Without Really Trying* in 1995 could not even fill some supporting roles adequately, though much of the original 1961 support, including Bonnie Scott and Ruth Kobart, are not fabled in the remotest way.

The show's original star, Robert Morse, is still very much in the business; this didn't happen all that long ago. Yet the three so to say inventors of the entertainment, Frank Loesser, Abe Burrows, and Bob Fosse, could take for granted performers of a sort that must be as over as Lyda Roberti and Bobby Clark.

At least the new director, Des McAnuff, had the right star for today in Matthew Broderick. An actor who is also a comic, Broderick pulled out his lovable city-bumpkin figure, a match for the part. In 1961, Morse's costar was Rudy Vallee, who by then could claim three decades of popularity on radio, film, and disc. He had never made top stardom, and had been on standby status long enough to be a kind of familiar novelty. So his trick entrance was one of those audience-does-take-then-cheers moments: the aspiring yuppie accidentally runs down the boss in the office-building lobby. It was staged so that the spectators didn't see Vallee come in, only a stage hubbub followed by the chorus' gasps as the view cleared and we noted Vallee on one side of the floor and Morse on the other. Audience did take, then cheered.

It's not Ronn Carroll's fault that he hasn't had Vallee's odd career as Yale man, saxophone player, bandleader with megaphone, catch line

("Heigh-ho, everybody!"), and theme song ("The Vagabond Lover"), with a disastrously lifeless film debut in early talkies but persistent returns leading to a key role in a classic Preston Sturges comedy (*The Palm Beach Story*), and so on. That's a lot of there, and it was the audience's recognizing the man who had it that made the lobby accident such a telling moment.

McAnuff had none of this to work with in 1995, because our time doesn't look back on show biz as thirty years of fun, as the public did in 1961. Show biz has got complicated since then, troubling and divisive. It has lost the good-natured mischief that was once its central quality, lost the jobs that someone like Rudy Vallee could fill, even if—even *because*—he was so wooden in his feature-film debut, in *The Vagabond Lover*, that Marie Dressler ate him with a spoon and cigar-store Indians feared for their jobs.

At least McAnuff had Victoria Clark on hand. Her Smitty, a sidekick of sorts, took a more even tone than did Claudette Sutherland in 1961. But that *How To Succeed* was played as a cartoon. This one was overplayed, too, with some realistic foundation, which explains some actors apparently taking genuine leaks in the men's room scene, not to mention the chorus' jungle noises in "Coffee Break," indicative of drug deprivation.

After Broderick and Clark, the leads were miscast. Megan Mullally, Karen on *Will & Grace*, is one of the funniest comics on TV; what was she doing playing the *ingenue*? Lillias White's Miss Jones was completely wrong. This character is supposed to be a wall of frozen doom to everyone except the hero: he instantly melts her. It's an old show-biz wheeze, designed to convey the level of this con man's accomplishment. White played not doom but *serious*, so her kindness to Broderick was simply confusing.

These comedy musicals should be easy, because even when Virginia O'Brien vanishes, they still have funny people, don't they? Many of Hollywood's biggest hits today are comic vehicles. But *A Funny Thing Happened on the Way To the Forum* was much less funny in 1996 than originally. True, Nathan Lane knows of the Great Tradition and can draw on it at will. True as well, director Jerry Zaks thought of a spectacular new joke to add to an essentially respectful view of the text, while elaborating the one-set work with a second piece of scenery. When Lane's Pseudolus called, in "Comedy Tonight," for the raising of the curtain, it went up on Euripides at his grimmest. "Tragedy *tomorrow!*" cried Lane in rebuke, as the curtain came back down blushing.

All the same, the original *Forum* featured one-of-a-kind support to Zero Mostel, and Lane's was a variable crew. Once again, we have Ruth Kobart irreplaceable, as 1962's Domina. They've been casting the Shrewish Wife for thousands of years. Is this character suddenly out of our reach?

Maybe the comedy musical is too specialized, and the easiest show to revive is the one that used to be the easiest to write: a musical comedy with a tuneful score, lots of dancing and carousing, and a cast with charm. Roundabout brought back one of the best of these, *The Boys From Syracuse,* in 2002, directed by Scott Ellis and with an entirely new book by Nicky Silver, and everything was completely wrong. This may be Rodgers and Hart's most satisfying score, as melodious as *Babes in Arms* and as smart as *Pal Joey,* but richer in lyricism than either. However, in 2002 the music did not fare well; and of dancing there was little. This was originally a Balanchine show, remember—but for Roundabout, choreographer Rob Ashford supplied little more than a pas de deux for "This Can't Be Love" and some marching around now and again.

The cast was so small that leads Erin Dilly and Lauren Mitchell (the original Spider Woman, in the failed tryout) could be spotted in the opening crowd scene trying to swell the back row, looking anonymous in coolie hats. As for the new script, it had exactly three laughs. One was when Toni DiBuono was pushed into the orchestra pit. Another was when Chip Zien gazed into a sorcerer's crystal ball and saw Auntie Em. The third was when a scene for Dilly, Mitchell, and DiBuono ended when the first two exited but DiBuono started a plangent reprise of "Falling in Love With Love." The public stirred at this odd turn of events—the comic scamming a share in the big ballad? Suddenly, the other two, in the wings, shouted for her to get off the stage; and she did.

The original score, save one minor number, was wholly present, along with two interpolations for the courtesans, "You Took Advantage of Me" and "A Lady Must Live."* The additions at least supported this staging's

---

* A lyric in the second song was changed, from "If I looked like Aimee McPherson" to "If I had the face of Medusa." Is even Aimee Semple McPherson, the Pentecostal revivalist of the 1920s, now another of the Great American Joke Celebrities that no one living can place?

promotion of the original's courtesans and policemen into an ensemble integrated into the action—like, say, the lovesick maidens and Dragoon Guards in Gilbert and Sullivan's *Patience*. It's sensible. But too much of the revisal's expedients created rather than solved problems.

This suggests that the fault lay entirely behind the scenes. After all, Encores! had had a great success with the original *Boys From Syracuse* in 1997, not only because the original is better than remakes, but because Davis Gaines, Rebecca Luker, Malcolm Gets, Sarah Uriarte Berry, Debbie Gravitte, and Patrick Quinn landed those numbers, and because Michael McGrath and Mario Cantone jested correctly. Perhaps Roundabout is hiring people who just don't get it.

A 1989 *3 Penny Opera*—so billed—had a unique Not Get It problem: the audience. Kurt Weill and Bertolt Brecht's play with songs is one of the twentieth century's absolutely central works of theatre. It's known even beyond the borders of the theatregoing world, with a hit tune that became global wallpaper. It's political, yet it also claims a Warm and Fuzzy, from the Theatre de Lys revival that popularized off-Broadway in the 1950s. It has Lotte Lenya's ghost. Anyone with intellectual pretensions has to cite it now and again.

However, this confection of English ballad opera, Weimar cabaret, Brechtian kleptomania, Neue Sachlichkeit, and Communist propaganda is not the piece that most New York theatregoers expect when they buy their tickets. It's an enraged harangue interrupted by demented musical numbers; correctly performed, it doesn't make a lot of friends.

And this *3 Penny Opera* in 1989 was performed correctly, right down to the Brechtian half-curtain running across the stage. This was no Greenwich Village Lotte Lenya love-in, nor a Lincoln Center "Come slum with us, it's fright night" special. This was *Die Dreigroschenoper* as close as Broadway can get it: and its would-be admirers were appalled. They didn't like the half-curtain, the craziness, the politics, the people breaking into disagreeable songs for no reason. And what about that dingy dance of big bald Ethyl Eichelberger, grinning and bumping around to an echo of the Tango-Ballade while a set was changed? He looked like someone who would sauté a puppy for breakfast.

What did you people think Brecht and Weill had in mind, *Sail Away* with a half-curtain? In Michael Feingold's excellent translation and John Dexter's direction, this very misunderstood work came to light. We

Americans saw it, for once, as it was meant to be seen. Yes, there were a few alterations. The Eichelberger dance is not in the original 1928 score. Nevertheless, given the "translation" from anti-Nazi Berlin to democratic America, this was, authentically, the experience its authors intended us to have, and that's why it failed, at 65 performances.

There was one flaw, a large one, though the craft would probably have sunk in any case: each of the leads came from some different area of show biz, and they didn't play well together. That would seem to impeach Dexter's staging. But what can he do if his Macheath (Sting) is from rock, his Ballad Singer (Eichelberger) is from off-off, his Peachum (Alvin Epstein) is from Yale, his Mrs. Peachum (Georgia Brown) is from *Oliver!*, and his Polly (Nancy Ringham) is the understudy? Heigh-ho, everybody! The indisposed Polly, Maureen McGovern, eventually reclaimed her role, but this was no help, with Kim Criswell performing the restored "Lucy's Aria," an operatic spoof, without the opera muscle needed to flex the joke into hearing, and with the rest of the cast hailing from those dueling venues.

I can offer the reader a more engaged ensemble, in a sadly forgotten title. This is the sort of show that might have run perhaps half a season in the 1950s, moving on to summer stock and graceful retirement in the Samuel French catalogue: *Wind in the Willows* (1985), from Kenneth Grahame's children's classic. Jane Iredale's book and William Perry and Roger McGough's score followed Grahame's plot while deleting most of his nature rhapsody and the details of animal-world etiquette. The dancey overture suggested old-time musical comedy, with its noisy duets and trios and its charm songs. One of the latter, "I'd Be Attracted," sug- gested something Irving Berlin might have written in imitation of Bock and Harnick. But the inspiration was not consistently strong enough— the weasel villains utterly defeated the authors—and the subject matter was rather tender for Broadway.

On the other hand, *Wind in the Willows* marked Nathan Lane's first full-size lead in a musical, as the lordly yet maniacal Toad. Lane had not quite edged into the signature style that puts him on the short list with Bert Lahr and Phil Silvers; one felt that his Toad knew where to go but wasn't yet certain they'd let him in this age of rationalized comedy. Iredale did flatter Lane with a fine set of ancestors—"the great philoso- pher Platoad," "George Washingtoad," "the famous psychiatrist Sigmund

Toyd," and of course "Sweeney Toad." But anyone who knows Lane's voice will hear him in the punch line of this encounter with a furious Frenchman whose automobile Toad has just wrecked:

TOAD: Oh, my good man, I'm terribly sorry. I'm sure we can settle this in an amicable manner.
FRENCHMAN: (ferociously) *Gendarmes!*
TOAD: Maybe not.

As Grahame provides no possibility for a romance, the authors made Mole a woman, and while her relationship with Ratty was never overtly sensual, it was very deeply felt, and gave Vicki Lewis a chance to create something special. Those who know Lewis only from comic roles (such as *Damn Yankees'* reporter) have no idea what depth she brought to this born-yesterday creature who finds a mentor and source of love in the Rat. David Carroll also got one of his very best roles here, letting his radiant tenor bind the contradictory mix that is Ratty. We all know someone like this: generous yet thoughtless, able to identify every failing except his own, yet somehow indispensable. Ratty loves boating, as in Grahame—but travel? No, he's just "a lazy riverbank dreamer," he says. Then, one day, he gets an urge and simply abandons poor Mole.

From her opening of the show, leaping out of her den to pour her belt-with-soprano-extension voice into the rambunctious waltz "The World Is Waiting For Me," Lewis was wistful, expectant, and determined, an odd match for the complicatedly unsettled Rat. Similarly, Mole closed Act One alone, with the impassioned "The Day You Came Into My Life." It is a song of tragic realization: a solitary being, redeemed by friendship, must return to solitude. It made a heartrending intermission curtain, the kind one is eager to describe to friends. But the show didn't last a week.

Another trio of performances has been somewhat overlooked—as a unit, at least. But these three were in a smash: Heather Headley, Adam Pascal, and Sherie René Scott of *Aida* (2000). Uncle Scrooge McDuck opened his main vault to put this one on, because a kind of workshoppy tryout in Atlanta was arranged just to assess the show's qualities—no New York theatre had been booked at that point. This was just as well, for the Atlanta stand was built around the unit set of a working pyramid that could not be got to work. Performances were jammed, canceled. Even

Titanic finally got launched, but the Atlanta *Aida*, entitled *Elaborate Lives*, was junked and a new production team put together, with Robert Falls directing and Bob Crowley designing.

It's Disney!, the customary skeptics cried. It's cheesy pop (by Elton John and Tim Rice)! They don't complain about the cheesy pop of *Hairspray*. Moreover, *Aida* does something unusual in Opera on Broadway. Most readers will know of *Carmen Jones* (1943) and perhaps *My Darlin' Aida* (1952), using the operas' original music to new English lyrics and reset in America. There was as well *Once Over Lightly* (1942), *Il Barbiere di Siviglia* in English though still in Seville. However, this John-Rice *Aida* is a *new* work *based* on an opera plot, retelling for those with the knowledge a familiar story in unfamiliar ways. It is comparable to *Marie Christine*, except without LaChiusa's intricate musicality and realism of setting.

Aida is as basic and wild as a rock concert. It is worth remarking that while Headley and Scott were retained from Atlanta, the Radames, Hank Stratton, was replaced by Pascal to get more rock into the sound. Stratton is a fine singer, a Nashville tenor when he ventures into pop. But Radames' vocals call for the raucous inflection of a *Rent* alumnus such as Pascal, not someone who, like Stratton, would be ideal in Sondheim or LaChiusa. There were changes in text as well, more of emphasis than kind. The Ethiopian slave who plays confidant to Aida was switched from a wise-guy squirt into a nervy young man; and Scott's establishing song, "My Strongest Suit," grew from a dance around a clothes rack to an elaborate fashion show in Ancient Jejune.

Still, this is a piece built solidly upon a romantic triangle: besides the confidant and the three principals' fathers, there is nothing but chorus and décor. Highest honors go to Crowley for keeping the men from looking ridiculous, an all but inescapable snare in musicals set in years B.C. And the opera's tragic ending was adjusted with a conciliatory frame.

For those who know their Verdi, the first scene of this *Aida* is a marvelous shock: a modern-day Egyptian museum, with Pascal and Headley shy strangers very aware of each other. At stage left, in a case, is a model of a regal Egyptian woman, facing upstage. While Pascal and Headley distract us, the model—Scott, completing the all-important trio—turns to us to start the first number, "Every Story Is a Love Story." Later, as Aida and Radames expire in each other's arms, entombed alive, the lights fade only to come up on the by now forgotten museum. There at last the two lovers can find each other across the centuries as the story ends.

"Overlooked" may be the wrong word, considering that Headley won the Tony for her intense and finely shaded portrayal. But opinion makers are unhappy praising performers in works they don't approve of. Pascal was not much varied in his acting—the part entirely lacks nuance—but his singing matched Headley's ecstatic power. Scott had the odd role, a partly comic one, for one of the changes that book writers Linda Woolverton and the team of Robert Falls and David Henry Hwang rang upon Verdi was the expansion of Amneris from the Soprano's Bitter Rival into a kind of Nile Valley Girl who matures through her exposure to heroic tragedy. Scott can sing rock, as here, or post-Sondheim theatre music, as in Jason Robert Brown's *The Last 5 Years* (2002), and her comic style is based on delivering the funny lines as if they weren't. This is old show-biz thinking—Gracie Allen made her career on it; and George Abbott was at pains, with the young talent that he was always breaking in, to remind them not to "play" comedy. Just *say* comedy. It's a virtually lost art, and therefore all the more effective, as when slave Aida and princess Sherie establish a bond out of mutual understanding. Or has the princess been too open? And with a slave! "Keep it to yourself," she warns Aida:

AIDA: I promise. But now you have to promise me something.
AMNERIS: (scandalized) You're *audacious*! (but curious) What?

A pattern emerges: of a lack of the lovable zanies that musical comedy used to count on; and of a difficulty in justifying old shows with modern performance practice. *Wind in the Willows* and *Aida* prove that we are richest in serious singing actors. But every so often a truly odd piece can make use of what one might call zany singing actors, of the kind that could scarcely have existed even a generation ago. But then, *Urinetown* (2001) couldn't have existed a generation ago, even though its cast included John Cullum, who was playing lead on Broadway *two* generations ago, taking over Mordred in *Camelot* in May 1961.

First of all, that title! The narrative concept is worse: to avoid wasting water during a shortage, toilet flushing is limited by a fee, causing discomfort among the penniless class.* Let's let two of the characters explain it, in dialogue heard over choral humming during the opening number. Grim Officer Lockstock listens as naïve yet dubious Little Sally invokes "the drought":

> LITTLE SALLY: A shortage so awful that private toilets eventually become unthinkable. A premise so absurd that—
> OFFICER LOCKSTOCK: Whoa, whoa, whoa there, Little Sally, not all at once. . . . Nothing can kill a show like too much exposition.
> LITTLE SALLY: How about bad subject matter?

Aside from the pleasant lunacy of these characters' open acknowledgment that they're in a musical, we have the deft collaboration of two different comic styles. Little Sally (Spencer Kayden), a roller-skating street urchin with gigantic black braids and a teddy bear, is direct in her delivery. She quibbles with everything, as if anticipating the public's wariness, yet she's willing to crash into a wall and go boom when the show needs a laugh. She's almost in the story. Officer Lockstock (Jeff McCarthy), a cop whose uniform suggests the Nazi Schutzstaffel, plays the entire evening in quote marks. He's almost not in the theatre.

Then, too, the overture is a freak on Kurt Weill's German style; and dead people appear as visions while someone pumps an aerosol spray can (for "vision" effect); and the "Snuff That Girl" dance finds the cast in the rear stage-right corner looking exactly like a famous moment in *West Side Story*'s "Cool" number; and the curtain calls are followed by a square-dance hora.

Mark Hollmann and Greg Kotis wrote *Urinetown*'s score (Kotis alone wrote the book) to satirize no one genre of musical. The target is the musical itself—its idealism, its easy solutions to unresolvable problems, its liberal politics, its belief system made of music. John Cullum was the corporation president, so—as in any self-respecting E. Y. Harburg show—he's the bad guy. And he has a daughter (Jennifer Laura Thompson) who must be involved with the proletarian hero (Hunter Foster), in a reverse of the

---

* This is not only repellent but implausible. Why not set up communal troughs in remote areas with drainage rather than a sewer plan? But as we'll see, part of *Urinetown*'s glee is that, like old-time musical comedy, it's fun *because* it doesn't make sense.

twenties Cinderella show. Again we find a useful conflict of performing styles, as Cullum casually exhibited the absolute power of star charisma while the two kids worked like heck. Strange that a show presented on off-off (at the American Theatre of Actors) before its transfer to Henry Miller's Theatre should present such confidence. As director John Rando and choreographer John Carrafa could probably tell us, mixing styles is the easiest way to confuse one's audience. *Urinetown* goofs on clichés, but it turns straight for the love plot, then persuades the hero that he bears the healer's art. Uh-oh. He urges a crippled girl to throw off her leg brace, miming a kind of "You can walk, my sister!" as he turns to the public with an idiotic grin, not even bothering to check his handiwork as she of course crashes to the floor in the evening's biggest laugh. And then he dies.

One knows how easily *Urinetown* might have been unappreciated. Recommending it to friends, at least when it was new, was like recommending *Watership Down*. (Friends: "It's about *what?*") Little Sally foresees this in the finale:

LITTLE SALLY: I don't think too many people are going to come to see this musical, Officer Lockstock.

OFFICER LOCKSTOCK: . . . Don't you think people want to be told that their way of life is unsustainable?

LITTLE SALLY: That, and the title's awful.

But the piece caught on, partly because of Rando's superb production, but also because the writing is consistently excellent. The authors know how silly musicals used to be and how serious they are now: so they combined them. *Urinetown* is a silly show with a serious story, the very opposite of what some people think the musical has turned into: a serious show with a silly story.

"Can't we do a happy musical next time?" Little Sally asks Officer Lockstock. How about *The Producers* (2001)? This isn't just a happy musical, but one that, like *La Cage aux Folles*, returns us to the unreal reality where life is carefree, even crime, jail, Nazis. It's one of the many reasons why *Show Boat* is outstanding as a musical of 1927: those who suffer in *Show Boat* really suffer, and racism is not carefree.

But the typical twenties musical lives in the same alternate universe that Toon Town occupies in the movie *Who Framed Roger Rabbit*. Toons may get banged up, but on their own turf they're invulnerable and free of moral comprehension. So the cheating of investors is not really cheating; and jail is summer stock. At the end of *Chicago*, a realistic show performed as if in the alternate universe, we are supposed to be appalled that show biz enables two killers to strike the big time. At the end of *The Producers*, we delight in the two stars' grand old finale with hats and canes, because they didn't really cheat: they entertained.

Of course, this show uses a lot of outdated fixtures. There's the Extremely Blatant Opening Number, in which chorus people set the scene in a tone combining omniscient author and village gossip. This genre became popular in the 1950s, when the Rodgers and Hammerstein revolution made the insipid opening chorus too vague to live. The smart shows replaced them with a dance (e.g., *Guys and Dolls*, *West Side Story*), a book scene (*The King and I*), a curious solo (*Kismet*, *The Most Happy Fella*), or an intelligent chorus to kick in plot action or introduce characters in a provocative way (*Wonderful Town*, *Plain and Fancy*, *Li'l Abner*). *The Producers* places us at the start of this fifty-year-old revolution, in a primitive way, in "Opening Night," as two usherettes set it up and the spectators come out of the first (and last) performance of Max Bialystock's *Hamlet* musical, *Funny Boy*.

Max himself appears, in first-night cape and slouch hat. Who ever dressed like this, Morris Gest in 1915? *The Producers* takes place in 1959, yet already it is crazy, or let's say stylized, or maybe piquant: but not naturalistic. Indeed, the entire show will walk out of frame for a joke, as when Ulla, the Swedish secretary hired to assist the new office of Bialystock and Bloom, asks the worried Bloom, who has just moved away from her, "Vy Bloom go so far downstage right?" For all that, isn't *The Producers*, among other things, another of those offshoots of burlesque in which comics and broads form the content? The leads count five males and Ulla. All the rest is ensemble, and all six leads are comics, Ulla especially included.

That is: not actors who can utter humorous lines with accomplishment but giddy toons who usher us into their alternate universe. The musical used to be rich in them—but they were another item that Rodgers and Hammerstein put out of business. This is one reason why *The Producers* seemed not old-fashioned but refreshing. As the cliché tells, it was so old it was new.

That was not the case in the 1968 movie, despite its cult popularity. Why do people claim to "love" the movie? What do they love, its degrading view of humanity, in which everyone is an ugly stereotype? Do they love the revolting Zero Mostel as Max? The Leo Bloom of Gene Wilder, who seems like a rat having a bad day in a Skinner box?

Maybe the inherent "reality" of cinema cuts one off from that alternate universe. Otherwise, why were Nathan Lane and Matthew Broderick so charming in the same roles? Why is the movie's drag-queen director, played by Christopher Hewett, so unpleasant? Hewett makes one feel that he's just about to scream the place down. The musical's Gary Beach made one feel that he's about to pull taffy with Bernadette Peters.

But then, this material was reshaped for the musical; and music rounds out stereotypes. Anyway, the book that Mel Brooks and Thomas Meehan got out of Brooks' screenplay gives us types only in the supporting leads. Bialystock and Bloom are characters with Wanting Song weight, Bialystock's "The King of Broadway" and Bloom's "I Wanna Be a Producer." The latter even shows us how Bloom envisions show-biz success: chorus girls literally coming out of the woodwork of his accounting office.

It's sexy and spoofy but also clever, for it tells us how Bloom sees the world. We don't "see" anything along with Bialystock, because he's already in show biz. He knows what American success looks like. It is Bloom who must have the vision without which the plot has no enabler. It was always the musical's certain gift to express . . . well, the expressible. But with *style*. That's partly what Lane and Broderick have that Mostel and Wilder lack. In musical comedy, the crazier you are the more power you possess.

Lane's high-powered Max effects a crucial change in the character. In the film, Max is predatory; Lane is beleaguered. It's not that he tries to portray his fraud as the product of a cultured love of theatre, for this kind of show doesn't work that way. His fraud is a plot device, and what he loves is a good line. Unlike so many of the Golden Age comics, Lane has the singing voice for the score, and he can act. Phil Silvers could sing and act, too; and for Encores! Lane played Silvers' role in *Do Re Mi*, another show about a loser getting into legal trouble while trying to make it. But *Do Re Mi* is also a self-respecting show, with a Boy Meets Girl and small speaking roles for characters who bustle about doing sensible things. *The Producers* isn't sensible and there is no Boy Meets Girl.

True, there is a romantic liaison between Ulla (Cady Huffman) and Leo. He sings "That Face" about her, he runs off to Rio with her, and they marry. But "That Face" is an up tune, not a love song, and Leo comes back from Rio to Max, which is why these two are more effectively evoked by their first names. They aren't a producing firm. They're friends. The show's one ballad, "'Til Him," is a duet for Max and Leo. *Do Re Mi* had to apportion its comedy, know when not to joke. *The Producers* was billed as "the new Mel Brooks musical," and Mel Brooks does not know when not to joke. So, after Leo's chorus of "'Til Him," Max says, "I never realized . . . [the naïve spectator might expect a sentimental moo here] . . . You're a *good singer!*"

Broderick matched Lane with less a portrayal than a roguish parergon of a portrayal, something jumping off from it into other places. So while Lane played his character, Broderick did a kind of imitation of his character. This gave their relationship an arresting tension, of not only two different temperaments but two opposing styles. Yet the styles defined the difference in temperament, in effect creating a reality by other means.

To put it another way, it was not essential that Lane and Broderick encompass an honestly observed reading of a friendship between two men who have no reason to feel anything for each other. It was instead essential that Lane and Broderick convey to us the self-fulfillment of playing together in a smash hit that reminds the audience why the form we call "musical comedy" was once thought to contain the very spirit of American culture.

Of course, that spirit always needed its best wits and musicians to give the presentations their content; so what exactly does "Music and lyrics by Mel Brooks" mean? Yes, Brooks wrote spoof numbers for his films, for instance Madeline Kahn's Marlene Dietrich act, "I'm Tired," in *Blazing Saddles*. But this succession of double meanings is tuneless, a lyric to be declaimed in Sprechstimme. When *Blazing Saddles* needed a title song for the credits, it had to be singable, and we note that suddenly Brooks wrote only the lyrics, to the music of John Morris.

Glen Kelly, who got major billing on *The Producers*' poster on a line by himself in the next-to-closing spot just above director-choreographer Susan Stroman, was credited with "musical arrangements and supervision." In the CD notes, Brooks makes a point of thanking Kelly, "who took my rude, simple 32-bar songs and made them sound like glorious and memorable Broadway show tunes." What is Brooks saying? Did he map out a potential number with a set of lyrics and a starting melody for Kelly to complete? Did Brooks write, or at any rate hum, a whole refrain for Kelly to harmonize? Did Brooks compose the verses and trios, too?

However it was contrived, the score has to be credited with inventing music for a story that cannot be called latently musical. There are some plot numbers—"We Can Do It," "Where Did We Go Right?"—and the production number of crones on walkers, "Along Came Bialy." The up tune and ballad have been mentioned. There are character songs. Still, this is a score consisting almost entirely of comic numbers. This, too, roots *The Producers* in ancient musical comedy; numbers promoting laughter used to be daily bread on Broadway. They were often generical, however, like Alan Jay Lerner's sardonic patter on l'amour, or E. Y. Harburg's social observations; or list songs; or a woman's story ("Katie Went To Haiti," "The Hostess With the Mostes'"). *The Producers* sings with fresh ideas, partly because the *Springtime For Hitler* material is so unusual and partly because Mel Brooks apparently doesn't have a fixed idea of what a musical is. Surely only a neophyte would dream up the score's singular item, "Betrayed," a kind of pointillistic "Rose's Turn," in which the jailed Lane regurgitated bits of the entire show, book and score, to that point. With a sudden cry of "Intermission!," Lane went still for a few seconds, then exploded back into his geschrei.

Another reason that the score never seems thin and contrived is the production itself. Stroman's staging is so clever, and the ten-and-a-half-million-dollar budget so well spent, that one's guard goes down at once. Indeed, that opening sequence seems designed to worry us, with its perky usherettes and audience proceeding out of the scenic little playhouse to tell us what they thought. A number not unlike this one was dropped from *On the Town*'s second act because it was terrible. *The Producers'* opening is worse than terrible: it's basic and pleasantly direct in a time when all the best musicals are strange and furtive. *The Producers* says, This is how flops used to begin. And then Nathan Lane enters.

So the Chicago tryout was a smash, and Internet sites grew robust with reports on previews at the St. James, and the reviews were what everyone who was clued in had thoroughly expected. The only thing New York loves more than a big ugly bomb is a big fat hit, and *The New York Times* began to give the show blowjobs on an almost daily basis. About half a year into its run, tickets for the eleventh and twelfth rows of the center orchestra and the first three rows of the mezzanine went up to $480 each.* *The Producers* looked to be the hit of all time—till Lane and Broderick had to be replaced.

Henry Goodman, in Lane's place, was a disaster. An actor of Shakespearean power, he could not get into the alternate universe. Goodman's view of Max led him to literalize a character who is less an individual than a collection of show-biz legends, zany business, and Mel Brooks' worldview, something one plays but cannot act. Brad Oscar, Lane's understudy, took over with a capable performance in correct style. But he lacked Lane's groggy clarity, that rue of Cassandra in Troy. Broderick's successor, Steven Weber, brought a goofy honesty to a part that worked much better when Broderick simply wondered what goofy honesty might be like. Has anyone considered letting Mel Brooks play Max himself?

Replacing almost any first-division star during a run is a delicate matter. Who, for instance, could have replaced Ethel Merman in the original *Gypsy*? Certainly not Angela Lansbury, for the obvious reasons— age, fame, experience. But after *Mame* (1966), Lansbury in a *revival* of *Gypsy* seemed alluring, even if Lansbury would have to undergo Procrustean transformation to assume a role that was written around Merman. Tyne Daly, the next Rose on Broadway, was closer to Merman's, with more charm. And Bernadette Peters, in 2003, returned us to the Lansbury approach: not a natural-born Rose, Peters must formulate an entry *into* Rose, get hard, vehement, reckless.

To know what Rose is, one need only know what Ethel Merman was: a phallic woman with an utter lack of patience and a filthy mouth at a

---

* This is an ancient practice that had fallen out of use by the 1940s. Since the mid-nineteenth century, a gentlemen's agreement among producers had held the top ticket price to two dollars. However, the astonishing expansion of the theatre world around the turn of the century made progressive economic policies welcome. The two dollars top held in general, but flash hits could jump it to as much as six or seven dollars. Producer Charles Dillingham, an adherent of this philosophy, built the Globe (today the Lunt-Fontanne) Theatre with an extra-large orchestra specifically to accommodate big spenders for his series of extravaganzas (as the genre was called) with Fred Stone and David Montgomery, later with Stone by himself. By the 1920s, when the parvenu Celeb Society of drunks and toffs made a hobby of attending opening nights, producers accordingly jumped the top again for that night only. This climaxed at the premiere of *Up in Central Park* in 1945: those paying the premium attended the cast party at Tavern on the Green.

time when few men above the rank of trucker swore at all. There is no question that authors Jule Styne, Stephen Sondheim, and Arthur Laurents were writing Rose on Merman. Laurents especially had in mind the Merman tank-assault delivery in composing such lines as "They're real dreams and I'm gonna make 'em *come* real for my kids!" or *"Because I was born too soon and started too late, that's why!"*

In terms of job description, Merman was not an actress, though she maintained a confident delivery of banter and plot development alike. And she did extend herself on *Gypsy* particularly. Merman was a singer, exemplary in the days before miking, when projection rather than electronics filled the house. She had excellent diction, faultless pitch, and amazing stamina.

So building Rose around Merman made it not only a great role but one with demanding prerequisites. Roses need a splendid instrument but, like Merman, have to extend themselves in the portrayal. We ask of each applicant: What did she sing and when did she sing it?* And among Bernadette Peters' other qualifications, we do not find a genetically appropriate Rose horn.

At least Peters was working with director Sam Mendes, though from the first preview the Internet sizzled with reports of a slow-moving, empty-looking production. And Peters? These early "reviews" were divided. Some attached themselves to the notion that, as she was miscast, she could not satisfy. After all, Peters is Broadway's sweetheart—sister Josie Cohan in *George M!*, Ruby (Keeler) in (downtown's) *Dames At Sea*, Gelsomina in *La Strada*, Mabel Normand, the more complicated but still loving roles in *Sunday in the Park With George*, the plangent heroine of *Song & Dance*. Her Hildy in Ron Field's *On the Town* revival was richly feisty, however, and she had a lot of tough love to offer as the Witch in

---

* Betty Buckley, one of our great voices, played Rose at Paper Mill Playhouse in 1998. She invited Sondheim and Laurents out to scrutinize, as she needed their approval to play *Gypsy* in London, according to different versions of this story her life's dream or a passing whim. After the show, she asked what *Gypsy's* authors thought. Sondheim, ever the gent, said he'd seen better stagings of the show. Buckley absorbs this, then turns to Laurents. "You were execrable," he tells her. In the car going back to New York, Sondheim rebukes Laurents' brutality. "I'm eighty," says Laurents. "I can say whatever I please." Of course, Buckley wasn't execrable. Some of her actress' choices were questionable, such as the violent gum chewing in the penultimate book scene, in Gypsy's dressing room. Why the gum? Buckley's powerful singing was, as the *Michelin* puts it, "worth the detour." But Sondheim was right: we've all seen better stagings of this show.

Into the Woods. But then: was her unsatisfying Annie Oakley proof that Peters had limits?

Another group of preview critics attached themselves to the notion that Peters is an inherently interesting performer in any role, and cannot be less than wonderful in anything.

Stop! You're both right: Peters was miscast *and* giving the greatest performance of her career, her thespian imagination shooting her into warp speed to catch up to Rose while pulling the character itself into a new place in its history. For once, Rose's fragile interior could be glimpsed under the the cowcatcher ego defenses; and the voice was carefully placed, to overcome its lack of belt density. It was certainly a different Rose—but also a different Peters.

In the event, Mendes' staging turned out extremely well, very fast-moving and not at all empty. The changes of scene, conducted by the players themselves moving at top speed in half-darkness, excited the narrative tempo; and the aforementioned miniature proscenium was lowered for the onstage numbers, giving us a chance to follow events backstage at the same time. The two teenage girls, Tammy Blanchard and Kate Reinders, were for the first time directed to underline how differently they view their mother. Blanchard adored her and Reinders hated her. Before "If Momma Was Married," Reinders, with scornful disregard, lit up a cigarette as a kind of objective correlative of her anger. And there was one arresting novelty in the establishing of the burlesque house: a pair of baggy-pants comics way upstage, doing their act in pantomime when Rose Louise and Her Hollywood Blondes hit—so the variety cards at the sides of the stage warned us—"The Bottom."

Of the four Broadway Roses, Peters had the most to prove. Merman, again, *was* Rose. Lansbury was expected, Daly permitted, then encouraged. If Peters was doubted, it was not by Arthur Laurents. The Bernadette Rose was his idea, formulated when she appeared in an *Anyone Can Whistle* concert: with her dolly charm, she'll *show* how Rose gets away with it! All right, Peters hasn't the voice to make "Rose's Turn" a shattering musical climax. Yet she, more than anyone else, brought that "born too soon and started too late" into her staging of the number by taking on some of the stripper's attitudes—in the way she toyed with and finally threw off her sweater, or rolled her shoulders, or stalked the stage.

Best of all, Rose and Louise did not walk into the wings for their last exit, as always before, but went onto a little balcony leading to an exit door upstage. This gave Peters a chance to pause and survey the empty stage of her life. After all the conniving and pushing and trying to get her people to understand that if you *will* it enough you'll get there, Rose is exactly where she started: as a stage mother barred from the theatre.

And finally, she comprehended what she had been all along: to put it behind her and walk through that door into nothing.

Now, *that* is Gypsy.

9

FIVE SPECIAL SHOWS

Vicki Baum's play *Menschen im Hotel* follows the intersecting lives of four people in Berlin's Grand Hotel, each at a moment of life crisis. The fabulous ballerina is suddenly in decline. The dashing but penniless young baron is being forced into thievery. The business tycoon faces ruin. And his lowly clerk is terminally ill.

Within a span of thirty-six hours, each of the four has come through his crisis, to a big helping of joy or woe. The ballerina has rediscovered her life force. The clerk and a temp secretary hired by the tycoon are entraining for a fling in Paris. The tycoon has been arrested for murder. The baron is dead.

Baum named her characters as demonstratively as any Restoration dramatist. The ballerina is Grusinskaia ("Georgian"), underlining the glumly volatile temperament popularly associated with the folk of the Caucasus. The baron is Felix Von Gaigern, which reads, roughly, as "Blessed by the violin," a kenning for his Apollonian grace. Herr Preysing, the tycoon, is "Mr. Priceman"; the clerk, Herr Kringelein, is "Little Curly Head"; and the secretary is Flaemmchen, "Flame Baby."

A sensation of Broadway's 1930–31 season (at 459 performances) in an English adaptation by W. A. Drake, *Grand Hotel* was an MGM property before it opened, for the studio's genius, Irving Thalberg, wanted to use it to launch a new phenomenon of star bunching. Thus far, Hollywood movies were filmed with a single headliner or a couple, the other principals drawn from the journeyman ranks.

But what if?, Thalberg asked. What if MGM, studio of studios, were to give you not one or two helpings of the ambrosia but five helpings?

A banquet! The Barrymore brothers are the baron and the clerk and Wallace Beery is the tycoon—this is more charisma than any movie had had. Now, what if we throw in Joan Crawford as the secretary and Greta Garbo, star of stars, as the ballerina? This is more *movie* than any movie had had.

Grand Hotel would become a musical sooner or later, of course. But musicals were not based on movies in 1932, when Thalberg's *Grand Hotel* appeared, and by the time they were it was the Rodgers and Hammerstein era, when silent film was thought irretrievable and the early talkie simply dowdy.

So it took a quarter of a century till they got to the property, at that in vastly different form, as *At the Grand* (1958). Luther Davis' book moved the action to Rome and focused on the ballerina (now an opera singer) and the clerk (now a lowly employee at the hotel) as star roles for Joan Diener and Paul Muni. Robert Wright and George Forrest wrote the score, the director was Mr. Diener, Albert Marre, and the piece never made it to New York.

Comes now one of the oddest resuscitations in the musical's history. Victor Herbert's *Algeria* (1908) closed as a failure, underwent extensive revision, and reopened a year later as *The Rose of Algeria* with an entirely different cast and director. In modern times, *The Scarlet Pimpernel* (1997) pulled off a similar coup, albeit quickly reopening, with only certain cast changes. And a long forgotten out-of-town casualty, *Chu Chem* (1966), another Diener-Marre show, found its way to Broadway in a humble staging in 1989. But when else has a road dropout come to town not only a generation later but in a full-scale mounting put on by members of Broadway's leadership class in a concept production by Tommy Tune?

At that, the new *Grand Hotel* (1989) put all of Baum's original characters back into rotation. The ballerina was respelled Grushinskaya, and her servant, Suzanne, was now named after the actress who had played her on Broadway and for MGM, Raffaela Ottiano, though for some reason *her* last name, too, was altered, to Ottanio.

Peter Stone, unbilled, rewrote Davis' book, and Wright and Forrest's score was amplified by Maury Yeston, who had worked with Tune on *Nine*. Out of town in Boston, Tune felt he had his story and his staging but needed sharp, stinging new numbers in place of a few of those from 1958, and Wright and Forrest were slow workers. "A couplet a day," one of them cheerfully told Tune. Yeston was faster.

Actually, it's odd to think of one of our most progressive directors working with material from so long before. But Wright and Forrest were innovators. They aren't ever thought of as such, because they favored operetta, which, by the time they even started writing it, in *Song of Norway* (1944), was regarded as corny and demented. Still, their *Kismet* (1953) reinvented operetta as a form as sexy as it is romantic. They wrote for it Broadway's first truly erotic piece of music, "Rahadlakum"—an entirely original composition, by the way, in a score otherwise borrowed from Borodin.

Tune himself was making *Grand Hotel*'s score innovative, by cutting it up for dialogue inserts, cutting the dialogue up for music inserts, cutting up the dancing, the scene plot, the very show itself: to twist a fifties fourth-wall musical comedy into a modern concept piece. Yet Tune kept the musical-comedy elements alive. Most dark shows of this time are simply dark. *Grand Hotel* crazed and larked about from time to time, though its intermissionless two hours, so packed with schemes and confrontations, gave a sense that the action itself was under sentence of death. Vicki Baum's irony is that for all the disasters and triumphs that we witness, it is just another day in *Grand Hotel* (i.e., the great world stage). "People come, people go," snorts the Doctor, used in the movie and by Tune as a narrator. "Look at them! Living the high life! But time is running out!" At show's end, he adds, "Nothing ever happens."

A great deal happens: everyone trades destinies. The secretary is brought into Baum's fantastic symmetry of troubled souls with her own life crisis: she is unmarried, pregnant, and without the means to raise a child. Now each principal can exalt or destroy at least one of the others. The ballerina can redeem the baron's wastrel existence with her love just as he reanimates her self-belief. The tycoon kills both their futures, and his own, when he shoots the baron. But the baron, busiest of the five leads, rehabilitates the clerk as well with generosity. All that he gives is a flash of good manners and a stock tip. But the clerk has known so little kindness in life that the baron's welcome transfigures him. The baron's death is a sacrifice—for, as the clerk leaves for Paris with the secretary, he acts as if he has had a reprieve. He must have: because now he will protect the secretary, who, remember, is pregnant. New life blesses all around it.

If Tune's cast was challenging the film, the first set of Broadway players, in the 1930 production, hadn't a single star. The names of Eugenie

Leontovich (as Grusinskaia) and Henry Hull (the baron) alert only the connoisseur. The musical's baron, David Carroll, at last had a hit; his steely tenor and easy glamour reclaimed the character from John Barrymore's Garbo-besotted brooder, transforming him back into Vicki Baum's male in the wild cry of his youth and power. This is essential if we are to understand how intensely his intimacy affects the clerk (Michael Jeter). "Already I've met my first baron," he says when Carroll intercedes with impedient management to get Jeter a room, "and I'm only in the lobby!" This is merely bemused wonder. But when the baron ensures that the "room" is a suite fit for a noble, Jeter's response is heartfelt, awed by the generosity of a stranger: "Thank you. Thank you, my good friend, I thank you." His growing love for the wondrous being who befriends clerks creates a terrible event later, when Jeter can't find the wallet that holds his fortune. Reproached by Jeter's panic, Carroll hands the wallet over, reminding Jeter that he had given it to Carroll to hold.

But he hadn't. Jeter had dropped it, and his great friend the baron stole it and is now giving it up. Jeter accepts Carroll's absurd alibi, but he is absolutely crushed by the betrayal. How well Michael Jeter browsed the moment for its nuances of innocence pleading not to be made wise even as it learns.

Liliane Montevecchi played the ballerina, giving the show a taste of continental style, along with expertise in ballet. Karen Akers, promoted from Baum's maid to more of a personal assistant, was billed as the Confidante. More correctly, in her austerely tailored attire, Louise Brooks hairdo, and six-foot frame, Akers was the Lesbian Devoted To Madame. Indeed, the Confidante intends to spend her life's savings to provision their retirement. Like Maury Yeston a veteran of *Nine*, Akers is primarily known for cabaret. Yet she impressively embodied this curious individual, so self-effacing yet so *present*. One of her solos, "Villa on a Hill," sounds both controlling and intimidated. During the Boston tryout, it got the grand treatment, with the entire cast joining in on a second chorus; but Tune dropped that extra helping of music, determined to cut the gala to its throughlines, break the adventure down to its map.

Jane Krakowski enjoyed a wonderful look as the secretary, the perfect German flapper in a short red dress cut high above the knee and strapped red heels. From the first moments of her entrance, one seemed to recognize her. However, her original establishing song,

"Reflections-Flaemmchen," sung in the ladies' powder room to "the girl in the mirror," was too vaguely delineated. Wright and Forrest replaced it with "Flaemmchen." Infectiously rhythmic and chatty, it put over the character vividly, defining her as yet another would-be Hollywood vamp. But Flaemmchen is the only principal who owns nothing of material value, and Tune must have wanted to explore this. So Maury Yeston wrote the third number for this slot, "I Want To Go To Hollywood," a macabre Charleston with a middle section on the ugliness of indigence. This underscored a point only mildly made in earlier versions of the tale but voiced emphatically and repeatedly throughout the musical: society, especially that of Weimar Berlin, has but two conditions, poverty and liberty. Those in the former are little better than slaves of the latter, who are "nonchalantly table-hopping life away," to quote a line of "The Grand Waltz."

Like so many shows now, *Grand Hotel* made do with a unit set. This time the design was an eye-filler. Tony Walton placed the orchestra atop the playing area (as he had done for *Chicago*), creating the hotel out of four columns supporting the orchestra level, three glorious chandeliers, the revolving front door, and four rows of eight chairs each. The chairs were constantly moved to outline subsidiary playing areas—various principals' rooms, the hotel bar, the conference room, the roof—even, at one point, six locations simultaneously. For in recutting the show, so to say, Tune used a split-screen technique throughout. Akers even managed to traverse the front of the orchestra tier to look down on the tryst of ballerina and baron to sing "What You Need."

Of course, *Forbidden Broadway* found all this just so much spoof candy. *Grim Hotel* presented the ballerina, in a French accent thick enough to stuff into escargot shells, crying, "Raffaela, what kind of hotel *is* this? There are no walls in my room! Only a row of chairs!" To which Raffaela responded, "This is a concept hotel. It's German expressionistic. You have to imagine the walls."

The show itself began with a gentle cacophony of voices, the hotel switchboard operators. Then a vast doorman pushed the revolving door upstage and the Doctor (John Wylie) rushed out to take the compère's customary seat at stage right and shoot some morphine into his arm. (Later, his solo, "I Waltz Alone," punctuated plot action like the exhalations of the addict on his enchanted height.) "The Grand Parade," one of the new Yeston titles, brought the entire cast on as the Doctor rose to introduce the principals. Even after the number ended, the sequence seemed to continue as the orchestra struck up "The Grand Waltz" in Latin mode and began to underscore the dialogue. This musical presence would obtain through most of the book scenes, turning the direction—even simple entrances and exits—into choreography.

Thus, there wasn't all that much dancing per se—some strutting from two black American waiters (David Jackson, Danny Strayhorn) in the Moroccan Bar in "Maybe My Baby Loves Me"; a fox-trot for the ensemble in the Yellow Pavilion, where the clerk screams out a lifetime's frustration at the tycoon as the chorus, facing upstage, obliviously goes on fox-trotting; "We'll Take a Glass Together," Michael Jeter's comic tour de force as he, the baron, and the ensemble celebrate the clerk's stock plunder (that is, his promoted status in the Grand Hotel of life); and the bolero of the Gigolo (Pierre Dulaine) and the Countess (Yvonne Marceau). The Doctor introduces this with "And once again, those two sworn enemies, love and death, come face-to-face and join hands." For the baron has been shot, the story is all but over, and Tune has to climax both the story and movement that have combined to narrate *Grand Hotel*. The story rises to the baron's "Roses at the Station," another Yeston number, in which the hero's life passes before his eyes in the moment of death. The movement then takes over, "in the bedchamber of the Countess and the Gigolo," in something like a *danse apache* performed by Leni Riefenstahl and Mack the Knife.

How does one assess this extraordinary piece based on relatively ordinary material? And what if its revision had come along a few years after the failed 1958 tryout and not in 1989? Stephen Douglass as the baron, Jeanmaire as the ballerina, perhaps Nathaniel Frey as the clerk but surely Pat Stanley as the secretary: a conventional show, on the light side, with discrete musical structures and some giddy dance numbers, including a set-piece ballet for Jeanmaire. *At the Grand*: a new musical.

"State of the art" underrates how deftly Tune reinvented that historian's obsession, the integrated musical. From *Oklahoma!* on, the well-wrought show had a score that jumped into a dialogue scene to seize its characters' feelings; and dance to express what the book and songs couldn't. For example: the way "Goodnight, My Someone" floods Marian's thoughts during a piano lesson; or *Mame's* "Open a New

Window" dance. Still, dialogue, song, and dance were separate entities to a great extent.

Grand Hotel dissolves the borders between the entities. Songs seize each other. The whole show is a dance. The story is a set of throughlines developed concurrently. Form is thus so liberated that the work of the ambitious but conservative Wright and Forrest sits well next to the post-Sondheim investigations of Maury Yeston.

It should be said that Wright and Forrest bring elegance to the subject, as in the tangoing "Table With a View" or a cut twenties pastiche, "You Can't Cry On My Shoulder (and cry for somebody else)." Yeston wields a coiled-spring power, as in the frantic stream-of-consciousness raving in the aforementioned "Roses at the Station." Yet it was Wright and Forrest who wrote the biting love song "Crescendo," and Yeston who wrote its soaring replacement, "Love Can't Happen."

Further, Yeston's "At the Grand Hotel," for Michael Jeter, plays a simple melody over a subtly complex harmonic foundation. Performed at first in A Flat, the song freely uses added seconds and fourths in its chording, reaching a temporary resolution on the straightforward F^7 only after the wildly baroque F^9_{-5}. The effect twists the tune's innocence, as if mating elegance with dire need. Thus the two scores merge, toying with each other. And note as well that while Yeston's minor-key glowering beauty of a theme song, "The Grand Parade," frames the action in the modern manner, the last music heard, during the curtain calls, was "The Grand Waltz," Wright and Forrest's jubilant alternate theme song: "And life goes *on!*"

Running 1,077 performances—exactly as long as the original *Kiss Me, Kate* (1948)—*Grand Hotel* naturally sustained cast changes, though not as many as other titles that have lasted nearly two and a half years. Barons Brent Barrett, Rex Smith, and John Schneider romanced René Ceballos and, in her Broadway debut, Cyd Charisse. Chip Zien and Austin Pendleton were other clerks getting to know secretary Lynnette Perry. Anthony Franciosa played the Doctor on the national tour, and Leslie Caron headed the Berlin cast.

The shows touted in this chapter all have wonderful music—still the essential quality in a genre that, back in the First Age, cared only for the star comic and les girls. It took more than fifty years to institutionalize the lasting value of a good song: the standard. What absolutely does not last, of course, is everything else: the staging. This chapter is also about shows that are all but unrevivable because they were mounted so well when new that they'll never be as effective again. One of these stagings was of the concept kind, two were somewhat small-scale, and one was a monster that, throughout its New York tryout, kept not working because of technical problems.

This was *Titanic* (1997). At its first preview, director Richard Jones came out to warn the audience of potential glitches and announced also that some of the music was not yet orchestrated. More than once, the action stopped as a woman apologized to the public over the loudspeaker or asked the cast to vacate the stage. At a point in Act Two, the stage went blank while the pianist turned the Lunt-Fontanne Theatre into a piano bar over the chatting of well-wishers and Schadenfreude Künstlers. "Ladies and gentlemen," the announcer finally said, "we are seconds away from completing this change"—to a response of laughter and applause.

After that, however, the response turned into derision as the town gossips reveled in catastrophe. *Titanic* should not have begun performances with Stewart Laing's complex scene plot yet unregulated. But the public should not have confused these presumably physical drawbacks with flaws in Maury Yeston's score and Peter Stone's book. Perhaps everyone simply made the assumption that the stage cannot represent the events of April 10 to 15, 1912. How was *Titanic* to bring the ocean and liner into view? The assumption was based on the notion that *Titanic* was about a boat. No: it was about the people on it.

A very class-conscious piece, *Titanic* draws a cross section of the passengers as if analyzing Western society at a time when it was decisively moving from oligarchical monarchies to democratic republics. And, naturally, the *Titanic* identified its people literally by class—first, second, third. The last are the poor, immigrants in search of the future, embodied in "the three Kates" (Jennifer Piech, Theresa McCarthy, Erin Hill), Irishwomen full of youth and fun, but also in two of the staff, stoker Frederick Barrett (Brian d'Arcy James) and radioman Harold Bride (Martin Moran), who make a shy bond out of Moran's telegraphing a marriage proposal for James.

Second class concentrates on two couples, Charles Clarke (Don Stephenson) and Caroline Neville (Judith Blazer), and the Beanes, Edgar (Bill Buell) and Alice (Victoria Clark). Here, class both unites and divides, for the aristocratic Blazer has "lowered" herself in union with sportswriter Stephenson, while Clark's obsessive worship of her social "betters" destroys her marriage to Buell. In first class are the millionaires, though we mainly get to know only the nice ones, retail tycoon Isidor Straus (Larry Keith) and his wife, Ida (Alma Cuervo).

The huge list of characters—there were forty-three in the cast—meant that the authors had at times to paint in broad strokes. When the Strauses are out promenading in the moonlight, Mrs. Straus asks if Mr. Straus (so they call each other) can find the Big Dipper:

MR. STRAUS: The Big Dipper? I can't find my own stateroom.

Thus the point of view must glide like a camera among the decks and interiors, collecting group impressions (as in the Third Class' anthem of ambition, "Lady's Maid") but often dawdling to rate the details of an individual or two, as in the prologue, "In Every Age," a visionary solo by the ship's architect, Thomas Andrews (Michael Cerveris). The group and individual portraits are brilliantly combined in "The First Class Roster," a ship's officer's recital of the names and suites of the elect, with Clark's breathless commentary on their curricula vitae. Thus we are initiated into the sociopolitical panorama while making Clark's acquaintance, in her adulatory yet nicely sympathetic etchings.

There is as well plenty of massed choral singing, sometimes in bits, sometimes in shortish numbers, and, in particular, in "The Launching," an eighteen-minute sequence following the prologue: the loading, boarding, and embarkation. Again, the score moved from individuals to classes of people and, finally, to "Godspeed Titanic," with virtually the entire company in view as the ship sails out of Southampton harbor. In Jones' staging, this abundant climax snapped off an extra coup, as a little boy ran on clutching a toy boat and, in time with the last tonic chord, raised it triumphantly on high.

Many things made *Titanic* special. But surely that prologue of Cerveris calmly walking into view with his blueprints at stage right to sing in awe of the achievements of builders, followed by "The Launching," is the most sheerly musical opening of the era. A panoply of melodic styles— matching the social heterogeneity of the people who are singing—the series of numbers moves from wonder to confidence to excitement, culminating in the hymnlike majesty of "Godspeed Titanic." Is this show the last of the operettas, with its period décor, extremely romantic saga, and gigantic score? Bits of music pulse through the work like Leitmotiven— a *Titanic* theme, a disaster-at-sea theme, a Morse code theme. But this is above all an evening of bold gestures, density, sweep. Unlike pop opera, *Titanic* stands entirely within the Great Tradition as a kind of modern Jerome Kern or Richard Rodgers score. In fact, one of the cut numbers, Blazer and Stephenson's "I Give You My Hand," is a fox-trot ballad very comparable to what Kern and Rodgers wrote when feeling expansive. Retained, it might have been a highlight.

On the other hand, Yeston can set anything to music; anyone can write a ballad. *Titanic*'s score finds numbers in, for instance, the stoker's world-view as he toils in boiler room number six, in a steward's analysis of the din-ing habits of the luminaries in first class, even in "Dressed in Your Pyjamas in the Grand Salon," as these same grandees are roused after the collision. Symmetrically, the first act was the sailing and the second act the sinking— or, rather, the tilting, as the entire cumbersome set box suggested the grad-ual submerging of the bow below the water line in the raising of the stage-right section. This became so precarious that, as architect Cerveris envisioned the full extent of the catastrophe while alone in the first-class smoke room, the furniture—including a grand piano—came crashing past him. The most hair-raising moment in the tilting arrived early in the act, during "Dressed in Your Pyjamas," when the passengers angrily insisted that the ship must be in some minor difficulty, then cut off as, in the silence, a tea cart solemnly rolled from stage right to stage left all on its own. As if refusing to make the obvious deduction, the ensemble returned to its chorale of four different melodies, building to a worried defiance as, on the last note, the orchestra struck up the Morse code theme, a musical S.O.S.

Another special quality of *Titanic* lay in the consistency of the social theme. The notions of mankind glorifying itself in material achievement, of the helplessness of humans confronted by the policies of the natural world, and of the passing of an age of owners to one of voters all resonate throughout both book and score. Another unfortunate loss in the editing of so much music during previews was a number late in Act Two for four millionaires, "Behind Every Fortune." This quartet was developed over an ostinato suggestive of the moaning of a vast machine, the noise becom-ing ever more elaborate with each strophe. Facing imminent death, and citing Balzac's familiar line about great fortunes being created by crimes, the four confessed to sins against the public good and even mused on how hard it would be for their successors in malfeasance to get away with it. This is especially pertinent, for the sinking itself was a crime, compounded of arrogance and stupidity.

One thing the original production lacked was a sense of the sheer luxury of the first-class experience. But for Laing's costumes, the dining saloon of the upper crust didn't appear all that different from the third-class commissary. Perhaps yet more decoration is too much to ask of a scene plot that already has to show us the Southampton dock, the Titanic's bridge, upper promenade, crow's nest, radio room, and other spaces, and finally even the deck of the Carpathia that picked up the survivors. And there was one astonishing visual, at the very end of Act One. Having presented three levels of the ship at once just before the collision, Laing suddenly swept that stubborn monster of a set out of sight. The stage was miraculously empty but for a small model of the liner, moving into the stage-left wing space as orchestrator Jonathan Tunick sounded great apprehension in the pit. Smash! And curtain.

"A new musical" was the poster billing. But Titanic was really "A modern musical play with the customary extra helping of music and not a lot of humor." There were amusing moments here and there, and Victoria Clark's celebrity gazing was a recurring gag. One genuine ironic laugh came after the opening sequence, when a lone man came running out with his bags, screaming that he'll be "the laughingstock of Poughkeepsie." The Titanic's maiden voyage, and he missed it! "If that isn't the story," he wailed, "of my entire goddamn life!"

It may sound curious that the show's second half deals with the sinking, because, obviously, there is no way to show that, beyond the ever more perilous tilting of the floor. Again, however, Titanic is about the character relationships within the passenger list, the society, the civilization. So the action is occupied with, for instance, the shockingly graceful last champagne taken by the Strauses in their duet, "Still"; and the argument among the architect, the owner (David Garrison), and the captain (John Cunningham) about who is guilty of the disaster; and that dire scene in the smoke room, where the architect redraws his blueprints: as if the scratch of a pen could avert the deaths of 1,517 souls. Isn't that the moment that Titanic has been heading for from the first entrance, not coincidentally that of the architect? He thought that art and science could run the world, master nature, command God. Then that grand piano comes screaming past him as the *Titanic*'s stern reaches straight up to heaven and the ship breaks in half and dies.

But how to end it? At that first preview, some spoken lines from the ensemble led to a reprise of the first number, "In Every Age." Followed then some lines from a diver in 1985, "the first human being to lay eyes on her" in seventy-three years. To an orchestral peroration, one seemed to see modern-day oceanographic apparatus approaching the wreckage, but the effect was so feeble that some spectators giggled. The intent of the paradox—the great "floating city" reduced to a statistic of nature—was underlined in the very last note, a quietly jagged chord that had been flowing all the way through the score as if in warning.

An interesting idea: but it didn't play. By the premiere, all but the reprise of "In Every Age" had vanished. The survivors, bundled in blankets from the *Carpathia*, were joined by the dead to close with a last chorus of "Godspeed Titanic," still thrilling but now rhapsodically tragic as well. The little boy ran on to flourish his toy boat as before. And the curtain fell.

Though it lasted 804 performances and is currently enjoying productions overseas (in less elaborate décor), *Titanic* very nearly closed after almost all the critics failed to get it. As so often today, there was too much music for the dull ear to absorb. Worse, there were all those characters to keep track of, not to mention the show's portentous atmosphere. Stupid people like stupid things, which explains why musicals with a bit of story and songs about nothing much are greeted as if Cole Porter and the Gershwins were writing them for Ethel Merman and the Astaires.

Important Tony nominations, including Best Musical, allowed *Titanic* to go for a run; and it eventually took the award. But it is typical of modern theatregoing that some of our best shows are bound to challenge, with their dense blocks of music, their diffuse harmony, their ensemble commentary cutting in like knives. The stories lack familiar cues, and their characters are drawn from the freak show of life, tabloid crime shockers, Proust. The audience is as mystified and fidgety as the critics, which is one reason why the rest of this chapter praises flops.

It's easy to flop today: write *The Wild Party*. Michael John LaChiusa's version, one of two that appeared in the spring of 2000, is an adaptation that is also an original, because its source material, Joseph Moncure March's lengthy poem of 1928, presents no more than a gallery of off-kilter types very lightly delineated. Queenie and Burrs are vaudevil-lians with a high-stakes personal life and the most eclectic bunch of friends imaginable: the lesbian Madelaine True; the "ambisextrous" Jackie; Eddie the boxer and girl friend Mae; yet more gays in the piano-playing d'Armano brothers, who treat each other like miffed lovers; Dolores, "a singer without a voice"; two Jewish producers; Queenie's "red-headed running mate," Kate; Kate's escort, the classy, dev-astating Black. Queenie and Burrs throw a party for these and others, in a climate best summed up by a couplet that thrills in when Queenie and Black get it on:

Some love is fire: some love is rust:
But the fiercest, cleanest love is lust.

With LaChiusa and George C. Wolfe on book, LaChiusa on score, and Wolfe directing, *The Wild Party* came down as the most deranged evening in the musical's history. The piece is so brilliantly bizarre that despite the precise rivalry of Andrew Lippa's Manhattan Theatre Club version of the poem, the LaChiusa-Wolfe reading was a unique event.

For one thing, March's character sketches turned into fully developed studies of people living in the absolute freedom of a Jazz Age. Jazz, in the 1920s, meant music, but also sex, also race, also lies and showing off and cheating. LaChiusa's *Wild Party* helps itself to all this, but it also wants to expose the lies. LaChiusa employs a bit of twenties pastiche here and there to engender the timeplace, but he really intends his for the most part absolutely modern music to convey the erotic abandon that folks heard in jazz when it was new. The restless moving-bass lines and blats of brass chords suggestive of pelvic thrusts remind us why the disapprovers of the time wanted the music outlawed: it sounded like sin.

And this is truly a sinful show. Its single act flies by more or less in real time, as LaChiusa and Wolfe discuss their throughlines: on the twenties as the divide between old and new cultures; on American life as a form of show biz; on the easy dishonesty of styling oneself versus the difficult hon-esty of being oneself. Indeed, the 1920s was a cultural divide, as everything from before 1914 seemed to have changed—music, clothes, attitudes toward religion, morality, gender. A few of our greatest shows have con-sidered how deeply show biz has penetrated American life—*Show Boat*,

Follies, Chicago. Many of *The Wild Party*'s spoken lines underscore this perception, as when Dolores, eager to meet the producer pair, tells the helpful Burrs, "You play the overture and leave the rest of the score to me"; or when Queenie, on a scenic inset of a fire escape, looks out on the city and cries, "With so many lights, you can actually pretend one of them's shining on you!"

Of course, too much show biz is bound to foster dishonesty, or at least a "Let's pretend." Most of the show's characters are in the profession, or involved in a form of it (Eddie), or recently out of it (Mae). But Queenie and Burrs especially emphasize this; they make a living inventing themselves. Queenie is a dancer. Burrs, a clown in March, is in this version a blackface performer—the most dishonest niche in all of entertainment, with its overwrought makeup and implausibly robust dialect. In his black suit trimmed with white—shirt, gloves, lips—he is Al Jolson, who hid the egomaniac's bullying under the amiable black wise-guy portrayal. Queenie, too, has a makeup problem: but offstage, not on. She styles herself, "reads lines" instead of conversing, obsessively paints her face. Burrs is *too* honest offstage. He holds nothing back. Even violence. Even murder.

We first see these two doing their acts in a prologue in the form of a variety show, with billing cards at stage left. An opera-house curtain parts at the center and dimples up as the empty stage fills with men of various kinds, singing the first lines of March's poem. Ladies of burlesque in orange undies join them, in an atmosphere of such easy-come sex that we soon see the men running their hands over Queenie herself. She pulls off her top and stands thus before us, somewhat obscured by the lighting but blatantly available.

"Opening Act," the billing sign had read; now it changes to "Burrs the Clown," to present him in his Jolson kit. "A Comic Interlude" offers an actual set, a flat cartoon studio whose Murphy bed tumbles in with Queenie inside it. It's a typical morning, with lazy Queenie and impatient Burrs, played for over-the-top comedy till he grabs a shoe to beat her with and she holds him off at knifepoint. Then, as Burrs suggests they throw the titular party that night, director Wolfe organizes the all-important transition (in the "show-biz" throughline) from antique theatre mannerism to a naturalism that will "play" the 1920s for an audience at the millennium. The idea of a party interests Queenie, as we hear in a new movement from the orchestra—"Fast, hot, urgent" the score demands, for the ripples of dangerous sixteenth notes in both piano bass line and high-pitched woodwind skediddles.

The show itself is getting urgent now, the action serious and the music "real." Wolfe pulls off a last flourish of silly fun as Burrs and Queenie take their bows near the billing sign. Burrs is still in his morning T-shirt and shorts, but he has found a cane and straw boater somewhere, and he even milks our applause with one hand as if turning a dial. The two gain the wings as the sign reads "Olio Promenade by Guests." A show curtain drops and the men and women of the prologue reappear in costume as March's revelers to sing "(Don't lemme go) Dry." This prepares us for the appetitive, even predatory events to follow. The vaudeville is over and the wild party has begun.

Robin Wagner's set design smartly illustrated the show's jump in tone from the fanciful to the realistic when he revealed Queenie and Burrs' actual apartment. To avoid the monotony of unit set–itis, Wagner arranged much of it on a revolve, to take the eye from bedroom to kitchen, to view the living room from different angles. The cramped feeling, strangely, did not limit Joey McKneely's choreography, consisting of incidental bits or the characters' manic response to the jazz, the new fun in new times. If *La Cage aux Folles* represented a pleasantly reactionary aesthetic in the construction of musicals in a kind of integrated separation of parts—here the dance number, there the vocal, the joke, the plot points—*The Wild Party* is the innovative and difficult show, its elements raucously blended because its subject is raucous.

There is a dance number, "Black Bottom" (not, of course, the number of that title from the 1926 *Scandals*), and there are a few vocals sung as set pieces, such as Dolores' "When It Ends," performed before the house curtain in a reminiscence of the opening vaudeville sequence. Still, most of this two-hour one-act is an apparently effortless glide through the possibilities of composition, with dialogue scenes containing songs that contain dialogue. As the party guests slip into and drop out of alliances, the score seems to do the same. Thus, the d'Armano brothers' hot satire "Uptown" so captivates Burrs that he joins them in some black scatting; and when Black and Queenie put the jazz behind them in a duet on the fire escape, "People Like Us," the music eases into a powerfully diatonic *andante* in this evening of chromatic slitherings and itchy razzmadoodles.

The scatting was inevitable in a piece designed to mix the races as March had not done. In LaChiusa, not only the d'Armanos but Kate, Eddie, and Dolores are black, although—in that modern view of racial bigotry as something that occurred only in Dixie—the characters generally seem not to notice. Are they that liberated? In 1928? LaChiusa's version of the poem's characters is extreme overall, bringing everyone up to a heightened reality in which naturalism games with symbols. Jackie becomes a fluttery live wire of addictions. Dolores intensely seduces the producers. Kate is a sensualist of such appetite that her "Black Is a Moocher" sounds like sextalk in both words and music. "I like it like that," she moans.

It is a mark of greatness in a musical when every number lands. Not simply every number is tuneful, as in, say, *The Boys From Syracuse*. Not even every number exhilarates character, as in *My Fair Lady*. Rather: every number makes the experience so vivid that we are reminded that music theatre is our highest—our most complete—art. As befits a miscellany of people reacting to a transitional moment in American cultural history, no single *Wild Party* number overcrowds the others. This is a party of songs as of people, an exhibition of *objets trouvés*. Like Oscar Hammerstein, LaChiusa knows that characters express themselves in their own wording as well as their own music. So "Best Friend," the loving duel of Queenie and Kate, is a list song of bitchy parallel constructions comparable to a richly nuanced hug of welcome at the door. While introducing Kate and developing Queenie, the number links them in a unique bond. Or consider "More," Jackie's solo as he snuffles cocaine just before trying to rape Mae's younger sister. It's absolute Jackie, yet it sums up a part of the 1920s, the Jazz Age in its gimme-gimme avidity.

And what a cast! There were subtle performances, crazy performances, total performances. Mandy Patinkin and Toni Collette were Burrs and Queenie, he at his most astonishingly intense and she shivering in fear of having to give herself away. He stalked; she vogued. Of the guests, Marc Kudisch's Jackie was alarmingly brilliant; Nathan Lee Graham and Michael McElroy brought a wonderful period-but-now quality to their black-entertainers-at-the-white-party roles; and ageless Eartha Kitt made a regal Dolores. The definitive guest is Kudisch, because Jackie *is* the 1920s. But the most important guest is Kate, because she brings Black, the truth maker. Tonya Pinkins played a Kate of worldly grandeur, and

Yancey Arias was the ideal Black, an empty vessel of beauty that fills with humanity and love at the very sight of Queenie.

As Black's appearance at the party changes the story, the musical structure must change as well. One of the d'Armanos praises Kate's know-how in accessorizing: "The shoes and the dress and the man *all match!*" However, Black is more than a trophy date. He's the guy who replaces Burrs in Queenie's limited world, the sensitive gent as opposed to the hysterical performer: the honesty that Queenie must embrace in order to find redemption.

Director Wolfe made certain that Black got entrance insurance, almost freezing his company as this looker in his dynamite tuxedo crossed all the way from stage right to stage left. One of the d'Armanos scoped the audience with a "Who is *that* number?" look. It's comic but it's also major punctuation, a warning that something besides party is going to happen now. As the d'Armanos, at the piano, go into "Tabu," Black shows off his hustler skills to Queenie. She is skeptical, denigrating, alluring: her typical poses. But something in him touches something in her, and his "Taking Care of the Ladies" moves into a dance for the two of them. She's tickled. She waves a naughty-boy finger at him. Then—suddenly—it's serious motion, their eyes locked even in the turns, a lark become a mating ritual. But simple, basic: the thing that Queenie needs to learn how to become.

It marked the climax of *The Wild Party*'s dance element. Later came the climax of the vocal element, the aforementioned "People Like Us." It is not only a moment of serenity amid the jazzomania but a piece of intimate revelation, the pair taking each other's confession as all LaChiusa's energy now moves toward the climax of the thematic element. Back in his Al Jolson blackface—the dishonesty again—Burrs pulls a gun on Queenie, Black interferes and turns the gun on Black, it fires, Burrs dies . . . what then? March's poem gets it over with in two lines, for a neighbor has complained of the noise to the police, and now is when they arrive:

The door sprang open
And the cops rushed in.

The musical unfortunately rather evaporated at this point (without the cops), for its throughlines were intellectual rather than dramatic, and thus could not find a satisfying conclusion. However, this is not why the critics panned the piece. LaChiusa's musical hocus-pocus and his dazzling mixture of art and fuck in a musical are probably a generation ahead of most theatregoers. And how many today can keep up with, for instance, the quatrain in "Uptown" that cites Martha Graham, E. B. White, and Ethel Waters, then refers to Langston Hughes' pretending "he's one of Mrs. Astor's daughters"? Don't these summoning terms of the day speak only to the elite? And how many get the joke that Hughes was gay and given to putting on airs? When Cole Porter wrote something like this, audiences were better read than those of today. Better heard. *Informed.* This is one reason why so many new musicals are adaptations of movies that everybody has seen, some more than once. Thus, the stories won't be hard to follow, and the music will be simple, and the allusions will reach back no further than last Thursday.

One didn't have to know who Walter Winchell was to appreciate *Sweet Smell of Success* (2002). One needn't even have screened the 1957 film it was based on, from Ernest Lehman's short novel. And the invoked names of the day, 1952, were those that still have ring—Ike, Adlai Stevenson, Dorothy Kilgallen, the Actors Studio. There was one notable reference that many might have missed in a hand puppet called Bobo, a recollection of Ed Sullivan's recurring guest Topo Gigio, the "Italian mouse" (though he dates from later than 1952). And 1952 generally really was another country, as L. P. Hartley called the past. The chorus men were dressed in suits and hats, a fashion so bygone they seemed as exotic as Mamelukes.

Still, this show made itself comprehensible from the very first moment. "Someone started a rumor," ran the first lyric of Marvin Hamlisch and Craig Carnelia's score at some preliminary point in composition, launching a playful earful about how much fun it would be to sin up a scandal with someone hot. But the show isn't about love or sex. It's about power. So the curtain rose on designer Bob Crowley's 3-D backdrop of New York, a semicircle of skyscrapers looking down on the acting space. Around the edges stood the chorus, tensely watching columnist J. J. Hunsecker (John Lithgow) dictate the next day's column to his secretary (Joanna Glushak). After a few items, the music began, and now the lyric quoted above, reconstituted, ran, "Gotta get in the column." For here was another musical about America's show-biz culture. And in show biz, you're on the marquee or you're dead. Or worse: unknown.

"How did they build *Titanic?*" was a fair question in the second of our special shows; another would be How did they make a musical out of *Sweet Smell of Success,* the bleakest and darkest of films, Burt Lancaster's crusade against Walter Winchell, portraying the columnist as a megalomaniac nursing plans to run for president? Critic David Thomson calls Hunsecker "the first heartless titan of corrupt organisation in American films." That is, not the tycoon villain that Edward Arnold embodied in Frank Capra's films, but something vast and insidious, "a foreshadowing of Watergates." On the other hand, Lancaster was one of the many Hollywood stars who saw fascism everywhere in America but nowhere in Russia, Cuba, North Vietnam, Cambodia. Stalin killed more than twenty million human beings. How many did Walter Winchell kill?

But I digress with pleasantry. One of the fascinations in "singing" the *Sweet Smell of Success* movie is its implausible naturalism, so late-night Manhattan of the *Guys and Dolls* era yet so fantastical. Think of its almost unbearably flawless vernacular ear (in the screenplay by Lehman and Clifford Odets), countered by Hunsecker's own idiom, Winchellisms that Winchell himself never uttered, such as "Conjugate me a verb, Sidney: to promise." Or think of the way the film's director, Alexander Mackendrick, contrasts the elaborate etiquette of the well-lit social spaces (Winchell's "office" was the Stork Club) with the ugly battlefield of the streets.

One way to make this movie into a musical was to explain it: for the film seems to take place in a fast-moving hell where everyone already knows the other people. How about Boy Meets Girl? Or even Sidney meets J.J.? Actually, book writer John Guare assumed that Boy (Jack Noseworthy), a jazz pianist, has recently met Girl (Kelli O'Hara), J.J.'s halfsister. This gradually comes into view in a scene establishing the two as well as giving us a taste of how press agent Sidney Falco (Brian d'Arcy James) operates.

We are in an empty club, the boy at the piano and the girl listening. The owner is one of Sidney's clients, but the hopelessly unconnected Sidney can do nothing for him. Still, he fakes a buddy-buddy call to J.J., tries to sign the boy and seduce the girl. Sidney is all but invisible to them, as the boy goes into "I Cannot Hear the City," a ravishing ballad written to recall the best of what might have been heard in a fifties jazz club. But more: it's a love song, his, to her. So Boy doesn't Meet Girl. *We* meet them, even as we watch Sidney work his hustle. Then J.J. drops in, on his all-night rounds, like a vampire; he takes a fancy to Sidney. Even: he likes him. Even: he *dates* him, in the next sequence, set to the dashing and slightly worried "Welcome To the Night." Already, the musical is giving us more people than the film does, not in population but in individuality, and we see why the authors saw a musical in such unlikely territory. Brilliant as the film is, after the musical it will always be missing something that it thought it had: reality.

It's the score that does it. With the scatting showpiece "One Track Mind" and the importunate "Don't Know Where You Leave Off," the boy is re-created as a passionate talent and lover, far more of a threat to J.J.'s domination of his sister than Martin Milner gets a chance to be in the film. Kelli O'Hara's sister is life-embracing, where the movie's Susan Harrison is made into a stick figure. Lancaster, taking his energy level down to a kind of chilling boil, does present an effective metaphor for evil power. But the musical's writers gave John Lithgow the opportunity to play the character, not the symbol. Lithgow's J.J. was mixed of the ebullient and the vindictive, the appreciative and the controlling. Rather late in the show, we learned how murderous he is; but by then he had taught us that even violence has feelings.

Least changed from the film was Sidney. The fixing and flattering that Tony Curtis performs so nimbly in the part somewhat defeated his musical potential. Sidney is great in the staccato of wangling and lying; but a Hero's Wanting Song, "At The Fountain," seems to glorify a creep. The melody is ecstatic, even noble.

Another way to make the movie a musical was to spin its late-night Manhattan into a sound: jazzy in the performing spots and jaggedly nervous in the plot numbers, with dazzling love music for the romantic pair and a lot of period gossip-column jargon in the lyrics. The chorus is used in concept-show style, now as people in the story and now as warnings and coaxings in Sidney's brain.

They have a song of their own, "Dirt," which arrives rather late in the proceedings for a piece with opening-number feel to it. But the bulk of the score is character numbers for the principals, even when they are performing—the boy in his club spots and J.J. on a telethon, when, after a sketch with the aforementioned mouse, he dons red-and-white checked jacket and straw boater for "Don't Look Now." The title is a pun, for J.J.'s cheap magic tricks* share the stage with an assault on the boy by crooked cops. We watch the boy's comatose form roll out of sight as the telethon dancers obliviously work around him in that concept-show geography that can show us several places at once.

Nicholas Hytner directed, expertly ringing in stage furniture when necessary—the hot club of choice to humiliate the aforementioned dead club, J.J.'s penthouse but then Sidney's mean little lair. Still, the main playing space was the open stage and the way the night moved through it, arranging and menacing. It was a classy production, one that saw through what "glamour" meant to J.J.'s readers yet rose above it with the glamour of what the word "Broadway" still means to those who labor there. Hytner had a lot to work with; the score is so rich that the lovely "That's How I Say Goodbye" (for the boy and girl) could be dropped as extraneous.

Perhaps you enjoy my personal notes, boys and girls; here's another. The second time I saw *Sweet Smell of Success*, I was in a box overlooking stage left. The scene in J.J.'s apartment makes several points of plot and character not touched upon in the film. The most important of them reveals how tenderly he regards his sister. In the movie, we infer that J.J. nurtures incestuous fantasies about her—but only dimly, because very little sensuality can be discerned in Lancaster's relentless imitation of a bank vault. Does he even have girl friends? Winchell did. John Lithgow's J.J. loves the girl as a father. Yes, he's too controlling: but he *loves*. "For Susan," a gentle waltz sung for Sidney's benefit, brings out a box of souvenirs that, to Lithgow, show how special she is. Lovingly, J.J. presents Sidney with the proofs. Bogie, FDR, and Groucho are among her admirers—and because I was sitting right overhead, I could see, as almost nobody else was able to, that every testimonial that Lithgow adduced to his reverie was fairly embodied in that box. At a reference to sheet music autographed "by Kern and Berlin," Lithgow plucked from the box a *Show Boat* song sheet in exactly the physical form that it would have had if autographed by Kern before his death, in 1945. This production troubled thus to authenticate its props even though only a very few of us would

---

* The musical supplies a vaudeville background for J.J., which brings him closer to the real-life Winchell than anything in the film. Winchell got his start in vaudeville; it's hard to imagine Lancaster's ironclad zombie of a J.J. as having started in anything as lively as show biz.

know. This is not only integrity; this is intelligence in an age so stupid it thinks "impact" is a verb.

Unlike *Grand Hotel* and *Titanic*, but like *The Wild Party* and *Sweet Smell of Success*, our last special show was a failure. However, the previous two titles at least ran a few months. *Amour* (2002) lasted two weeks. This is a historically instructive show even so in its return to first principles, as a modern version of what Jacques Offenbach was doing when he invented musical comedy in the 1850s and '60s: not in his format but in his spirit.

Based on Marcel Aymé's short story "Le Passe-Muraille" (roughly, "He Walks Through Walls"), *Amour* was first given in Paris in 1996 under Aymé's original title. His tale proposes a man suddenly given the power to get into any place he fancies. Defying the authorities, he becomes a popular hero, then loses his power while he's moving through a wall and must live out his life thus immured.

Even the French, for whom the story is a classic, are not sure how to take it. Is it droll or tragic? Political? Spiritual? As adapted by composer Michel Legrand to the words of Didier van Cauwelaert, the musical became as uncategorizable as the original, daffy but touching, deep yet light, chic, captious, sour, grand, facetious, witty, charming. In short: French. As long as one can admire French culture while loathing the French themselves, *Amour* stood out as a delightful oddity, the sole time that anything with a genuine French savor appeared on Broadway during the Fourth Age or after.

Of course, there had been evenings of French cabaret now and again, and Robert Dhéry's authentically French variety shows *La Plume de Ma Tante* (1958) and *La Grosse Valise* (1965). But of story musicals we have seen only *Irma la Douce* (1960), at that in a thoroughly Anglicized edition. One reason why Broadway has hosted so few French story musicals is that the French don't see many either. French musical comedy all but died out after a heyday between the world wars. Most French composers prefer variations on opera or operetta or the contentless spectacles favored at the Mogador and Châtelet.

But here is the very inventor of pop opera, Michel Legrand, writing in a tidy, playful little sound. *Amour* is through-sung, but it abjures the intrusive Big Tune and just-sing-everything conversations that he introduced in *Les Parapluies de Cherbourg*. Instead, *Amour* is comprised of separate and clearly structured numbers. Melodies may be repeated, but there is no

"I Will Wait For You" smash and grab. The tuneful score is orchestrated (by the composer) for only three players. The New York pit added two others, bringing woodwinds and percussion novelties into the texture. Jeremy Sams translated the text. Scott Pask designed a unit set, a square in Montmartre that managed to change into all sorts of things, such as a bedroom open to a star-filled black heaven. And James Lapine directed as Aymé had narrated way back at the start of it all: simply and clearly.

Why did *Amour* run only two weeks, then? We've heard this before: too special.* Special isn't a genre anymore, as it was when Rodgers and Hammerstein originated the idea that each show should be unlike all your other shows, or anyone else's. Today, dance pieces are a genre. Live movies are a genre. Revivals are a genre. Even junk, as we'll see in the next chapter, is a genre. And audiences seem less adventurous than they used to be. They don't attend theatre; they attend genre.

Set in 1950, *Amour* faithfully followed Aymé's parable while filling it out with incidental figures—officials, office workers, people of the street. Dusoleil (Malcolm Gets) becomes the hero of Montmartre for his Robin Hood thievery. The newsboy (Christopher Fitzgerald), the whore (Norma Mae Lyng), and the strolling painter (Norm Lewis) personify the little people who benefit from these exploits. Dusoleil is worshiped as Passepartout ("Goeverywhere"). Yet he is a little person himself, "the office nerd" who cultivates a passion for the beautiful young wife (Melissa Errico) of a corrupt prosecutor (Lewis Cleale).

It's almost a daffy miniature of another show set in Paris, *The Phantom of the Opera*: a romantic triangle in which the lead character has a super-natural gift. In a subtle throughline, the authors have arranged for all the principals to want to be someone else. The nerd would be hero, the wife would be single, the husband acts out erotic bondage fantasies, and even the painter at one point confides that he would like to be Salvador Dalí. Doubling and tripling among the nine actors kept the stage busy, and the intermissionless ninety minutes never lagged, for the absurd story hopped from number to number. Even the fateful ending, as poor Dusoleil made an exhibition dash at a wall for the television cameras and got

* Coming near the start of what turned out to be an unexciting season, *Amour* ended up with five of the musical's potential top six Tony nominations, everything except Best Director.

permanently stuck in the masonry of the eighteenth arrondissement, was played as a prank, a bit of lamentable persiflage. After all, the office nerd, socially isolated from even his co-workers, had found physical expression of what he always had been: half in and half out of life.

Supporting this weightless Gallic curio was a thrill of melody. Lapine's staging improved on the French original by building up the young wife with new solos, especially her Wanting Song, "Other People's Stories." Lapine also cut down an interminable monologue from the doctor (John Cunningham) who treats Dusoleil's condition. The evening was launched by a new vocal arrangement for the overture that recalled the Swingle Singers of the 1960s, and there was as well many an offbeat number that wouldn't quite suit an American show. For instance, the painter's solo, "One Splash of Paint," was a quietly intense rumination that seemed utterly irrelevant to the plot. And the two leads' waltzy love duet, explicitly staged in bed, enjoyed a vertiginous flute obbligato and percussive punctuation, as if here, too, that French habit of observing even while feeling must be honored. Indeed, don't the modest forces and dizzy plotting recall Offenbach's one-acts at the Bouffes-Parisiens in the 1850s? Aren't they *meant* to? French art has a long memory—and Legrand shares with his predecessor that rare ability to joke *in music* just as his librettist jokes in words. The composer has in fact termed *Amour* "an opéra-bouffe"—Offenbach's own form.

Sams got little praise for his work, though this must be the best set of English lyrics in all the through-sung musicals of the Lloyd Webber–Schönberg era. There is plenty of frisky enjambment; Sams matches "I can hear you" with "loud and clear, you [disgusting man]," a carryover unknown to the lyricists of the megahits. Another lyric mates "Jeez, Louise" with a quotation from Shakespeare.

However, Sams did try to get away with a few easy lines—a cliché, an old rhyme. And of course there are those who will jump on a chance failing with "I *knew* it wasn't good!" Are some people going to musicals hoping to hate them? Are some people not having fun unless it's stupid fun? *Amour* wasn't stupid, and that may be a problem. How did the *Chicago* film hit so big? *Chicago*'s a smart show, and the film's smart as well. Does its Blitzkrieg editing style disarm the fears of those who can't follow a story with intellectual content? Are they skipping the words and just browsing through the pictures? Or are they not having a good time because they're not sure what their Opinion is?

What's your idea of a good time? Mine is when the *Amour* ensemble got on Malcolm Gets' case and demanded that he seduce the young wife after all. Gets temporized, so Norma Mae Lyng, the prostitute, started pulling his clothes off:

GETS: Wait a minute!
LYNG: (brushing this away) I'm a professional.

It's fun in passing, an ironic smile, which the musical used to have plenty of, even in *Show Boat* and *Oklahoma!*. But one has to listen to catch it, and the public may have lost its concentration, like potheads zoning out halfway through a sentence. This is not an audience that dotes on Shakespearean quotation. Write me a sound bite, baby.

JUNK IS A GENRE

Or even: junk is the Tony Awards committee, endorsing what I call the New Stupidity by not knowing what the word "book" means when applied to a musical.

Years ago, no one had a problem with this word. The book comprised the spoken lines between the songs and the dance.

Then came shows that were nothing but songs and dances, or shows with so much music and underscored dialogue that "between" all but disappeared. However, the Tony people seem to believe that somewhere, somehow, every musical has a book, even if it be some indefinable—in fact, nonexistent—"something."

So *Cats* must have a book. Now, *Cats* consists entirely of song and dance and thus in reality cannot have a book. Some might say that *Cats'* "book" inheres in an overriding throughline. But a throughline isn't a book. And *Cats'* throughline—which is: will Betty Buckley ride on a big tire tonight? Yes—is scarcely even a throughline. Nevertheless, *Cats'* Tony nominees included T. S. Eliot, cited with Andrew Lloyd Webber for Best Score but also, by himself, for Best Book. Yet after Eliot's contribution to *Cats'* score—specifically his poetry, used as lyrics—there *is* no Eliot contribution to *Cats*. If one wants to nominate *Cats* for Best Throughline, that would go to Trevor Nunn, *Cats'* director. Laying down throughlines, however, is understood in the job description of "director," so a Best Throughline nomination is supererogatory: because Nunn was nominated as *Cats'* director. And a Best Book nomination for *Cats* is illiterate, because by any understanding of what the word "book" denotes, *Cats* does not have one.

Tony nominators nevertheless went on to nominate John Weidman for his book to *Contact*, though *Contact* has very little book. It has three throughlines, one for each of its three parts. Of dialogue as such there is little. Too little, I'd say, to consider for nomination unless one is living in a time when the simple communication of English is breaking down because no one knows what words mean.

Another Tony committee nominated Matthew Bourne, the choreographer of a *Swan Lake* seen on Broadway in 1998, as both Best Director and Best Choreographer. Do these Tony loons think *Swan Lake* is a musical? A musical may have a director and a choreographer; if one person serves as both, they remain two different jobs nonetheless. But a ballet's choreographer already is its director, because the "direction" of ballets consists entirely of choreography.

These erroneous Tony citations are not isolated gaffes. They reflect what is happening in the theatre, just as the theatre reflects what is happening in the culture. Broadway used to be the place where the nation's smartest writers achieved self-fulfillment. Now it's the place where writers have to figure out how to address a people whose polls reveal that most high-school students believe that the Vietnam War was fought in Bayonne, New Jersey in the fourteenth century.

The New Stupidity is this culture's accommodation of the irresistible—ignorance, illiteracy, laziness. An assistant at a publishing house had written copy citing as a song title "Somewhere Over the Rainbow." When I told him that this was the first line of the song and not its title, he made no move to correct the error, because "Everyone will know what I mean."

This incident is typical. Thus, the pride that the business class used to take in hiring people to write correct English for them had to be retired, as one can read on TV headline crawls: even the major networks routinely spell phonetically, as if in Shakespeare's day. The discipline of history becomes a menu of crazy lies. A member of Congress asserts as fact that President Bush knew in advance of the 9/11 attacks, and no storm of disgusted rebuttal follows on. The New Stupidity isn't just stupid: it's unchallenged. Intelligent people have given up battling it because there's too much of it, and thus an absolute lack of knowledge becomes effectively as valid as knowledge, innocent of shame. It points toward a society in which there is no reason to be educated at all.

"Nucular." "Mischievious." "Step foot in." "Trodding the boards." And the problem is not only words, but music as well. The critic's ear seems to have frozen at somewhere around "Ribbons Down My Back": a cue line, an orchestral vamp, an easy melodic structure in something like AABA. ("Ribbons" actually sings through in AA^{1}A^{2}BBAA^{1}C. But it *sounds* easy.) The more creative of today's composers have moved past "Ribbons" in structure, harmony, and, often, character content. There is no place in *Passion* or *Marie Christine* for a Jerry Herman song any more than the shows written by Cole Porter for Ethel Merman could use something in the style of Karl Hoschna. Art grows.

How is it to do so in the New Stupidity, especially when so many of the younger writers seem unaware of the most basic rules of composition? Encouraging them are the usual revolutionists, to whom anything untraditional is praiseworthy, regardless of its quality. But much of this work seems different from typical Broadway fare not because it reveals a new style but because it's no good.

"Just saw *Runaways!*" ran the caption of a photograph in that show's publicity, the illustration featuring exuberant families pouring out of the Plymouth Theatre. A revue of 1978 about abused kids that started at the Public Theater and moved to Broadway, *Runaways* aimed a candid look at a difficult subject. It wanted to startle, to create anguish and awareness. Unfortunately, the piece was the work of composer Elizabeth Swados, whose music recalls the concerts your five-year-old nephew gives by humming while blowing bubbles in a glass of water. I always envisioned a different photo for that "Just saw *Runaways!*": a host of lepers and re-dead crawling out of the Plymouth, with medical teams rushing the comatose into ambulances, Anne Frank beseeching heaven with a "This, too?" look, and a few destroyed souls on their knees, praying for death. Just saw *Runaways!*

Swados' sound was no more ingratiating in the more commercial *Doonesbury* (1983), which Swados wrote with Garry Trudeau, the creator of the familiar comic strip. The comics have been singing on The Street for a century—Victor Herbert and Harry B. Smith turned Winsor McKay's *Little Nemo* into a musical in 1908, and Maggie and Jiggs of George McManus' *Bringing Up Father* provisioned a series of shows in the following decade and into the 1920s, though few were seen in New York. George Herriman's *Krazy Kat* went not to Broadway but Town Hall, as a ballet-pantomime, with scenery by Herriman, in 1922. More recently,

Li'l Abner, *Peanuts*, and *Little Orphan Annie* have had notable success as musical theatre. *Doonesbury*, which lasted three months, was seldom theatre and never musical. This pop material might have worked as a television series or a comedy disc; nothing of what made the strip amusing was transformed into what makes musicals amusing. *Li'l Abner* came to Broadway in 1956 in the form of a fifties musical with fifties musical-comedy talent, the whole made on Al Capp's characters and attitudes. *Doonesbury* played Broadway but never came to it in any real sense.

Leader of the Pack (1985), a review of the romantic and professional partnership of songwriters Ellie Greenwich and Jeff Barry, came with its pop built in. The pair created "Chapel of Love," "Hanky Panky," "Da Doo Ron Ron": another sound that, whatever its charms, does not suit musical theatre. As the years pass and more of these items turn up, one starts to see a genre on the rise, one of music that comes from Somewhere Else. Frank Rich called the show "a revival of *Your Hit Parade*" put on in some "banana republic." Staged on rotating platforms representing 45 RPM discs, *Leader of the Pack* tried to run on very little story—the Greenwich-Barry partnership falters too bad the end—while hijacking a contentless series of old songs.

Leader of the Pack makes *Footloose* (1998) and *Saturday Night Fever* (1999) look rather gala by comparison. But do these movies need to be musicals? Can't they stay in the Somewhere Else for which they were conceived and where they found success?

At least *Footloose* had to be written. The score, mainly by Tom Snow and Dean Pitchford, was all new but for four numbers, and the script, by Pitchford and Walter Bobbie, who also directed, was not the film's script (by Pitchford, incidentally). No, *Footloose* was *based* on a film, while *Saturday Night Fever* truly *was* the film, with soundtrack "atmosphere numbers" now serving as character and situation spots. This was ludicrous: the lyrics didn't match the characters, and situations that couldn't use music had music crowbarred into them. The verisimilitude of director-choreographer Arlene Phillips was so haphazard that a character contemplating suicide (Paul Castree) took part in an ensemble number wearing a mild smile, as if he had nothing on his mind. Worse, the movie's outstanding quality—the authenticity with which it explored New York's outer-borough working-class Catholic youth culture—had utterly vanished even as the characters spoke the movie's lines.

Footloose had better source material in the first place, another of those American tales in which the nice people take on the haters. True, much of the film's ambivalence and edge were lost in the adaptation, and the breezy athleticism of the title song, a series of trick shots of Kevin Bacon virtually dancing on air, could not be staged. But *Footloose* was a book musical with a story score. And unlike some of *Saturday Night Fever*'s cast, *Footloose*'s people came through impressively, especially the kids. Hero Jeremy Kushnier seemed a suitable musical version of Kevin Bacon, with a nice voice and an easy presence, only gently heroic. The three girl sidekicks (Stacy Francis, Kathy Deitch, Rosalind Brown) were solid musical-comedy helpers, digging into the lines and putting over the numbers. Billy Hartung was wasted in the villain's part, and his character's violence was gentled down to snarls; he even disappeared from the story line just when—in the film—he becomes a real menace. Still, Walter Bobbie knows how to cast kids. One of his ensemble—and understudy to Kushnier and Hartung—was Hunter Foster, fated to lead the cast of *Urinetown*. And linking *Footloose* with *Saturday Night Fever* was Paul Castree, another of the ensemble.

Like *Leader of the Pack*, *Mamma Mia!* (2001) came with its pop built in: the ABBA song catalogue. Why not invent a story with which to flaunt the Swedish pop group's hits? Better, why not just use the story of Burton Lane and Alan Jay Lerner's *Carmelina* (1979), which was already the story of the 1969 movie *Buona Sera, Mrs. Campbell*? There was no copyright violation, for the tale comes from a newspaper report. An Italian woman has told each of three American servicemen that he has sired her daughter—apparently she told Alan Jay Lerner, too—and the three all visit at once. At least the setting is new: Greece. And the mother now has a backstory, as the former member of a singing trio; her two ex-partners visit as well. It seems that the daughter is getting married, and the girl's dustup with her fiancé can provide plot suspense, just as in the old days.

One can easily fit ABBA song hits into such a roomy scenario. "Dancing Queen" will be the trio's old standby, for instance; and "Gimme! Gimme! Gimme!" will furnish state-of-the-art with book scenes between the verses as suspicions quicken among the three fathers, who to that point don't even know that one of them has a daughter about to be married.

Add in a relatively small cast, no need for expert thespians, and a revolve offering only two boring sets. *Mamma Mia!* became an international hit, and caretakers at the cemetery where David Merrick rests report convulsions emanating from his grave: because how did the cheapest of the great showmen miss out on this piece of stupid junk that will gross so grandly that they've stopped filling out the royalty checks because they ran out of digits?

Something must explain *Mamma Mia!*'s great success, and doubtless it's the music. Many theatregoers were kids when ABBA was new, and *Mamma Mia!* is a painless way for them to revisit their youth. Then, too, Catherine Johnson's book turns on the six older people, and while they don't pair off at the end as if in *Iolanthe* (one of the men is gay, anyway), the show's viewpoint is senior. It is the music that is young, for ABBA always had a lot of energy even when singing about nothing. This may be the only show whose pit players actually sound "produced"—that is, with that balance and polish that careful studio work achieves. (Martin Koch—working, presumably, with the two ABBA men, Benny Andersson and Björn Ulvaeus—seems to be the musician responsible.)

Still, all this does create a show without genuine character songs—or perhaps, rather, a show with zesty ABBA character songs but no characters. The daughter's two sidekicks jump-start the exposition by climbing over the roof of the unit-set house to elicit some background from the daughter (Tina Maddigan). But this will be no *Footloose* trio; after that first scene, the two friends dwindle into ensemble work. Worse, the mother (Louise Pitre) and *her* sidekicks (Judy Kaye, Karen Mason) make no attempt to establish a reality behind that singing-group past. Were they a hit? Did they record well? Why did they break up? This past is simply assigned to them, as is the happy-ending wedding: the two kids never make up their quarrel. Boy (Joe Machota) loses Girl, but he never really gets her back. He just shows up and they get married, because it's time for *Mamma Mia!* to get to Nostalgic ABBA Medley Finale.

At least one could say that ABBA doesn't come from Somewhere Else, not after *Chess*. But country music is definitely strange on Broadway when not put to theatrical use. The country sound heard in *The Robber Bridegroom* or *Violet* imbues those works with a powerful sense of place, but both have strong dramatic scores. *Urban Cowboy* (2003) did not. A glum repetition of the 1980 movie with an anthology score, the piece was a dismaying example of how far into Somewhere Else producers are now straying. Are all the good twenties and thirties plays suitable for adaptation used up? There isn't another title by Lynn Riggs?* The Ibsen Sequel Cycle can't be over yet; how about a *Big Eyolf?* Isn't there another Fellini or Bergman film, a virgin Dickens title, a comic strip? What made *Urban Cowboy* an enjoyable film was something that only film can do: allow the spectator to experience a subculture as a native. You learn what they know. The musical's great quality, on the other hand, is not to reveal a community but to imagine one. You learn what sorcerers wish for.

Hairspray (2002) is a different case altogether. Unlike most of the shows in this chapter, it was put together adroitly, albeit from a film that is as Somewhere Else as it gets. It may be that the current era of the American musical is simply turning into Somewhere Else itself, for after *Show Boat*, *Candide*, and *Hello, Dolly!* we come to a lot of nothing, some fine scores too rich for the average ear, and *Hairspray*.

If one can make a hit musical out of a smug little mustache, this would be the one, though the Rediscovery of Musical Comedy—launched with *Crazy For You* and redeveloped in *The Producers*—has much to do with it. With a book by Mark O'Donnell and Thomas Meehan, music by Marc Shaiman, and lyrics by Scott Wittman and Shaiman, *Hairspray* is set in Baltimore in 1962. Some white kids want to integrate a televised dance party, ending "Negro Day" in favor of a kind of permanent Everybody Day. This is admirable, if strangely progressive for Baltimore in 1962. As one of *Hairspray*'s characters observes, "Every day is White Day—you've got to be more specific."

For a piece with such grand illusions, *Hairspray* is less specific wherever possible; this is a Marc Shaiman, not a Marc Blitzstein, show. Director Jack O'Brien kept it quick and snazzy, with a first visual that will fix the memory of a generation: the heroine (Marissa Jaret Winokur) awakening to start "Good Morning, Baltimore," but "shot" from above. One might call *Hairspray* the modern equivalent of a George Abbott show, but for the perfunctory talents of the cast's youngsters. *Hairspray* generally has Abbott's light touch in treating serious themes (*On the Town*'s wartime regrets; management's cheating the union in *The Pajama Game*) and the easy-listen music that Abbott preferred. The pacing, too, suggests

---

* Unfortunately, there was: *Roadside* (1930), which turned up on off-Broadway in 2001 as a musical by Harvey Schmidt and Tom Jones. The plot rather resembled that to their *110 in the Shade*, but the score seemed—unusually for this team—ordinary.

Abbott—but he got credit for this simply because he cut down the verbose book-writing style of the 1920s and '30s. Musical comedy plodded till Gower Champion, in *Bye Bye Birdie*, instilled the ideal of the very tight book moving as quickly as possible to the next music. O'Brien is Champion's custodian, which is one of *Hairspray*'s clever points.

Another is the collection of chance fun, such as the rainbow-colored socks on Dick Latessa's feet during the finale, or the two quotations of *Gypsy*. One number ends with Harvey Fierstein crying, "For *me!*," and another moment finds the heroine saying, "I'm a pretty girl, Mama." There are also self-referential jokes, in which the characters betray a worldly knowledge of not Baltimore in 1962 but race relations since then and the fact that they know they are characters in a musical. Of course, any show whose star is a man portraying a woman—not dragging but impersonating her—is bound to spoof itself. But *Hairspray* wants us also to revere its ideals about social tolerance in a number George Abbott would have cut, the grandiose "I Know Where I've Been."

I still think that *Hairspray* is stupid junk. It's clever stupid junk, true, despite one floppo number "(The Legend of) Miss Baltimore Crabs," and a very lengthy denouement. A Champion show concluded in a jiffy. "The Pop Alchemist" was the sobriquet bestowed upon Marc Shaiman by *The New York Times Magazine*. He was seen as an energizing genius, when he is more likely another of the younger talents who can do a little thisa and a little thata. The *Times* called Shaiman "perhaps the most remarkable pop music savant to try his hand at a Broadway show since—well, you'd have to go pretty far back." No, *Times*, you can't go back at all, because pop "alchemists" like Shaiman formerly did not write for Broadway because they weren't good enough to share The Street with Frank Loesser and Frederick Loewe. The *Times* went on to praise the *Hairspray* score as one giving "old-fashioned instant pleasure." No, *Times*. Old-fashioned instant pleasure was what Frank Loesser and Frederick Loewe gave. What Marc Shaiman gives is instant stupid junk.

Which brings us to Frank Wildhorn, one of the maximum leaders in the "popping" of the Broadway sound. Composer Wildhorn, with various collaborators, gave Broadway three scores at the millennium, *Jekyll & Hyde* (1997), *The Scarlet Pimpernel* (1997), and *The Civil War* (1999). The second has the distinction of being the only Broadway musical to be revived during its original run, as previously mentioned. In fact, each of this trio is unique in some way. These may be terrible shows, but they are not mediocrities.

Jekyll & Hyde claimed as its source Robert Louis Stevenson's short story of 1886, "The Strange Case of Dr. Jekyll and Mr. Hyde." However, besides the premise of the good doctor with the evil "twin," the musical used nothing of Stevenson and, like the movie versions, added two women leads for heart interest, mirroring the protagonist with females "good" and "bad." These were, respectively, Christiane Noll and Linda Eder, forming a unit, so to say, "opposite" Robert Cuccioli, who formed his own unit by playing Jekyll wearing his hair long and playing Hyde wearing his hair crazy. The storytelling was almost completely incoherent, but the staging was arresting. Director Robin Phillips and his co–set designer, James Noone, placed the main action in a center square, allowing deranged pantomimes to occur on the sides. Actually, deranged things occurred *in* the square, too. In the first scene, in a laboratory, white-coated technicians seemed to be examining cadavers on gurneys. However, if one looked closely, the cadavers turned out to be naked men moving very slightly in slo-mo, and the technicians seemed to be giving them the kind of massage one looks for in a demimonde passion shop.

The show at the sides was even wilder, as the ensemble engendered the lewd atmosphere of Hyde's nightworld haunts: couples gone from the world in intertwined bliss; a shirtless man, trousers undone, lasciviously drying himself as if after a bath at a public fountain.

Unlike such titles as *Saturday Night Fever* and *Hairspray*, "Dr. Jekyll and Mr. Hyde" is classy. It's lit, after all, and as cinema it has attracted, at various times, John Barrymore, Rouben Mamoulian, Fredric March, Miriam Hopkins, Spencer Tracy, and Ingrid Bergman. Such names! Even the actory Hopkins seems a reproach to today's talents, so bland that one never sees imitations of women movie stars any more. John Barrymore was actory, too, but with what vivacity! And Mamoulian's pictorial imagination! Were those days in which directors spoke only to actors, and actors spoke only to God?

Frank Wildhorn speaks to people who don't know what music and theatre were, and will thus accept anything sung on a stage, especially a scream-the-theatre-down! score. The books are no better, as when *The Scarlet Pimpernel*'s heroine tells the hero, about the villain, "I first met Chauvelin the day we stormed the Bastille." *The Civil War* largely avoided dialogue and was, surprisingly, not untuneful. But while *Jekyll & Hyde* and *Pimpernel* gave their leads some sort of motivational throughline, *The Civil War* folded its players into an unpopulated epic. Robert Cuccoli may or may not have enjoyed singing his climactic Jekyll-Hyde duet, "Confrontation," by flinging his hair from neat to crazy and back again, but he (and his replacements) will be remembered doing so by 1,585 houses, counting previews. And Douglas Sills became a star playing the Pimpernel. But *The Civil War*'s idea of pathos was to present two enemy soldiers in a shoot-out, the wounded one dying in the arms of the other—his brother, of course. The dead man's ghost sings "Tell My Father," which means to move us. How can we care when, except for a bit of introduction in the crowded opening number, the two have never been established as characters?

The popping of Broadway reached its height in *Dance of the Vampires* (2002), a veritable pop theme park, with the dippy lyrics that don't rhyme; the high-tech sonic pranks (one solo's big last high note seemed to have been tracked in, and other notes were unmistakably "faded"); the inflated star power (Michael Crawford was rumored to be taking home $180,000 a week, not much less than twice the highest previously known salary, Reba McEntire's for *Annie Get Your Gun*); and a pervasive illiteracy, as in a spoof poster seen in the final set, of a New York City of the future, announcing the show *Bats*, "now in it's 34th smash year." Can't anybody in the company spell?

From its first preview, *Dance of the Vampires* was Eurotrash, shrieking and freaking at its own vulgarity, *The Phantom of Las Vegas*, *The Flying Hun*. Before this, however, it was simply another of those romantic continental spectacles with a pop-opera score such as we never get over here despite their tremendous success in Europe. One such is *Elisabeth* (1992), on Franz Josef I's wife, Elisabeth of Bavaria, in a very creative scenario in which Elisabeth's anarchist assassin and Death himself have principal roles. Another is our own *Der Glöckner von Notre Dame* (1999), an elaboration of the Walt Disney cartoon *The Hunchback of Notre Dame*. Michael Kunze, a standard translator of English-language musicals into German, himself created the *Elisabeth* text and translated *Hunchback*. It was Kunze who wrote the words for *Tanz der Vampire*, to the music of American Jim Steinman. Roman Polanski directed the German premiere of this work of dark grandeur, completely unlike its source, Polanski's giddy spoof film of 1967, *The Fearless Vampire Killers*.

The American version took the material back to giddy spoof, with Steinman now writing his own lyrics and collaborating on the book with David Ives and Kunze. John Rando and Jim Carrafa were hired to lend the piece the sportive wit they had revealed as director and choreographer of *Urinetown*. But what was this revision spoofing, exactly? Campy horror with greasy pop, suitable for singing by that Steinman favorite Meat Loaf? *Dance of the Vampires* was the first example; it isn't a genre yet. It did appear to be spoofing itself, and perhaps it deserved to, with its risibly overblown star who couldn't draw crowds in New York in any case. With a heavy scene plot yet some set changes so awkward that one wondered if Chipmonck had got loose backstage. With a huge cast of vampires, a few of whom made their first entrance climbing *down* the sides of the proscenium, and virtually all of whom came ghouling into the orchestra aisles for one exit, so close one could hear the hum of their microphone battery packs. But hold: was the impressive castle-gate set at the end of Act One part of the spoof or accidentally excellent? Later, when a gay vampire (Asa Somers) tried to seduce the young hero (Max von Essen) in front of a mirror and we saw the hero's reflection while the vampire—of course—had none, didn't this lightly clever touch belong to some other show, one with style? Did the Dream Ballet have dancing counterparts for von Essen and his love (Mandy Gonzalez) because Carrafa was locking up an homage or because von Essen and Gonzalez can't dance?

Are the pop Frankensteins taking over Broadway, just as the vampires do at the end of this show? Worse: are they doing harm to the Great Tradition? It's worth noting that its reigning masters and their junior partners have not been having the commercial success we wish for them. I can name three failures that should have fascinated the public bored with the easy stuff, the way people supported *Porgy and Bess* (for four months, anyway), *Lost in the Stars*, *West Side Story*. That public is gone, isn't it? Yet the three recent shows I invoke now had wonderful music. One is slowly being rediscovered as an outstanding score of the age. Another enjoyed a superb staging with a big cast and plenty of dancing. The third was the tale of the little guy who learns to like himself, a classic conceit.

Stephen Sondheim's *Passion* (1994) is the one with the important score, based on a variation of *Beauty and the Beast*, Ettore Scola's 1981 film *Passione d'Amore*. Truth, at first, is beauty in this story. Then truth is beast—or is truth an idea beyond reach, as celebrities have been telling us since Pontius Pilate? *Passion* juxtaposes two couples. The first, Giorgio and Clara, are God's favorites exulting in the perfection of their mating, sin without guilt. The second couple is Giorgio and Fosca, an impossible proposition, for Fosca is the beast. Nothing can happen, yet Sondheim and his book writer and director, James Lapine, decided to happen it.

Was this a mistake? Because Sondheim lavished a unique score on a difficult story. When Clara abandons Giorgio, he suddenly responds to Fosca; surely this does not occur. Fosca has a beauty of intelligence, but not a beauty of soul. She is not only ugly: she bedevils Giorgio, even vindictively. Perhaps the tale suits one of those weirder-than-life nineteenth-century novels, in which form the material originally appeared. Perhaps a post-neorealistic Italian film like Scola's can actualize it with some artistic hocus-pocus. But the addition of music must prove the emotional content—not test it, *deliver* it.

So audiences giggled at Fosca's insistence and remained unconvinced when Giorgio finally succumbed. But then, were they even trying to attend to this very small, very dark, and very beautiful piece? Their laughter expresses anger that they're not getting *Company* and *Follies* again. They want Sondheim the gadget, with concept staging and ghosts and Elaine Stritch.

Passion offered a new sort of Sondheim, in music integrated not only with the action but with itself, elusive musical structures stirring up musical ideas and verbal themes. Never had so much singing occasioned so few numbers as such, so few titles. The tunestack favors the generic: "First Letter," "Second Letter," and so on; "Transition" and "Soldiers' Gossip," each a number of times; "Garden Sequence"; "Flashback." The score is so concentrated that merely interesting lines such as Fosca's telling Giorgio "I do not dwell on dreams" and "You are why I live" become, in context, enlightening, thrilling. Aren't the two lines the opposite of each other? She dwells on a dream of his love; she lives only long enough to experience it for a single night. She does dwell on dreams, and he is why she dies: like the butterflies she sings of, that tarry as they taste the nectar of a flower with a secret cache of poison. He is that flower because even she knows that the story is implausible. It cannot be happening.

Perhaps *Passion* is meant as a metaphor. On that level, its story is not only plausible but necessary. We must hear of dreams; art is dreams.

Passion is a dream, in which the most superb sex lacks physical contact and intelligence creates happiness.

The staging was simple, emphasizing the cast. Jere Shea turned down the lead of the *Damn Yankees* revival to play Giorgio, and Marin Mazzie enjoyed her first prominent role as Clara. The show began with the two of them in bed, unmistakably nude under carefully draped covers, to establish the sensuality that they take so for granted and that Fosca can only imagine.

As Fosca, Donna Murphy gave one of the musical theatre's greatest performances. There were arresting details, as when she snatched a needlework circlet from a maid with a look as guilty for the rudeness as it was too miserable to apologize, or when she tenderly tried to touch Giorgio even as he raged at her. In London in 1997, playing to the Giorgio of Michael Ball, Maria Friedman gave another epochal performance, though Judy Kuhn, in D.C.'s Sondheim festival in 2002, took the role way down. It's an unusual choice, but as audiences are still feeling their way through this uncanny piece, there is no Final *Passion*.

Steel Pier (1997) was the wonderful staging, under director Scott Ellis but mainly because of choreographer Susan Stroman, set designer Tony Walton, and lighting master Peter Kaczorowski. David Thompson's book, a cross section of the lives of people associated with a dance marathon* in Atlantic City in 1933, tells an interesting story that runs out of content in Act Two, as if for production by George Abbott. But the Kander and Ebb score is one of their best, with that strange concoction of the captivating and the meaningful that, of their generation, only Jerry Bock and Sheldon Harnick have also mastered (and Bock and Harnick broke up twenty-seven years before *Steel Pier* premiered).

---

* Readers who know what dance marathons are, please stop here and return to the text. Others: dance marathons are popularly thought to be expressions of capitalist degeneracy that arose when the hard times of the 1930s caused the penniless to endure an insanely punishing physical oppression that paid off, in a small way, for more or less the last contestant left alive. In fact, the marathons, though a feature of the Depression, were invented and popularized in the 1920s, when times were good. They were regarded as a kind of outpost of show biz, as much a talent show as an endurance contest. *Steel Pier* honors this with a number of entertainment spots, such as a harmonica number for John C. Havens and a mock wedding in which Kristin Chenoweth's coloratura rose to Cunegonde's high E flat. Those of you who know what dance marathons are but read this footnote anyway, scorning my instructions, just remember: I know where your kids go to school.

"Second *chance!*" rings out in the orchestra on an upward-driving perfect seventh as the show begins—a quotation of one of the numbers, and an explanation of the work's premise: someone gets the opportunity to change a destiny. Depending on how one sees it, this could be Rita Racine (Karen Ziemba), a nice kid involved with the lying manipulator (Gregory Harrison) who runs these marathons. Rita's dance partner in the marathon is Bill Kelly (Daniel McDonald), an aviator; and others include Shelby (Debra Monk), one of those Ready Ladies, born to sing Fred Ebb's raciest lyric ever, "Everybody's Girl" (which is nonetheless cultured enough to take off on the fanfare to the prelude of the fourth act of *Carmen*, besides quoting *Carmen*'s Gypsy Song in the verse); Happy (Jim Newman), a farmboy; and Precious (Kristin Chenoweth), Happy's wife, more interested in show biz than in farm life.

Actually, that melodic cell describing a seventh occurs throughout the score, but it's really singing about the aviator's second chance: because he's dead. His plane crashed during an air show when he was holding a raffle ticket for a dance with Ziemba, an attraction at the show. He can yet claim it, with the understanding that he will help her break with the odious Harrison and walk out on the marathon, the Steel Pier, the cheat in her life. It's a bit reminiscent of *Cabaret*, especially in the two shows' title songs, invitations to ignore life's realities in a place of entertainment. But it's also a very Oscar Hammersteinian notion, a spiritual idea: that love creates redemption through minders, so to speak, who interfere in our lives in times of need. Yet when Ziemba finally realizes what has been happening and asks McDonald, "Who are you?," all he says is "Just a guy. Who wanted a second chance."

The marathon setting obviously gave Stroman many places to go, and she found them all. The marathon itself is made of dance, of course. But the story is a fantasy in part, and the second act opened with a dream sequence modeled on a Hollywood idea in a *Flying Down To Rio* number, "Leave the World Behind." McDonald in his aviator's outfit piloted a biplane lined with the chorus women in blue swimsuits while Ziemba danced for joy. The very start of the evening also took the action out of reality, as chorus men and women gently stepped out from the wings in a formation framing McDonald, prone on the stage floor. This uncanny visual poetry made nothing clear, but it was intriguing. The audience must also have missed the lovely pun in McDonald's solo about Ziemba early in the marathon, "The Last Girl (I'll ever love is over there)." It's a typical Boy Meets Girl effusion but for the fact that he means it literally: because he'll be gone forever in three weeks.

Perhaps the fantasy felt too contrived for some, or perhaps it was another case of the public's impatience with well-made story musicals with strong emotional foundation. Those listening to the cast album in the future will find it hard to understand why such a beautifully organized show lasted only two months.

The third title was inspired by a movie, like *Passion*. The 1994 film *A Man of No Importance* starred Albert Finney as Alfie Byrne, a bus conductor in sixties Dublin. A closeted homosexual who lives largely in wishful reverie, he has but one positive outlet, directing plays for a theatre group housed at his parish church.

It's a small story, again like *Passion*, fit indeed for the intimate quarters of the Newhouse. Without the film's real-life Dublin to revel in, Stephen Flaherty and Lynn Ahrens and their book writer, Terrence McNally, built up the supplementary characters. They individualized the amateur thespians as (mostly) comic roles and haunted the action with the embodiment of Alfie's hero, Oscar Wilde. They gave full play to three people of personal importance to Alfie: his sister; his bus driver and secret crush, Robbie; and his leading lady (in Wilde's *Salome*). So Alfie's world was well imagined—it's people, not things—and the moral was clearly stated. As one song puts it, "Love Who You Love."

Alfie (Roger Rees) believes that that must be Robbie (Steven Pasquale). But first Alfie must love himself—a problematical truism, for the aging and socially awkward Alfie simply cannot function as protagonist to the homophobic chorus (using the terminology of the earliest Greek tragedies). Theatre nurtures him, but as his cloister, his refuge. Is he even the hero of his own piece? Or isn't that Wilde, the man of importance who was also probably the first uncloseted gay man in modern history? Half of a dual role, Wilde is played also by the villain of the piece, an anti-intellectual butcher (Charles Keating) who denounces *Salome* as blasphemy and gets the church to close down the theatre group. The typical religious bigot, preaching Christ while denying His tolerance, the villain-hero, butcher and poet, makes a statement about the hetero world: it stands as far from gay as possible, yet much closer than it knows.

As I've said, Flaherty and Ahrens work best with an ethnic idea, though the score's savor of Dublin lives as much in the chamber scoring, by William David Brohn and Christopher Jahnke, as in such Irish numbers as "Confusing Times" and "Man in the Mirror." Ever since *Cabaret*, the important show must test its songwriters above all in the first number. In the 1920s, even major shows, titles still performed today, thought nothing of bringing up the curtain on a chorus that does no more than check in as Moroccan Riffs, flappers, or college students. *A Man of No Importance* opens with its title number, and from the first notes we know we are the guests of masters of the form. Like Sondheim in *Passion* and Kander and Ebb in *Steel Pier*, Ahrens and Flaherty know precisely where the action should start, how it sounds, and what it says. *Passion* begins in the erotic beauty that the work will ceaselessly challenge. *Steel Pier* begins in its fantasy, then cuts to the heroine frisking in the water at the ocean's edge as she takes us into her confidence.

And "A Man of No Importance" unveils the timeplace, the characters of note, and even, subtly, the authors' plan. It's a day in Alfie's life, this number, a gallery of his people, a look at the toothsome Robbie, and at last the entrance of his Salome (Sally Murphy), which will hasten Alfie to his agon, the central contest in the drama of his life.

Elsewhere in the score, audiences strongly responded to Robbie's "The Streets of Dublin," something comparable to a rave-up by the Irish rock group the Pogues and with a thrilling vocal coda. They may have been unhappy with "Art," an anthology number in which the members of Alfie's troupe enjoy individual comic turns. Mrs. Grace (Katherine McGrath), designing the poster, describes Salome's mother, Herodias, as "earth mother, tigress, empress, woman." Amusing enough. But Mrs. Curtin (Patti Perkins), *Salome*'s choreographer, taps through the Dance of the Seven Veils, a lead balloon of a joke. Interesting almost despite itself was "Tell Me Why," the rebuke of Alfie's sister (Faith Prince) after he is outed in a gay-bashing. Alfie didn't trust her enough to be honest—but why should he have trusted her? The ally of the loathsome butcher, she was as much a part of the prevailing homophobia as everyone else. Do the authors think she's right? Both music and lyrics sound sincere even as the character strikes a hypocritical pose.

The moment marked the narrative climax, for by then everything had been taken from Alfie—his theatre, his relationship with Robbie, his self-respect. Novelty Star Rees sang quite well enough for numbers obviously crafted around his vocal range, which lies somewhere between Walter

Huston and Tony Randall. Alfie's music is deflating, even self-flagellating. In "Man in the Mirror," he nears the end of the first act trying to get a look at himself: a soul outliving his years of promise, and what promise ever was that, anyway? It's a dire moment, even in the soothing Irish lilt of a piccolo dancing over the lower strings.

So Rees came through as an eloquent singing actor, a trim and frankly more estimable version of the pitiable mess that Alfie had been in the film. More important, Rees had originated the lead in the Royal Shakespeare Company's *Nicholas Nickleby*, so memorably that, ever after, no matter what he's playing, he seems to heed a Dickensian morality. Rees—rather, Alfie—knows what's fair in the world. That guided one's attention, fed one's worry. Then, too, Joe Mantello's direction sited the piece very smartly in its space, basically that of Alfie's little theatre, his life. Rees stood at its center at the end, when, surrounded by his pro-scribed players, he had Robbie—still his friend after all—read out a bit of Wildean poetry. The company quietly sang the title line of the title song. And Rees looked out at the public with shy happiness. Good: the show's title is meant ironically. One was no longer worried; and the lights faded to black.

Three treasurable music boxes that failed to delight. True, none of this trio was of that kind associated with the classic titles of old. *Passion* is too questingly newfangled to achieve wide popularity, and the other two have some weak numbers. Still, all three uphold that Great Tradition that I take for my text: in which gifted people try to explain the world to us by singing their stories.

So, frankly, one ought to comment on the huge success of a show with little story to tell and no song for it. *Contact* (1999), a triptych of dance pieces seen downstairs and then upstairs at Lincoln Center, and credited to Susan Stroman and John Weidman, didn't even have a live orchestra: the music, taking in both classical and pop, was canned. A jazzy rendering of "My Heart Stood Still" brought the lights up on "Swinging," a touch of Fragonard with an aristocrat, his lady love, and his male servant, pushing them on the swing and then having sex with the woman (on the swing, in full flight) while the master is offstage. The title is a pun, for the master is actually the servant and vice versa; the three have thus been "swinging" in the sense of acting roles to intensify erotic satisfaction.

It was a stylish piece, extremely well staged with hair-raising athletic stunts—the timing of the swing bar's arrival, just missing the head of the "aristocrat"; the daredevil "servant" on the swing ropes.

But that chic little throwaway is followed by a deadly expansion of the kind of skit one used to see on television's *Carol Burnett Show*, a restaurant sketch in which Carol would be Harvey Korman's mousy wife, Korman an impatient husband, and Tim Conway an exasperatingly bumbly waiter. There would be a suggestion of pathos and even social commentary, and the whole thing would be over within five minutes. But "Did You Move?" takes up the rest of *Contact*'s first act, with Karen Ziemba as the wife and Jason Antoon as her now truly loathsome husband. A mixture of dream and reality, the sequence used "Anitra's Dance" from Grieg's *Peer Gynt* music, the famous ballroom waltz from Chaikofsky's *Yevgyeni Onyegin*, and the Farandole from Bizet's incidental accompaniment to *L'Arlésienne* to contrast the fun that a liberated Ziemba could be having with the miserable life she actually leads.

After the intermission came the so-to-say title piece, which begins with a playing of "You're Nobody Till Somebody Loves You," the message that the musical theatre has been obsessively conveying for a century. Nobody loves the protagonist, an advertising executive (Boyd Gaines) who is the terror of his downstairs neighbor, an unseen woman kept awake at odd hours by his stamping on his wooden floor. As she begs for peace on his answering machine—in the middle of the night, by the way—he ignores her, continuing to stamp around and then trying to hang himself in a comic attempted-suicide scene.

Boys and girls, am I the only one who finds this contemptible jerk disgusting? Would you like someone stamping all over your head? And do you think suicide is a matter for comedy?

Note, by the way, that there have been a few spoken lines in this section. That, apparently, is what John Weidman believes constitutes the "book" of a musical. So did the Tony nominating committee, of course. What other "books" deserve this honor? How about the book of the Eiffel Tower? Its book is the comments that tourists make as they scan the view. How about the book of Geraldo Rivera, a cabbage, Go Fish?

Meanwhile, Boyd Gaines, having failed to die, now visits a dance parlor. Stroman, again, is at her best in a dazzling set change: leaving his apartment, Gaines walks the perimeter of the circular stage apron, followed by the chorus men. A huge WALK/DON'T WALK sign suggests by synecdoche a foot trip to somewhere in Manhattan, and another sign reads VINNIE'S. The signs turn, the walk is over, and somehow the dance place simply materializes. It's a pool hall that converts to a funky ballroom at night.

"You're nobody till you can dance" could be the motto of the American musical, and naturally Gaines can't: a metaphor for his lack of love, sharpened by the entrance of the Queen of Dance Night, the spectacular Girl in a Yellow Dress (Deborah Yates). All men want her, but Gaines *especially* can't have her, till he eventually figures out the moves and wins her—in his dreams. It was all phantoms, and the club dancers deposit him in his apartment, back in the noose that failed. But now his neighbor comes banging on his door, and it will be Yates, so there will be contact. And Boyd Gets Girl after all.

But *Contact* is not a musical. To be fair, it never claimed to be one; it was the Tonys that called it so. And Stroman's choreography was eye-catching, especially in the stragglers-get-shot challenge dances of the danceteria. But one wonders if *Contact*'s popularity was based more on the public's distaste for the complexity of the modern book musical, with its seething characters and concept-show cross-cutting. *Contact* is the equivalent of a fifties Percy Faith LP: easy to take, with no distractions and little content. It's not junk by any means. But it's a dance piece, and that seems to be as much "musical" as today's audience can handle. We used to have shows so smart they were flops. Now we have shows so dumb that they're hits.

Why Can't Susan Smith and Timothy McVeigh Have a Musical? Hitler Has One

One notices it first of all, perhaps, in the aforementioned *Grind*. Timothy Nolen's character, encountered as a drunken bum, is haunted by the death of his wife and son. His establishing song, "Katie, My Love," is couched in a Gaelic lullaby with "Lu tara lee" refrains. The lovely tune is disquietingly set to the words of a man bent on suicide. Much later, in Nolen's other solo, "Down," we learn that he is an Irish terrorist who blew up a train carrying English soldiers, not knowing that his wife and son were on it. He has murdered his own family.

What is odd is not that he sees the soldiers (and, presumably, other civilian passengers) he killed as no more than broken things flying high in the air: for he actually drew back to look up at his handiwork as if at a painting. No, what is odd is that *Grind* itself doesn't seem to find his multiple homicide appalling. The show's authors aren't glorifying terrorism. They aren't forgiving it or making any aruguments whatsoever in its favor. But they don't seem to mind that it's there, and they don't see Nolen as a villain. On the contrary, his reclamation as a burlesque straight man is part of the show's happy ending.

The musical has long had anti-heroes, of course. Pal Joey Evans is probably the most famous of them. But he is a user, not a terrorist. Billy Bigelow gets himself involved in a would-be robbery-murder; but the rules in operation in *Carousel*'s 1945 demanded that he die the death in return. And so it is with all the other characters in musicals who are not scapegraces or rogues but outright destroyers of life. In serious shows, such as *Street Scene*, they are viewed within a frame of moral judgment; in satiric shows, such as *Chicago*, they are identified as symbols of the corruption of society.

But *The Capeman* (1998) was conceived to tell the story of a thrill killer without any judgmental perspective. The murder of two teenage boys by another teen—why? because—is simply gazed upon, like the butchery flying out of the blown-up train in *Grind*. The musical's political history lies in its relationship with the liberal thinking of its times; and the musical now seems to have begun adopting the moral relativism promulgated by the wrecking left. One saw this in the befuddled look on the face of the author of *The Capeman* every time someone asked him why he wanted to write about a killer. What's wrong with a killer?, his confused look appeared to reply.

This was Paul Simon, who composed *The Capeman*, writing as well the book and lyrics in collaboration with Derek Walcott. The teaming of one of the nation's most enduring musical voices and one of the most distinguished poets of the day suggested a major song-cycle album, perhaps even a breakthrough piece like *Tommy*. And perhaps one day, just like *Tommy*, that cycle would find its way to the stage. (As it was, *The Capeman* shared with Des McAnuff's *Tommy* staging the casting of the title role with three players, to catch him at different ages.)

However, in bringing his piece directly to the stage, Simon was combining absolute artistic control with the rocker's disdain for the Great Tradition. Perhaps he anticipated making unique rather than traditional art—but that's hard enough for the experienced thespian. The novice may be stumped just trying for the conventional.

In the end, the two authors never digested the subject matter, though Walcott, a veteran writer and director of theatre, may have been limited by Simon's mania for listening to no one but himself and giving his various directors no room in which to challenge or even question his views.* Susana Tubert, then Eric Simonson, then the show's choreographer, Mark Morris, were the serial directors, all superintended by Walcott and all finally superseded by an unbilled Jerry Zaks. However, the work was so incoherent that it could be shortened and clarified but never integrated.

---

* What if *The Capeman* had enjoyed the protection of a strong director with full directorial power right from the start? Someone like Hal Prince, say? One visualizes Paul Simon performing some of the weaker numbers, perhaps the letter songs meant for Wahzinak, Indian maid. Whereupon Prince says, "What kindergarten pageant did you write that for?" *Variety*: HAL PRINCE ON UNEMPLOYMENT.

This was because Simon began work with not a meaningful story but a meaningful musical style. He wanted to dramatize his enthusiasm for Latin music, especially that of the time covered in the show, from 1949 to 1959 (when the murders occurred), then from 1962 to 1979, when the Capeman, Salvador Agrón, died. Again, this is thinking meant for Top 40, not for Broadway. The project had such cultural traction even so that *The New York Times* felt impelled to preview it in a cover story for the Sunday magazine. Interviewing Simon, Stephen J. Dubner noted not a confused look but exasperation at mention, once more, of the controversial story. "This is *all* about music," Simon insisted. "The story, I think, is an interesting story. But I'm not a sociologist, or even a playwright. So I'm interested as a composer in things that I love, and this is all about how I fell in love with music and who I was when that love happened."

That was the problem: a feeling rather than a perspective, and an utter lack of response to the implications of headline crime. The kid with the troubled background getting into gang violence and murder, the tabloid circus-trial, the escape from prison, and, nevertheless, the parole that set him free early enough to die at the age of forty-two—all of this was in the show, observed yet unexamined. Vincent Canby, the *Times'* spectacularly clueless movie critic who had by then moved over to theatre, made a rather sensible mistake in discussing *The Capeman.* "Mr. Simon," he reported, "was drawn to the tale not only by Agrón's redemption following the commutation of his death sentence but also by the 'great musical environment.'"

In fact, the musical showed no redemption. Agrón starts as a young thug, takes two lives, and ends as a middle-aged nothing who shows not a shred of remorse for or even knowledge of what he has done. Canby, who often missed strategic narrative developments, must have assumed that there was some remorse somewhere or other in the piece: because otherwise why would anyone want to write it?

Some of the lyrics suggest a social and racial framework that was only tenuously supportive, and "Shopliftin' Clothes," in which Agrón and his pals burgle a store right in front of the helpless owners, was clearly designed to amuse. If that didn't appall, real-life footage of the freshly arrested Agrón, a reptile in human form, showed the audience in a few moments what Simon evidently hadn't noticed for years. It isn't all about music.

"As a show, *The Capeman* is a great album," said Canby. There he was right. Perhaps Simon refused to let anyone but Walcott near his work because he knew how well the music was going to come out, albeit with some lyrics as lumpishly declarative as those in pop opera, and with a second act in chaos. Typical of the first act is, say, "The Santero," a musical scene in which Agrón's mother (Ednita Nazario) applies to a fortune-teller to learn of her son's destiny. To the massed singing of the chorus, the mother arrives at the Santero's house. A few lines of recit and we reach the song proper, "So Say the Shells." The shaman tosses seashells and then predicts it all in music as eerily beautiful as a cave painting.

Such fine preluding suggests a dramatic playing field that *The Capeman* never reached, even as designer Bob Crowley delighted with his arresting perspectives, even as excellent numbers—as music per se—kept coming. One such was "Bernadette," rock's version of what used to be called a charm song, and a nifty exhibition piece for Marc Anthony, the salsa singer who played the middle (and most important) of the three Salvadors. His elder, Ruben Blades, spent the first act tramping around with a mysterious package (a book he wrote in prison, we finally learned). As in *My Life With Albertine*, the two didn't seem like versions of a self. Anthony gave a vital performance and Blades offered little. On at least one night, he executed a little hopping step with a half-smile during the bows; it was more than he had done all evening to that point.

The show fell completely apart when the narrative followed Agrón's time in prison. Here, the typical number might be "You Fucked Up My Life," Agrón's confrontation with his former gang, during which he suddenly claims that he took the rap for *their* killings. One thought back to the murder scene in Act One: was that why it was staged so confusingly? Still, nothing in the text anticipated this startling announcement, and the show itself took no notice of it, tooting right along to more non sequiturs. For all that, "You Fucked Up My Life" followed Agrón's escape from prison—how? because—and unfortunately led directly to yet more of a strange figure, billed as Lazarus, who apparently had the same job as Ruben Blades, wandering about the stage, now here, now there.

"Murder is not entertainment," read the picket signs outside the Marquis Theatre. Comedian Joy Behar was on hand to remind us that plenty of musicals have had murders. *Oklahoma!*. *West Side Story*. *My Fair Lady*. A single CD of some of the *Capeman* numbers had come out, basically a Simon studio release with a stingy use of the production's three leads (and Sara Ramirez, who played Wahzinak) and its theatre orchestrations, by Stanley Silverman. But the critics all noted the show's great shortcomings, and it closed after a two-month run. A complete cast album was recorded, but Simon refused to release it. We are left with the work's final image: Nazario and the three Salvadors alone at center stage, the Santero's warning bootless after all, as oracles are in the best of stories. Simon should have heeded warnings. His show seemed all the more a failure because so much thought had gone into the music and so little into everything else.

While *The Capeman* was simply irresponsible, Stephen Sondheim and John Weidman's *Assassins* (1991) is a serious inquiry into the motivations that created America's unique rogues gallery of presidential assault. A number of Sondheim shows are misunderstood, most notably *Company* and *Follies*. But *Assassins* is thought by some—just because of its subject matter—as "the glorification of slime," to borrow a line from *The Capeman*.

Assassins doesn't glorify. Nor does it excuse or sympathize. It gathers up the indicated historical figures, from John Wilkes Booth (Victor Garber), Charles Guiteau (Jonathan Hadary), and Leon Czolgosz (Terrence Mann) to the more contemporary "Squeaky" Fromme (Annie Golden), Sara Jane Moore (Debra Monk), and John Hinckley (Greg Germann, later the goofy lawyer Fish of *Ally McBeal*). Finally, the show brings all before Lee Harvey Oswald (Jace Alexander) to beg him to apotheosize their movement.

Obviously, Weidman was not breaking his subjects into chronological cameos, but creating a kind of *Grand Hotel* of assassins. At one point, the lights came up on a saloon with Czolgosz and Hinckley at the bar (though Hinckley was born fifty-four years after Czolgosz's execution), and Booth at a table reading *Variety*. For those unversed in the history, it was interesting to see how varied were the subjects' backgrounds—immigrants and native sons, an actor and a housewife, some crazy, some angry, some crusaders, and some happy idiots:

"SQUEAKY" FROMME: Charlie says that fast food is the stinking swill
    Americans lap up the way a dog returns to its own vomit.
SARA JANE MOORE: . . . Who's Charlie?
FROMME: Charlie Manson!
MOORE: Charlie Manson, *the mass murderer*? Is he a friend of yours?

FROMME: I'm his lover and his slave.
MOORE: Far out!

For some odd reason, *Assassins* boasts Sondheim's catchiest score. Because the work is a longish one-act, there is no room for expansive Sondheimorama. Everything must be nailed quickly, concisely, in numbers less about character and plot than about theme. The opening, "Everybody's Got the Right," picks up material in later solos from Booth and Giuseppe Zangara (Eddie Korbich), eventually to develop the theme in a quartet, the "Gun Song." Other assassins have their numbers, till the score reaches a full statement of the theme in "Another National Anthem." The title refers not to a supplementary hymn but to the sputterings of enraged losers nourishing feelings of injured merit. Fixed social systems have no losers. But American democracy, with its big-win show-biz religion, inspires self-righteous freaks to seek revenge for what they see as a monumental cheat aimed at them personally. One line of "Another National Anthem" runs, "The usherette's a rock star." This, no doubt, led another piece of filth to kill John Lennon, the "president" of music. But Sondheim and Weidman's show is about those who take aim at the head of the country as a whole: at the liberty that gave them nothing while "the mailman won the lottery."

Directed by Jerry Zaks at Playwrights Horizons, *Assassins* played three weeks as the hottest ticket in town but did not transfer to Broadway despite the fine production and the work's astonishing power. Most musicals dawdle a bit in filling out an evening, or simply blunder into traps. But here was a work conceived to be short because it's tighter and truer. Who isn't interested in this topic? Who doesn't want to hear the newest Sondheim?

Despite Zaks' sure-footed leadership and superb cast, *Assassins* is not easy to pull off. The London staging, at the Donmar Warehouse in 1992, lacked tension. The original used simple sets till the final scene, just after "Another National Anthem," when the singing died away and the darkness was broken by a sight as logical as it was shocking: Lee Harvey Oswald in that room in the Texas School Book Depository. How better to recollect the old Greek idea of theatre as a dangerous and necessary function of democracy? The London *Assassins* went undecorated, with the principals onstage throughout, posed in niches. Henry Goodman's Guiteau, at least, arrestingly unveiled the madman's belief in his own clarity. But New York's structure of a theme gathering evidence for a presentation was lost.

Assassins itself was almost lost after 9/11 (though it finally did get to Broadway, in 2004). But I think that new day of infamy makes *Assassins* all the more relevant. The show is not irresponsible or unpatriotic. It wants to know why people would commit such an atrocious crime; and it tells us. *Assassins'* losers are like Islamists killing the symbol of the success they cannot have. The show reveals the freak vindictively trying to destroy the cynosure.

The musical has long championed the downtrodden, though they tended to be more like Flora the red menace than Leon Czolgosz. The favorite downtrodden group, of course, was blacks, sometimes in their own stories, such as *Lost in the Stars* (1949), sometimes as an important element of stories with white leads, such as *Finian's Rainbow* (1947), sometimes just with a few lines or a number to fill out the social context, such as Samuel E. Wright's Pullman porter in *Over Here!* (1974).

One doesn't attain liberation until one is graduated from downtrodden status into full citizens' rights to stories about individuals, not race. The breakthrough piece in this matter was *The Tap Dance Kid* (1983), a domestic tale entirely about a single black family, the Sheridans. Unlike, for instance, the Youngers of *Raisin* (1973), *Tap Dance Kid's* father (Samuel E. Wright once again), mother (Hattie Winston), daughter (Martine Allard), and son (Alfonso Ribeiro) are not striving to start a business or flee the ghetto: father is a well-to-do attorney and they live on Roosevelt Island, a surburban enclave in the middle of New York City.

The Sheridans are so assimilated that they have white people's problems: father is too strict, daughter is unappreciated and overweight, and son, the title character, defies father in a wish to get into show biz like his uncle (Hinton Battle). Henry Krieger and Robert Lorick's score indulged in too much empty soft rock. But their theatre-music character songs were good, especially a long musical scene for Wright that earned him a Tony nomination. Finally letting go after an evening of almost primly buttoned-up self-control, Wright blazed away in disgust for what he sees as the ultimate black humiliation, the jim-crow nigger—yes, he uses the word—servility of . . . *dance!* The black "Rose's Turn," "William's Song" was thrillingly gruesome, all the more so after the mild irony of Wright's *Over Here!* solo, "Don't Shoot the Hooey To Me, Louie."

So there was race in the piece, after all. And, true, when young Martine Allard ripped with surprising vocal power into her establishing song, "Four Strikes Against Me," one strike she cited was her race. Even so, *The Tap Dance Kid* generally saw black as something the characters happened to be rather than the subject of the discourse. William sees his children as underachievers, and perceives this as a racial problem. But from the kids' point of view, the show is about an intensely controlling father, a universal theme.

One might see the universal also in Cy Coleman and Ira Gasman's *The Life* (1997), for while this look at the working girl's world had an almost all-black cast, the characters were black because they were black, not because they had a statement to make. This recalls a venerable tradition, dating back to the late nineteenth century but solidified in the black musicals of the 1920s and heading on to such titles as *Cabin in the Sky* (1940) and *Jamaica* (1957). Whatever problems bedevil the characters, they are never of racial derivation, because the stories take place in environments in which blacks make the rules.

In *The Life*, more exactly, men make the rules, and the women are victims until, like *The Life*'s Pamela Isaacs and Lillias White, they rebel. Isaacs actually kills her outrageously villainous pimp (Chuck Cooper), and White takes the rap, presumably to get off on self-defense. No doubt the Production Code would have been unhappy, but it is all the same a moral outcome.

The Life had first been workshopped in 1990, and thus took seven years to reach the Ethel Barrymore Theatre, where the show played 466 performances and lost seven million dollars. That's not a bad showing for a piece whose underworld setting lacks the charm of *Guys and Dolls*' Runyonland or *Chicago*'s rugged ironies. In particular, the grooming of *The Life*'s cast favored a provocative realism from the chorus girls that utterly upended one of the musical's oldest essentials.

The Life's book, by David Newman, Gasman, and Coleman, treats an unhappy place, one with few loyalties and countless broken promises. Typical is Jojo (Sam Harris), who charms us by leading a zesty opening, "Use What You Got," then spends the evening double-crossing all the people we like. As well, Coleman's music throws off almost entirely that puckish use of satiric pastiche with which he personally defines musical comedy. There is no "Real Live Girl" or even "Big Spender" here. Much of the music has a bluesy quality, as befits the somber dissatisfactions of almost everyone in it.

"Use What You Got," in the minor, is familiar Coleman, its vamp built on an orchestral version of piano chords over a bass fiddle walking between the first and fifth of the tonic, then cutting to the leading tone, and the verse moves from the tonic to the submediant seventh. This is simply a technical description of the way the best composers make the familiar innovative. They love tradition, but it's in their nature to surprise: so they combine the two in new tradition. This is what made the musical great from 1920 to about 1980.

But the villain's "Don't Take Much (to turn a girl into a woman)" is a piece of minor-key meanness with a threateningly simple melody and angry chording, so that the verb in the phrase "buy her a beer" sits on a major seventh chord with both the second and sixth tones flatted: a creep fondling breasts with a pulp-fiction smile. This is a Coleman we had not heard before, creative in a post-traditional way.

Perhaps the outstanding black show of the era was *Jelly's Last Jam* (1992). Here, race was an issue. As with *The Tap Dance Kid* and *The Life*, there was no racial conflict; whites (except the gangsters) are to get along with or ignore. But much of the work discussed the relationship between a people and a music in highly ethnic terms. The protagonist was Jelly Roll Morton, but the *subject* was Morton's music and its dissemination in American culture. Logically, then, *Jelly's Last Jam* drew its score from Morton's music itself, arranged and amplified by the indispensable Luther Henderson to the lyrics of Susan Birkenhead.

Yes, another evening on new Broadway with old composition. However, this was not a recapitulation of Gershwin or Porter. There was a great deal of fresh Luther Henderson amid the Morton, and Morton's work is hardly overfamiliar, except, *possibly*, the once ubiquitous "King Porter Stomp"—the "After the Ball" of jazz—used to create the first number, "The Jam." And Birkenhead's sly rhymes groove so meetly that it's difficult to believe that any of the score predates the production.

Henderson and Birkenhead are here the Wright and Forrest of jazz, with a black *Song of Norway* on the life and work of Jelly Roll Morton. They and book writer (and director) George C. Wolfe come down a bit hard on their man. Yes, he was arrogant; but he was arguably the first influential progenitor of jazz, at a time when the recording industry hadn't yet begun popularizing the new sound. One had to travel to make revelation, most often up the Mississippi to Chicago, thence eastward to New York.

So Morton (Gregory Hines) takes the same classic jazz journey invoked in a forgotten seventies show on the same general subject, *Doctor Jazz*. This title, too, mixed old and new music, similarly curated by Luther Henderson, and the two shows even share a number, "Doctor Jazz," composed by Morton's coeval Joe "King" Oliver. The earlier show, however, was so empty of content that Henderson had nothing to point up except music as an autonomous energy. Wolfe wants Henderson and Birkenhead to tell what this music is. So "The Jam" recalls the explicit union of sex and pleasure in the very word "jazz" that so alarmed puritans in the 1920s. Later, "That's How You Jazz," a new number by Henderson and Birkenhead, gave Hines the opportunity to define this all but indefinable music while cajoling the ensemble to imitate a backup band. It's a familiar genre of vocal arrangement, but this time it's a recipe for art. Hines calls for "a lowdown foundation"—the basses doing the tuba. Next, a charm "of syncopation"—the girls plunking like the banjo. Last, "a bluesy variation"—the brasses. Yes, that's how you jazz.

There were as well some character numbers, such as Hines' eleven o'clocker, "Creole Boy," another Henderson and Birkenhead piece, this one sounding like something Kurt Weill might have composed had he been black. But this score is far more interested in describing a historical context for the music, even unto projecting as a backdrop the familiar black Victor label of Jelly Roll Morton's Red Hot Peppers' 78 of "The Chicago Stomp" as Hines and the ensemble got a dance rave-up out of it.

Dark in the literal sense as well as in its mood, *Jelly's Last Jam* sat in the modernist's big black box as Wolfe conjured up his places in the saga, and as the Chimney Man pursued Morton. His life seemed to take him from one underworld to another, from Storyville's Too-Tight Nora and Three-Finger Jake to his New York music publishers, played as a vaudeville duo and just as crooked as Nora and Jake. Morton may not be Where It Started; no one person ever is. But Morton is probably the nearest big name to When It Spread, and there is a great story in this.

Art about art, like *Sunday in the Park With George*, *Jelly's Last Jam* would have been a succès d'estime at the very least, but in fact it ran 569 performances, a fine showing for the unique these days. Wolfe got robbed at the Tonys, however. Gregory Hines and Tonya Pinkins won as Jelly and his Anita. But Wolfe lost the director Tony to Jerry Zaks for *Guys and Dolls* because that revival was a big hit, and the book Tony to *Falsettos*, which doesn't have one. Perhaps the revival of the movie musical, in *Moulin Rouge* and *Chicago*, will encourage some studio to let Wolfe try turning this already quite cinematic piece into a film.

The newcomer sympathetic group, after blacks, is gays, and here, too, was a breakthrough work, in *Kiss of the Spider Woman* (1993). After the constipatedly presentable gay airline stewards in *Dance a Little Closer*, the "married" couple of *La Cage aux Folles*, and neurotic Marvin of the *Falsettos* shows, *Spider Woman* offered the screaming faggot as anti-fascist. It did so with dignity, odd as that sounds, but also with humor, and that cannot be easy. Indeed, the show got off to a false start in a Westchester tryout, in 1990. John Rubinstein played the window dresser obsessed with movies, and Kevin Gray was the hetero political prisoner. The action was overwhelmed by Rubinstein's "narration" of a film, scenes from which were interspersed with the real-life scenes, reflecting something of their content. However, this is a Latin American work, based on a novel by Manuel Puig and treating that culture of film, that complex of politics. Why was the WASPy North American Lauren Mitchell playing Rubinstein's diva? Shouldn't it have been Chita Rivera?

So director Hal Prince reinformed his concept, Terrence McNally restructured the book, and Kander and Ebb amended their score. The new *Spider Woman* played Toronto and London first, in 1992, and Chita took on her birthright role of Aurora, with Brent Carver and Anthony Crivello as the cellmates who change each other's lives. Instead of a single Aurora movie plot running through the action, Carver now evoked one, two, many Chitas, and she constantly referenced the outer action. Her lyrics alone can be cut down to an outline of the show: a "handsome hero" will ensnare the man whose love was the art of escape, and to please that hero he will learn the art of belief, even be willing to die for it. And he will die.

Given the plot inherited from Puig, Kander and Ebb had to slip all the fun in in Aurora's film spots—a Birdcage Number for "Gimme Love" in beads, feathers, and platform heels with four shirtless boys; or even just enjoying a surprise entrance by running into the action to sing about a visit to a gypsy fortune-teller. This is Kander and Ebb's most serious show. Their other anti-fascist piece, *Cabaret*, is the place where the showmanship of old-time musical comedy married the power of the musical play most decisively, and *Spider Woman*, their offspring, favors the powerful side. The showmanship is still there, but this is a work devoted to proving the theorem ("Her name is Aurora") + Spiritual Redemption = ("His name was Molina"). That is, Carver goes from "Dressing Them Up," one of the new numbers for the second version and the flippant tirade of a shallow mind, to a realization that the ideals of the man he loves outclass hedonistic fantasies. He doesn't become political. He simply becomes heroic, the star of his own movie. In a brilliant coda, the murdered Carver dances the tango with Rivera before an audience made of the cast, including the prison warden who killed him; Carver's mother is an usherette with flashlight.

Spider Woman touches *Assassins* for a moment here—Prince Meets Lapine—because both center at last on the same being in, respectively, his virtuous and destructive avatars. *Assassins* takes place during a century of American history, and *Spider Woman* treats "sometime in the recent past" in "a prison in Latin America." Yet the two works share a look at nobodies who fulfill ego wish by becoming the guy in the close-up: the mailman won the lottery. Carver, however, is the innocent caught in a riot; *Assassins* is about the rioters. The latter work, of course, deals with its subject at an intellectual remove, considering. *Spider Woman* is a romantic presentation, sympathizing. Its guy in the close-up not only doesn't kill but sacrifices himself in death.

Another subhead in the file on the unempowered community came to Broadway in *Side Show* (1997), about real-life Siamese twins the Hilton sisters. Anticipating another of those anthology scores, as for *Crazy For You* and *Play On!*, one visualized a tunestack of old show songs: "Alone Together," "My Own Best Friend," "And I Am Telling You I'm Not Going," "Stuck With Each Other," and, of course, "Tea For Two." But, lo, the show was entirely new, with music by Henry Krieger to Bill Russell's book and lyrics. There was very little book. Krieger's *Dreamgirls* music had swallowed much of that show's story, and he did even more so here. This show, too, was a backstager: the life and loves of conjoined women (Alice Ripley, Emily Skinner) who fall under the protection of two entrepreneurs (Jeff McCarthy, Hugh Panaro). The men become involved with the girls, but the physical intimidation alienates them, and the girls must face life as a lonely set of two.

On this outing, Krieger composed conservatively, with little rock, and Russell's lyrics avoided the *dummkopf poésie* of pop opera. In truth, the reason why Americans never got into the pop-opera business in a major way is because shows like *Dreamgirls* and *Side Show* can create comparable sensation by other means. These works feature the extra music and Big Idea scenario favored by Lloyd Webber and the French guys. But *Side Show*'s director, Robert Longbottom, is also a choreographer, and unlike the typical (or even exceptional) pop opera, *Side Show* enjoyed dance numbers and a playful side, including some not entirely uncampy vaudeville spots. As in *Dreamgirls*, many conversations were sung. There were also violent upheavals in the music that *Dreamgirls* did not have, as when the Quarrel Duet "Leave Me Alone" broke into the merry big-number vamp to the onstage cutup number "We Share Everything," or in the rutting percussive hunger of "Tunnel of Love."

Despite a truly superb score, an invigorating production, and strong support from the *Times*, *Side Show* barely eked out its 91 performances. Preview audiences—the truest theatregoers, who don't wait to be told what's hot—were enthusiastic. But the shall we say, ticket-buying community was wary of the subject matter. In "Overnight Sensation," McCarthy sang, "Wait till your doubt turns to fascination." No. This was a case of *Watership Down* Syndrome, and the doubt stayed doubtful.

Ironically, the show made stars of Ripley and Skinner. Those doubters asked how they pulled "it" off. A trick costume? Lighting? Was it done with strings? No. They just stood next to each other. The irony at *Side Show*'s center is that Violet and Daisy Hilton know that they are a unit yet keep hoping to be taken for individuals. Like so many modern plays, *Side Show* is about the relationship of distinctive people to "normal" people, its view of life already concentrated on the distinctive. They don't, at first, seem so. They look normal, framing the story as they sit on bleachers for a number called "Come Look at the Freaks." And we notice that McCarthy and Panaro, the men who adopt, then love, and then abandon the sisters, are not in the frame: because *Side Show* is not about "normality."*

Let me tell you of the most terrible line in musical-theatre history. It is in this show. It occurs when, late in Act Two, the girls are disappointed

---

* Only in the framing sequences on the bleachers were Ripley and Skinner not "attached"—except during McCarthy's "Private Conversation," when Skinner appeared as a vision in McCarthy's thoughts, by herself.

once again by McCarthy and Panaro. Suddenly, a major Hollywood director—from MGM!—shows up. He wants the girls in his next picture. Daisy, trying to conquer her romantic despair to focus on show-biz success as the Great American Cure For Everything, asks him, "What's the title of our film?"

And he says, "*Freaks*."

Yes. It's Tod Browning, and the Hilton sisters did make the film, which is even more ghastly than its title suggests. It's a terrible letdown for the *Side Show* audience, who have fallen completely under the spell of the oddest of heroines. Some years from now, Encores! will try it, and the public will cheer the hall down.

Considering other minority groups awaiting redemption, we find Rodgers and Hammerstein's *Flower Drum Song* returning after forty-four years, in 2002, to reconvene its conflict of assimilationists and conservatives among San Francisco's Chinese community. But hold. The work was not revived, nor revised, but given a completely new libretto—new scenario, even—by David Henry Hwang. And the Rodgers and Hammerstein office fought this vandalism in the courts? No: they commissioned it.

It may be that the motivation was simply to bring back a delightful score in a commercially valid framework. After all, unlike the R&H classics, *Flower Drum Song* is a musical comedy, not a musical play; and the former dates much more surely than the latter. Still, some made the inference—encouraged by Hwang—that the original book, by Hammerstein and Joseph Fields, was condescending to Chinese people and thus needed "correcting."

In fact, Hammerstein was the only librettist and lyricist in the Golden Age who never joked or sang in stereotype; rather, we should credit his wish to bring Chinese culture to Broadway when he knew that casting the show would be all but impossible. For all that, the author of the source novel, *The Flower Drum Song*, C. Y. Lee, was part of the production team as an unbilled consultant. Surely he would have spoken up if he thought his people besmirched.

So this new *Flower Drum Song* is an ungrateful pastiche. Worse, it was boring—and it had its own stereotype, in the gay character Harvard (Allen Liu). Some were offended at this irony, but as Harvard was cute, smart, and independent, it's hard to see what harm was done. However, like so many of today's writers, Hwang has no conception of the chronology of slang, of how the use of a term or phrase strongly associated with a particular era cannot be used anachronistically without jarring the ear. Though set in 1960, the new script gave Jodi Long the line "Footbinding? What was that about?" One didn't speak that way in 1960. The Capeman says, "You fucked up my life." Oscar Hammerstein says, "You fucked up my show?"

One minority group seldom celebrated on the official short list is the white working-class male, so The Full Monty (2000) and Movin' Out (2002) were not viewed in a sociopolitical light. However, in a culture in which special-interest groups, lone-ranger spoilers, and the ACLU make war on everything from the Pledge of Allegiance to Christmas, the appearance of shows told from the viewpoint of the guys who fix your car and fight your wars is, if inadvertently, a political statement of a kind.

The Full Monty and Movin' Out have dance in common, but are otherwise utterly unlike each other in denomination. The Full Monty is the kind of show they've long been doing on Broadway, based on something and with book, score, choreography, and direction by talents that entertained us previously, allowing perhaps one newcomer. Where's Charley? (1948) was like that: a star package for Ray Bolger made on a classic farce by George Abbott and George Balanchine with a name new to Broadway in Frank Loesser. The Pajama Game (1954) was like that: another Abbott show, staged with both Jerome Robbins and Bob Fosse, from a coeval novel; again, the score, by Richard Adler and Jerry Ross, introduced a new byline. New Girl in Town (1957) was like that, as Abbott now drew on Eugene O'Neill to introduce the songwriter Bob Merrill.

Clearly, Abbott loved this form, but it was universally generic, and comes down to us in The Full Monty's David Yazbek (another songwriting debutant), Terrence McNally, Jerry Mitchell, and Jack O'Brien, working from the well-known film. The six guys who become strippers will be cast with more or less experienced actors, not entirely George Abbott tyros. Five of them solo in the first number, a men's chorus called "Scrap" that describes the state of being helplessly unemployed and one of those out-of-the-handbook set-it-up pieces. Annie Golden and Emily Skinner will be on hand as wives of two of the guys, and Skinner will warm the folks with her solo, "Life With Harold." An acidulous old gal who helps the guys with their act, Kathleen Freeman completely lacked the exhilarated scorn that (her replacement) Jane Connell brings to such a role, but Freeman was lopsided enough for all that; and she had been around for so long the audience all but gasped when she entered. Wasn't she on *Topper?*

Movin' On, by contrast, is the kind of show they've only recently started doing on Broadway, and everybody will be unfamiliar to most of the public. Twyla Tharp is an outstanding name in ballet, but this is Broadway's first experience of what Tharp does when she is free to do it, after her galley service on *Singin' in the Rain*. *The Full Monty* got a pleasantly traditional staging; *Movin' On* looks like nothing yet seen on The Street. Orchestras have been onstage since the 1970s, but this band is playing Billy Joel, not Kander and Ebb, and in a swing-easy cool that finds them at times as fascinating as the dancing going on below. At the center of the upper story sits Michael Cavanaugh at the grand, performing the numbers with the sharp attack and confidence of the Piano Man himself.

The two shows examine different aspects of prole culture. *The Full Monty* tells of married couples and teaches homo tolerance.* Really, what it speaks to is the feeling of having been degraded that minorities share with, here, husbands and fathers who can't support their families. *Movin' Out*, however, recalls the youth of the Vietnam generation, and its characters undergo vaster tragedy than those of *The Full Monty*. *Movin' Out* ends happily enough, in a reaffirmation of a circle of friends, yet Tharp hears raging ironies in Billy Joel—"We Didn't Start the Fire," "Angry Young Man," "Big Shot," "Captain Jack (will get you high tonight)." Oddly, after the comparable rage of "Scrap," *The Full Monty* gets light. There is an attempted suicide scene as insufferably comic as the one in *Contact*, and then the show becomes pure musical comedy as the guys stop worrying about powerlessness and start wondering how far their strip act ought to go.

Movin' Out's superb marriage of pop music and classical dance made it a sensation. Yet many have failed to appreciate how sleekly Tharp has blended ballet with the thing we have no word for yet that denotes what happened to "hoofing" after Balanchine, de Mille, and Robbins adopted it. This aesthetic blend takes in the music as well, mildly in a quotation

---

* It is but lightly touched on: two of the six guys turn out to be gay. We learn this during the Funeral Number, "You Walk With Me," when Ethan (Romain Frugé) moves to Malcolm (Jason Danieley) to comfort him by publicly taking his hand. We are expected to have anticipated this as, earlier, the two expressed a lifelong fondness for the cast album of *The Sound of Music*. Is this the new go-everywhere gay title? It used to be *Ankles Aweigh*.

of the slow movement of Beethoven's *Pathétique* Sonata but also in Joel's classical suite for solo piano, *Fantasies & Delusions*, few pieces of which are heard in *Movin' Out*, on tape (by pianist Stuart Malina), while the bandstand goes dark and the dancers temporarily own the show.

Revolutionists apply politics to the theatre by preferring works that beat Broadway with a stick. One such would be, it was hoped, the Public Theater's dance piece by George C. Wolfe and Savion Glover, *Bring in 'da Noise Bring in 'da Funk* (1995). "It all depends on how much you like tap dancing," wrote John Simon, putting it mildly. In *The New Republic*, Robert Brustein thought it depended on whether or not you "are beginning to find theatrical expressions of [black racist] anger a little opportunistic and not a little boring."

Partisan hopes for the so-termed *Noise/Funk* were dashed when *Rent* (1996) came along two months later, presented by New York Theatre Workshop. By the time both titles had moved to Broadway, it was clear that *Rent* must overwhelm its funkier-than-thou rival. *Rent* was East Village, anti-bourgeois, and of ethnicity so mixed that it had automatic Victim Superiority. Besides, its author, Jonathan Larson, had died of an aortic aneurysm at the age of thirty-five on the eve of the show's very first night. It was not just an untimely death but an outrageous one, as he was cheated of learning what impact his vision would have on the world.

For here is another of those American pieces of a precise time and place for a certain audience that blithely tours the world. Does the term "East Village" have any meaning for audiences at Reykjavík's Þjóðleikhúsið in 1999, when the tunestack included "Eins Lags Sigur" ("One Song Glory"), "Út í Kvöld" ("Out Tonight"), and of course the title song, "Skuld"? Do the Icelanders understand that Angel is a cross-dresser and Maureen a performance artist? And do they know that Larson updated Puccini's *La Bohème* and reset it in Manhattan's urban waste not for color but because that is where *La Bohème*'s alienated artists and lovers would be today?

The parallels with Puccini are not only general but precise, at times in tight correspondence. For Rodolpho and Mimì there are Roger (Adam Pascal) and Mimi (Daphne Rubin-Vega), and the second couple, Marcello and Musetta, are Mark (Anthony Rapp) and Maureen (Idina Menzel). Colline (Jesse L. Martin) and Schaunard (Wilson Jermaine Heredia) are on hand with almost those very names, only now they are lovers; and Colline still has a thing for his overcoat. Landlord Benoît is landlord Benny (Taye Diggs), and Mimi's first duet with Roger ends "They call me Mimi"—in the opera, the first line of her first aria. Even the chance narrative about the killing of an Akita named Evita—which many must take as Larson's invention—is a tweak of the original, in which Schaunard murders a parrot.

Larson's intention was not to render a gigantic homage to opera, but to find a way to filter a real rock sound into use for music theatre. Previously, this had been done by faking the rock (as in *Hair*), spoofing around so the music didn't matter (as in *The Rocky Horror Show*), or making messes (as in *Marlowe*, *Rockabye Hamlet*, and other horrors of the 1970s). Rock has not worked artistically for musicals because the percussive sound, driven by The Beat, makes characterization impossible.

Larson found a way to dramatize in rock. Mimi actually sounds daintily sensual in "Light My Candle," and Maureen displays a humorously appetitive terror in "Take Me or Leave Me." One of Maureen's exes, Joanne (Fredi Walker), joins another ex, Mark, in "Tango: Maureen," which really is a tango. So some of *Rent* isn't at all rock; but the setting is, and the attitudes are, though the lyrics are as smart as anything in the Great Tradition. Interestingly, what was most rock about *Rent* was the length of time needed to perfect the transmission of those lyrics through the sound system—virtually right through Theatre Workshop's previews and performance run. Spitting out the syllables like Royal Shakespeareans, the *Rent* cast, with ever more nicely calibrated miking, made the breakthrough in time for a triumphant Broadway premiere.

The musical theatre has many classics and cult flops but few phenomena. *Rent* was one. Like many a smash, it added something new to the experience of theatregoing: rush tickets for "*Rent* heads," who kept all-night vigils before the box office to buy front-row seats for the coming performance. Some of these were folk unused to the stage, and the production unfortunately—no, reprehensibly—readjusted its PR in television commercials that called *Rent* "the musical for people who hate musicals." This was Broadway beating *itself* with a stick. Who did they think would respond to these TV spots, Renata Adler?

What were the politics of *Rent*? Was it a revolutionary piece, or downtown going to a Broadway ball? A Social Lesson, or Instant Plastic Compassion? There was that elitist Puccini connection, perhaps an exploitation of AIDS.

Whom was *Rent* against? Starting with some black shows of the early 1970s, and such anti-war pieces as *Blood Red Roses* (1970) and Michael Cacoyannis' *Lysistrata* (1972), the political shows identify themselves by isolating the side they oppose—white people, democratic governments, and, here, the loft rent that Mark and Roger refuse to (in any case, can't) pay. The enemy is in truth more of an abstraction. "Everything is rent!" the two cry in the title song's final line. *Rent*'s people are more forthcoming about what they're in favor of, in the nervously feel-good chorale of the bourgeois-baiting "La Vie Boheme."* Hearing the list of favorite things, one takes in a rain of unobjectionable idiosyncrasies. Is *Rent* the show of the age or a sermonette?

One wonders if anyone asked that of *Show Boat* when it was new. Its mixed-race cast and treatment of such indexed behaviors as alcoholism and family abandonment must have seemed ostentatiously progressive to some. But even if *Rent* bedecks itself in misery too adorably—an arguable view at best—it cannot rival the potentially controversial nature of our last political title. It is all the more worrisome a piece in that its love of racism and terrorism in fact excited no controversy: *Ragtime* (1998).

The *Ragtime* saga takes us first to 1810, when Heinrich von Kleist published his novella *Michael Kohlhaas*. Set in Germany in the middle of the sixteenth century, based on actual events, and narrated in an oddly detached tone in paragraphs of such sweep that all spoken dialogue is trapped inside them rather than set forth individually, the tale is simple and extremely violent. Kohlhaas is a horse dealer cheated by a knight. When Kohlhaas fails to get justice from the state, his wife attempts to intercede for him with the Elector of Saxony and is viciously jabbed with the blunt end of a spear by a bodyguard. She dies, and the spiritually broken yet physically energized Kohlhaas goes on a rampage to bring his enemy knight to judgment. All who bar his way are killed, with their wives and children. Whole towns are savaged; von Kleist likens Kohlhaas to a dragon. Finally, Kohlhaas gets justice, but he must pay for his crimes. At the scaffold, he has his revenge by swallowing a bit of paper on which an infallible gypsy fortune-teller had written when the house of the Saxon Elector would fall, who would be the last of his line, and what foe would fell him. Von Kleist leaves us thinking

---

* It's correctly "la vie bohemienne" or "la vie de bohème." Larson could have retained the preposition in the second alternative for the French would actually sing it as "la vied' bohème," to the same four notes.

that the Elector is doomed to die in horror: but, the author adds, in his very last line, the descendants of Kohlhaas live among us.

It would seem that E. L. Doctorow decided to expand von Kleist's plot and format for his 1975 novel *Ragtime*, similarly treating historical subject matter in a tone that suggests a voice-over guiding one through a documentary. As von Kleist included Martin Luther in his story, Doctorow found roles for Harry Houdini, J. P. Morgan, Evelyn Nesbit, Henry Ford, Emma Goldman, Theodore Dreiser, Sigmund Freud, Booker T. Washington, and many others, some for repeated appearances, others for a sequence, even a paragraph or two. For narrative throughlines, Doctorow invented an unnamed white family in New Rochelle and an unnamed immigrant Jewish family.

However, unlike von Kleist, Doctorow paints pictures, lavishing a playfully descriptive eye on these encounters and interceptions of eccentrics, villains, daredevils, bores. The narrative rhythm has the feeling of ragtime itself, perhaps: foppish melodizing over the plainest of foundations in rondo form and ever driving forward. To make certain that the reader would catch the source of his prestidigitation, Doctorow turned Kohlhaas into Coalhouse, the first name of the father of a third invented family, a black one to balance the native bourgeois and immigrant Jewish groupings. And he had Coalhouse pursue a certain adversary, here not a noble but the chief of a New Rochelle fire company. And he had Coalhouse's love die very much as von Kleist's Lisbeth Kohlhaas does. Doctorow may have enriched his tale with other allusions to classic German lit, for the mother of Coalhouse's child decides to murder the newborn, much as does Goethe's Margarethe in *Faust*.

Margarethe succeeds, and pays with her life. But Doctorow's Sarah is foiled when the white family saves the baby and takes both it and Sarah to live with them. Coalhouse reappears, to court Sarah, and eventually the Jewish family—now reduced to a father and daughter—is also drawn into this central driveline. Around them, the historical figures dance the ragtime of being Americans doing interesting things. Doctorow's melting pot is one not only of ethnicities but of personalities with crazy needs. Younger Brother (the sibling of white Mother) stalks Evelyn Nesbit and at one point masturbates in a closet while Emma Goldman massages Nesbit's spectacular young body and then comes helplessly cascading out as if a kite flown by climax; Father takes part in Peary's expedition to the North Pole; Coalhouse, in his scorched-earth quest for justice, becomes a terrorist who finally seizes and threatens to destroy the J. P. Morgan Library and there meets Booker T. Washington, emissary from the authorities.

Coalhouse kills fewer people than Kohlhaas. But he is, to say the least, a dubious choice as hero of a musical—and, no mistake, this show regards Coalhouse as its hero. The novel has no protagonist; there's too much everybody in it for that. The musical, too, has a lot of everybody, but it centers on Coalhouse, who stages murderous raids on firehouses. Worse, we are clearly meant to accept with a delighted shiver the moment when Younger Brother gains an audience with Coalhouse with the intention of becoming his only white operative. "I can make bombs," he announces. "I know how to blow things up."

If these are the good guys, who's the villain? Father, of course: because he's white and a male. Here's another dreary blast of self-hatred from the left, and another defense of barbarism, as long as it's committed by members of a pet group. If it had been Father who was abused and Mother who had been murdered, no one would care, no one would forgive Father's terrorism, and no one would give him a musical.

It's odd to think that when I started this line of books by writing of the 1920s, Fred and Adele Astaire were mischievous and Marilyn Miller was Cinderella. Their musicals weren't about anything, so they were easy to assemble. The novel *Ragtime* is about the passing of the stable white bourgeois America amid the rise of the volatile minority culture of blacks and recent immigrants, peppered by the private lives of people who actually lived through that time. How does one assemble that musical?

First came *Ragtime* the movie. Doctorow wrote a screenplay for director Robert Altman, but in the end Milos Forman made the film, from Michael Weller's script. Many found it disappointing, but it has its partisans. Most interesting is Randy Newman's score, pointing the way to how music may suit a view of American culture as a form of American music. Newman used only one number of the period, "I Could Love a Million Girls," from *Mamzelle Champagne* (1906), by Cassius Freeborn and Edgar Allan Woolf. One of the many one-act revues produced in a "roof" setting (a prehistoric form of dinner theatre, in fact), *Mamzelle*

Champagne was the show that Stanford White was enjoying when Harry K. Thaw shot him, an event vividly presented in the film.* Otherwise, Newman created his own period flavor. He does some antiquing, in the waltz, polka, music-box tinkle, and Chopin's A Major prelude, a staple of the turn-of-the-century parlor. There is more modern material as well, in an homage to Nino Rota's Fellini style and some very dramatic passages when Coalhouse takes over the Morgan Library. There is ragtime, of course, and a theme song, a lightly mournful waltz called "One More Hour" that has nothing to do with Doctorow's panorama of epochs crunching each other like the earth's tectonic plates. Indeed, the number seems absurdly pretty and petite; *Ragtime* the musical will theme up with an anthem worthy of history, "Wheels of a Dream." "One more sad song," Newman's waltz pleads, "play for me." Perhaps it is meant to remind us that Doctorow's Kohlhaas has been upgraded from horse trader to musician; it is Coalhouse's piano playing that warms Sarah's hardened heart.

Stephen Flaherty and Lynn Ahrens did not blend much outright antique into their *Ragtime* score, and there is no time for the pretty and petite, not with six principals and the historical cameos to delineate. With book writer Terrence McNally, they retained Doctorow's kaleidoscopic presentation while cutting his events down to the three families, five historical figures (Harry Houdini, Evelyn Nesbit, Emma Goldman, Henry Ford, Booker T. Washington), and certain aspects of cultural transformation (assembly-line industrialization, immigration, baseball, the movies, and the latest invention, the Pointless Celebrity). Filling the piece with character and plot songs, they also wrote numbers of, one might say, synoptic explanation, as in "Journey On," in which Father (Mark Jacoby), on his steamship with Peary, passes the Jewish father,

---

* *Mamzelle Champagne* started as a Columbia varsity show, with the typical all-male cast. (Both Oscar Hammerstein and Richard Rodgers got their start writing these.) A producer bought the rights and recast it with the customary comics and babes, but the drag jokes didn't play when biological women uttered them. Worse, a high wind on opening night was drowning out the dialogue, and Woolf's mother—noting unkind remarks by those sitting behind her—feared that his promising career was over. This was the performance at which Thaw killed White. As the pistol discharged, Woolf's mother leaped to her feet, shouting, "My God, they've shot my son!" Of course, the crime's notoriety made *Mamzelle Champagne* a must see, and Woolf went on to a successful career taking in three shows with Jerome Kern and a stint as a screenwriter at MGM. He shares a script credit on *The Wizard of Oz*.

Tateh (a towering Peter Friedman), in the steerage of his boat. Father admires his opposite's courage, but, says Tateh of Father, "He is a fool on a fool's journey." That is, one accomplishes nothing by planting a flag on a patch of ice; the accomplishment is to flee oppression for liberty. Father is on a nineteenth-century quest, confirming the existence of irrelevant things. Tateh is on a twentieth-century quest, trading isms.

For a book musical, *Ragtime* has an astonishingly spacious score. Even the opening number, the title song, is itself gigantic, throwing everything at the audience at once—but cogently—in order to present the leads, the cameos, and the central concept of eras in battle with each other. Taking their seats, the public saw an empty stage dressed to resemble a train station, overlooked by a great clock. One recalled a line from *Grand Hotel*, another show that began with the curtain up: "Time is running out."

The Little Boy (Alex Strange) started up this great machine, to the quiet sounding of the show's ur-theme, four rising notes outlining a perfect or diminished fifth. (Other themes are freely quoted throughout the score.) Looking into a stereopticon, the Little Boy "produced" its view for us, of a Victorian house in front of which a group of whites in summer togs and parasols posed for a photograph. Thus the show begins with a posed still, an attempt to freeze time. It will end with the arrival of the *motion* picture, whose contents include time.

As with the novel's three families, this opening number was divided into three groups—the bourgeois whites, the blacks, and the immigrants—all joining in the chorus. Is "Ragtime" anything like the music of Scott Joplin's day? The first two vocal measures are too chromatic, though the third measure employs the sixth of the scale in the melody, a taste of period. Certainly, the syncopations recall the old style. The lyrics, oddly, bear traces of Doctorow's staccato narration; and the leading players take turns between strophes directly addressing the public with grand or pungent flourishes, such as Washington's description of himself, "the most famous Negro in the country": or Grandfather's "He was thoroughly irritated by everything."

The number at first kept the groups separate, each in its own sphere. The blacks, for instance, were colorfully dressed and drawn to the piano playing of Coalhouse (Brian Stokes Mitchell), while the immigrants were all in brown and black and seemed to huddle where they could find room. The three groups occasionally showed signs of integrating, or at least being aware of one another, and the number built in power and the speakers kept on identifying the many throughlines. It was very much like those books literally opening before us with which Old Hollywood used to start adaptations of classics—the feeling that a great novel could actually be performed, retaining its literary qualities while being enriched by the new format. Ford (Larry Daggett), Morgan (Mike O'Carroll), Goldman (Judy Kaye), Nesbit (Lynnette Perry), White (Kevin Bogue), Thaw (Colton Green) . . . and Houdini (Jim Corti). "Warn the Duke!" the Little Boy called to him. Houdini didn't get it: the Little Boy, characterized by Doctorow as a clairvoyant, is warning all of us that the key event in the future of Western Civilization is the assassination of Archduke Franz Ferdinand of Austria-Hungary in 1914. This will trigger the Great War, altering forever social values in the West. Now everything is ready, and the song rises to a tremendous climax as everyone on stage is singing, "The people called it Ragtime!," the last syllable hurled out on tonic B Major harmony with the sopranos and tenors on a high B. Warn the Duke: for time is running out.

Director Frank Galati, choreographer Graciela Daniele, and set designer Eugene Lee knew they had a pageant on their hands, and they put on one of the biggest shows of the day. Strangely, the dancey strain of "The Crime of the Century," Evelyn Nesbit's vaudeville act, inspired no fancy walkabout: the serious shows continue to be shy of big dance numbers. Rather, Lee's sets danced, as in the arrival of immigrants at Ellis Island. Step by step, they make their way through the bureaucracy of admission, each stage represented by not medical staff or clerks with forms but a series of metal barriers, each falling to detain the newcomers, then rising to let them inch forward, the last of the barriers going up on the latest Americans, with their certificates of entry.

A sequence called "Atlantic City" was especially apt in its evocations: a huge backdrop of a painting of the boardwalk in period manner, while a band of blacks in red uniform plays ragtime for strolling whites. The two lighthearted cameos, Evelyn Nesbit and Houdini, took the vocal after having erupted into the previous book scene—on Coalhouse's terrorism—with jarring frivolity. But if "ragtime" is meant as a portmanteau term combining "American culture" with "nothing stands still in the twentieth century," the show quite rightly builds itself on juxtapositions and turnabouts. Out of town, in Toronto, Nesbit and Houdini had a number called "The Show Biz," an enjoyable lament that slowed the plot when it was at its most suspenseful. So "Atlantic City" gives the pair some narrative scope, as we catch up with the fading relationship of Father and Mother (Marin Mazzie). Then, as the chorus hits the end of the number—*right* on that last vocal note—a wagon bearing a cameraman and a movie director with megaphone rolls in from stage right: Tateh, in the most American of acts, reinventing himself in The Show Biz.

Thus *Ragtime* narrated as much in its staging as in dialogue and song. The score is a buff's favorite for its wealth of melody, the richest Flaherty and Ahrens by size alone. It is possible, though, that Ahrens' work has been a bit taken for granted, for while the music has an immediate appeal, not till the huge work has been fully absorbed does one appreciate the words, one of the finest sets of lyrics in the musical's history. Ahrens never forgets that each of her characters is a different illustration of how America happens. Tateh, in "Buffalo Nickel Photoplay, Inc.," describes the movies' appeal as "People love to see what people do," an aperçu of piquant charm. Then, in Tateh's duet with Mother, "Our Children," they watch his daughter and her son playing on the beach: "Toward the future . . . from the past"—and everything that the show is sings in that simple line.

Flaherty and Ahrens gave Coalhouse's beloved, Sarah (Audra McDonald) an act of atonement for her attempted murder that she lacks in the novel: "Your Daddy's Son." It would be unthinkable not to, for a musical such as *Ragtime* cannot use the observantly uninvolved tone that Doctorow adopts. Music is about feelings. More interesting, the unusual subject matter in general led the authors to unusual song ideas. *Ragtime* buffs might think of the title song or "Wheels of a Dream" as the central number. But thematically the center of *Ragtime* is "New Music," at once a plot number, a character song (for several characters at once), and a throughline administrator. For here, as Coalhouse cajoles the resistant Sarah with his piano playing, the white family confronts black art. That is, the people who run the culture meet the people who are changing it. At the edge of the action stands poor Father, who dimly grasps what's happening but cannot take part in it. *Ragtime* punishes his lack of vision by booking him on the *Lusitania*'s last voyage (as in the novel), so that the more adventurously American Mother can marry Tateh and raise an ethnically mixed family, including Coalhouse and Sarah's orphaned son.

Assassins may have missed out on a good thing by giving *its* Emma Goldman no music of her own, for in *Ragtime* she ends up in fascinating numbers. "The Night That Goldman Spoke at Union Square," marking the political inculcation of Younger Brother (Steven Sutcliffe), writes a new page in the epic theatre handbook, as Younger Brother sings to the audience and Goldman stays characterologically within the narrative. Yet at some point she focuses on him in particular, making the show's sole reference to the masturbation episode otherwise left behind in the novel. How does Goldman know that about him? She knows yet more, reminding us that even beside its concept-show freedom *Ragtime* is a somewhat fantastical piece, with its symbolic figures crossing paths like deities in some enchanted glade, its "Warn the Duke!" Even as Younger Brother continues to sing to the public of Goldman's effect on him, she announces and confides at once, "I've been waiting for you."

Thus summoned to enter his own legend, Younger Brother makes his way to Coalhouse's hide-out: but he is too shy to speak. The orchestra has struck up and a number is clearly under way. Yet Younger Brother stutters till Emma Goldman simply appears, starting the refrain of "He Wanted To Say." By now, we are all used to the concept-show convention of characters turning up anywhere they want to—not corporeally, but rather as messengers, guides, inquisitors, or, as here, an inspiration. Each concept musical twists the magic innovatively at least somewhere; and Goldman's sudden manifestation is one such. She is singing what Younger Brother cannot articulate. He is presumably thinking it, if inchoately. But then even Coalhouse and his gang take over this unspoken refrain—or, rather, the show as a whole has become Younger Brother's inspiration, which unfortunately climaxes as he at last speaks his mind, taking Doctorow's line "I know how to blow things up." As he and Coalhouse shake on it, there is a blackout and a tremendous explosion, unmistakably the sound of another firehouse destroyed and more firefighters incinerated. *Ragtime* expects us to find this gratifying, just as the action has built to the line quoted above as something momentous and thrilling.

That line marks *Ragtime*'s decisive departure from Heinrich von Kleist, for the author of *Michael Kohlhaas* takes no sides, while the authors of *Ragtime* surely do. All those firefighters killed for what? The destruction of an automobile? Some of *Ragtime*'s chorus women in the ensemble number "Coalhouse Demands" voice their rejection of terrorism in exactly those terms, but they are little more than a woodwind toot in a symphony whose title is Coalhouse. True, the car is presumably an objective correlative of racial oppression, and it is Sarah's murder rather than the auto that sets Coalhouse off. Still, these assaults on firehouses are unforgivably disgusting, and to see terrorism exalted in American theatre—even before 9/11—reveals how slavishly Broadway buys snake oil from the wreckers and stooges of the hard left. This is truly the glorification of slime.

I Dreamed I Saw Fosse in My Maidenform Bra; or, the Last Five Years

Jane Eyre (2000) could be called a typical musical of the millennium, though it was unappreciated and closed quickly. The source material, Charlotte Brontë's novel, might recall the more serious fifties shows such as *Fanny* (1954) and *The Most Happy Fella* (1956)—except fifties shows were still at least partly musical comedies, and this *Jane Eyre* had virtually no humor, and little light. Fifties shows dealt with tribulation of certain kinds, but they had their sunny side. *Jane Eyre*'s "Children of God," dealing with Jane's ghastly backstory as a child abused by life-hating ghouls, marks the show almost from the first as less a romance than an ordeal. The number reaches a superb climax, with the little schoolgirls and the adults in an operatic ensemble; but the music is virtually slashing at us.

There is plenty of such music, too, another quality identifying the present-day musical play: Jane's liltingly sorrowful "Forgiveness"; her soaring "Sweet Liberty"; Rochester's "As Good As You" and duet with Jane called "Secret Soul"; his unworthy fiancée's establishing song, "The Finer Things," a coloratura waltz in which the music delights in her while the lyrics despise her, expose her; Jane's duet with this rival, "In the Light of the Virgin Morning," one melody with two different sets of character lyrics; Rochester's "The Proposal," the center of the work, in which the typical Big Dark Man of the old Gothic novel admits that the Tortured Heroine is truly his love, in a hymn that suddenly breaks into *stile concitato* without screaming. Compared with the pop-opera style, *Jane Eyre*'s score is almost Mozartean.

These are only eight of the twenty-four separate numbers (not counting reprises) listed in the program, and like most of the others this octet finds expression in earnest and intimate revelation. With a score by Paul Gordon and book (and some lyrics) by John Caird, *Jane Eyre* is yet another dark show. How many have we seen in these pages? For light relief, we can count only on the housekeeper's two numbers, "Perfectly Nice" and "A Slip of a Girl," both somewhat comic in $\frac{6}{8}$ time and suggesting Marion Lorne on speed. There is as well "The Gypsy," in which a disguised Rochester tells fortunes in merry waltz meter.

This direly intense and very faithful adaptation is opera in all but name. One wonders, however, what opera singer could dare the immense title role, very memorably played by Marla Schaffel; but then, such talent is one of this era's strengths. The farther back one goes in the musical's history, the less versatile the talent appears: but the roles themselves were less needy. Even *Show Boat* was designed not for actors but for singers, dancers, and comics who could finesse their way through the dialogue. Ours is the age of the art musical and its singing actor.

Here's another serious show, but one with odd problems. *Jane Eyre* had no problems; one either liked it or one didn't. But *Thou Shalt Not* (2001) was so flawed that the well-warned came to jeer. It was an interesting piece even so, one that tried to pull off something different, a restoration of the all-important dance component of the musical play of the 1940s and '50s. It should be remembered, however, that much of the dance in the early musical-play era was simply decoration. *Paint Your Wagon* (1951) filled out its second act with two irrelevant dances almost back-to-back, the "Rope Dance" for Gemze de Lappe and James Mitchell, then a "Can-Can" for Mary Burr and James Tarbutton. *Fanny* worked a "Cirque Français" into a birthday party, with acrobats, clowns, an aerialist, a pony act, and musical seals, all for novelty's sake only. (*Street Scene* [1947] and *Candide* [1956] in part derived their uniqueness by isolating dance in a single number, respectively in the "Moon-Faced, Starry-Eyed" jitterbug pas de deux and the "Paris Waltz.") But of course this was the day of George Balanchine, Agnes de Mille, Jerome Robbins, Michael Kidd, Bob Fosse: such talent must not be wasted. And note that all but Fosse came from the world of ballet, where dance isn't integrated into something but rather *is* the thing itself.

Today's public would be restless at dance for its own sake. The choreographer of a serious show cannot decorate, but must interpret and even narrate along with the authors. So *Thou Shalt Not* was billed as "A new

musical by Susan Stroman, David Thompson and Harry Connick Jr."
though Connick was singly credited also for the score, Thompson for the
book, and Stroman as director-choreographer. Clearly, the three wanted
to state how collaboratively they had authored this adaptation of *Thérèse
Raquin*, Emile Zola's novel of 1867. For instance, had Thompson laid out
a psychological guideline for the heroine's establishing scene—a dance;
the vocal itself came along later—from which Connick and Stroman
worked? (Connick wrote his own dance arrangements and orchestrations.) Such ambitions often create a more enjoyable experience—
bungling and all—than do more popular shows made of spare parts and
faking. For those who truly love the musical—basically, gay men and
Frank Rich—a mistaken piece such as *Thou Shalt Not* can fascinate especially on the analytical level. One deconstructs the work as it unfolds, trying to understand what its makers' intentions were. If nothing else, this
was a chance to see what one of our foremost director-choreographers
would do with her "art" show, a glowering portion of dark music cut from
a still vital piece of classic lit.

Bref, Laurent helps Thérèse escape her loveless marriage to Camille in
passionate adultery. They murder Camille. Literally paralyzed by grief,
Camille's mother can only gaze upon them with hatred, but Camille's
spirit haunts them, ruins love and life. They kill each other in despair,
before the gloating silence of the mother, who, Zola says, "could not feast
her eyes sufficently" all that night on the sight of the corpses.

One of the first great psychological novels, *Thérèse Raquin* obviously
lends itself to dance theatre. The setting was moved from Zola's France to
postwar New Orleans to take advantage of Connick's love of Bourbon
Street jazz while maintaining a French flavor and even Zola's character's
names. With the hero of Stroman's 2000 *Music Man* revival, Craig
Bierko, and Kate Levering as the guilty pair, and Norbert Leo Butz and
Debra Monk as les Raquin *mère et fils*, the cast was a ready one, though
only Butz won praise and poor Monk had to spend the second act in a
stroke victim's disfiguring mouthastuck grimace, without the slightest
hope of taking part in an eleven o'clock song.

The show's worst mistake lay in Connick's lack of interest in character
and plot numbers, favoring jazzy ensembles of the Quarter or Frank
Sinatra snap-your-fingers goodtime solos. Debra Monk's establishing
song, "My Little World," is a fine number in itself, but it establishes

nothing. It was a performance piece, leaving this bossy but not uncharming lady with the crush on her weakling of a son to manifest herself entirely in her book scenes and, later in the act, in their duet, "I've Got My Eye On You."

The score was not wholly unintegrated. "(Who are you in) The Other Hours," Bierko's seduction of Levering; her acceptance of him, "Sovereign Lover"; and their despairing duet near the end, "I Like Love More," certainly described the arc of their affair. Yet too much of the music was atmosphere, often of glancing or no relation to the plot—the jive session "It's Good To Be Home"; the two Mardi Gras numbers, "Light the Way" and "Take Her to the Mardi Gras"; Butz's folklike "Tug Boat," just before he is murdered; and his funeral tune, "Won't You Sanctify." Even the ghost Butz's "Oh! Ain't That Sweet," his snigger at the discomfort he has brought to his killers, and sung in an ironically natty white suit on their bed, seemed like yet another concert spot because it so resembled the other ones.

Again, the music itself is pleasurable, a successful attempt to mate pop with the Great Tradition as sheer sound. Connick's lyrics rhyme—pop usually doesn't—and he is a craftsman of the sound he works in. But his songs don't often enough relate to the action. That is the difference, one might say, between Harry Connick and Kander and Ebb. The difference, even, between Somewhere Else and Broadway. We have been paying for the success of *Hair* for thirty-five years.

Thou Shalt Not's staging was interesting. Bierko's first number, "While You're Young," was a performance spot at the keyboard. As the rest of the cast moved to Bierko's fancy beat, the lights dimmed on them while Levering sang the slow ballad "I Need To Be In Love." The ensemble continued to dance *against* her rhythm, isolating her in her spotlight as if warning us that she is dangerously out of tune with her surroundings—unaware, so to speak, of the risks, the penalties, of love.

Then, too, there were all those wonderful dances, genuine set pieces such as in Rodgers and Hammerstein's day, when dance episodes proudly bore titles. *Thou Shalt Not* named its dances after the songs they expanded upon, although the most dramatic of these was named for the show itself.

In Zola, the degeneration of the adultery finds expression in Thérèse's reading habits: she displaces her feelings for Laurent onto the heroes of novels. That would have made an arresting ballet, perhaps; Stroman instead showed her Thérèse sinking into a sexual mire, culminating in the suggestion of an involvement in gang sex. When, not long after, Bierko and Levering embraced downstage center as if each were trying to crush the life out of the other, they slowly revolved to reveal Levering clutching a giant knife behind her back. Involuntarily, I gasped. Because the story is involving, and the authors' wish to make something special out of it is admirable, and their mistakes are more thought-provoking than all the gimmickry in *Hairspray*.

At least musical comedy is an ageless form. *Jane Eyre* is a work of this era, and *Thou Shalt Not*, even as a descendant of the old musical play, is as well. But a fast, springy piece with tuneful songs and crazy dances is *Good News!* (1927), *Finian's Rainbow* (1947), *Li'l Abner* (1956), *The Wiz* (1975), and *Thoroughly Modern Millie* (2002). True, the book of this last is uneven, the interpolations are irritating when the composer is so ready herself, and the use of a surtitle screen for inane translation "fun" becomes a device of tomato-baiting incitement. Still, like *Crazy For You* and *The Producers*, *Millie* took the top Tony for restating musical comedy without modern rationality, not to mention disillusionment. It's Boy Meets Girl, period.

Another personal note: I was at one of those New York dinner parties in someone's garden behind a brownstone some years ago, and guest Dick Scanlan mentioned that he was working on a stage version of the *Thoroughly Modern Millie* film. This suggested that the cycle of making flop stage musicals out of classic movie musicals was over. Now, I thought, we're to get flop stage musicals out of terrible movie musicals.

Bud's wrong again. Though a piece of Universal Pictures afterbirth, the stage *Millie* ended up energetic and colorful, with many long-lost elements of traditional musical comedy cleverly rediscovered. Director Michael Mayer actually framed the two acts with the oldtime curtain up and curtain down, and choreographer Rob Ashford's ensemble worked numbers in the matching costumes (by Martin Pakledinaz) that amused our grandparents. Touches of operetta in the vocal parts recalled the shoving match between pop and "classical" in the stage and film musicals of the 1930s and '40s. (One of countless examples is the "I Like Opera/ I Like Swing" duet of Betty Jaynes and Judy Garland in the *Babes in Arms* movie.) Then, too, there was the general lack of horror in the subplot involving hotelière Mrs. Meers (Harriet Harris) and her slavery ring, because in unreconstructed musical comedy, nothing is real but Boy Meets Girl. Here Boy (Gavin Creel) met Understudy (Sutton Foster), who replaced Erin Dilly before the La Jolla tryout's first night. The second couple was Marc Kudisch and Angela Christian, and the madcap millionairess shtick went to Sheryl Lee Ralph.

There was no attempt to reproduce the film in the *Saturday Night Fever* manner. The new *Millie* really was new, especially in the leads' performances. Foster made a high-powered heroine where the film's Julie Andrews was so low-key that she might have intended her portrayal as sardonic commentary of an arcane nature. Andrews' Jack Armstrong–like boss was John Gavin, playing entirely in cartoon; Kudisch didn't turn him into Hamlet, but he did give the guy some variety. In the end, of course, Millie falls for not the boss but the penniless guy (who turns out to be a society scion, another forgot cliché of the old school). Jimmy is given a new personality, meanwhile, as a womanizer who Gets Girl only after some reluctance about Commitment.

The greatest change involved Mrs. Meers, for the film relied on Beatrice Lillie to be funny by nature. She had little to do, but Harriet Harris enjoyed a solo, "They Don't Know," and far too much business with two Chinese assistants, whose lines and lyrics were the reason for those surtitle screens.

Despite its great success, *Millie* is not a consistently excellent show. The book, by the film's author, Richard Morris, and our partygoing Dick Scanlan, is short in good lines. One piece of business stood out, when Sheryl Lee Ralph showed up as a decoy at Harris' registration desk. Ralph is disguised as a Scandinavian in blond wig and summer boater, and of course the idea is totally zany because Ralph was one of Michael Bennett's original dreamgirls, the great Deena Jones. It's a delirious laugh that only a stage musical could program; on film, only the *genere fantastico* of the Marx Brothers could get away with it. As the audience's laughter dies down, Ralph gives Harris some ridiculous false name, and Harris just waits.

RALPH: (trying to move the plot along) It's Swedish.
HARRIS: I thought you were Finnish.

Scanlan wrote lyrics to nine new songs with composer Jeanine Tesori. Two titles from the movie were heard as well—but there were also four numbers from other sources. (A fifth, a dance number called "The

Nuttycracker Suite," jazzes up the Sugar Plum Fairy's theme and the main strain of the pas de deux from Chaikofsky's ballet *The Nutcracker*.) The movie itself utilized period interpolations, but that's no excuse, especially when Scanlan called upon that insufferable Al Jolson number "Mammy" for another drop-in by the surtitle screen so that the two Chinese guys could Jolsonize in Mandarin.

After the variety of styles that Tesori had sampled in other stage works, the old-fashioned *Millie* must have felt limiting; but nuns fret not at their convent's narrow room. Tesori freshens genre in the playboy's "What Do I Need With Love?" and in Ralph's hymn to Musical Comedy's Official Location, "Only In New York." Tesori's especially apt in verses. "Jimmy," left over from the movie (and written by Jay Thompson), is given a new intro whose thought processes are suddenly invaded by the title line of the film's title song (by James Van Heusen and Sammy Cahn). Thus, the movie's sentimentality is enriched with psychological reality: Millie has distracting ambitions. Later, Jimmy himself starts the verse to "I Turned the Corner" on a ledge of Millie's office building, looking down on the crowds below. Tesori actually catches this in her music—the scurrying of the tiny figures, the lofty grandeur of the view—and then glides into the most romantic of ballads, of the old sort. It's Victrola Mozart.

Jane Eyre, Thou Shalt Not, and *Thoroughly Modern Millie* typify currents running through the musical today: one, the extra-musical musical play that encroaches on opera; two, the rehabilitation of dance after years of neglect; and, three, the musical-comedy revival.

The first of the three is the most vulnerable, not only because the searching intelligence of its creative staff has outstripped the public's indulgence, but because it seems obsessed with disasters and tragedies. Finally it got to a lynching, in *Parade* (1998), on one of America's most famous miscarriages of justice. In Georgia, in 1913, a black man killed a young girl, but charges were filed against a harmless white man, a Jewish northerner. Convicted on false testimony, he got the death sentence, commuted to life imprisonment by the governor. But a mob dragged him out of jail and strung him up. The first thing that *Parade* shows us is the oak tree from which he swung.

And the first thing we hear is "The Old Red Hills of Home," sung by a Confederate soldier to an evil relentless rumbling in the orchestra, something immutable and unlistening, clinging to a handful of folk wisdoms, all of which are wrong, something impervious to proofs. That rumbling is the bad guys—the south itself, perhaps—for *Parade* is yet another of the countless works of American art about decency taking on depravity. This is the core of the western, till relatively recently a ubiquitous American genre; and *Parade* is exactly like a western but for its setting. It is a form of *Ox-Bow Incident*, with the credulous mob and the manipulative liars and the hating fanatic and the guy who starts on the bad side but crosses over to good.

Written by Jason Robert Brown and Alfred Uhry, *Parade* was directed by Harold Prince, but it is not a concept musical. Its title contains a concept, for it refers literally to the statewide parade long popular throughout the deep south on each April 26, in memory of the Final Capitulation of the Confederate Army.* Presumably, the title refers metaphorically to the obtuseness of a people that make a holiday of a catastrophe because they have mythologized themselves into a history-book martyrdom, as some Germans did after World War I. So these people parade their colors, their heroes, their ignorance. It's good weather for bad guys.

Leo Frank (Brent Carver) and his wife, Lucille (Carolee Carmello), are the good guys. Mary Phagan (Christy Carlson Romano) is the victim. The bad guys are, at first, more or less everyone else. The district attorney (Herndon Lackey) knows he is prosecuting an innocent man but nourishes political ambitions. The reporter (Evan Pappas) tries Frank in the press. Frank's lawyer (J. B. Adams) scarcely defends him at all. The real murderer (Rufus Bonds Jr.) delivers the convicting testimony in court. The victim's schoolmate Frankie Epps (Kirk McDonald) joins the lynch mob and is the one who kicks the chair out from under Frank to hang him. The governor (John Hickok) eventually becomes the man with a conscience. Prodded by Lucille Frank—and the judge, who repents of having rushed the proceedings toward the death penalty—the governor throws away his political career in trying to save Frank. Still, many others in the cast add to the monolithic nature of the Parade against Frank, the determination to destroy him even if he is innocent. Uhry

---

* Contrary to popular belief, Robert E. Lee's surrender at Appomattox Courthouse on April 9 concluded hostilities between the North and Lee's forces only. Other Southern generals had yet to yield. But when Joseph E. Johnston defied Jefferson Davis' order to pursue the conflict and surrendered to the North's General Sherman near Durham Station, North Carolina on April 26, the war was officially over.

throws us a line to explain why the black man who was the apparent culprit was not charged and an apparently guiltless white man was: the victim's defiled innocence demands a show trial:

THE CORRUPT DISTRICT ATTORNEY: Hangin' anoher Nigra ain't enough this time. We gotta do better.

This must be the most appallingly tragic story in musical-theatre history. Carmello in particular put us through great anxiety as Lucille rises to greatness from housewifely trifles. Her half of "What Am I Waiting For?," a "segregated duet" with Leo, recalls his courtship in a fluttery waltz marked "*Delicato.*" Later, her dismissal of the reporter's attempt at an interview, "You Don't Know This Man," bears the uncrushable dignity of a decent person facing The Beast; and the ironically challenging "Do It Alone," though subdued, reveals her strength. Most dramatically, she takes her husband's case to the governor during a dance number, "Pretty Music," the charming ragtime re-creation intercut with tense stanzas of dialogue.

In some ways, Lucille holds the show's center. It is she who most grows and most acts, although, ironically, she is part of the culture that produces that Parade. Also, she is the only character allotted a full evening's worth of music. For Jason Robert Brown gave his score a documentary flavor by giving camera time to relatively unimportant people—the kind that wouldn't get, for example, an establishing song in a more traditional tunestack. Thus, an entire number, "The Picture Show," is given to the murder victim and Frankie Epps, who tries to arrange a movie date with her as they travel the length of the stage in a trolley car.

To those who regard serious musicals as Transylvanians regard Dracula, "The Picture Show" may look defective, an excrescent idyll. Obviously, it establishes Mary Phagan for us; she otherwise has only one short book scene. But the number also gives us Frankie Epps, and lets us see these two not as figures in a murder case but carefree teens, he an amusingly goofy swain and she scoffing at his approach. The number poses an interesting question: how do such charming kids figure in the Parade? Mary's friends give false testimony in court, and Epps, we know, will be Leo Frank's murderer.

Does "The Picture Show" humanize monsters? In a kind of mutation, its music reappears in Leo's trial as his solo, "Come Up to My Office," a fantasy version of Leo corresponding to that false testimony, a human turned into a monster. But then, the Parade itself has the aforementioned "The Old Red Hills of Home," as disturbing as "The Picture Show" is disarming. The entire show is disturbing; it is the only musical I can think of that has stirred real anger in people, though none that I've spoken to could articulate exactly what had incensed them. It may be that Brown, Uhry, and Prince created theatre too powerful for theatregoers. Another Prince show, *Sweeney Todd*, might seem like the all-time terminal musical, in which officers of the court connive at an innocent man's destruction: as in *Parade*. But *Sweeney Todd* speaks from a remove, as an antique urban legend belonging to another country. Then, too, *Sweeney Todd* is about a revenge: a melodrama. *Parade* is about an outrage: the truth.

For a serious show, many prefer something like *A Class Act* (2000), also drawn from real life but lifted by a musical-comedy spirit. The subject is composer and lyricist Edward Kleban. Apparently destined to be one of the noted alumni of the B.M.I. workshop because of his lyrics to *A Chorus Line* (1975), Kleban somehow never got another show on during the following twelve years before his untimely death. Moreover, *A Class Act* studies not only Kleban's talent but the busy little worries and demands that vexed his personal life.

With a book by Linda Kline and Lonny Price, songs culled from Kleban's catalogue, and Price directing as well as playing Kleban, *A Class Act* was a success at the Manhattan Theatre Club but failed on its transfer to Broadway. One problem was the small scale of the eight-person staging. True, Price rescaled it smartly. On off-Broadway, in the opening scene at Kleban's funeral, the subject himself materialized for his establishing song, "Light On My Feet," by simply rising from a chair in the audience. At the Ambassador Theatre, he more engagingly appeared in a box at stage right and elevatored down to the deck.

Another problem was this B.M.I. workshop thing itself. Few people outside the profession know what it is, and for them the work was mystifying. Who was this Lehman Engel (Jonathan Freeman), tall and dapper and vaguely like Cyril Ritchard? Why were these people writing songs for Lehman Engel? Shouldn't they be writing songs for Florenz Ziegfeld or David Merrick? And who were these people in the first place?

Let us consider the B.M.I. workshop, because it has had some impact on the musical since the 1970s. Lehman Engel was a southerner who came to New York during the Depression to forge a career in musical theatre. After jobs writing incidental music for plays and one composer credit for a musical—*A Hero Is Born* (1937)—Engel concentrated on conducting and, eventually, writing books on the making and performing of musicals.

He was a superb conductor. Goddard Lieberson chose him as musical director of Lieberson's series of of studio-cast readings of classic Broadway (including the first full-scale recording of *Porgy and Bess*). Harold Rome wouldn't open a show without Engel in the pit. Stephen Sondheim wanted him for *Anyone Can Whistle*, though the producer screwed that up and Herbert Greene got the job. Conducting on Broadway has long been divided among a handful of first-class musicians, and Engel was as good as any of his colleagues. Listen to the dashing whiz that he lays on the over-tures to *Li'l Abner*, *Destry Rides Again* (1959), *Do Re Mi* (1960). This is the very sound that "Broadway" makes in its Golden Age: the crazy excitement of the next bunch of wonderful tunes coming into one's hearing.

As a teacher, however, Engel was compromised. His respect for and encouragement of talent is undeniable. But his expertise found expression in silly rules, such as The First Number Must Be Written Last. Like, he insisted, the slow introduction to the opening allegro of a Haydn symphony.

But a symphony is abstract and a musical is narrationally precise; it is specious to compare the two. Besides, the first number has become so thematically central in the modern musical that it defines and creates the show. It must be written first, or early on, whereas Haydn's intros are no more than assertive welcomes, excrescently included.

More: Engel decreed that a comedy song only delineates the lament of a character with a problem that is disaster to him or her and amusing to us: "I Cain't Say No." I vividly remember classmate Brooks Morton ask-ing Engel how "Always True To You In My Fashion" suits the definition. It's not a lament, yet it's obviously meant to be funny.

"It's not a comedy song," said Engel, trapped in his own sophistry.

Actually, even with the musical-comedy handbook rewritten into tat-ters, there still are genre numbers. They just aren't as fixed as they used to be. One of *A Class Act*'s jokes found Engel assigning "a charm song for *A Streetcar Named Desire*." But Engel did ask the writers in the elemen-tary class to write a number for *Streetcar*: a ballad. The charm song was for

The Member of the Wedding. And the comedy song was for *Come Back, Little Sheba*.

And where did all this practice take one? At semester's end came several matinée showcase revues, in which Engel's students would see their work performed by Equity talent before, presumably, important listeners. It must have worked, because we have seen how many writers started with Engel and ended on Broadway.

Somehow, little of this came through in *A Class Act*. The real Lehman, grand, fussy, and easily piqued, was nothing like Jonathan Freeman (or, on Broadway, Patrick Quinn). The loving beehive surrounding Kleban in the show—some of whom travel to Toronto for the tryout of the 1973 *Irene* revival just because Kleban wrote the dance arrangements—never existed. It was not till two years later, when *A Chorus Line's* immense popularity validated the B.M.I. classes, that a certain community spirit finally emerged. In effect, those who had not been Kleban's intimates befriended his success.

That said, *A Class Act* was a wonderful adventure in the world of Ed Kleban—and a book musical, at that. The uninformed would never have guessed that the songs had been rounded up for the occasion—even if, like many Shire and Maltby pieces, they have the revue-oriented tendency to create tiny one-act plays. "Paris Through the Window" is typical, almost cinematic in its three American guys driving a car into their first view ever of this great cultural capital. The variety and vitality of Ed Kleban urges upon us the wonder that he never got to Broadway again while he lived. We get details of his career, as in a first encounter with Michael Bennett (David Hibbard), in which the monster genius writhes on the floor like a reptile. That *is* the moment: Kleban meets Bennett! But why didn't anything else happen after? Could Ed Kleban's tragedy be that of the musical in general? Producers hear one's name and say, Yes, but what revivals have you written?

Scott Wise was credited with *A Class Act's* choreography, but there was little of it. Musicals used to dance because they were musicals; now they have to have a reason. Mark Dendy's reason for filling The "other" *Wild Party* (2000) with dance was the revue-like format, one welcoming set pieces and chance entertainments. This was the off-Broadway *Wild Party*, preceding Michael John LaChiusa's version and entirely the work of Andrew Lippa. His party offers no collision of past and present, show biz and reality. But it does see a lot of opportunity for movement, even reviving the New Dance Sensation so popular in the 1920s. With the retirement of "The Monkey Doodle-Doo" and "The Varsity Drag," Lippa saw an opening for "The Juggernaut," which, true to the genre, pleads "Jug with me" without actually revealing how one jugs. One has to attend the show and watch Dendy's troupe open up.

True, LaChiusa's *Wild Party* has its New Dance Sensation, the aforementioned "Black Bottom." But Lippa's gang was crazed for dance, one of the many ways in which his version read March's poem differently than LaChiusa and Wolfe did. This one took two acts in a unit set, and it even included the guy complaining about the noise who calls the cops. (They never showed up, however.) Lippa also used his ensemble to narrate during the numbers, as in "What a Party," when those on stage named each arriving guest, who then gave a terse description of himself. "Lesbian." "Pugilist." Jackie (Lawrence Keigwin) was here a sweet-natured dancer, and mute at that. Dolores (Kena Tangi Dorsey), Eartha Kitt's tear-the-house-down turn in LaChiusa, was in Lippa just "a hooker," as she announced upon entering; she had little to do. Michael Gibson's orchestrations, too, varied greatly with Bruce Coughlin's for LaChiusa, employing electric guitar and winds among his nine players, while Coughlin slipped violins, banjo, and a tuba into his sixteen-person pit. And Lippa's Black (Taye Diggs) was no beautiful unanswered question but a fully realized character, which sounds great but complicated the flow of the show's last half hour. In March's poem, Black is just a guy. In LaChiusa, he's anything you want him to be: the ultimate hustler/savior. In Lippa, he's the Boy who Meets Girl, which doesn't suit this odd material.

Before the story line slowed up, Lippa really did throw a wild party, a vaudeville of showstoppers. Idina Menzel's establishing number as Kate, "Look At Me Now," starts "I was born in a ditch in West Virginia" on an aggressive blues recit over chopping chords, a classic genre. This is the Great Tradition, especially when Madelaine True (Alix Korey) gets to "An Old-Fashioned Love Story." Madelaine's the lesbian, as twisted as anyone in this twisty tale, and the music is twisted, too, letting the scan of "love story" fall incorrectly for the merrily dire lesbian flip of it all: "Boys stay out to sea" is Madelaine's utopia. "A Wild, Wild Party" is even bolder. Marked "Tempo di Sunday Morning (Gospel Jump)," it's a review of Bible stories in the idiom that P. G. Wodehouse invented in the 1910s: applying modern lingo to ancient affairs for comic effect. In this retelling, Sodom and Gomorrah were just another wild party, "loving it loud and fast." LaChiusa's party is America in cultural revolution. Lippa's is musical comedy as the second oldest profession, "and hoping the beer would last."

With Julia Murney and Brian d'Arcy James as Queenie and Burrs, Lippa's edition of March had very strong contenders. But it must be said that the other party gave its cast comprehensive playing room, which they filled to repletion. It's not unlike competing versions of *Show Boat* in the 1920s. You could be the Gershwins: you're still going up against Kern and Hammerstein.

The dance revival has found its happiest place in the anthology revue, where folks don't have to get into a story in order to participate in a big number. Most of these shows reheat a songwriter's leftovers; *Fosse* (1999), like *Jerome Robbins' Broadway*, substantiated a choreographer. However, as its title implies, the earlier work devoted itself to a kind of Robbins history, taking in not only the obvious points of reference but some interesting footnotes. *Fosse*, "conceived" and put together by Richard Maltby Jr., Chet Walker, and Ann Reinking, less ambitiously devoted itself to Fosse's *Dancin'* (1978), with a few outstanding Broadway numbers ("Steam Heat; "Big Spender" and "Rich Man's Frug"; the pertly ghoulish Manson Trio from *Pippin*) and some of Fosse's Hollywood stuff. There was virtually nothing from some shows in which Fosse developed his history—the erotic Dream Ballet from *New Girl in Town* (1957), for whose integrity he had to fight the entire production team; the "Uncle Sam Rag" from *Redhead* (1959), in which Fosse embodied the music's counterpoint in groupings of "counterpointed" dancers; "Coffee Break" or "A Secretary Is Not a Toy" from *How To Succeed in Business Without Really Trying* (1961);* "Rich Kids' Rag" from *Little Me* (1962). Gwen Verdon served as "artistic advisor" on *Fosse*; didn't she want to see more of the

---

* The following is the most genuine of footnotes: extremely inconsequential yet unfortunately unavoidable. Fosse was *How To Succeed*'s co-director, not choreographer; the dancing was credited to Hugh Lambert. In fact, Fosse had been called in during *How To Succeed*'s rehearsals to take over the choreography, but after his Tony-gorging success as the director-choreographer of *Redhead*, Fosse's byline could not fall below the "musical staging" level. From 1959 on, excluding *How To Succeed*, Fosse accepted only auteur credit for stagings, including for the tryout casualties *The Conquering Hero* (1961) and *Pleasures and Palaces* (1965). Thereafter, he became co- and even sole author as well, the one director-choreographer to bar collaborators from his theatre.

Fosse that she was a part of? Too much of the program emphasized the sentimental Fosse—yes, he had a soft side—which never impressed the way the cynically life-loving Fosse did. The first act finale (of three) was that tiresomely wistful "I Wanna Be a Dancin' Man," introduced about a half-century earlier by Fred Astaire in the film *The Belle of New York*. Even by then, this was show-biz hokum forgiven only because Fred Astaire had well earned wistful rights. Fosse had used it in *Dancin'*, and that staging turned up in *Fosse*, as the show's predominantly dark look brightened up. The black costumes and black space overseen by two mobile prosceniums outlined by lightbulbs gave way to white suits, gloves, and boaters against a gold-and-white backdrop.

And this is not Fosse. Yes, he made it: but it turns on one of those stupid frauds that American show biz can't get enough of, that "You haven't lived until you've played the Palace," that "You'll never make the big time because you're small-time in your heart," that MGM dream of a culture made entirely of show biz, for which Mickey and Judy filmed manuals for do-it-yourself stardom while, behind a prop tree, little Jackie Cooper was fucking Joan Crawford. It's naïve—a condition that has nothing to do with Bob Fosse. Yet, came *Fosse*'s third act, there was "Mr. Bojangles," again from *Dancin'*, and another risibly sentimental number. Fosse wasn't a romantic; Fosse was a satirist. *Fosse* was enjoyable, of course, and a thrilling showcase for the dancers. But it was an incorrect piece, not dishonest but concentrating on rather a lot of irrelevant material.

I vastly prefer *Swing!* (1999), which had the advantage of lots of vocals and instrumentalizing along with the dancing. *Swing!* had also the benefit of one of the outstanding vocalists of the day, Ann Hampton Callaway, and a snazzy staging conceit that integrated the band members with the performers, the lead singers with the dancing corps. Thus, Laura Benanti didn't simply sing "Cry Me a River." She duetted on it with Steve Armour's trombone. Just before the release, he blatted out some vigorously lame excuse on his ax. "*What?*" the incredulous Benanti cried, making a face before she returned to the melody.

A look at the song and dance styles of the period between, say, James Reese Europe and John Coltrane, *Swing!* was a fresh breeze in all ways. Yes, the Andrews Sisters standby "Boogie Woogie Bugle Boy" was performed—but by three black men in suits, bearing attachés. Only after that did three women appear, in skirted army uniforms, for "G.I. Jive." There was plenty of scatting—Duke Ellington's "Bli-Blip" was almost nothing else—but in the most fastidiously clarified scatalogue, as Callaway and Everett Bradley dated for dinner, quarreled, and made up. On the way, there was a cute quotation from another title on the evening's jukebox, "I Won't Dance," and the number ended with "In other words, Bli-Blip": the ontology of scat, if you think about it.

The extremely appealing program of old standards (with a few new pieces In the Style) never felt twice-told as in other shows, partly because of the strong vocal readings but also because of director-choreographer Lynne Taylor-Corbett's imaginative production. So many of these nostalgia revues just play that old music. *Swing!* explored the forms of swing as if asking why pop was so much more enjoyable in the 1930s and '40s: when instrumentalists created music while they played it instead of surviving on rudimentary guitar chords and a hook borrowed from Eric Clapton. When writers and singers communicated.

Though *Swing!* got good reviews, the public did not flock in appropriate measure; and *The Gershwins' Fascinating Rhythm* (1999) was utterly destroyed. As said before, one very noticeable error can prejudice reviewers against everything else you do, no matter how effective, and this Gershwin revue suffered from a cheap-looking stage design. The costuming was acceptable; but the relentlessly dead look of the stage sabotaged an otherwise enjoyable show making the most of some of Broadway's best talent at the not-yet-star level: Michael Berresse, Darius de Haas, Orfeh, Sara Ramirez, Patrick Wilson. Directed by Mark Lamos with especially intriguing choreography by David Marques, *Rhythm* sometimes dramatized the songs and sometimes simply sang them, taking in a few rarities, including a vocal version of the B Flat trumpet blues from *An American in Paris*. The little dramas tended to the playful, as in a lesbian flirtation for "Isn't It a Pity?" and a psychiatric session for "Just Another Rhumba" in which the patient's dance fever infects the doctor.

The songs were occasionally mated in combinations, but never reduced to medley snippets in the seventies manner. They were heard full out, complete with their verses. However, the singers performed in modern style, with a certain amount of black pop inflection and even scatting. I repeat: a certain amount, not a sensory overload. Nevertheless, this irritated the critics, though these songs have enjoyed more than half a century's worth of renderings in strict Broadway style and could profit from a contemporary boost. One possibly wouldn't want to hear Jerome Kern done this way. But when Third Age Broadway was concocting a sound out of European leftovers, Victor Herbert, and "jazz," Gershwin led the jazz end of the movement, as Harold Arlen was to after Gershwin. Jazz brings us to black music. So isn't there a logic in giving Gershwin a mild dose of later black style? Or did Cole Porter write *Porgy and Bess*?

True, the show got unnecessarily contempo in some spoken ad-libs—a "Check it out! Check it out!" here and an "It's the bomb!" there. Is this supposed to bring in more of those people who hate musicals? Some of the singing in this show—Sara Ramirez's "I've Got A Crush On You," for instance—was as good as any Gershwin I've ever heard. Why cheapen the event with pop-sleaze dialogue? No one who hates musicals is going to buy a ticket to something on Broadway.

But, once again, I digress with pleasantry; and we're up to *By Jeeves* (2001), boys and girls. It's the thrill of Andrew Lloyd Webber, the ghost of P. G. Wodehouse. The latter is actually one of the musical's inventors; what a culmination. *By Jeeves* itself marked a culmination, for it began as a Great Big Bomb in London in 1975, and took all this time to reinvest itself. Lloyd Webber's original collaborator, Alan Ayckbourn, came along to revise for small stages, but Bertie (John Scherer) is absurdly energetic for Wodehouse's slow-witted protagonist. And butler Jeeves (Martin Jarvis) is disloyal. In Wodehouse, Jeeves has tiffs with Master in private only.

As for the score, while it's amusing to hear playwright Ayckbourn turn lyricist and listen to Lloyd Webber making do without a Big Tune, *By Jeeves* probably should have been a revival of a *thirties* English musical— say, by Vivian Ellis and A. P. Herbert. Ayckbourn himself staged *By Jeeves*, inventively enough. For a garden scene, an assistant handed out six huge flowers to the first row of the audience, to be picked later, and in the last number, "Banjo Boy," the cast backed Bertie in *Wizard of Oz* costumes. At the line "Snap your fingers," all did so, except the Witch, amusingly hampered by Turandot fingernails.

A home team did no better with *Seussical* (2000), Stephen Flaherty and Lynn Ahrens' chowder of throughlines involving Horton the elephant (Kevin Chamberlin), the microscopic Whos, Gertrude McFuzz (Janine LaManna), Mayzie LaBird (Michele Pawk), and others of Dr. Seuss' inventions. The Cat in the Hat (David Shiner) played host rather as Ed Wynn used to in his revues, horning in on the acts and joking with the audience. At one point, he got into a stage box to molest a female spectator, then took a call on his cell phone. "No," he said into the receiver, "I'm happy with my present long-distance carrier."

It sounds like a sharp evening of musical comedy, and certainly promised unique subject matter and style. Flaherty and Ahrens, who wrote the book as well, may have been hobbled without an established port of call to develop, as with the Caribbean jamboree of *Once On This Island*. The show's pre-opening shakeout was dire: as both set designer and director were replaced, by Tony Walton and Rob Marshall, as one throughline evaporated, leaving principal Eddie Korbich in the chorus, and another so cut down that the Grinch (William Ryall) barely checked in. In the end, it's hard to say what went wrong, for *Seussical* ended up not flawed so much as soft in appeal. It was perhaps typical of the piece that a musical-comedy zany of the 1960s, Alice Playten, turned up in a small role with little to do.

The musical play, the dance show, musical comedy . . . and what of the lost art of off-Broadway? It remains undefinable, a genre without a format. But one does note two enduring qualities: small and offbeat. Small was definitely Jason Robert Brown's *The Last 5 Years* (2002): just two characters, played by Norbert Leo Butz and Sherie René Scott, recounting the breakup of a romance in skewed time. Her side of the story moves from present to past, his—simultaneously—from past to present, thus framing the show in hope and disillusion at once. Meanwhile, offbeat is undoubtedly *Avenue Q* (2003): the love-and-work problems of twentysomethings, played in the style of *Sesame Street*. Jim Hensonesque hand puppets teach lessons on tolerance, illustrate the meaning of such words as "purpose," and generally solve their problems, though these are well above the *Sesame Street* age level. Television monitors spell things out—things like "One night stand."

Clearly, *Avenue Q* is a grown-ups' show that had no trouble moving to Broadway. (At the same time, the children's show *A Year With Frog and Toad* failed in its uptown move.) Another product of the B.M.I. workshop, *Avenue Q* has a soft-rock score by Robert Lopez and Jeff Marx that entirely lacks Jason Robert Brown's sophistication. Brown's off-Broadway is, so to say, B.M.I. *artiste*; *Avenue Q* is B.M.I. parody. But expert puppetry is always seductive, especially when the lead puppeteers (John Tartaglia,

Stephanie D'Abruzzo, Rick Lyon) act along with their charges, animating themselves. Then, too, the romantic plots alluringly combine the traditional and the funky: the main couple is Boy Meets Girl, and the second couple, once the headquarters of Harold Lang and Helen Gallagher, is Gay Comes Out To Straight Best Friend. Interestingly, the physical production, in a unit set of *Street Scene* tenements, needed only an upgrading of the television-monitor material to move from off-Broadway, as the difference between The Street and Off continues to evaporate.

At least there still is an off-Broadway. A piece of Broadway has dropped away, because writers we admire can now create shows that don't show up on The Street. It's not that they closed in tryout. They languish in the New Tryout, regional limbo, performed yet not seen. "When you're far away from New York town," ran a lovely lyric in *Jennie* (1963), "you're nowhere at all." So why are brand-name bylines falling into this new hell?

Aren't musical versions of *Our Town* (1938) and *The Skin of Our Teeth* (1942) the kind of thing that Broadway was bound to get to in this age of recycling? There may be greater American dramas (especially by O'Neill and Williams), but Thornton Wilder's pair of mini-epics is very classic, the one so often revived and the other so often Discussed, as a rare example of Broadway trying out something like absurdism. Aren't Harvey Schmidt and Tom Jones ideal for *Our Town*, with their Rodgers and Hammerstein aura of community and wholesomeness? And wouldn't *Skin*'s merrily crackpot anthropology suit the musical-comedy strut of Kander and Ebb?

Or wait. Don't all those those unsatisfying *Cyrano* musicals tell us that some plays shouldn't sing? *Skin* is obstinate, didactic, ridiculous, ponderous, daring, and farcical. It's a food fight of a play; a musical version would emphasize its contradictions. *Our Town*, at least, is more consistent. Its sentimentality is married to the world-despair of a pious cynic, but it does have feelings to express in music.

So Schmidt and Jones are well-grounded; and Jones' book follows the original very closely, even verbatim at times. Many of the songs are what one must expect, given the nature of the play and how Schmidt and Jones see the world: the full company opening the action with the all but inevitable "Our Town," a wistful duet on travel for the two homebody mothers called "Somewhere," and a number for their husbands, "All At

Once You're Getting Married." There is a great deal of choral work in the last third of the story, in the churchyard, and Emily's deflating return to her childhood takes in "Birthday Girl," "Goodbye, World," and "Now You Know." Of course. But the authors have faithfully restated the simple beauty of life that Wilder used as his foundation. The score should not "stretch" Wilder, expand him. Anyway, how could one possibly expand *Our Town*? The end of Wilder's first act—the famous recitation of a return address that starts traditionally only to reach through "the Western Hemisphere" and "the Earth" to "the Universe" and "the Mind of God"— typifies not only Wilder's vastness but a chance for Schmidt and Jones to add music with a nice ear for what the play is "feeling" at this point. So, keeping the Stage Manager out of the action, the authors just put an "Amen" on the end of the church-choir rehearsal that has underscored the scene. It is the perfect touch, an understatement of great heart.

Of course, there must be a love song, and "I Notice You," for George and Emily, sets a Kern-like melody dancing over cascades of triplets, a lovely idyll. Still, Wilder means to trouble us in the play, and Schmidt and Jones do not. Nothing in the music suggests Wilder's belief that man was born to die before he knew that he was alive, a terrible aperçu, blasphemy so vast as to outrage atheists. There is even this: when Wilder's Stage Manager refers to "this play," it states the obvious—that Wilder wrote the first concept musical without a note of music. When one adds music and lets the Stage Manager speak of "this musical," as happens here, something disturbs Wilder's scenario, sophisticates it. And sophisticated is the one thing *Our Town* cannot be.

Even so, don't Broadway's theatregoers have the right to see for themselves? After a Westbeth workshop in 1985, the musical—entitled *Grover's Corners*—was to have made the big time with Mary Martin as the Stage Manager, an idea at once arresting and silly. But who doesn't want to see Mary Martin again? The onset of Martin's fatal cancer killed the project, and *Grover's Corners* was seen instead in Illinois in 1987, with both authors in the cast. With its modest production values, the show would be ideal fare for Encores! if that program ever decided to revive a premiere. Wouldn't John Cullum make a wonderful Stage Manager?

Our Town's Boy Meets Girl treats a childhood romance that reaches marriage and then death. *The Skin of Our Teeth* has no love plot at all, not even sortakinda love such as in *The Human Comedy* (Saroyanesque world love), *Raggedy Ann* (a doll's selfless devotion to her owner), or *Titanic* (no central romance but a number of couples, one of whom, the Strauses, do come up with a love song).

This is a dicey prospect in a story musical, though *Pacific Overtures* and the somewhat "beyond story" *Assassins* function without love plots. And *Skin*, like them, is a work on a big idea. In an odd way, Kander and Ebb wrote a B.M.I. workshop sort of score, with a comedy number, an establishing number, and various other genres (some of their own invention), as if satisfying Lehman Engel's pedagogy while reinstructing his field.

One anticipated an Apocalypse Number for the Fortune Teller who predicts the Flood in Wilder's second act; this is too ripe a character to refuse. And of course Sabina would get a Seduction Number with Mr. Antrobus, starting on the customary Kander and Ebb vamp and the wordless vocal notes (here on "la") forming a structural entity, "You Owe It To Yourself." (Note the idiosyncratic Kander and Ebb title, a cliché to be revitalized by a characterological irony in the lyrics.) Given that the Antrobuses were built up in the music, one might expect them to officiate on the jaunty Kander and Ebb up tune, as they do in "As You Are Is As You Were." There are other wonderful songwriters, but this is the last remaining team that makes one want to dance all the way home.

There are fetching numbers throughout the score. It's more an impish than romantic one, generally avoiding the emotional power of songs like *The Rink*'s "Marry Me" or *Steel Pier*'s "First You Dream." But then, impish and anti-romantic itself, *Skin* must defeat any attempt to make music the *feeling* of the piece. Rather, music must be the entertainment of the piece. *Our Town* has the feelings; *Skin* is vaudeville acts. That's why the score has B.M.I. workshop ideas in it: like *Chicago*, but much less overtly, the *Skin* songs celebrate established forms.

Keep in mind that Wilder's anthropological gag with a James Joycean subtext is only deceptively simple; this is the project that Leonard Bernstein and Betty Comden and Adolph Green gave up on. Instead of asking his students to find a ballad in *A Streetcar Named Desire*, Lehman Engel should have assigned an opening number for *The Skin of Our Teeth*. Now, that's an *étude*. Bernstein and company thought up a frame number, "Here Comes the Sun," to express in tumultuous simplicity man's unconquerable ability to survive. Good enough. Kander and Ebb went in the opposite direction, avoiding Wilderian Theory. They even changed the

New Jersey setting from Wilder's portentous Excelsior to the more quo-
tidian Freeport. The music, a kind of suburban tango, pitters sweetly away
as the principals introduce themselves between media announcements of
the impending ice age. Wilder's detractors in 1942 thought his play just
too darn grand, and to an extent the Bernstein version would have been,
too. Kander and Ebb are cagey and casual. The piece gets grand enough
as it goes along. Why *start* there?

The Kander and Ebb *Skin* was given regionally, in 1999, but New York
has yet to see it. Another show denied us is *Paper Moon*, which reached
the Paper Mill Playhouse in 1993. Based more on Peter Bogdanovich's
film than on its source, Joe David Brown's novel *Addie Pray*, *Paper Moon*
had music by Larry Grossman, lyrics by his *Grind* partner, Ellen Fitzhugh,
and also Carol Hall, and a book by Martin Casella. Too many movies are
made into musicals, but this movie is ideal ignition material, for the
relationship between Bible salesman Ryan O'Neal and his young ward
(who may be his daughter), Tatum O'Neal, was stuffed with the resentful
affection that provisions strong character numbers.

With a Bible Belt setting at the time of the Depression, Bogdanovich
used thirties 78s for his soundtrack—Bing Crosby's "One More Chance,"
Ken Darby and Ramona on "A Picture Of Me Without You," the Boswell
Sisters on "I Found a Million Dollar Baby" when O'Neal hooks up with
good-time gal Madeline Kahn. Grossman largely avoided period pastiche
and wrote solid, timeless musical comedy in styles prevalent since the
1960s. The orchestra struck up the overture with the reassuring fanfare
on the would-be hit, "Some Day, Baby." The first story number, "God
Bless the Widow Women," intercut plot exposition with the growing
relationship between Gregory Harrison and little Natalie DeLucia.
"Entrepreneur" was a guileless charm song that put the pair over as surely
as Bogdanovich did the O'Neals.

So what went wrong? Nothing—and Christine Ebersole, in Kahn's
part, stole everything but the house curtain. Her black maid, who hates
her, was also on hand, to stick in such conversation boosters as "Tell them
about that time you danced naked at that truck stop, Miss Trixie."
Ebersole knows that small-time hustling is her destiny; but the authors
know that no one is born a hustler. In "Girls Like Us," Ebersole took control of the show's emotional energy with the autobiography of every
woman maligned because she trades in coin other than marriage: "We

learn to smile when other girls learn to read." In a passing reference to Harrison as "men like you," she tells us she realizes that he's a rare good guy, out of her reach. *Paper Moon* is an unimprovable film, but Grossman and his partners improved upon it. Wouldn't the show make a dandy complement to *Grover's Corners* and *The Skin of Our Teeth* in Encores!'s season devoted to Broadway's lost first nights?

William Finn's *Elegies* (2003) played only the two dark nights a week at the Newhouse during the run of *Observe the Sons of Ulster Marching Towards the Somme*, but it did play. One had hoped for a story musical from Finn, but this song cycle, semi-staged by Graciela Daniele, bubbled up with stories. The very title *Elegies* suggests dirges; these were more like valentines to the missing. These included animals, celebs, older relatives, an Asian couple, and of course close friends lost to AIDS. Five of New York's best singers, some young and some older, soloed or shared in the numbers, taking them on as character parts. Keith Byron Kirk played the protégé of the Asian couple in "Mister Choi & Madame G," as Finn conjures up his usual reality of detail in their "irritated grins" and "their children practicing violins." Michael Rupert recalled "Mark's All-Male Thanksgiving," sang "The Ballad of Jack Eric Williams (and Other 3-Named Composers)," and set before us one of those friends you don't know what you'd do without but you'd rather, a Pole named Bolek, in "Venice." Betty Buckley portrayed in "Only One" a terminally ill English teacher absolutely unsentimental about death ("I do not like scenes") but admirably proud that she'd made her kids learn their stuff. Christian Borle cited his five dead dogs, including a Dandy Dinmont he hated, leading to a closing joke capped by the most moving line of the evening. Carolee Carmello reminisced about family in "Passover," so different from Mark's gay Thanksgiving. For echo texture, Finn employed a lot of wordless vocal material—Borle barked—but *Elegies*' great charm lay in how well it sang about life. Some writers' autobiographical trivia come off as maudlin. Finn's unique voice makes everyone seem glamorous.

Meanwhile: the revivals, some faithful and some rebellious in the extent of modification. *Man of La Mancha* (in 2002) had a rebellious set (by Paul Brown) that simply wouldn't stop doing things. *Annie Get Your Gun* (1999) had rebellious concept-show veneer and ethnic issues in its new book, turning a heretofore unwreckable classic into a mishmash. *The Music Man* (2000) and *Kiss Me, Kate* (1999) had rebellious scripts, the one drawing on the screenplay and the other pointlessly rewritten to say the same things the original did using different words.

Even *42nd Street* (2001), faithful in the main, had a rebellious Julian Marsh. Michael Cumpsty is too modern an actor to content himself with the largely uninflected God of the Lightning that Jerry Orbach presented in the original. Cumpsty wanted to discover Marsh, inhabit him; and were he playing the 1933 movie he could no doubt sample the many rhythms and meanings that Warner Baxter brings to the role. But Gower Champion's *42nd Street* isn't that Warner Bros. Depression-era slice of life. Champion's show is character types and dance numbers; developing Marsh as a human being only emphasizes Marsh's inconsistencies, heartlessly firing the heroine one minute and inflaming her with "Lullaby of Broadway" the next.

When good shows go bad. Experience tells us that altering works *for the sake of altering them* vitiates their energy. I recently encountered someone who was putting on *Allegro*, and I asked if all the dances would be included. The reply was a vaguely surprised "The dances?," as if we'd been talking about *The Iceman Cometh*. Rodgers and Hammerstein wrote *Allegro* to be a culmination of all the musical's arts, a kind of ballet of a play in three hours of real time, a jazzy Gesamtkunstwerk. To leave out the dancing is to leave the Cotton Blossom out of *Show Boat*. Stung at my inadvertent implication that a danceless *Allegro* might be questionable, my correspondent proudly disdained "the puristic approach." Purism, apparently, means performing what the authors wrote.

To illustrate; one of the charms of *Annie Get Your Gun* is the casual introduction into the action of "There's No Business Like Show Business." It's insinuated, really. Today, this is the American entertainer's motto song, another national anthem. But in the original script, Ethel Merman asks, "Show business? What's show business?," and without so much as a bell tone, someone is ticking off the parts of the answer: "The cowboys, the wrestlers, the tumblers, the clowns," and so on. It's conversational, incidental. In 1999, the number launched the show as a Big Motto Song (besides showing up again in its original spot), turning what had been a deft coup into a bombastic cliché.

Oklahoma! (2002) came from England's National Theatre in what we might call "restudied" form. There was no hacking around, though director Trevor Nunn pasted chunks of script into unusual places. So many spoke of a new dark feeling in the triangle of Curly (Patrick Wilson), Laurey (Josefina Gabrielle), and Jud (Shuler Hensley) that it became common knowledge, begetting another of those mendacious factoids. *Oklahoma!* has always been dark; it was written dark. What was new was Hensley's take on Jud, so often your average rodeo psychopath but here zoning in and out of schizoid awareness in trancelike mutterings and distracted looks. Gabrielle, too, broke with casting tradition in that she not only enacted but danced Laurey, a rare ballerina soprano.

One revival truly reinvented its material, because *You're A Good Man, Charlie Brown* (1999) turned Clark Gesner's bare-stage off-Broadway bit into a smallish Broadway show with a lot of décor. Set designer David Gallo kept the view very much in the style of Charles M. Schulz, so that the school bus, flowery sofa, piano, and flying doghouse (actually, the hut was stationary; the earth tilted behind it) approximated a flat Sunday-color comic-strip background. It was good planning to exchange the vapid role of Patty for that of Charlie Brown's little sister, Sally; and Andrew Lippa built up the first number and wrote two new ones, one a humdinger for Kristin Chenoweth's Sally, "My New Philosophy." Very much in the character of Schulz's Sally, the song finds her happily, even intensely seizing upon various comeback phrases as her all-purpose retort—from "Why are you telling me this?" through "*No!*" to the ultra-Schulzian "I can't *stand* it!" Unfortunately, Lippa's other contribution, "Beethoven Day," is a rock piece, absolutely incorrect for the musically reactionary Schroeder. Still, the production stands as a rare case of a purely off-Broadway event— in the sixties meaning of tiny, spoofy, and cheap—transformed into an eyeful, at that with such gaining headliners as Chenoweth, *Rent's* Anthony Rapp, Stanley Wayne Mathis, and Roger Bart.

The most unexpected revival brought back a piece last seen in the 1912–13 season, John Philip Sousa's *The American Maid* (2002). The New York City Opera gave it under the title of its original 1893 version as *The Glass Blowers*, reconstructing the work from archival materials. Sousa's famous marches have overwhelmed his "comic opera" scores, but he was a tuneful dramatist, even in another of those generical plotlines in which an American tycoon wants to marry his daughter to an English duke while she prefers her American hero. Christopher Alden's sagely amusing production set it all in a black-and-white factory enlivened by colorful costuming, juggling themes of labor relations, class war, and military exploits and keeping the horribly busy libretto in trim. At one point, dreary but unavoidable plot development involving two villains was intoned at stage right while the rest of the cast watched a ballerina give good recital. Interestingly, Alden's use of footage of the Spanish-American War screened to Sousa marches—surely the remark of the modernist—was in fact a feature of the 1913 production.

Some chapters ago, we considered the appeal of *Big River*, having no idea that the Roundabout would play host, in 2003, to a production by Deaf West Theatre of North Hollywood. A troupe ecumenically using deaf, hearing-impaired, and hearing actors, Deaf West had earlier revived the musical *Oliver!*. Of course: the adventure of a helpless orphan in apparently insensitive (or worse) surroundings mirrors the experience of the deaf in a hearing world.

Big River is even more apropos, for Huckleberry Finn is nature's child unable to follow the (to him) tortuous lanes of civilization, and Jim is an escaped slave, prey to any predator. Director-choreographer Jeff Calhoun was at pains to emphasize an enlightening moment in which Jim tells how he brutally punished his very young daughter for disobeying a command, not realizing that scarlet fever had left her deaf. As the Jim, Michael McElroy, recounted the event, it resonated through the auditorium. Have a little patience, the production seemed to say, and we can keep up with you.

The format was simple, though its permutations created considerable variety of presentation: some actors spoke and sang. Some were mute, their portrayals given voice by the speaking actors. Every line was signed, by the deaf or the hearing. Unlike the signing we get at public events by a specialist on the sidelines, Deaf West's signing was incorporated into the staging. Part of the experience was watching the deaf "act" their signing, because no two individuals sign exactly alike (except in ensemble numbers, when Calhoun wanted symmetry).

The physical production was relatively modest, based on squares bearing reproductions of the pages of an antique illustrated edition of the novel. The staging's complexity lay most truly in the relationship between the actors and the signing and between the deaf and the hearing, as when the signing Pap (Troy Kotsur) took a swig from the corn jug and the speaking Pap (Lyle Kanouse) wiped his mouth.

There was a relationship as well with the hearing in the auditorium. It is Christian and democratic to give the disadvantaged a chance to make art in their own way, and it is inspiring when they succeed—and on our terms, no less. For this was, on a basic level, a *Big River* of what Italians call *valido* quality, meaning not just okay but what one hopes for in a performance of the work. On the grander level, it was a dramatization of what Mark Twain had in mind in the first place: a sample of the experience of folks who aren't secure among the rest of us. Shamefully, on the night I saw it, a couple down front in the center of the orchestra walked out after five minutes. If you have no compassion, haven't you at least some curiosity?

That couple missed a tremendous performance from Daniel Jenkins in particular. Broadway's original Huck and later the hero of *Big*, Jenkins was now playing Mark Twain, narrating and sounding for the signing Huck, young Tyrone Giordano. Jenkins aged handsomely into his Twain kit, and was so genially intent on interpreting this product of his own imagination that many spectators felt compelled to keep one eye on him while following the rest of the show.

Perhaps the best revival ever was a New York Philharmonic concert, not of Beethoven or Mahler but of *Sweeney Todd*, in 2000. The work's musical sophistication of course recommends it for full-scale symphonic rendering, but one wonders if there aren't more possibilities in this line— a Philharmonic *Show Boat* with *all* the music, or a *Golden Apple* (for Encores! has been shy). Perhaps the Phil might try such an evening once a season, though it's hard to imagine any work but *Sweeney Todd* creating such excitement. The work itself is "demented" (in the old opera buff's argot meaning "so brilliant it's crazy and so crazy it's brilliant"), and the announced leads of opera's Bryn Terfel and our own Patti LuPone offered two of today's few demented performers. Terfel canceled, and George Hearn, who had succeeded to the title role during the original run, took over as if rejuvenated by some shady apothecary. Never before had the opera baritone sound that Sondheim composed been so clearly placed, in an assumption fit for legend.

Patti Lu brought all her native intelligence and show-biz strategies to Mrs. Lovett, matching Hearn's barbaric grandeur with twisted bourgeois cabaret. Like Hearn, she gave more voice to the part than we usually get. She also had the advantage that lines that were purely functional in 1979 tickle the public now that we know the show. Considering what to do with their first corpse, Hearn says they'll dispose of it after dark. "Well, of course, we could do that," Patti Lu replies, not really agreeing and readying a countersuggestion. This naturally gets a laugh, because everyone today knows that she wants to grind the flesh into hambuger for her pie ware, and he's going to let her. Indeed, "A Little Priest" is coming right up, so that laugh is huge and sustained and punctuated by guffaws of absurd pleasure. *Sweeney Todd* may not be many theatregoers' favorite musical, but it's on everyone's short list, and it holds up remarkably well for a work that is now a generation out of date. But then, it is our "other" opera (alongside *Porgy and Bess*), and operas don't age as popular theatre does.

True enough, with a cut book and skeletal staging, this was a spectacular *Sweeney Todd*. The supporting cast, including Davis Gaines, Heidi Grant Murphy, Neil Patrick Harris, and Audra McDonald, was the best yet, and conductor Andrew Litton led a fast, tight reading. One wonders if audiences at the vindicating 1942 *Porgy and Bess* revival comparably jumped for joy.

Not a revival but definitely a reinstatement of old art was *Elaine Stritch At Liberty* (2001), probably the best-liked one-person show in history. It really was one person alone. As George C. Wolfe staged it, first at the Public Theater and then uptown, it was Stritch and a chair. No filler of superannuated vaudeville acts as in the forties style, no docile little dance trio spelling the star in the fifties style, no lighting by Chipmonck or translation by Martha Morton Conheim. The evening went almost strangely ungimmicked. In a floppy white blouse over black stockings, Broadway's most redoubtable "I'm Still Here" doyenne looked back on life and work in anecdote and song. "Constructed by John Lahr" and "Reconstructed by Elaine Stritch" was the author credit. But it sounded as though Stritch was using a highly personal form of psychodrama (as they used to call it) to experience a life that, she says, she missed most of.

The stories took in Marlon Brando, Gig Young, Ben Gazzara, Richard Burton, and Ethel Merman, but the story was Stritch Without Euphemisms. As she paced the stage, dragging that chair along on the longer jaunts, she dealt honestly with her disasters. Of course, she sang well and often. Some were "her" numbers: "Civilization," "Why Do the Wrong People Travel?," two from *Company*, "Zip," which she sang in the 1952 *Pal Joey* revival, "Broadway Baby," which she claimed at the 1985 Philharmonic *Follies* concert. Other numbers became story songs. Barbara Cook sang "This Is All Very New To Me" in *Plain and Fancy* (1955) as an Amish girl after her first kiss; Stritch made it a woozy reflection after her first drink. "There Never Was a Baby Like My Baby," a plain old love song for Dolores Gray in *Two On the Aisle* (1951), was now a torch song mourning Stritch's husband's death.

Considering that its sole accessory was a red curtain that rose and fell opera-style, the show gave a full helping of theatre. Alas, Stritch marred her history at the Tony Awards, flouting the honorees' time limit with laundry-list thankyou droning and saying "Please don't do that" as the orchestra cut in to chase her off the stage. No doubt Stritch saw this moment as a culmination of her career. But viewers see these dreary recitations as Bad Television. They vitiate one of Broadway's last remaining connections with the national culture, and thus harm theatre in general.

Every American awards show has its thankyou; why do they seem so boring at the Tonys? Because all those producers insist on dragging the rest of us through a catalogue of their family members as millions of viewers surf off to more congenial video? What drives these idiots to seek ego validation at the expense of the first essence of the meaning of Broadway, entertainment?

A few days before the 2003 Tonys, MTV aired its movie awards show. Hosted by twentysomethings Seann William Scott and Justin Timberlake, and devoted to youth, rock, and irreverence—the three essentials of the meaning of MTV—the show observed the by now venerable format for these celebrations in its own prankish way. There is always a movie spoof splicing parody into actual footage, and this year the subject was the *Matrix* sequel, with the cooperation of actors from the film itself. There is as well goofy behavior from some of the presenters and winners, and even a token grown-up—Harrison Ford, mainly because he has been dating young (Calista Flockhart) and co-starring young (with Josh Hartnett). Like it or not, the show states and develops the spirit of MTV, and is thus less another awards show and more of a thing itself.

By comparison, the Tony show is a dead imitation of itself. Theatre is the last piece of American society that still has glamour; that, talent, and the vitality of live performance inform the spirit of Broadway. Shouldn't there be much less thankyou and much more song and dance? Why not hire some dance captain to revive numbers from past Tony winners? Why not commission spoofs from *Forbidden Broadway*'s Gerard Alessandrini?

As the Tonys approached in 2003, *The New York Times*' Jesse McKinley ran an only partly facetious list of suggestions to enliven the show—a Best

Song award, with the four nominees performed; tributes to the recently deceased; more celebrity presenters, including those with little or no Broadway connection; Kevin Spacey doing his Christopher Walken imitation, topped (one imagines) by Walken imitating Spacey; a taste of the sleazy contest-reality formats currently trendy on TV, with the national Tony audience voting for Best Musical while "a snooty Englishman and a faded diva [as on *American Idol*] offer critiques" of the nominees.

Well, why not? McKinley also thought that Elaine Stritch should have been allowed to ramble away. No. The thankyou must go, and I in turn propose two major revisions in the awarding itself. One: no producers are permitted on stage at any time. Their prize can be accepted by someone else—Kevin Spacey, Kyme, Jesse McKinley, the scary clown monster. Two, the honored must limit their acceptance speech to illustrative anecdote, touching braggadocio about shaking an addiction, eerie personal reminiscence, and so on: but one generic thankyou to everyone, or gratitude to *one name only*. Here's the whimsical twist—those who try to take attendance of their personal thankyou membership instantly lose their Tony to the runner-up. *Physically* lose it, to a corps of big rufftuffs, who themselves could pay homage to some great old show—cowboys from *Whoopee*, S.S. guards from *The Deputy*, Charenton inmates from *Marat/Sade*, Samurai warriors from *Pacific Overtures*. Ratings would soar in the first few years of this regime, as even those with no theatregoing commitment would tune in just to see the violence, the screaming, the zero tolerance for thespians' excruciating thankyoumania.

As I write, at the end of the 2002–2003 season, devotees are collecting replacement casts. *The Producers* is playing better now, with Lewis Stadlen and Don Stephenson. Stadlen used to do Groucho Marx; now he opens a grabbag of comic voices with an occasional grand line in the Jimmy Durante manner. Don Stephenson—unwillingly, at director Susan Stroman's insistence—imitates Matthew Broderick and even looks like him. John Treacy Egan's Roger De Bris is only capable, reminding us how much voice and crazy *gloing!* Gary Beach brought to the role; but Peter Samuel's Nazi has presence as a most convincing old Brownshirt, almost defying Mel Brooks' alternate universe.

Aida now stars Toni Braxton. It would be unfair to compare her with Heather Headley, who gave a performance that doesn't just earn but defines the Tony. Braxton comes from another part of show biz, where nobody has to act; and she has matinée alternates. Headley didn't. Will Chase is a sound Radames and Mandy Gonzalez, fresh from *Dance of the Vampire*, gamely takes on the impossible task of following actress/model/rack diva Sherie René Scott's Amneris.

Over at the *Chicago* revival, Melanie Griffith is now Roxie Hart. Why? My guess is that the besotted Mrs. Banderas wanted to cling to her husband and thus asked her people what show was playing within a hundred yards of *Nine*. "*Chicago*," they replied, and she said, "Get me that." Show biz, just show biz. Melanie sang, yes, and she danced. True. She did not extend herself, but then she doesn't do a lot in her movies, either. I'd call it cute and boring. The rest of *Chicago* still zings, though some of the principals are overplaying, trying to bang the sluggish audience of tourists into laughing at jokes too sharp for them. They greatly cheer at the end, even so.

Isn't this the best revival since *No, No, Nanette* launched the cycle with a faithless restyling? It was of the Tradition all the same. In fact, all three of the last-named shows spring from historical sources, though they typify aspects of the musical today. *The Producers* is of a truly ancient line; its reliance on comics and babes and its risky fun celebrate instruments of the First Age; the spirit is Weber and Fields burlesque. *Aida*'s form was invented in the 1920s, put on hold in the Depression, then redeveloped in the 1940s, and while its songwriters come from Somewhere Else, they extended themselves to dramatize and exalt the material. *Chicago* is the revival, too often perfunctory or out of style. Not here. In truth, it's astonishing how crisply the ensemble plays—regardless of who's in the leads—in such an intricately animated staging. Maybe they should institute a Tony for Best Dance Captain.

So there still is a Broadway of musicals. But the fad police have begun hijacking it, ordering it to change its music, its subject matter, its audience, its *age*. This assault on the Great Tradition reminds one of the demolition of the old Pennsylvania Station: let's kill something beautiful with our greed for *now*. It's sacrilegious, or something: but it's so *now*. It's yes *now*, so pop Parade. Yes, the theatre has its Parade. Pop morons shit their pants and say, Look, it's my Broadway musical.

INDEX

ABBA, 225–26
Abbott, George, 21, 32, 32n, 127, 128, 146, 183, 227, 228, 255
Abraham, F. Murray, 175
Adams, Lee, 46–47, 122
Adams, Roger, 127
Adler, Bruce, 116
Ahrens, Lynn, 136–38, 235, 262, 265, 285, 286
Aida, **181–83**, 298–99
Ain't Broadway Grand, **122–23**
Ain't Misbehavin', **123**
Aint Supposed To Die a Natural Death, 106
Akers, Karen, 94, 95, 198
Alden, Christopher, 293
Alden, Jerome, 58
Alessandrini, Gerard, 297
Alexander, Jace, 245
Alexander, Jason, 38, 62
Allard, Martine, 247, 248
Allen, Debbie, 65
Allen, Peter, 53–54
American Maid, The (The Glass Blowers), **293–94**
Amour, **216–19**
And the World Goes 'Round, 156
Anders, Darlene, 31
Anderson, Stephen Lee, 145
Andreas, Christine, 32, 54, 161
Andrews, George Lee, 49
Andrews, Julie, 115, 173
Anker, Charlotte, 45–46
Annie, **123**
Annie Get Your Gun, 15, 230, **291**, 292
Annie 2: Miss Hannigan's Revenge, **162–63**
Annie Warbucks, **162**, **163–64**
Anthony, Marc, 244
Antoon, A. J., 61

Antoon, Jason, 238
Anyone Can Whistle, 192
Applause, 12, 23, 134
Arias, Yancey, 211
Arlen, Harold, 115, 156, 285
Armitage, Richard, 86
Armour, Steve, 283
As the Girls Go, 122
As Thousands Cheer, **155**
Ashford, Rob, 178, 273
Ashley, Christopher, 42, 123
Ashman, Howard, 59–60, 161, 162
Aspects of Love, 73, 74
Assassins, 41, 136, **245–47**
Astaire, Adele, 96, 173, 261
Astaire, Fred, 96, 169, 173, 261, 283
Austin, Beth, 45
Avenue Q, **286–87**

B.M.I. workshop, 278–80. *See also* Engel, Lehman
Baby, **112–13**
Bacall, Lauren, 12, 13, 14, 38
Bacon, Kevin, 225
Bailey, Melissa, 52
Baker, Becky Ann, 42
Baker Street, 99n
Bakula, Scott, 52
Banderas, Antonio, 96
Baral, Vicki, 57
Baranski, Christine, 162
Barnum, 90
Barrett, Brent, 11, 54, 129, 201
Barry, Gene, 4, 5, 6, 8
Barsha, Debra, 167
Bart, Roger, 174, 175, 293
Barton, Steve, 82, 114
Bassett, Rick, 146

Bat Boy, **156**
Batatunde, Obba, 105
Batt, Mike, 73n
Battle, Hinton, 247
Beach, Gary, 187, 298
Beauty and the Beast, **111, 112**
Bécaud, Gilbert, 99–100
Beckwith-Smith, Susan, 141
Beechman, Laurie, 73
Beery, Leigh, 161
Behar, Joy, 244
Bells Are Ringing, 23–24, 127
Benanti, Laura, 283
Benedict, Paul, 175–76
Bennett, Michael, 2, 83, 96, 105, 106,
    109–10, 158, 274
Bennett, Robert Russell, 34, 131, 131n
Benson, Jodi, 60, 117
Bernstein, Elmer, 49
Berresse, Michael, 126, 129, 284
Berry, Sarah Uriarte, 179
Besoyan, Rick, 166
Betts, Doris, 145
Bickley, Graham, 81
Bierko, Craig, 271, 272, 273
Big, **112**
Big Deal, **101–02**
Big River (Deaf West Theatre production),
    294–95
*Big River: The Adventures of Huckleberry
    Finn*, **143–45**
Billington, Ken, 24
Billion Dollar Baby, 115
Birch, Patricia, 57
Birkenhead, Susan, 174, 249, 250
Björnson, Maria, 81
Black, Don, 49, 176
Black and Blue, **115**
Blades, Ruben, 244
Blair, Janet, 45
Blake, Josh, 27, 63
Blanchard, Tammy, 192
Blane, Sue, 149
Blazer, Judy, 22, 151, 202, 204
Blitzstein, Marc, 2, 31–32, 101, 160
Blood Brothers, **87–88**, 90
Blood Red Roses, 259
Bloomer Girl, 129
Blues in the Night, **115**
Blum, Joel, 119
Bobbie, Walter, 128, 224, 225
Bobby, Anne Marie, 60
Bock, Jerry, 125, 233
Bogardus, Stephen, 134
Bogue, Kevin, 264
Bohème, La (Broadway version), **159**

Bohème, La (Public Theater version),
    158–59
Bolton, John, 110
Bone Room, The, 16
Borle, Christian, 291
Bostwick, Barry, 171
Boublil, Alain, 73, 73n, 78, 79n, 85, 90
Bourne, Matthew, 222
Bowab, John, 129
Boy Friend, The, 96
Boyd, Julianne, 155
Boys From Syracuse, The, 55, **178–79**
Bradley, Everett, 284
Bramble, Mark, 31
Brecht, Bertolt, 179
Brigadoon, 22, **33–34**
Brightman, Sarah, 82
Bring Back Birdie, **46–49**
Bring in 'da Noise Bring in 'da Funk, **257**
Broderick, Matthew, 176, 177, 187, 188, 298
Brohn, William David, 82, 117, 236
Brook, Peter, 66
Brooks, Mel, 187, 188–89
Brown, Georgia, 100, 180
Brown, Jason Robert, 276, 277, 278, 286
Brown, Rosalind, 225
Browne, Leslie, 114
Brustein, Robert, 257
Brynner, Yul, 123
Buckley, Betty, 65, 138, 175, 191n, 221, 291
Buell, Bill, 202
Burch, Shelly, 94
Burge, Gregg, 125
Burgett, Sharon, 141
Burnett, Francis Hodgson, 141, 143
Burns, David, 169
Burr, Mary, 270
Burrell, Deborah, 109
Burrows, Abe, 146, 176
Burstyn, Mike, 122
Bussert, Meg, 33
Butterell, Jonathan, 95
Butz, Norbert Leo, 271, 286
By Jeeves, **285**
Bye Bye Birdie, 228
Byers, Bill, 22

Cabaret, 38, 80, **123**, 236
Cage aux Folles, La, **3–8**, 9, 12, 24
Cahn, Sammy, 275
Caird, John, 270
Calhoun, Jeff, 294
Callaway, Ann Hampton, 283, 284
Callaway, Liz, 31
Camelot, 12, 82, **123**
Campbell, R. M., 18

Candide, 40, 66, 90, 101, 166, 227, 270
Cantone, Mario, 179
Cantor, Eddie, 170
Capeman, The, 68, **242–45**
Cariou, Len, 10, 11, 58, 59
Carlisle, Kitty, 39
Carlton, Bob, 157, 189
Carmelina, 225
Carmello, Carolee, 151, 276, 277, 291
Carmen Jones, 182
Carnelia, Craig, 56, 212
Carnival!, 132n
Carousel, 2, 25, 72, 102, **103–04**, 241
Carradine, Keith, 121
Carrafa, Jim, 231
Carrafa, John, 185
Carrie, **65–69**
Carroll, David, 55, 73, 84, 85, 111, 161,
    181, 198
Carroll, Ronn, 176
Carver, Brent, 165, 166, 251, 276
Casella, Martin, 290–91
Casnoff, Philip, 84
Cassidy, David, 30
Castree, Paul, 224, 225
Cats, 73, **74, 75, 76**, 79, 83, 221
Cauwelaert, Didier van, 216
Cavanaugh, Michael, 256
Cavett, Dick, 123–24
Ceballos, René, 201
Cerveris, Michael, 104, 203, 204
Chamberlain, Richard, 102
Chamberlin, Kevin, 174, 175, 285
Champion, Gower, 228, 292
Channing, Carol, 12, 45
Chaplin, 119
Charles, Walter, 7
Charmoli, Tony, 13, 38
Charnin, Martin, 162, 163
Chase, Will, 299
Chenoweth, Kristin, 233n, 234, 293
Chess, **82–85**, 226
Chicago, 80, 90, **128–29**, 186, 218, 241–42,
    289, 299
Chipmonck, 123, 125, 231
Chong, Rae Dawn, 125
Chorus Line, A, 108, 158, 278, 280
Christian, Angela, 273
Cilento, Wayne, 102
City of Angels, **172–73**
Civil War, The, **228, 229**
Clark, Victor, 177
Clark, Victoria, 202, 205
Class Act, A, 155, **278–80**
Cleale, Lewis, 217
Close, Glenn, 79

Closer Than Ever, 112
Cohan, George M., 30, 104n
Cohen, Lawrence D., 65
Cohenour, Patti, 138, 159
Coleman, Cy, 101, 121, 172, 173, 248, 249
Colette, 16, 17, 23n
Colette, **15–22**, 29–30
Colette Collage, 21–22
Collette, Toni, 210
Comden, Betty, 22, 23–24, 289. *See also*
    Applause; Bells Are Ringing; Doll's Life,
    A; Will Rogers Follies, The
Company, 90, **123**, 245
Connecticut Yankee, A, 3
Connell, Gordon, 27
Connell, Jane, 29, 87, 116, 256
Connick, Harry, Jr., 271
Contact, 222, **237–39**, 256
Cook, Barbara, 65, 111, 141, 296
Cook, Roderick, 14
Coombs, Kristi, 51
Cooper, Chuck, 248
Cooper, Marilyn, 14
Copperfield, **47–48**
Corti, Jim, 264
Cotsirilos, Stephanie, 94
Coughlin, Bruce, 281
Cradle Will Rock, The, **31–32**, 71
Crawford, Michael, 79, 82, 230
Crawley, Brian, 145
Crazy For You, **116–18**, 227
Creel, Gavin, 274
Criswell, Kim, 31, 180
Crivello, Anthony, 151, 152, 251
Crowley, Bob, 103, 182, 212, 244
Cruise, Julee, 167–68
Cuccoli, Robert, 230
Cuervo, Alma, 203
Cullum, John, 123, 141, 183, 184, 185
Cumpsty, Michael, 292
Cunningham, John, 205, 218
Curry, John, 156
Cyrano: The Musical, **88–90**

D'Abruzzo, Stephanie, 287
d'Amboise, Charlotte, 65, 66, 128
Daggett, Larry, 264
Daly, Tyne, 123, 190, 192
Damn Yankees, **126–28**, 129
Dance a Little Closer, 3, **8–12,** 50
Dance of the Vampires, **230–31**
Daniele, Graciela, 61, 73, 136, 151, 264, 291
Danieley, Jason, 144
Danner, Dorothy, 34
Davis, Bruce Anthony, 102
Davis, Howard, 86, 102

Davis, Lindsay W., 140
Davis, Sammy, Jr., 54
de Haas, Darius, 284
de la Peña, George, 32, 114, 117
de Mille, Agnes, 33, 95, 104n, 270
Deitch, Kathy, 225
DeLaria, Lea, 124
DeLucia, Natalie, 290
Dendy, Mark, 280, 281
Denniston, Leslie, 48
Derricks, Cleavant, 105
Desert Song, The, 39
Destry Rides Again, 279
Devine, Loretta, 101, 105
Dexter, John, 179
Dhéry, Robert, 216
DiBuono, Toni, 178
Diener, Joan, 196
Diggs, Taye, 258, 281
Dilly, Erin, 178, 273
Do Black Patent Leather Shoes Really Reflect Up?, **48–49,** 55
Doctorow, E. L., 260, 261, 262, 266
Dokuchitz, Jonathan, 104, 167
Doll's Life, A, **22–26,** 28
Doonesbury, **223–24**
Dorsey, Kena Tangi, 281
Douglas, Jerry, 150, 151
Douglass, Stephen, 200
Dreamgirls, 83, **105–10,** 252
Driver, Donald, 55
Du Shon, Jean, 115
Dubner, Stephen J., 243
Duke, Vernon, 101
Dulaine, Pierre, 200
Dumaresq, William, 26, 27, 28
Dunlop, Frank, 73
Durante, 119
Dvorsky, George, 52

Eagan, Daisy, 142
Ebb, Fred, 13, 14, 14–15, 61, 156, 233, 234, 236, 251–52, 289–90. *See also And the World Goes 'Round; Cabaret; Kiss of the Spider Woman; Rink, The; Skin of Our Teeth, The; Steel Pier; Woman of the Year*
Ebersole, Christine, 120, 122, 290–91
Edelman, Gregg, 172
Edwards, Randall, 54
Egan, John Treacy, 298
Egan, Susan, 175
Eichelberger, Ethyl, 179, 180
Eikenberry, Jill, 45
Elaine Stritch At Liberty, **296–97**
Elegies, **291**
Eliot, T. S., 74, 75, 221

Eljas, Anders, 84
Ellington, Duke, 118, 119, 284
Elliott, William, 29
Ellis, Scott, 61, 125, 178, 233
Elmslie, Kenward, 161
Emick, Jarrod, 124, 126
Encores!, 129–30, 131–32, 170, 179, 187, 288, 291, 295
Engel, Lehman, 94n, 136, 278–80
Epps, Sheldon, 118
Errico, Melissa, 102, 111, 217
Esparza, Raúl, 42, 124
Evans, Harvey, 163
Evita, 73, 91, 104
Eyen, Tom, 105, 106, 107, 108–09

Falk, Willy, 52, 53
Falls, Robert, 182, 183
Falsettoland, **134–35**
Falsettos, **133–35,** 251
Fanny, 22, 270
Fantastics, The, 16, 18, 164
Feingold, Michael, 179, 180
Fiddler on the Roof, **29,** 123
Field, Ron, 38–39, 64, 191
Fields, Herbert, 146
Fields, Joseph, 254
Fierstein, Harvey, 4, 54, 228
Finian's Rainbow, 247, 273
Finn, Terry, 38
Finn, William, 132–36, 157–58, 291
Firman, David, 80
First Lady Suite, **150, 151**
Firth, Tazeena, 23
Fitzgerald, Christopher, 217
Fitzhugh, Ellen, 99, 290–91
Flaherty, Stephen, 136–38, 235, 262, 265, 285, 286
Flavin, Tim, 33
Flora, the Red Menace, 21
Flower Drum Song, **254–55**
Floyd Collins, 136, **144–45**
Follies, 90, 147, 245
Footloose, **224–25**
Forbidden Broadway, 199
Fornes, Maria Irene, 135
Forrest, George, 196, 197, 199, 201
42nd Street, 48, 80, **292**
Fosse, Bob, 2, 95, 101–02, 104, 128, 129, 176, 255, 270, 282–83, 282n
Fosse, **282–83**
Foster, Hunter, 184, 225
Foster, Sutton, 273
Fowler, Beth, 59
Francis, Stacy, 225
Fraser, Alison, 134, 141

Freeman, Cheryl, 118
Freeman, Jonathan, 278, 280
Frey, Nathaniel, 169, 200
Friedman, Maria, 233
Friedman, Peter, 263
Fry, Stephen, 86
Full Monty, The, **255–56**
Fuller, Penny, 157
Funny Thing Happened On the Way To the Forum, A, 55, **177–78**
Funny Face, 96
Furth, George, 37

Gabrielle, Josefina, 293
Gaines, Boyd, 125, 238, 239
Gaines, Davis, 54, 79, 130, 179, 296
Galati, Frank, 264
Gallagher, Helen, 155
Gallagher, Peter, 25–26
Gallis, Paul, 88, 89
Gallo, David, 293
Garber, Victor, 42, 126, 128, 245
Garner, Jay, 4, 5, 7
Garrison, David, 31, 42, 205
Gasman, Ira, 248
Gelbart, Larry, 172
Geoffrey, Stephen, 27
Gerard, Will, 52
Germann, Greg, 245
Gershwin, George, 96–97, 101, 116, 124, 285
Gershwin, Ira, 124
Gershwins' Fascinatin' Rhythm, The, **284–85**
Gesner, Clark, 155, 293
Gets, Malcolm, 110, 157, 179, 217, 219
Gibson, Michael, 281
Gibson, William, 56–57
Girl Crazy, 116
Gleason, Joanna, 149, 171
Glöckner van Notre Dame, Der, 230
Glushak, Joanna, 212
Goblin Market, **155–56**, 163
Golden, Annie, 245, 255
Golden Apple, The, 71, 129, 295
Gonzalez, Mandy, 231, 299
Good News!, 273
Goodbye Girl, The, **175–76**
Goodman, Henry, 190, 246–47
Goodman, John, 144
Gordon, Paul, 270
Gordon, Ricky Ian, 164, 165–66
Gore, Michael, 65
Goulet, Robert, 123, 156
Goz, Harry, 84
Graham, Nathan Lee, 210
Grahame, Kenneth, 180, 181

Grand Hotel, **195–201**, 263
Gravitte, Debbie (Shapiro), 122, 132n, 179
Gray, Dolores, 296
Gray, Kevin, 251
Grease, **123**
Green, Adolph, 22, 23–24, 289. *See also Applause; Bells Are Ringing; Doll's Life, A; Will Rogers Follies, The*
Green, Colton, 264
Greene, Ellen, 162
Gregory, Gillian, 87
Grey, Joel, 12, 119, 128
Griffith, Melanie, 299
Grind, 22, **98–99**, 143, 241, 242
Groenendaal, Cris, 82
Groener, Harry, 55, 56, 117–18, 120
Grossman, Larry, 22, 24, 99, 155, 290–91. *See also Doll's Life, A; Minnie's Boys; Grind; Paper Moon; Snoopy!*
Grover's Corners, 20, **287–88**
Guardino, Harry, 12–13, 14
Guare, John, 213
Guettel, Adam, 144, 145, 146
Gunton, Bob, 100
Guys and Dolls, **123**, 251
Gypsy, 18, **123**, 164, 166, **190–93**

Hackady, Hal, 155
Hadary, Jonathan, 245
Hair, 27, 258
Hairspray, 182, **227–28**, 273
Hamill, Mark, 120
Hamilton, Lawrence, 118
Hamlisch, Marvin, 59, 175, 176, 212
Hammerstein, Oscar, II, 2, 9, 24, 34, 103, 217, 254, 262n, 292. *See also Allegro; Carmen Jones; Carousel; Flower Drum Song; King and I, The; Oklahoma!; Show Boat; South Pacific; State Fair*
Hanan, Stephen Mo, 119
Haring, Keith, 167
Hariton, Gerry, 57
Harney, Ben, 105
Harnick, Sheldon, 88, 125, 233
Harper, Wally, 52
Harrigan 'n Hart, **119–21**
Harris, Harriet, 273, 274
Harris, Neil Patrick, 296
Harris, Sam, 248
Harrison, Gregory, 234, 290
Harrison, Susan, 214
Hart, Charles, 73n
Hart, Lorenz, 31, 32, 178
Hart, Moss, 5, 35, 36, 36n, 37, 38, 39, 41, 102
Hartung, Billy, 225

Harum, Eivind, 14
Haskell, Molly, 15
Hateley, Linzi, 65
Hathaway, Anne, 132n
Hauptman, William, 143
Havens, John C., 233n
Hayden, Michael, 42, 103
Headley, Heather, 110, 181, 182, 183, 298, 299
Hearn, George, 4, 5, 6, 8, 12, 23, 26, 295–96
Hedwig and the Angry Inch, **156**
Hello, Dolly!, 1, 227
Hello Again, **150–51**
Henderson, Luther, 118, 249, 250
Henning, Doug, 49
Henshall, Ruthie, 128
Hensley, Shuler, 293
Herbert, Victor, 50, 130, 196, 223, 285
Heredia, Wilson Jermaine, 257
Herman, Jerry, 4, 8, 12, 23, 115, 135, 172.
    *See also Cage aux Folles, La; Hello,
    Dolly!; Mame*
Herman Van Veen: All Of Him, **111**
Herrmann, Keith, 46
Hewitt, Tom, 124
Hibbard, David, 280
Hickok, John, 276
High Society, **111**
Hill, Erin, 202
Hillner, John, 116
Hines, Gregory, 118, 250
Hofmann, Peter, 82
Holdridge, Lee, 51
Holliday, Jennifer, 105
Hollman, Mark, 184
Holmes, Rupert, 138, 139, 143
Horowitz, Jimmy, 50
Hoty, Dee, 121
*How To Succeed in Business Without Really
    Trying*, **176–77**, 282n
Howard, Peter, 117
Hudson, Richard, 149–50
Huffman, Cady, 121, 188
Hughes, Dusty, 80
Human Comedy, The, **26–29**, 85, 288–89
Hume, Nancy, 58
Hutton, Bill, 73
Hwang, David Henry, 183, 254–55
Hytner, Nicholas, 77, 83, 102, 103, 104,
    146, 215

I Do! I Do!, **155**
Idiot's Delight, 8–10
Ikeda, Thomas, 137
Illmann, Margaret, 114
In Trousers, **133**
Innvar, Christopher, 144

Into the Light, **50–51**
Into the Woods, 147, **148–48**, 165
Iredale, Jane, 180
Irma la Douce, 216
Is There Life After High School?, **55–56**
Isaacs, Pamela, 248
It Ain't Nothin' But the Blues, **115**
IT Girl, The, **166–67**
Ives, David, 231

Jablonski, Carl, 17
Jackson, David, 200
Jacoby, Mark, 262
Jahnke, Christopher, 236
James, Brian d'Arcy, 202, 213, 282
Jane Eyre, 68, **269–70**, 273
Jans, Alaric, 48
Jarvis, Martin, 285
Jbara, Gregory, 126, 156, 174
Jekyll & Hyde, 68, **228, 229**
Jelly's Last Jam, **249–51**
Jenkins, Daniel, 112, 113, 144, 174, 295
Jerome Kern Goes To Hollywood, **115**
Jerome Robbins' Broadway, **115–16**, 282
Jerry's Girls, **115**
Jesus Christ Superstar, 73, 76, 80
Jeter, Michael, 198, 200, 201
Jett, Joan, 124
Joel, Billy, 256
John, Elton, 182
Johnson, Catherine, 226
Jolson, Tonight, 119
Jolson & Company, 119
Jones, Dean, 51
Jones, Elinor, 16
Jones, Leilani, 99
Jones, Richard, 149, 202, 203
Jones, Simon, 156
Jones, Tom, 15, 16, 18, 20, 287–88. *See also
    Bone, Room, The; Colette; Fantastics,
    The; Grover's Corners; Roadside*
Jordan, Hal, 150
Joseph and the Amazing Technicolor Dreamcoat,
    73–74
Joslyn, Betsy, 21, 23, 26
Jude, Patrick, 50
Just So, **155**

Kaczorowski, Peter, 233
Kahn, Madeline, 130, 188
Kalmar, Bert, 170
Kander, John, 13, 14, 61, 156, 233, 236,
    251–52, 289–90. *See also And the World
    Goes 'Round; Cabaret; Kiss of the Spider
    Woman; Rink, The; Skin of Our Teeth,
    The; Steel Pier; Woman of the Year*

Kapp, Richard, 58–59
Karnilova, Maria, 47
Kaufman, George S., 5, 35, 36, 37, 38, 41, 135
Kayden, Spencer, 184
Kaye, Judy, 22, 55, 82, 130, 141, 161, 226, 264
Kaye, Stubby, 99
Kazan, Lainie, 137
Keagy, Grace, 14
Keating, Charles, 235
Kehr, Don, 27
Keigwin, Lawrence, 281
Keith, Larry, 203
Keller, Jeff, 11
Kelly, Glen, 188–89
Kelly, Jean Louisa, 167
Kern, Jerome, 34, 56n, 75n, 101, 115, 131, 215, 262n
Kert, Larry, 63, 119
Keyes, Ralph, 56
Kid Boots, 3, 170
Kidd, Michael, 95, 270
Kiley, Richard, 130
Kimball, Chad, 165–66
Kindley, Jeffrey, 56
King, Denis, 156
King and I, The, 104n, **123**
Kirk, Keith Byron, 291
Kiss Me, Kate, 127, 201, **291**
Kiss of the Spider Woman, 67–68, 165, **251–52**
Kitt, Eartha, 210, 281
Kleban, Edward, 278, 280
Klein, Sally, 38
Kline, Kevin, 29–30
Kline, Linda, 278
Klotz, Florence, 24
Koch, Martin, 226
Kolinski, Joseph, 27, 31
Koltai, Ralph, 67, 102
Korberg, Tommy, 83
Korbich, Eddie, 103, 246, 286
Korey, Alix, 122, 130, 281
Kotis, Greg, 184
Krakowski, Jane, 96, 198–99
Krieger, Henry, 105, 107, 108, 247, 252, 253
Kudisch, Marc, 210, 273
Kuhn, Judy, 63, 64, 81, 84, 85, 125, 233
Kunze, Michael, 230, 231
Kushnier, Jeremy, 225
Kyme, 125

LaCause, Sebastian, 124
LaChiusa, Michael John, 150–52, 182, 206, 210, 211, 212, 282

Lackey, Herndon, 276
Lady in the Dark, 1, 134
Lahr, John, 296
Laing, Stewart, 202, 205
LaManna, Janine, 285
Lambert, Hugh, 282n
Lamos, Mark, 284
Landau, Tina, 144
Landesman, Heidi, 102, 143
Lane, Burton, 225
Lane, Nathan, 49, 177–78, 180, 187
Lang, Barbara, 26
Lang, Lise, 52
Lansbury, Angela, 29, 190–91, 192
Lapine, James, 42, 134, 146–47, 148, 217, 218, 232
Larkin, Peter, 61, 116
Larson, Jonathan, 257
Last 5 Years, The, **286**
Latessa, Dick, 63, 121, 126, 228
Laurents, Arthur, 4, 7, 171, 172, 191, 191n, 192
Lawrence, Stephanie, 87
Layton, Joe, 31, 47, 95, 119
Leach, Wilford, 27, 29, 140, 158
Leader of the Pack, 143, **224**
Lee, Baayork, 52
Lee, Eugene, 264
Legrand, Michel, 71, 216
Legs Diamond, **53–54**, 152
Leigh, Mitch, 101, 122
Lemper, Ute, 128–29
Lena Horne: The Lady and Her Music, 111
Lerner, Alan Jay, 8, 10–12, 189, 225. See also Brigadoon; Camelot; Carmelina; Coco; Dance a Little Closer; My Fair Lady
Leveaux, David, 95
Levering, Kate, 271, 272, 273
Lewis-Evans, Kecia, 137
Lewis, Marcia, 63, 128
Lewis, Norm, 54, 104
Lewis, Vicki, 126, 181
Li'l Abner, 132, 224, 273, 279
Life, The, **248–49**
Lindsay, Robert, 86, 89
Lion King, The, **111–12**
Lippa, Andrew, 207, 280, 281, 293
Lithgow, John, 212, 214, 215
Little Johnny Jones, **30**, 34
Little Me, **125–26**
Little Shop of Horrors, **161–62**
Litton, Andrew, 296
Liu, Allen, 254
Loesser, Frank, 101, 124, 176, 228, 255
Loewe, Frederick, 101, 228. See also Brigadoon; Camelot; My Fair Lady

Lola, **161**
Long, Jodi, 255
Longbottom, Robert, 253
Lopez, Robert, 286
Lorick, Robert, 247
Lost in the Stars, 247
Loudon, Dorothy, 115, 162, 163
Louise, Merle, 4, 5, 7
Lucky Stiff, **136**
Ludwig, Ken, 116
Luhrmann, Baz, 159
Luker, Rebecca, 130, 142, 179
LuPone, Patti, 29, 31, 76, 79, 111, 295–96
Lynch, Thomas, 164
Lyndeck, Edmund, 24
Lyng, Norma Mae, 217, 219
Lyon, Rick, 287
Lysistrata, 259

MacDermot, Galt, 26, 27, 28, 85. *See also*
   Hair; Human Comedy, The; Via
   Galactica
Machota, Joe, 226
Mackintosh, Cameron, 79, 162
MacLaine, Shirley, 111
MacMillan, Kenneth, 103
MacRae, Heather, 42
Maddigan, Tina, 226
Magruder, James, 174
Malina, Stuart, 257
Maltby, Richard, Jr., 78, 112, 171, 280, 282
Mame, 4–5, 23, **29**, 190
Mamma Mia!, 83, **225–26**
Mamoulian, Rouben, 104n
Man of La Mancha, 18, **291**
Man of No Importance, A, **235–37**
Mandelbaum, Ken, 71
Manheim, Camryn, 174
Mann, Terrence, 63
Mantello, Joe, 237
Marceau, Yvonne, 200
March of the Falsettos, **133**
Mardirosian, Tom, 137
Marie Christine, 150, **151–53**
Marilyn: An American Fable, **51–53**
Marlowe, **50**, 258
Marques, David, 284
Marshall, Kathleen, 132n, 170
Marshall, Peter, 7
Marshall, Rob, 125–26, 126, 286
Martin, Andrea, 137
Martin, Jess L., 257
Martin, Leila, 82
Martin, Mary, 288
Martin Guerre, 73, 73n, 79
Martins, Peter, 32

Marx, Jeff, 286
Mason, Karen, 226
Masteroff, Joe, 125
Mastrantonio, Mary (Elizabeth), 27, 55
Matalon, Vivian, 33
Mathews, Carmen, 47, 50
Mathis, Stanley Wayne, 125, 293
Matterson, Diana, 141
Matthews, Brian, 48
Mayer, Michael, 273
Mazzie, Marin, 233, 265
McAnuff, Des, 104–5, 176, 177, 242
McCarthy, Jeff, 60, 184, 252, 253, 254
McCarthy, Theresa, 202
McDonald, Audra (Ann), 103, 110, 151,
   152, 265, 296
McDonald, Daniel, 234
McDonald, Kirk, 276
McElroy, Michael, 104, 145, 146, 210, 294
McEntire, Reba, 230
McGillin, Howard, 54, 138, 158
McGlinn, John, 131
McGough, Roger, 180
McGovern, Maureen, 180
McGrath, Katherine, 236
McGrath, Michael, 179
McKechnie, Donna, 163
McKee, Lonette, 34
McKibbins, Paul, 166
McKinley, Jesse, 297–98
McKneely, Joey, 209
McManus, George, 223
McNally, Terrence, 61, 235, 251, 255, 262
McNicholl, BT, 166
McQueen, Armelia, 120
Me and My Girl, **86–87**, 90, 118
Meehan, Thomas, 122, 162, 187, 227
Meet Me in St. Louis, **111**
Mendes, Sam, 123, 191
Menken, Alan, 161, 162
Menzel, Idina, 257, 281
Merlin, **49**
Merman, Ethel, 13, 190–91, 292
Merrick, David, 80, 125
Merrill, Bob (a.k.a. Paul Stryker), 101,
   114, 255
Merrily We Roll Along, 24, **35–43**, 147
Metro, 88
Metropolis, **80–81**
Michaels, Patricia, 51
Michell, Keith, 7
Mielziner, Jo, 36, 36n
Miller, Jonathan, 66
Miller, Roger, 143–45, 146
Minnelli, Liza, 61, 156
Misérables, Les, 72, 73, 73n, 76

Miss Saigon, 73, **76–79**, 82
Mitchell, Brian Stokes, 54, 110, 125,
    132n, 263
Mitchell, David, 47
Mitchell, James, 270
Mitchell, Jerry, 255
Mitchell, John Cameron, 142
Mitchell, Lauren, 178, 251
Mitzman, Marcia, 85
Monk, Debra, 157, 171, 234, 245, 271
Monroe, Marilyn, 51
Montevecchi, Liliane, 94, 95, 198
Montresor, Beni, 64
Moore, Larry, 131n
Moore, Maureen, 48
Moore, Robert, 13
Moran, Martin, 202
Mordente, Lisa, 50
Moreno, Antonio, 166
Morgan, Cass, 158
Morison, Patricia, 45
Morris, Anita, 94–95
Morris, John, 188
Morris, Mark, 242
Morrison, Ann, 38
Morrow, Tom, 80
Morse, Robert, 176
Morton, Brooks, 279
Morton, Jelly Roll, 249
Morton, Joe, 55
Moss, Kathi, 94
Most Happy Fella, The, 71, **124**, 126, 160
Movin' Out, **255, 256–57**
Mullally, Megan, 177
Murney, Julia, 282
Murphy, Donna, 28, 151, 156, 233
Murphy, Heidi Grant, 296
Murphy, Sally, 103, 236
Murray, Sharon, 99
My Fair Lady, **29**, 39, 80, **102–3**, 160
My Favorite Year, **137–38**
My Life With Albertine, 85, 136, **164–66**, 244
My One and Only, **96–98**
Mystery of Edwin Drood, The, 90, **138–40**

Napier, John, 77, 79–80
Nazario, Ednita, 244
Nelson, Richard, 83, 164
Neuwirth, Bebe, 126, 127, 128
New Amsterdam Theater Company, 130–31
New Brain, A, **157–58**
Newman, David, 248
Newman, Jim, 234
Newman, Randy, 261
Nicholas Brothers, 115, 170–71
Nicholas, Paul, 74n

Nichols, Mike, 96
Nichols, Peter, 156
Nick & Nora, 162–63, **171–72**
Nine, 90, **93–96**, 98
No Strings, 132
Nolen, Timothy, 99, 241
Norman, Marsha, 113, 141, 144
Noseworthy, Jack, 213
Novick, Julius, 155
Nunn, Trevor, 74n, 83, 83–84, 221, 292
Nussbaum, Mike, 48–49
Nype, Russell, 155

O'Brien, Jack, 126, 127, 227, 255
O'Brien, Richard, 123
O'Brien, Timothy, 23
O'Carroll, Mike, 264
O'Connor, Donald, 34–35, 47
O'Donnell, Mark, 227
O'Gorman, Michael, 60
O'Hara, Kelli, 165, 214
Ockrent, Mike, 86, 87, 112, 116, 118
Oh, Brother!, **55**
Oh, Kay!, **124–25**
Oklahoma!, 1, 9, 22, 104n, **292–93**
Oliver!, **29**
On the Town, 72, **123**, 227
On Your Toes, 31, 32n, **32–33**, 34
Once On This Island, **136–37**, 286
Once Upon a Mattress, **123**
One Touch of Venus, 130
Onward Victoria, **45–46**
Opel, Nancy, 174, 175
Orbach, Jerry, 292
Orfeh, 110, 284
Oscar, Brad, 110
Our Town (Wilder). *See Grover's Corners*
Out Of This World, 132

Pacific Overtures, 77, **155**
Paint Your Wagon, 71, 270
Pajama Game, The, 227, 255
Pakledinaz, Martin, 273
Pal Joey, 129
Panaro, Hugh, 54, 114, 252, 254
Paper Moon, **290–91**
Papp, Joseph, 26, 29, 30n, 158
Pappas, Evan, 119, 137, 276
Parade, 68, **275–78**
Parapluies de Cherbourg, Les (The Umbrellas of
    Cherbourg), 71, 216
Park, Michael, 145
Parlato, Dennis, 84
Pascal, Adam, 181, 182, 183, 257
Pask, Scott, 217
Pasquale, Steven, 235

Passion, 68, **231–33**, 236, 237
Patinkin, Mandy, 76, 111, 142, 147, 210
Pawk, Michele, 116, 151, 285
Payton, Caroline, 159
Peck, Gregory, 121
Peggy Lee, **111**
Peil, Mary Beth, 96
Pendleton, Austin, 201
Perkins, Patti, 236
Perry, Lynnette, 201, 264
Perry, William, 180
Peters, Bernadette, 79, 147, 148, 164, 175, 190, 191–93
Peters, Michael, 106
Petrified Prince, The, 150
Peyton, Caroline, 27
Phantom of the Opera, The, 73, 73n, 74, 76, **81–82**, 105
Phelan, Deborah, 6
Phillips, Eddie, 127
Philips, Mary, 36
Phillips, Mary Bracken, 88
Piaf, **86**, 90
Piech, Jennifer, 202
Pinkins, Tonya, 118, 210, 250
Pirates of Penzance, The, **29–30**, 48
Pitchford, Dean, 65, 224
Pitre, Louise, 226
Play On!, **118**
Playten, Alice, 30, 286
Plunkett, Maryann, 87
Polanski, Roman, 230
Porgy and Bess, 71, 279, 296
Porter, Cole, 36n, 71, 101, 111
Powell, Michael, 113
Powers, John R., 48
Praed, Michael, 31
Preston, Robert, 13, 58, 59
Price, Lonny, 38, 63, 119, 134, 278
Prince, Faith, 126, 134, 171, 236
Prince, Harold, 22, 24, 25, 35, 37, 38, 39, 83, 85, 98–99, 99–101, 104, 150, 166, 251, 276, 278
Privates on Parade, **156**
Producers, The, 85, **185–90**, 227, 298, 299
Promenade, 135
Pryce, Jonathan, 77, 79
Pump Boys and Dinettes, **157**
Putting It Together, **115**

Quilico, Louis, 124
Quilters, 143
Quinn, James, 48
Quinn, Patrick, 179, 280

Rachael Lily Rosenbloom and Don't You Ever Forget It!, 109
Radiant Baby, **167–68**
Raggedy Ann, **56–57**, 289
Rags, **62–65**
Ragtime, **259–67**
Raines, Ron, 16n, 34, 54, 58
Ralph, Sheryl Lee, 105, 273, 275
Ramirez, Sara, 244, 284, 285
Rando, John, 185, 231
Raposo, Joe, 56
Rapp, Anthony, 257, 293
Reams, Lee Roy, 134
Red Shoes, The, **113–15**, 117
Reed, Alyson, 51, 52–53
Rees, Roger, 114, 235, 236, 237
Reichard, Daniel, 167
Reid, Alexander, 67
Reilly, Charles Nelson, 169
Reinders, Kate, 192
Reinking, Ann, 128, 282
Rent, 77, 157, **257–59**
Return To the Forbidden Planet, **156–57**
Rice, Tim, 73, 73n, 83, 84, 182. *See also Aida; Chess; Evita; Jesus Christ Superstar; Joseph and the Amazing Technicolor Dreamcoat*
Rich, Frank, 13, 148, 224
Richards, Evan, 48
Richardson, Claibe, 161
Richardson, Ron, 125, 144
Rigg, Diana, 15, 16, 18, 19, 20, 21, 22
Ringham, Nancy, 180
Rink, The, **61–62**, 289
Ripley, Alice, 85, 104, 110, 124, 252, 253
Rivera, Chita, 47, 49, 61, 67–68, 115, 129, 156
Roadside, 16, 227n
Robber Bridegroom, The, 226
Robbins, Carrie, 57
Robbins, Jana, 21
Robbins, Jerome, 2, 95, 104n, 115–16, 255, 270
Robbins, Tim, 31
Robertson, Liz, 10, 11
Rock 'N Roll!: The First 5,000 Years, **115**
Rockabye Hamlet, 258
Rocky Horror Show, The, **123–24**, 258
Rodgers, Mary, 103
Rodgers, Richard, 9, 31, 32, 32n, 101, 103, 104n, 217, 254, 262n, 292. *See also Allegro; Boys From Syracuse, The; Carousel; Flower Drum Song; King and I, The; Oklahoma!; On Your Toes; South Pacific; State Fair*

Romano, Christy Carlson, 276
Romano, David, 82
Rome, Harold, 101, 279
Rondelay, 150
Ronstadt, Linda, 30, 158
Rose, George, 11, 30, 138, 140
Rose, Phil, 140
Rosenberg, Irene, 45–46
Ross, Diana, 105
Ross, Jamie, 7
Ross, Stuart, 167
Rostand, Edmond, 88, 88–89, 89, 90
Rothschilds, The, **155**
Routledge, Patricia, 30
Royal Family of Broadway, The,
    135–36
Roza, **99–101**
Rubin-Vega, Daphne, 124, 257
Rubinstein, John, 42, 251
Runaways, 223
Runolfsson, Anne, 88, 89–90
Rupert, Michael, 134, 291
Russell, Bill, 252, 253
Russell, Ken, 96, 104
Russell, Willy, 87, 90
Ryall, William, 286

St. Germain, Mark, 155
Saks, Gene, 64
Salmon, Scott, 4, 8
Sams, Jeremy, 217, 218
Samuel, Peter, 298
Saroyan, William, 27–28
Satchmo: America's Musical Legend, 119
Saturday Night, **159–61**
Saturday Night Fever, **224**
Scanlan, Dick, 274, 275
Scarlet Pimpernel, 196, **229–30**
Schaffel, Marla, 270
Scherer, John, 285
Schmidt, Douglas W., 126
Schmidt, Harvey, 15, 16, 18, 20, 101,
    287–88. *See also Bone Room, The;
    Colette; Fantasticks, The; Grover's
    Corners; Roadside*
Schmidt, Paul, 174
Schneider, Anne Kaufman, 135n
Schoket, Steve, 52
Schönberg, Claude-Michel, 73, 73n,
    78–79, 79n, 85, 90. *See also
    Martin Guerre; Misérables, Les;
    Miss Saigon*
Schulman, Susan H., 113, 142, 146
Schwartz, Stephen, 62, 101
Scott, Sherie René, 104, 181, 182, 183,
    286, 299

Secret Garden, The (1991 version), 113,
    141–43
Seussical, **285–86**
Seven Brides For Seven Brothers, **111**
1776, 126
Shaffer, Anthony, 172
Shaiman, Marc, 227, 228
Shapiro, Debbie, 115
Sharman, Jim, 123
Sharp, Jon Marshall, 114
Shaw, Bob, 140
She Loves Me, 71, 125, 129
Shea, Jere, 233
Shenandoah, **123**
Sherwood, Robert E., 8, 9, 11
Shire, David, 78, 112, 280
Short, Martin, 126, 175
Show Boat, 1, 5, 6, 9n, **34–35**, 75n, 90,
    100–101, 185, 227, 259, 270, 292, 295
Side Show, 68, 85, **253–54**
Sieber, Christopher, 175
Silliman, Maureen, 56
Sills, Douglas, 132n, 230
Silver, Joe, 54
Silver, Nicky, 178
Silverman, Stanley, 245
Simon, John, 57, 257
Simon, Lucy, 141, 144
Simon, Neil, 126, 175
Simon, Paul, 242–45
Simonson, Eric, 242
Singin' in the Rain, **111**, 256
Siretta, Dan, 124
Skin of Our Teeth, The, 287, **288–89**
Skinner, Emily, 85, 110, 252, 253, 255
Slater, Christian, 48, 49
Small, Michael, 166
Smile, **59–61**
Smith, Harry B., 146, 148, 223
Smith, Rex, 27, 30, 201
Smokey Joe's Café, **115**
Snoopy!!!, **155**
Snow, Tom, 224
Somers, Asa, 231
Sondheim, Stephen, 22, 35, 37, 39–40, 101,
    115, 146–47, 149, 160, 165–66, 172,
    191, 191n, 232, 236, 245, 246, 279, 295.
    *See also Anyone Can Whistle; Assassins;
    Company; Follies; Funny Thing Happened
    On the Way To the Forum, A; Gypsy;
    Into the Woods; Merrily We Roll Along;
    Pacific Overtures; Passion; Saturday
    Night; Sunday in the Park With George;
    Sweeney Todd*
Song & Dance, 73, 79
Song of Norway, 197

Sophisticated Ladies, 48, **118–19**
Sousa, John Philip, 58–59, 293–94
Spencer, David, 158
Spiner, Brent, 31
Stadlen, Lewis, 298
Stanley, Pat, 169, 200
Stapleton, Jean, 169
Starcrossed: The Trial of Galileo, 146
Starlight Express, 72, 73, **74–76**, 75n, 79
Starting Here, Starting Now, 112
Stasio, Marilyn, 21
State Fair, **111**
Steel Pier, **233–35**, 233n, 236, 289
Stein, Joseph, 146
Steinman, Jim, 230–31
Stephens, Lannyl, 137
Stephenson, Don, 202, 204, 298
Stevens, Leslie, 4
Stevens, Marti, 16
Stewart, Michael, 46–47, 119, 120
Stewart, Paul Anthony, 88
Stillman, Bob, 54, 161
Sting, 180
Stock, Jeffrey, 174
Stoller, Mike, 115
Stone, Peter, 13, 15, 96, 121, 196, 202
Stout, Stephen, 136
Straiges, Tony, 48
Strange, Alex, 263
Stratas, Teresa, 63, 64
Stratton, Hank, 182
Strayhorn, Danny, 200
Street Scene, 241, 270
Streisand, Barbra, 156
Strike Up the Band, 132
Stritch, Elaine, 296, 298
Stroman, Susan, 112, 116, 188, 189, 233, 237, 238, 239, 271, 298
Strouse, Charles, 8, 10–12, 46–47, 62, 64, 162, 171. *See also Annie; Annie 2: Miss Hannigan's Revenge; Bring Back Birdie; Dance a Little Closer; Nick & Nora; Rags*
Stryker, Paul. *See* Merrill, Bob
Styne, Jule, 22, 101, 113, 114, 191
Summerhays, Jane, 87
Sunday in the Park With George, 41, **147–48**
Sunset Boulevard, 73, **79–80**, 85
Sutcliffe, Steven, 266
Sutherland, Claudette, 177
Swan Lake, 222
Sweeney Todd, 18, 40–41, 278, **295–96**
Sweet Adeline, 129, 131
Sweet Smell of Success, 165, **212–16**
Swing!, **283–84**
Swinging on a Star, 115

Take Me Along, **123**
Tallulah, **155**, 163
Tanner, Tony, 73
Tap Dance Kid, The, **247–48**
Tarbutton, James, 270
Tartaglia, John, 286
Tatum, Marianne, 31
Taylor, Ron, 31
Taylor-Corbett, Lynne, 284
Taymor, Julie, 112
Teddy & Alice, **57–59**
Teek, Angela, 125
Teeter, Lara, 32
Tell Me More, 5
Tenderloin, 132
Tesori, Jeanine, 145, 146, 274, 275
Testa, Mary, 52
Thacker, Russ, 48
Tharp, Twyla, 111, 256
Thompson, David, 233, 271
Thompson, Jennifer Laura, 184
Thorne, Raymond, 163
Thoroughly Modern Millie, 29, 85, 146, **273–75**
Thou Shalt Not, 53, **270–73**
Three Musketeers, The, **30–31**, 34
Threepenny Opera, 164, 164n, **179–80**
Tintypes, 48
Titanic, 71, 182, **201–6**, 289
Todd, Mike, 122, 122–23
Tommy. See The Who's Tommy
Toner, Tom, 141–42
Tony awards, 297–98
Townshend, Pete, 105
Tree Grows in Brooklyn, A, 22
Triumph of Love, **174–75**
Trixie True, Teen Detective, **155**
Trudeau, Garry, 223
Tubert, Susana, 242
Tune, Tommy, 95, 96–98, 104, 121, 196, 197, 200
Tunick, Jonathan, 94n, 205
Twiggy, 96–98
Two Little Girls in Blue, 5
Tyler, Jim, 59
Tynes, Bill, 130–31

Uggams, Leslie, 115
Uhry, Alfred, 30, 276, 276–77, 278
Ukena, Paul, Jr., 121
Umbrellas of Cherbourg, The (stage version), 65
Uptown . . . It's Hot!, **115**
Urban Cowboy, **226–27**
Urinetown, 164, 175, **183–85**, 225

Valenti, Michael, 55
Vallee, Rudy, 176–77
Van Dijk, Ad, 88
Van Dijk, Bill, 88, 89
Van Dijk, Koen, 88
Van Heusen, James, 275
Verdon, Gwen, 33, 127, 127–28, 129
Vereen, Ben, 99
Vichi, Gerry, 122
Vicky For President, 45
Victor/Victoria, **173–74**
Vidnovic, Martin, 16, 19, 22, 33
Violet, **145–46**, 226
von Essen, Max, 231

Wagner, Chuck, 31, 149
Wagner, Robin, 83, 209
Walcott, Derek, 242
Walker, Chet, 282
Walker, Don, 124
Walker, Fredi, 258
Walker, Peter, 119
Wallace, Lee, 99
Wallace, Timothy, 170
Wallop, Douglas, 127
Walsh, Barbara, 112
Walsh, Thommie, 49, 52, 96, 136
Walston, Ray, 127
Walton, Jim, 38
Walton, Tony, 80, 199, 233, 286
Wanamaker, Zoë, 86
Ward, Lauren, 145
Warhol, Andy, 167–68
Waterbury, Marsha, 60
Webber, Andrew Lloyd, 24, 72, 73, 73n,
　　74–76, 75n, 81–82, 85, 221, 285.
　　See also Aspects of Love; By Jeeves; Cats;
　　Evita; Jesus Christ Superstar; Joseph and
　　the Amazing Technicolor Dreamcoat;
　　Phantom of the Opera, The; Song &
　　Dance; Starlight Express; Sunset
　　Boulevard; Whistle Down the Wind
Weber, Steven, 190
Weeks, Alan, 55
Weidman, John, 222, 237, 238, 245, 246
Weill, Kurt, 50, 179
Weiner, John, 4, 5
Weitz, Eric, 30
Welch, Raquel, 13
Weller, Michael, 261
Wells, John, 66
West, Cheryl L., 118
Westenberg, Robert, 145, 149

Where's Charley?, 255
Whistle Down the Wind, 73
White, Jane, 161
White, Julie, 136
White, Lillias, 110, 177, 248
White, Onna, 31
Who's Tommy, The, **104–5**, 242
Wilcox, Larry, 18
Wild Party, The (LaChiusa-Wolfe version),
　　206–12, 281, 282
Wild Party, The (Lippa version), 207,
　　280–82
Wildhorn, Frank, 228–30
Will Rogers Follies, The, **121**
Wilson, Julie, 54
Wilson, Lester, 31
Wilson, Patrick, 110, 284, 293
Wiman, Dwight Deere, 32n
Winchell, Walter, 212, 213, 215
Wind in the Willows, **180–81**
Winokur, Marissa Jaret, 227
Winston, Hattie, 247
Wise, Scott, 126, 127, 280
Wittman, Scott, 227
Wiz, The, **29**, 273
Wolfe, George C., 167, 206, 207–8, 211,
　　249, 250, 251, 257, 281
Woman of the Year, **12–15**, 38
Wonderful Town, 129
Wood, Douglas J., 175
Woodhull, Victoria, 45
Woods, Sheryl, 34
Woolverton, Linda, 183
Wright, Rebecca, 49
Wright, Robert, 196, 197, 199, 201
Wright, Samuel E., 247
Wylie, John, 199
Wyman, Nicholas, 82

Yates, Deborah, 239
Yazbek, David, 255
Year With Frog and Toad, A, 286
Yeston, Maury, 93, 94, 94n, 196, 198, 199,
　　200, 201, 202
You Can't Take It With You, 5
You're a Good Man, Charlie Brown, 155, **293**

Zaks, Jerry, 177, 242, 246, 251
Zaslow, Michael, 46
Ziegfeld, Florenz, 121, 170
Ziemba, Karen, 234, 238
Zien, Chip, 42, 134, 149, 157, 178, 201
Zippel, David, 52, 155, 172, 175, 176